MAN'S ETERNAL QUEST

PARAMAHANSA YOGANANDA
(January 5, 1893—March 7, 1952)

MAN'S ETERNAL QUEST

and other talks

by

Paramahansa Yogananda

SELF-REALIZATION FELLOWSHIP

Founded by Paramahansa Yogananda
Sri Daya Mata, President

1976

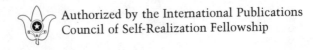

Authorized by the International Publications
Council of Self-Realization Fellowship

ISBN 0-87612-231-4
Library of Congress Catalog Number: 75-17183

Printed in the United States of America
1910-776-31.6M

Dedicated by Self-Realization Fellowship
to our beloved president,
SRI DAYA MATA
whose faithful devotion to recording the
words of her guru for posterity has
preserved for us and for the ages the
liberating wisdom and God-love
of Paramahansa Yogananda

PREFACE

*(By the president and spiritual head of
Self-Realization Fellowship/Yogoda Satsanga Society of India)*

The first time I beheld Paramahansa Yogananda, he was speaking before a vast, enraptured audience in Salt Lake City. The year was 1931. As I stood at the back of the crowded auditorium, I became transfixed, unaware of anything around me except the speaker and his words. My whole being was absorbed in the wisdom and divine love that were pouring into my soul and flooding my heart and mind. I could only think, "This man loves God as I have always longed to love Him. He *knows* God. Him I shall follow." And from that moment, I did.

As I felt the transfiguring power of his words on my own life during those early days with Paramahansaji, there arose within me a feeling of the urgent need to preserve his words for all the world, for all time. It became my sacred and joyous privilege, during the many years I was with Paramahansa Yogananda, to record his lectures and classes, and also many informal talks and words of personal counsel—truly a vast treasure-house of wondrous wisdom and God-love. As Gurudeva spoke, the rush of his inspiration was often reflected in the swiftness of his speech; he might speak without pause for minutes at a time, and continue for an hour. While his hearers sat enthralled, my pen was flying! As I took down his words in shorthand, it was as though a special grace had descended, instantly translating the Guru's voice into the shorthand characters on the page. Their transcription has been a blessed task that continues to this day. Even after such a long time—some of my notes are more than forty years old—when I start to transcribe them, they are miraculously fresh in my mind, as though they had been recorded yesterday. I can even hear inwardly the inflections of Gurudeva's voice in each particular phrase.

The Master seldom made even the slightest preparation for his lectures; if he prepared anything at all, it might consist of a factual note or two, hastily jotted down. Very often, while riding in the car on the way to the temple, he would casually ask one of us: "What is my subject today?" He would put his mind on it, and then give the lecture extemporaneously from an inner reservoir of divine inspiration.

The subjects for Gurudeva's sermons at the temples were set and announced in advance. But sometimes his mind was working in an entirely different vein when he began to speak. Regardless of the "subject for today," the Master would voice the truths engrossing his consciousness at that moment, pouring forth priceless wisdom in a steady stream from the abundance of his own spiritual experience and intuitive perception. Nearly always, at the close of such a service, a number of people would come forward to thank him for having enlightened them on a problem that had been troubling them, or perhaps for having explained some philosophical concept in which they were particularly interested.

Sometimes, while he was lecturing, the Guru's consciousness would be so uplifted that he would momentarily forget the audience and converse directly with God; his whole being would be overflowing with divine joy and intoxicating love. In these high states of consciousness, his mind completely at one with the Divine Consciousness, he inwardly perceived Truth, and described what he saw. On occasion, God appeared to him as the Divine Mother, or in some other aspect; or one of our great Gurus, or other saints, would manifest in vision before him. At such times, even the audience would feel deeply the special blessing bestowed on all present. During such a visitation of Saint Francis of Assisi, whom Gurudeva deeply loved, the Master was inspired to compose the beautiful poem, "God! God! God!"

The Bhagavad-Gita describes an enlightened master in these words: "The Self shines forth like a sun in those who have banished ignorance by wisdom" (VI:16). One might have been overawed by Paramahansa Yogananda's spiritual radiance, were it not for his warmth and naturalness, and a quiet humility, which put everyone instantly at ease. Each person in the audience felt that Gurudeva's talk was addressed to him personally. Not the least of the Master's endearing qualities was his understanding sense of humor. By some choice phrase, gesture, or facial expression he would bring forth an appreciative response of hearty laughter at just the right moment to drive home a point, or to relax his listeners after long and intense concentration on a particularly deep subject.

One cannot convey in the pages of a book the uniqueness and universality of Paramahansa Yogananda's vivid, loving personality. But it is my humble hope, in giving this brief background, to afford a personal glimpse that will enrich the reader's enjoyment and appreciation of the talks presented in this volume.

To have seen my Gurudeva in divine communion; to have heard the profound truths and devotional outpourings of his soul; to have recorded them for the ages; and now to share them with all—what joy is mine! May the Master's sublime words open wider the doors to unshakable faith in God, to deeper love for that One who is our beloved Father, Mother, and Eternal Friend.

DAYA MATA

Los Angeles, California
May 1975

INTRODUCTION

Mankind is engaged in an eternal quest for that "something else" he hopes will bring him happiness, complete and unending. For those individual souls who have sought and found God, the search is over: He is that Something Else.

—Paramahansa Yogananda

This volume of talks by Paramahansa Yogananda is for all who have ever known disappointment, dissatisfaction, discouragement, sorrow, or an unfulfilled spiritual longing. It is for those who have sought to understand the enigmas of life; for those who have held within their hearts an uncertain hope about the reality of God and the possibility that He could be known; and for seekers who have already turned toward God in their quest. May it be, for each reader, a ray of divine light on the path, bringing new life and inspiration and a sense of direction. God is all things to all people.

Man's Eternal Quest is a book about God: about God's place in man's life; in his hopes, will, aspirations, accomplishments. Life, man, achievement—all are but manifestations of the one omnipresent Creator, as inseparably dependent on Him as the wave is dependent on the ocean. Paramahansaji explains why and how man was created by God, and how he is immutably a part of God, and what this means to each one personally. Realization of the oneness of man and his Creator is the whole essence of Yoga. An understanding of man's inescapable need for God, in every aspect of living, removes the otherworldliness from religion and makes knowing God the basis of a scientific and practical approach to life.

As a man of God, and as an authority on the ancient divine science of Yoga, Paramahansa Yogananda has received the highest credentials from his spiritual contemporaries, and from readers of his works in all parts of the world—the literary and general public as well as his followers. That he has also received the ultimate commendation from the Supreme Authority is amply attested to by the manifest blessings of God on his exemplary life, and by the infinitely beautiful, uniquely edifying responses he received from God in vision and divine communion. This comment in *Review of Religions*, published by Columbia University Press, is typical of the acclaim received by Paramahansa Yogananda's earlier work, *Autobiography of a Yogi:* "There has been nothing before, written in English or in any other European language, like this presentation of Yoga." The *San Francisco Chronicle* wrote: "Yogananda presents a convincing case for Yoga, and those who 'came to scoff' may remain to pray." From *Schleswig-Holsteinische Tagespost*, Germany: "We must credit this book with the power to bring about a spiritual revolution." Of Paramahansa Yogananda himself, Swami Sivananda, founder of the Divine Life Society, Rishikesh, India, said: "A rare gem of inestimable value, the like of whom the world is yet to witness, Paramahansa Yogananda has been an ideal representative of the ancient sages and seers, the glory of India." His Holiness the Shankaracharya of Kanchipuram, revered spiritual leader of millions in South India, wrote of Paramahansaji: "As a bright light shining in the midst of darkness, so was Yogananda's presence in this world. Such a great soul comes on earth only rarely, when there is a real need among men. We are grateful to Yogananda for spreading Hindu philosophy in such a wonderful way in America and the West."

Paramahansa Yogananda was born in India on January 5, 1893. He had a remarkable childhood that clearly indicated his life was marked for a divine destiny. His mother recognized this and encouraged his noble ideals and spiritual aspirations. When he was only eleven, the loss of his mother, whom he loved above all else in this world, made firm his inherent resolve to find God and to receive from the Creator Himself the answers yearned for in every human heart. He became a disciple of the great *Jnanavatar* (incarnation of wisdom) Swami Sri Yukteswar Giri. Sri Yukteswar was one of a line of exalted gurus, with whom Yoganandaji had been linked from birth: Sri

Yogananda's parents were disciples of Lahiri Mahasaya, guru of Sri Yukteswar. When Yogananda was an infant in his mother's arms, Lahiri Mahasaya had blessed him and foretold: "Little mother, thy son will be a yogi. As a spiritual engine, he will carry many souls to God's kingdom." Lahiri Mahasaya was a disciple of Mahavatar Babaji, the deathless master who revived in this age the ancient science of *Kriya Yoga*. Praised by Krishna in the Bhagavad-Gita, and by Patanjali in the *Yoga Sutras, Kriya Yoga* is both a transcendent technique of meditation and an art of living that leads to union of the soul with God. Mahavatar Babaji revealed the sacred *Kriya* to Lahiri Mahasaya, who handed it down to Sri Yukteswar, who taught it to Paramahansa Yogananda.

When in 1920 Paramahansa Yogananda was deemed ready to begin his world mission of disseminating the soul-liberating science of Yoga, Mahavatar Babaji told him of the divine responsibility that was to be his: "You are the one I have chosen to spread the message of *Kriya Yoga* in the West. Long ago I met your guru Yukteswar at a *Kumbha Mela;* I told him then I would send you to him for training. *Kriya Yoga,* the scientific technique of God-realization, will ultimately spread in all lands, and aid in harmonizing the nations through man's personal, transcendental perception of the Infinite Father."

Paramahansa Yogananda began his mission in America as a delegate to the International Congress of Religious Liberals in Boston in 1920. For more than a decade he traveled the length and breadth of America, speaking almost daily to capacity audiences in all the major cities. On January 28, 1925, the *Los Angeles Times* reported: "The Philharmonic Auditorium presents the extraordinary spectacle of thousands...being turned away an hour before the advertised opening of a lecture with the 3000-seat hall filled to its utmost capacity. Swami Yogananda is the attraction. A Hindu invading the United States to bring God..., preaching the essence of Christian doctrine." It came as no small revelation to the West that Yoga—so eloquently expounded and clearly interpreted by Sri Yogananda—is a universal science, and that as such it is indeed the "essence" of all true religions.

In Los Angeles in 1925, Paramahansa Yogananda founded

the international headquarters for Self-Realization Fellowship, the society he had started in India in 1917 as Yogoda Satsanga Society of India.

In the early 1930's Paramahansaji began to withdraw gradually from nationwide public lecturing. "I am not interested in crowds," he said, "but in souls who are in earnest to know God." Thereafter, he concentrated his efforts on classes for serious students, and spoke mostly at his own Self-Realization Fellowship temples and the international headquarters. The selections in this volume are talks given primarily during this period.

Paramahansa Yogananda had often voiced this prediction: "I will not die in bed, but with my boots on, speaking of God and India." On March 7, 1952, the prophecy was fulfilled. At a banquet in honor of the Ambassador of India, B. R. Sen, Paramahansaji was a guest speaker. He delivered a soul-stirring address, concluding with these words from a poem he had written, "My India": "Where Ganges, woods, Himalayan caves and men dream God—I am hallowed; my body touched that sod!" He then lifted his eyes upward and entered *mahasamadhi,* an advanced yogi's conscious earth-exit. He died as he had lived, exhorting man to know God.

The Guru's talks in the earliest years of his ministry were recorded only spasmodically. But when Sri Daya Mata became a disciple of Paramahansa Yogananda in 1931, she undertook the sacred task, faithfully recording, for the generations to come, all of her guru's talks and classes. This volume is but a sampling: under the direction of Paramahansa Yogananda, many transcriptions—particularly those containing private instruction and meditation techniques and principles given to Self-Realization class students—were compiled along with some of his writings into a series of *Self-Realization Fellowship Lessons;* other talks appear as a regular feature in *Self-Realization Magazine.*

As most of the talks set forth in this book were presented before audiences familiar with Self-Realization teachings, some clarification of terminology and philosophical concepts may be helpful to the general reader. To this end, many footnotes have been included; also a glossary explaining certain

Sanskrit words, and other philosophical terms, and giving information about events, persons, and places associated with the life and work of Paramahansa Yogananda. It may be noted here that quotations from the Bhagavad-Gita in this volume are from Paramahansa Yogananda's own translation.

Paramahansa Yogananda could have said, with Jesus, "Think not that I am come to destroy the law, or the prophets: I am not come to destroy, but to fulfill" (Matthew 5:17). Paramahansaji honored all religions and their founders, and held in respect all sincere seekers of God. Part of his world mission is "to reveal the complete harmony and basic oneness of original Christianity as taught by Jesus Christ and original Yoga as taught by Bhagavan Krishna." (See *Aims and Ideals*, page 465.) Far from introducing a divisive dogma to the world, Paramahansaji showed that the practice of yoga establishes an inner attunement with God that constitutes the universal basis of all religions. Abstractions of theoretical religion pale before actual experience of God. Truth cannot be wholly proved to any seeker by anyone else; but by the practice of yoga, the aspirant can prove truth for himself through his own experience.

God is; and each man who will seek Him sincerely will know Him. Man can have no life or power to act, think, or feel without borrowing that power from God. Therefore, Paramahansaji pointed out, knowing God is not only a privilege and a divine duty, but a practical necessity. Why should man grovel in self-insufficiency when he can tap the Source of all power and fulfillment?

The wisdom in this volume is not the studied learning of a scholar; it is the empirical testimony of a dynamic spiritual personage whose life was filled with inner joy and outer accomplishment, a world teacher who lived what he taught, a *Premavatar* whose sole desire was to share God's wisdom and love with all.

SELF-REALIZATION FELLOWSHIP

Los Angeles, California
May 1975

CONTENTS

[xvi]

MAN'S ETERNAL QUEST

How Seekers First Found God

Self-Realization Fellowship international headquarters,
Los Angeles, California, November 11, 1934

We can readily understand how man first conceived of a science of medicine. He suffered physically and therefore sought a method to heal himself. But how did man happen to try to find out about God? The question gives scope for profound reflection.

In the Vedas* of India we find the earliest true concept of God. In her scriptures India has given the world immortal truths that have stood the test of time.

Every material inventor is actuated by material need—"necessity is the mother of invention." Similarly motivated by necessity, the early *rishis*† of India became ardent spiritual seekers. They had found that without inner satisfaction, no amount of external good fortune can bring lasting happiness. How then can one make himself really happy? This is the problem the wise men of India undertook to solve.

Three Aspects of Nature

Worship of God in prehistoric times began through man's fear of the various forces of nature. When it rained excessively, floods killed many people. Awed, man thought of the rain and wind and other natural forces as gods.

Later on, human beings realized that nature operates in three ways: creative, preservative, and dissolutive. A wave

---

* From the Sanskrit *vid,* "to know." The Vedas comprise a voluminous scripture of 100,000 couplets. The origin of the Vedas is lost in antiquity. They were passed down orally for millenniums until Vyasa, a sage who lived about 3000 B.C., committed them to writing and classified them into four parts: Rig Veda, Sama Veda, Yajur Veda, and Atharva Veda.

† Literally "seers." The *rishis* were the inspired personages to whom the Vedas were revealed in an indeterminable antiquity.

3

rising out of the ocean exemplifies the creative state; staying for a moment on the sea-breast, it is in the preservative state; and sinking back into the deep, it passes through the dissolutive state.

Just as Jesus beheld the universal force of evil personified in Satan, so the great *rishis* beheld the universal forces of creation, preservation, and dissolution personified in definite forms. The sages of old named them Brahma the Creator, Vishnu the Preserver, and Shiva the Destroyer. These primal powers were created as projections of the unmanifested Spirit to unfold His infinite drama of creation, while He, as God beyond creation, remains ever hidden behind their consciousness. In times of cosmic dissolution, all creation and its vast activating forces dissolve back into Spirit. There they rest until called upon again by the Great Director to reenact their roles.*

A Story About Brahma, Vishnu, and Shiva

In India there is a popular story about Brahma, Vishnu, and Shiva. They were boasting among themselves about their tremendous might. Suddenly a little boy came up and said to Brahma, "What do you create?" "Everything," Brahma replied grandly. The boy asked the other two gods what their work was. "We preserve and destroy everything," they answered.

The young visitor was holding in his hand a single piece of straw about the size of a toothpick. Placing it in front of Brahma, he asked, "Can you create a piece of straw like this?" After prodigious effort, Brahma found to his astonishment that he could not. The lad then turned to Vishnu and asked him to save the straw, which was slowly starting to dissolve under the boy's steady gaze. Vishnu's efforts to hold it together were fruitless. Finally, the little stranger produced the piece of straw again and asked Shiva to destroy it. But try as Shiva would to annihilate it, the tiny straw remained intact.

The little boy turned again to Brahma: "Did you create

* "They are true knowers...who understand the Day of Brahma, which endures for a thousand cycles (*yugas*), and the Night of Brahma, which also endures for a thousand cycles. At the dawn of Brahma's Day all creation, reborn, emerges from the state of non-manifestation; at the dusk of Brahma's Night all creation sinks into the sleep of non-manifestation" (Bhagavad-Gita VIII:17–18).

me?" he asked. Brahma thought and thought; he could not remember ever having created this amazing child. Suddenly the boy vanished. The three gods awoke from their delusion and remembered that behind their power is a Greater Power.

God, the Supreme Cause

In the Western world the idea of God developed through observation of the law of cause and effect. Man can materialize objects by taking materials from the earth and shaping them in accordance with a preconceived idea; therefore it seemed reasonable to conclude that this whole universe must have been created out of ideas. This led to the concept that everything must have existed first as an idea. Someone had to create that first idea or cosmic plan. Thus through the analogy of the law of cause and effect, intelligent men reasoned that there must be a Supreme Cause.

Science has learned that all matter is made of invisible building blocks—electrons and protons—just as a house is built of bricks. But nobody can tell why some electrons and protons become wood, and others become human bone, and so on. What Intelligence guides them? This line of questioning gives room for God in even the material scientist's theories about the nature of the phenomenal worlds. The sages of India say that everything proceeds from and goes back into its source: God.

Evidence of Order and Harmony Is Everywhere

Perceiving that every human being is a compound of matter and mind, the earliest Western thinkers believed that two independent forces existed: nature and mind. Later they began asking themselves, "Why is everything in nature arranged in a particular way? Why isn't one of man's arms longer than the other? Why don't stars and planets collide? Everywhere we see evidence of order and harmony in the universe." They concluded that mind and matter could not be both separate and sovereign; a single Intelligence must govern all. This conclusion naturally led to the idea that there is just one God, who is both the Cause of matter and the Intelligence within and behind it. One who attains the ultimate wisdom realizes that everything is Spirit—in essence, though hidden in manifesta-

tion. If you had the perception, you would see God in everything. Then the question is, how did seekers first find Him?

As the beginning step, they closed their eyes to shut out
immediate contact with the world and matter, so they could
concentrate more fully on discovering the Intelligence behind
it. They reasoned that they could not behold God's presence in
nature through the ordinary perceptions of the five senses. So
they began to try to feel Him within themselves by deeper and
deeper concentration. They eventually discovered how to shut
off all five senses, thus temporarily doing away entirely with
the consciousness of matter. The inner world of the Spirit began to open up.* To those great ones of ancient India who un-
deviatingly persisted in these inner investigations, God finally
revealed Himself.

Devotion and Right Activity Attract God's Attention

Thus the saints gradually began to convert their conceptions of God into perceptions of Him. That is what you must
do also, if you would know Him. You don't stay long enough at
your prayers. First you must have a right concept of God—a
definite idea through which you can form a relationship with
Him—and then you must meditate† and pray until that mental conception becomes changed into actual perception. Then
you will know Him. If you persist, the Lord will come. The
Searcher of Hearts wants only your sincere love. He is like a little child: someone may offer Him his whole wealth and He
doesn't want it; and another cries to Him, "O Lord, I love
You!" and into that devotee's heart He comes running.

Don't seek God with any ulterior motive, but pray to Him
with devotion—unconditional, one-pointed, steady devotion.
When your love for Him is as great as your attachment to your
mortal body, He will come to you.

In seeking the Lord, activity comes after devotion in importance. Some say, "God is Power; therefore let us act with

* "...for, behold, the kingdom of God is within you" (Luke 17:21).

† Meditation is that special form of concentration in which the attention has
been liberated, by scientific yoga techniques, from the restlessness of the body-
conscious state and is focused unfalteringly on God. Meditation is the concentrated flow of one's attention and consciousness toward communion and oneness with God.

power." When you are active in doing good, with the Lord ever uppermost in your mind, you will perceive Him in this way. But there is wrong as well as right activity even in doing good. A zealous churchman who brings more and more people into his congregation solely to satisfy his own ego is not going to please God through that activity. To realize the presence of the Divine Indweller should be the first desire in every heart.

It is when you persistently, selflessly perform every action with love-inspired thoughts of God that He will come to you. Then you realize that you are the Ocean of Life which has become the tiny wave of each life. This is the way of knowing the Lord through activity. When in every action you think of Him before you act, while you are performing the action, and after you have finished it, He will reveal Himself to you. You must work, but let God work through you; this is the best part of devotion. If you are constantly thinking that He is walking through your feet, working through your hands, accomplishing through your will, you will know Him. You should also develop discrimination, so that you prefer spiritually constructive, God-conscious activity to work performed without any thought of Him.

Meditation Is the Highest Form of Activity

But greater than activity, devotion, or reason, is meditation. To meditate truly is to concentrate solely on Spirit. This is esoteric meditation. It is the highest form of activity that man can perform, and it is the most balanced way to find God. If you work all the time you may become mechanical and lose Him in preoccupation with your duties; and if you seek Him only through discriminative thought you may lose Him in the labyrinths of endless reasoning; and if you cultivate only devotion for God, your development may become merely emotional. But meditation combines and balances all these approaches.

Work, eat, walk, laugh, cry, meditate—only for Him. That is the best way to live. In so doing you will be truly happy serving Him, loving Him, and communing with Him. So long as you let the desires and weaknesses of the physical body control your thoughts and actions, you will not find Him. Always be master of your body. When you sit in the church or temple, you perhaps feel a little devotion and a little discriminative perception, but that is not enough. The esoteric activity of meditation is necessary if you really want to be aware of His presence.

You might think that after two hours of meditation I would be bored to death. No, I couldn't find anything in the world as intoxicating as this God of mine. When I drink that aged wine of my soul, a skyful of happiness throbs in my heart. Divine joy is in everyone. Sunlight shines equally on the charcoal and the diamond, but the diamond reflects the light. Such are the transparent minds that know and reflect Spirit.

Thus in the esoteric activity of meditation you have the solution to the mystery of knowing God. I do not blame you for what you do, but for what you do not do. You think you have no time for God. Suppose the Lord were too busy to look after you? What then? Wrest your mind from the mirage of the senses and habit. Why be deluded like that? I am pointing out to you a land more beautiful than anything here can ever be. I am telling you of a happiness that will intoxicate you night and day— you won't need sense temptations to enthrall you. Discipline your body and your mind. Control your senses. Find God!

I often say that this body is a switchboard and the five senses are its telephone instruments. Through them I am in touch with the world; but when I don't wish to communicate, I shut off my five senses and live in the inexpressible joy of God. The Heavenly Father doesn't want you, His children, to suffer anymore. The sensory delusion in which you live must be overcome. You should conceive of God as the highest necessity of life. Break the shackles of limitation, of dark habits and mechanical daily routine. I condemn no man—only man's unbelief and oblivion of God. He can be known by using the technique of meditation. Then He shall throb as wisdom in your mind, and as joy in your heart, and you will be more active and more successful than you have ever been before.

Dear ones, I was once like you. I walked the earth seeking truth and happiness, yet everything that promised me joy gave me misery, and so I turned to God. You all must discover your own divinity and win the kingdom of God for yourselves.

The Self Is Your Savior

These deep truths are not for the inspiration of a passing moment but should be assimilated and made practical for your highest benefit. If only people knew wherein lies their own good! To those who act wrongly the Self is an enemy. Befriend the Self and the Self will save you. There is no other savior than your Self.* The fetters of ignorance and bad habits keep you bound. It is because you are determined to follow your wrong habits that you suffer. If only you would picture life a little ahead; lest the time, the precious time that is given you, slip away fruitlessly. The Hindus have a saying: "The child is busy with play, the youth is busy with sex, and the adult is busy with worries. How few are busy with God!"

Banish the imaginary hope that happiness will come from worldly fulfillments. Prosperity isn't enough, "gracious living" isn't enough. You want to be eternally happy. Seize the God within you and realize that the Self is Divinity. You must be able to answer with surety the highest question of your intelligence: "Whence did I come?"

God and immortality are not myths. It is the gravest insult to the Self within you to die believing you are a mortal being. How long will you let yourselves, sons of God, be helplessly mowed down by the sickle of death because you never tried during your lifetime to conquer *maya*,† ignorance?

Reason Gives Man the Power to Seek God

There is a God. He has given man independence, power, and reason. Man can find the Lord because of the gift of reason. To spend your time just playing with life and not finding God is wasting the divinely bestowed power within you.

Use the key of reason. It is not found in stones and animals. God gave man reason that he might find freedom from the delu-

* "Let man be uplifted, not degraded; let him transform his self (ego) into the Self (soul). The Self is the Friend of the (transformed) self, but the Enemy of the unregenerate self" (Bhagavad-Gita VI:6).

† Cosmic illusion; "the measurer." *Maya* is the magical power in creation by which limitations and divisions are apparently present in the Immeasurable and Inseparable. In God's plan and play (*lila*), the sole function of this delusive power is to cast a veil of ignorance over man to divert his awareness from Spirit to matter, from Reality to unreality.

sion of mortality. If you let your reason be trampled by ego and wrong habits, what then? If people bow to your will, what then? Happiness still eludes you. That is why Jesus chose God instead of Satan when the Devil tried to tempt him. Jesus realized that although worldly power has many attractions, it does not last. He had found something greater than all the riches of this universe. The things that most men desire are perishable. But God will never leave Jesus. He is still enjoying the omnipresent divine kingdom. So should each one of us choose the life that leads to God.

You are punishing the soul by keeping it buried, slumbering in matter life after life, frightened by nightmares of suffering and death. Realize that you are the soul! Remember that the Feeling behind your feeling, the Will behind your will, the Power behind your power, the Wisdom behind your wisdom is the Infinite Lord. Unite the heart's feeling and the mind's reason in a perfect balance. In the castle of calmness, again and again cast off identification with earthly titles, and plunge into deep meditation to realize your divine kingship.

Look within *yourself*. Remember, the Infinite is everywhere. Diving deep into superconsciousness,* you can speed your mind through eternity; by the power of mind you can go farther than the farthest star. The searchlight of mind is fully equipped to throw its superconscious rays into the innermost heart of Truth. Use it to do so.

Remember, it is you who must travel to the kingdom of heaven; it will not come to you by special delivery. Each man has to hie his own way alone. From this day make a resolution in your heart to seek God. When many devotees follow the path to Him, there will arise a "United States of the World,"† with God and His love as man's Director and Guide.

I want to give you more than the temporary inspiration of words alone; I want to shoot star-shells of wisdom straight into

---

* Soul-consciousness, which is intuitive and all-knowing. The superconscious mind is thus the omniscient power of the soul. (See also *spiritual eye* in glossary.)

† As the individual states of America maintain independence and yet are united in common ideals and goals, so if God's kingdom is to come on earth, the various countries of the world must similarly unite in a bond of harmonious cooperation and brotherhood.

your spiritual darkness, that by their bursting light you may see for yourself the truth of what I have said.

The Two Paths: Activity and Meditation

To summarize, there are basically two approaches to God-realization: the outer way and the inner, or transcendental way. The outer way is by right activity, loving and serving mankind with the consciousness centered in God; the transcendental way is by deep esoteric meditation. By the transcendental way you realize all the things you are not, and discover That which you are: "I am not the breath; I am not the body, neither bones nor flesh. I am not the mind or feeling. I am That which is behind the breath, body, mind, and feeling." When you go beyond the consciousness of this world, knowing that you are not the body or the mind, and yet aware as never before that you exist—that divine consciousness is what you are. You are That in which is rooted everything in the universe.

Why not inquire behind the darkness when you close your eyes? That is the place to explore. "And the light shineth in the darkness; and the darkness comprehended it not."* Vast lights and cosmic forces are moving there.

Skyfuls of Eternal Bliss Will Be Opened

Samadhi† is a joyous experience, a splendid light in which you behold the countless worlds floating in a vast bed of joy and bliss. Banish the spiritual ignorance that makes you think this mortal life is real. Have these beautiful experiences for yourself in eternal *samadhi*, in God. Auroras of light, skyfuls of eternal bliss will be opened to you.

All great teachers declare that within this body is the immortal soul, a spark of That which sustains all. He who knows his soul knows this truth: "I am beyond everything finite; I now see that the Spirit, alone in space with Its ever-new joy, has expressed Itself as the vast body of nature. I am the stars, I am the waves, I am the Life of all; I am the laughter within all hearts, I am the smile on the faces of flowers and in each soul. I am the Wisdom and Power that sustain all creation."

* John 1:5.
† Spiritual ecstasy; state of God-union experienced as the ultimate goal of meditation.

Realize that! My words may remain vibrating within you; but if you sleep on in delusion, you will not know it. If you awaken, you will be conscious that the truth I have spoken is ever throbbing within your soul. Meditate. Learn this liberating lesson. Wait no more. I came here not to entertain you with worldly festivities* but to arouse your sleeping memory of immortality. You do not realize the pain that comes to those who remain in delusion. I suffer for you, and will do everything to help you realize that illumination is within.

Free yourself forever!

* As a part of his effort to foster a broader understanding between the cultures of East and West, Paramahansa Yogananda occasionally arranged informal gatherings at the Self-Realization Fellowship international headquarters. He refers here to a "Hindu-American Banquet" that was to follow this talk.

The Universality of Yoga

Self-Realization Fellowship Temple,
Hollywood, California, May 21, 1944

Yoga is a system of scientific methods for reuniting the soul with the Spirit. We have come down from God, and we must reascend to Him. We have seemingly become separated from our Father, and we must consciously reunite with Him. Yoga teaches us how to rise above the delusion of separation and realize our oneness with God. The poet Milton wrote of the soul of man and how it might regain paradise. That is the purpose and goal of Yoga—to regain the lost paradise of soul consciousness by which man knows that he is, and ever has been, one with Spirit.

The world's various religions are based more or less on the *beliefs* of man. But the true basis of religion should be a science that all devotees may apply in order to reach our one Father-God. Yoga is that science. The practice of a *science of religion* is imperative. Different dogmatic "isms" have kept mankind divided, although Jesus pointed out: "If a house be divided against itself, that house cannot stand."* Unity among various religions may be brought about only when the individuals who practice those religions become actually aware of God within. Then we shall have a true brotherhood of man under the Fatherhood of God.

The great religions of the world all preach the necessity of finding God, of brotherhood among men; and all have a moral code, such as the Ten Commandments. What, then, creates the differences among them? It is the bigotry in men's minds. Not by concentrating on dogma may we reach God, but by actual soul knowledge. When men perceive the universal truths underlying various religions, there will be no more difficulties over

* Mark 3:25.

dogma. To me there is neither Jew, nor Christian, nor Hindu; all are my brothers. I worship in all temples, for each of them has been erected to honor my Father.

We should begin to build world unity with the idea that has been initiated by Self-Realization Fellowship: a "Church of All Religions"; not eclecticism, but respect for all religions as constituting various paths to God. Such temples, dedicated to the one God that all religions worship, should be built everywhere. I predict that this will come about. East and West should destroy forever narrow divisions in the houses of God. Attaining Self-realization through Yoga, men will come to know that they are all children of the one Father.

The Blind Cannot Lead the Blind

That unity of spirit is demonstrated in great men, those with God-realization. The blind cannot lead the blind; only a master,* one who knows God, may rightly teach others about Him. To regain one's divinity one must have such a master or guru.† He who faithfully follows a true guru becomes like him, for the guru helps to elevate the disciple to his own level of realization. When I found my guru, Swami Sri Yukteswarji,‡ I made up my mind to follow his example: to place God alone on the altar of my heart, and to share Him with others.

The Hindu masters taught that to gain the deepest knowledge one should focus his gaze through the omniscient spiritual eye. When concentrating hard, even the non-yogi wrinkles his forehead at the point between the eyebrows—the center of concentration and of the spherical spiritual eye, the seat of soul intuition. That is the real "crystal ball," into which the yogi

* One who is a master of himself—of the mind, emotions, senses, passions. His actions, unclouded by egoistic motives, are consonant with the will of God; and he knows himself as one with God, not in imagination but in actual experience of Divine Omnipresence.

† Spiritual teacher. The *Guru Gita* (17–19) aptly describes the guru as "dispeller of darkness" (from *gu*, "darkness" and *ru*, "that which dispels"). By divine right the title of *guru* is conferred only upon those exalted souls who, through their own Self-realization and oneness with God, are qualified to lead others from the darkness of ignorance to the everlasting light of Truth.

‡ In *Autobiography of a Yogi*, Paramahansa Yogananda describes his association with his divine guru, whom he called a *Jnanavatar*, "Incarnation of Wisdom." *Ji* added at the end of a proper name or title denotes respect.

gazes to learn the secrets of the universe. Those who go deep enough in their concentration will penetrate that "third" eye and see God. Seekers of truth therefore should develop the ability to project their perception through the spiritual eye. The practice of Yoga helps the aspirant to open the single eye of intuitive consciousness.*

Intuition or direct knowledge does not depend on any data from the senses. That is why the intuitive faculty is often called the "sixth sense." Everyone has this sixth sense, but most people do not develop it. However, almost everyone has had some intuitional experience, perhaps a "feeling" that a particular thing is going to happen, when there is no sensory evidence to indicate it.

It is important to develop intuition, or direct soul knowledge, for he who is God-conscious is sure of himself. He knows, and he knows that he knows. We must be sure of God's presence, as sure as we are that we know the taste of an orange. It was only after my guru had shown me how to commune with God and after I had felt His presence every day that I assumed the spiritual duty of telling others about Him.

The West has emphasized large temples of worship, but there are few in which the worshipers are shown how God may be found. In the East, the emphasis has been on the development of men of God-realization; but they are in many cases inaccessible to spiritual seekers, remaining in seclusion in remote and solitary abodes. Spiritual centers in which people may commune with God, and teachers who can show people how to do so, are both necessary. How may one receive knowledge of God from a teacher who himself does not know God? My guru impressed upon me the necessity of knowing the Heavenly Father before trying to tell others about Him. How grateful I am to have received his training! He himself truly communed with God.

* During deep meditation, the single or spiritual eye becomes visible as a bright star surrounded by a sphere of blue light that, in turn, is encircled by a brilliant halo of golden light. This omniscient eye is variously referred to in scriptures as the third eye, the star of the East, the inner eye, the dove descending from heaven, the eye of Shiva, and the eye of intuition. "If therefore thine eye be single, thy whole body shall be full of light" (Matthew 6:22).

The Lord must first be perceived in one's own bodily temple. Every seeker should daily discipline his thoughts and place on the altar of his soul the wildflowers of his devotion. He who finds God within will be able to feel His presence in every church or temple he enters.

Yoga Converts Theology to Practical Experience

Yoga enables man to perceive the truth in all religions. The Ten Commandments are preached, in various words, in every religion. But the two greatest commandments are those emphasized by Jesus: "Love the Lord thy God with all thy heart, and with all thy soul, and with all thy mind," and "Thou shalt love thy neighbor as thyself."*

Loving God "with all thy mind" means withdrawing one's attention from the senses and giving it to God; giving to Him one's whole concentration in meditation. Every seeker of God must learn to concentrate. A prayer that one utters while at the same time thinking of other things in the background of the mind is not a true prayer and is unheeded by God. Yoga teaches that in order to find the Father it is first necessary to seek Him with all one's mind, with concentration that is one-pointed.

Some people say that the Hindus are more adapted to the practice of Yoga, that Yoga is not suited to Westerners. This is not true. Many Westerners are at present in a better position to practice Yoga than many Hindus are, because scientific advancements have given Westerners much free time. India should more and more utilize the progressive material methods of the West to make life easier and freer; and the West should take from India the practical metaphysical methods of Yoga whereby every man may find his way to God. Yoga is not a sect but a universally applicable science by which we can find our Father.

Yoga is for everybody, for the people of the West as well as for those of the East. One would not say that the telephone is

---

* Matthew 22:37, 39. Krishna's teachings in the Bhagavad-Gita similarly stress these two commandments: "On Me [the Lord] fix thy mind, be thou My devotee, with ceaseless worship bow reverently before Me. Having thus united thyself to Me as thy Highest Goal, thou shalt be Mine Own" (IX:34); and "The best type of yogi is he who feels for others, whether in grief or pleasure, even as he feels for himself" (VI:32).

not for the East just because it was invented in the West. Similarly, the methods of Yoga, although developed in the East, are not exclusively for the East but are useful to all mankind.

Whether a man is born in India or in America, he someday has to die. Why not learn how to "die daily" in God, like St. Paul?* Yoga teaches the method. Man lives in the body as a prisoner; when his term is over, he suffers the indignity of being thrown out. Love of the body is therefore nothing more than love of jail. Long accustomed to living in the body, we have forgotten what real freedom means. Being a Westerner is no excuse for not seeking freedom. It is vital to every man that he discover his soul and know his immortal nature. Yoga shows the way.

The Soul Must Reascend to God

Before creation existed there was Cosmic Consciousness: Spirit or God, the Absolute, ever-existing, ever-conscious, ever-new Bliss beyond form and manifestation. When creation came into being, Cosmic Consciousness "descended" into the physical universe where it manifests as Christ Consciousness:† the omnipresent pure reflection of God's intelligence and consciousness inherent and hidden within all creation. When the Christ Consciousness descends into the physical body of man it becomes soul, or superconsciousness: the ever-existing, ever-conscious, ever-new bliss of God individualized by encasement in the body. When the soul becomes identified with the body, it manifests as ego, mortal consciousness. Yoga teaches that the soul must climb back up the ladder of consciousness to Spirit.‡

* I Corinthians 15:31.

† The Hindu scriptures refer to Christ Consciousness as *Kutastha Chaitanya,* universal consciousness or omnipresent intelligence.

‡ Yoga teaches that the abode of the soul—of man's life and divine consciousness—is in the subtle spiritual centers in the brain: *Sahasrara,* the thousand-petaled lotus at the top of the cerebrum, seat of cosmic consciousness; *Kutastha,* at the point between the eyebrows, seat of Christ consciousness; and the medullary center (connected by polarity to the *Kutastha*), seat of superconsciousness. Descending into the body (and body-consciousness) from these centers of highest spiritual perception, life and consciousness flow down the spine, passing through five astral spinal centers (see *chakras* in glossary) and branching outward into the physical organs of life, sensory perception, and action.

To regain the blissful realization of its oneness with God, the soul of man

Secret of Happiness Is Consciousness of God's Presence

It is all right to enjoy life; the secret of happiness is not to become attached to anything. Enjoy the smell of the flower, but see God in it. I have kept the consciousness of the senses only that in using them I may always perceive and think of God. "Mine eyes were made to behold Thy beauty everywhere. My ears were made to hear Thine omnipresent voice." That is yoga, union with God. It is not necessary to go to the forest to find Him. Worldly habits will hold us fast wherever we may be until we free ourselves from them. The yogi learns to find God in the cave of his heart. Wherever he goes, he carries with him the blissful consciousness of God's presence.

Man has not only descended into mortal sense consciousness but has become bound by abnormalities of that sense consciousness, such as greed, anger, and jealousy. Man must banish these abnormalities in order to find God. Both Easterners and Westerners should be free from sense slavery. An ordinary man may become angry because his morning coffee hasn't been brought to him and he is sure the deprivation will give him a headache. He is a slave of his habits. The developed yogi is free.

Everyone can be a yogi, right where he is now. But we are prone to think strange and difficult anything that is beyond the horizon of our own habits of life. We do not consider how our habits may appear to others!

The practice of Yoga leads to freedom. Some yogis carry this idea of nonattachment to extremes. They teach that one should be able to lie on a bed of nails without discomfort, and other forms of *tapasya*, physical discipline. It is true that one who can sit on a bed of nails and think of God shows great strength of mind. But such feats are not necessary. One may just as well sit in a comfortable chair and meditate on God.

Patanjali* teaches that any posture that keeps the spine

---

must retrace its downward course, ascending by the sacred spinal route to its home in the higher cerebral centers of divine awareness. This is accomplished by the practice of guru-given scientific techniques of yogic meditation, such as may be learned from the *Self-Realization Fellowship Lessons*. (See glossary.)

* Foremost exponent of Yoga. Patanjali's date is unknown, though many scholars assign him to the second century B.C.

erect is good for meditation, yogic concentration on God. It is not necessary to go through physical contortions or to practice exercises requiring extraordinary physical endurance and suppleness, as is advocated in *Hatha Yoga*. God is the objective; consciousness of His presence is what we should work toward. The Bhagavad-Gita says: "He who absorbs himself in Me, with his soul immersed in Me, him I regard, among all classes (of yogis), as the most equilibrated." *

Hindu yogis have been known to demonstrate obliviousness to extremes of heat and cold, and to mosquitoes and other annoying insects. Such a demonstration is not a requisite of being a yogi, but it is a natural achievement of the adept. Try to eliminate disturbing elements; or to endure them, if necessary, without being disturbed inwardly by them. If one can remain clean, it is pointless to be dirty. One may become attached to living in a hut as well as to living in a palace.

The greatest factor in achieving spiritual success is willingness. Jesus said, "The harvest truly is plenteous, but the laborers are few." † People of the world seek the gifts of God, but he who is wise seeks the Giver Himself.

To be a yogi is to meditate. The yogi doesn't think first of food for his body upon waking each morning; he feeds his soul with the ambrosia of God-communion. Filled with the inspiration found by his deeply diving meditative mind, he is able to perform happily all the duties of the day.

God made this earth as it is on purpose; in His plan it is man's part to make the world better. The Westerner tends to go to extremes in keeping constantly busy getting new and improved material comforts. The Easterner tends to go to extremes in being satisfied with what he has. There is something appealing about both the go-ahead spirit of the West and the easy, calm spirit of the East. We should take the balanced road between.

Meditation Makes the Yogi

To find God, one should meditate every morning and night, and whenever there is a little spare time during the day. In addition, it is important to meditate for six hours on one day out

* VI:47. † Matthew 9:37.

of the week. This is not unreasonable; some people practice at
the piano for ten hours every day of the week, and think nothing
of it. To become a spiritual master, it is necessary to give more
time to God. We have to make Him feel that we love Him more
than anything else. When you become experienced in meditation, able to go deep into superconsciousness, five hours of sleep
are enough. The rest of the night should be used for meditation.
One can use nights and early mornings and holidays for meditating on God. In this way anyone, even the busy Westerner,
can be a yogi. So become a Western yogi. You don't have to wear
a turban or to have long hair like me!

We need the "hives" of churches, but we also need to fill
the churches with the "honey" of our own Self-realization.*
God is present in the churches too, of course; but your just going there will not persuade Him to reveal Himself. Church-
going is good, but daily meditation is better still. Do both, because you will certainly have inspiration from going to church;
and from daily meditation you will receive even greater upliftment. It is when a devotee's heart is afire and when he throws
shell after shell of prayer that God surrenders to him. That unceasing devotion is essential to finding Him. In order to be a
yogi and still keep pace with the modern world, it is necessary
to meditate at home, to discipline oneself, and to perform all
duties with the attitude that they are a service to God.

My greatest desire is to build temples of God in the souls
of men; to see the smile of God on men's faces. The most important of all life's accomplishments is to establish a temple
of God in one's own soul. And it can be easily done. That is
why Self-Realization Fellowship was sent to the West.

Anyone who has established God in his soul temple is a
yogi. He can say, with me, that Yoga is for the East, North,
South, and West—for all people, that they may follow the by-
ways of theology to join the highway of Yoga. The right road
leads to the palace of God's bliss. He who once reaches there
shall "go no more out."†

* Knowing one's Self as the soul, and that the soul is one with God.
† Revelation 3:12.

The Infinite Nature of God

Self-Realization Fellowship international headquarters,
Los Angeles, California, January 28, 1937

The Hindu scriptures state that God is beyond comprehension by mind and intellect. Powerful as they are, their scope is insufficient to contain Him. So the human mind is incapable of a true conception of God. The question "Who made God?" arises only because mind cannot comprehend That which has neither beginning nor end.

When you are looking at the sun millions of miles away in the sky, that huge luminary seems smaller by far than our earth. Yet the diameter of earth is roughly 7,900 miles; and the sun is more than a hundred times that wide. If you could place our planet next to the sun, earth would appear by comparison a tiny dot. Let us suppose the giant solar orb is expanding, growing more and more huge, until the vast blue expanse of the sky is entirely swallowed up by its mass. The space thus filled is nevertheless but a particle, a mere speck, of the space that spreads through countless universes and into infinity. Were the sun to go on endlessly enlarging in space, still it would not be able to take the measure of infinity. The cosmic delusion of finitude prevents the mind from conceiving such vastness. Where are its boundaries? Whence came this endless void? The Originless Immeasurable is God. Omnipresent in the farthest reaches of space, He is in the distant stars, and in you and me; and He is conscious every moment of every place He is.

God is not mind—He created it and He is beyond it. Otherwise we could conceive Him in our minds. We can accurately call Him Divine Consciousness, Divine Joy, Divine Existence, but not mind.

Though mind is incapable of encompassing Omnipresence, it is nevertheless able to *feel* God. Feeling His presence and measuring it are two different experiences. The wave cannot measure the ocean, but there is a point of contact between them. So where the Infinite becomes the finite there is a point of contact: the superconscious mind. That mind can feel God. When we expand the ordinary mind until it impinges on the superconscious mind, we are able to feel His presence.

We Have Descended from the Infinite into the Finite

We have descended from the Infinite into the finite. Yoga is withdrawal of the attention from externals in order to focus it on the inner source of Truth. Only in this way can we discover how God has condensed His consciousness into the multitudinous finite forms of His creatures and the universes they inhabit. The human body is the most intricate of all His creations. A single original cell, the united sperm and ovum, divides; and by multiplication of the process builds up trillions of cells around itself to create the bodily temple that houses our divine soul consciousness.

You don't realize how much energy is locked in even one little gram of flesh. Its release would spread countless electrons far into space.* And the power and extent of the consciousness that is present in the body is beyond human conception. Though externally we are made of flesh, behind its gross cells are electrical currents, life currents. And behind these subtle energies are the thoughts and perceptions.

Thought is inexhaustible. Since the world began, thoughts in unimaginable numbers have passed through the ether. One could not begin to count them, but it is possible to get some idea if you reflect on how many thoughts and feelings you express during your own lifetime. Millions! Try to remember all you have thought in just one year, or even in one day. Consider the accumulation of thoughts of every human being through unrecorded ages past. God knows them all!

Mind cannot measure even the subtle phenomena of nature. How many electrons whirl in the electricity that flows into

---

* The awesome power of the release of nuclear energy was first demonstrated under controlled conditions within a few years after this talk, when the first atomic bomb was exploded at Alamogordo, New Mexico, on July 16, 1945.

the light bulbs here in the chapel? Trillions, dancing together, make this light you behold. These ultramicroscopic particles are moving at a speed equivalent to traveling from here to New York, or to any other part of the world, in a few seconds. Scientific experiments are proving this.

If you try to calculate how many protons and electrons are condensed in our earth, the mind goes only so far and then stops. What is revealed to the searching mind seems infinite, but there is a point beyond which ideas become too subtle to follow. From that sphere where the mind cannot penetrate, God is pouring forth His essential Light—the Cosmic Intelligent Vibration that structures finite creation.

God's True Nature Known Only Through Intuition

If we use the mind properly, we can understand how God is beyond mind and intellect; and how His true nature can be felt only through the soul's power of intuition. We must find His consciousness through the superconscious mind—the nucleus of mind and intelligence. His infinite nature is revealed to man through the intuitive superconsciousness of the soul. The joy felt in meditation reveals the presence of Eternal Joy spread over all creation. The light seen in meditation is the astral light* from which our tangible creation is made. Beholding this light, one feels a unity with all things.

The ordinary person lives in the world but is relatively unconscious of its nature and purpose. A life of such limited perception is not unlike that of the animals. We used to have here at Mt. Washington a goat that was invariably attracted by my voice. One day, while I was speaking in this chapel, the goat came trotting in and right on up the aisle to me! I am sure it didn't know what I was saying; it simply liked to hear my voice. But you come to these lectures not only to listen to the words, but also to feel the presence of God behind them. If you attune your consciousness with His consciousness, and remain in that current of bliss, you will feel at-onement with Him. Whatever understanding I have attained has been acquired by

---

* Everything on the material plane has a counterpart made of astral light, a light that is more subtle than the electromagnetic energies of the atom. Hindu scriptures called this energy *prana*, which Paramahansa Yogananda has translated as "lifetrons."

becoming attuned to God's consciousness within. This you too can accomplish.

As one develops spiritually and realizes his kinship with all that lives, his responsibility to share the suffering of others increases. Jesus was willing even to suffer in sharing the afflictions of others; we too must do what we can for those who are shivering with cold and disease. It is a nightmare for them; and whatever of their woes we can remove, we are removing them from God also. He is not happy when His children are in misery, for He suffers in them.

At this moment most of you are enjoying beauty and peace, but think of those in Louisville today! Thousands are suffering there because of the floods. Once long ago I was thinking how wonderful America is, without the disasters that afflict so many countries; then God showed me the floods that are occurring now. The vibrations of the thoughts* and feelings of thousands being killed in the fighting in Spain have caused atmospheric changes that are responsible for these floods and other disasters around the world. War spews out vibrations of wrong that throw all nature out of balance and harmony, causing "natural" catastrophes.

God gave freedom to man, and man has misused that freedom; this is the cause of all suffering. The misuse of our God-given free will has terrifying consequences. I would rather someone tell me that I am about to do wrong, than allow me to act and not wake up until years later to the harm I had done.

Satan Created Ignorance, Cause of All Suffering

Suffering is therefore not the work of God, but of Satan's power of *maya*, delusion. This force creates the ignorance that

---

* The power of thought, for good or ill, derives from the thought-essence of the universe. In manifesting creation, God first projects it as thought-patterns, the finest form of creative vibration, which condenses into forms of astral light and then into grosser atomic structures. Remove the primal thought of God and creation dissolves. Man's thoughts are a microcosmic borrowing from God's thought power and so have the ability, even when undeveloped, to affect significantly his own health, happiness, and success and, when strongly reinforced by kindred thoughts of others, the world in which he lives. The thought-patterns implanted in creation by God are thus affected harmoniously or inharmoniously by the thoughts of mankind. (See *karma* in glossary.)

blinds people to the consequences of their actions, causing them to err and thus bring suffering upon themselves. Those who are fighting in Spain—both the government forces and their opponents—think they are trying to do right. The only way to avoid error is to develop the discriminative wisdom to know what is wrong, and then resolve not to do it. One wrong fighting another wrong doesn't make a right. The true enemy of man is ignorance. It must be driven from this earth.

We have everything necessary in the world today to bring about the millennium. Only man's selfishness makes it impossible. Tremendous unnecessary suffering is created by man's shortsighted self-interest. Money that could feed and clothe needy people is used instead for destruction. The root cause of the world's troubles is this selfishness born of ignorance. Each person thinks he is doing right; but when he seeks to satisfy only his own interest, he is setting in motion the karmic law* of cause and effect that will inevitably destroy his own and others' happiness.

The more I see of world tragedies caused by man's ignorance, the more I realize that even if every street were paved with gold, happiness would not be lasting. Happiness lies in making others happy, in forsaking self-interest to bring joy to others. If each one would do that, then everyone would be happy; and all would be taken care of. This is what Jesus meant when he said: "All things whatsoever ye would that men should do to you, do ye even so to them."†

A federation of all religions and all nations is necessary. But such a union will come only when every individual engages in that meditation which leads to direct contact with God. Communion with Him is the solution. When one has realized God, he no longer feels that others are different from himself. Unless such wisdom comes, not to just a few, but to all men, there will be no freedom on earth. Even here in America freedom is not total; suffering still abounds. Each one of us has a responsibility to bring peace and happiness to our country and to all men. One should care, not only for his own nation, but

* *Karma* is the law of action and reaction. Whatever man sows by his behavior he will reap in like measure, in this life or in succeeding ones. (See glossary.)
† Matthew 7:12.

all countries; not only for one's own family, but for all mankind. The ordinary man's interest is limited to himself and his surroundings, but the man of God identifies with the whole world. Don't think the contribution made by your spiritualized consciousness is small. Your part may mean very much.

In order to know God you must become like Him. In spite of our transgressions, in spite of our forgetfulness of God and great indifference to Him, still He lovingly gives us life and all that supports life in this world. Nothing is greater than God; indifference to Him is the highest sin.

Those who are not willing to give up all they have to find Him, will not know Him. Whoever would know God must be able to forsake all else for Him. Jesus was trying to make his disciples understand this truth when he told them to keep watch and pray with him at Gethsemane. But when they fell asleep, he sadly observed: "The spirit indeed is willing, but the flesh is weak."*

Man is like a puppet. The strings of his habits, emotions, passions, and senses make him dance to their bidding. They bind his soul. He who is unwilling or unable to cut himself free in order to know God will not find Him. I see myself apart from these attachments. I eat, and sometimes I don't eat; I sleep, and sometimes I don't sleep. I gave up all physical necessities to prove to myself that I do not need them. God doesn't eat or sleep; He isn't bound by senses and habits. This is what makes Him God; and we are made in His image. We should be able to give up everything to know Him: "Seek ye the kingdom of God; and all these things shall be added unto you."† Despite all the tests I have gone through for Him, in the end God has given me everything I wanted or needed of this world. And I have given it all back, for He has bestowed on me a gift infinitely greater: Divine Joy, day and night. In that Joy all desires that come into my heart are satisfied.

Meditation Lifts the Fog of Ignorance

In the Bhagavad-Gita, recorded by Sage Vyasa, Lord Krishna explains that if your innate wisdom is covered over with igno-

* Matthew 26:41.
† Luke 12:31.

rance, you are deluded and thus stumble through life: "Tamasic [ignorant] action is that which is instituted through delusion, without measuring one's ability, and disregarding the consequences—loss to oneself of wealth and influence, and harm to others."* When the fog of ignorance is removed by meditation you will see the right path. You will be troubled no more; you will find fulfillment eternal. "Verily there exists in this earth nothing more sanctifying than wisdom. In due course of time, the devotee who is successful in yoga [meditation] will spontaneously realize this truth within his own heart."†

These truths are all real to me. Truth is Reality. Self-realization is not something one can learn from books; it comes only through personal experience. Realization of Truth, experience of God—not dogma merely—is what every religion should bring to its followers. What Jesus Christ realized, we too must experience. He didn't teach that we should worship him as a personality, but rather that we should experience what he experienced in his oneness with God. That can be attained only by meditation and by following God's laws. To worship Jesus because he is Jesus is not enough. We must embrace the universal ideals he taught, and strive to be like him.

We are here on earth in this particular body-form for just a little while, to learn our lessons and move on. Whither are we headed now? Think how many pages have already been turned in the Lord's dream novel of creation! When I visited Salt Lake City I saw in vision a great ocean, and mammoths walking on the shore. Later I learned that the skeleton of an ancient mammoth had recently been found there.

As human beings we have God-given power to cast away every habit and limitation and spread our consciousness throughout creation, penetrating not only the hearts of all creatures, but reaching out beyond the stars. Our native vastness encompasses even greater space. Such tremendous possibility lies within us! We are infinite! I live in that sphere of infinity, and am conscious of the body only once in a while.

You are limited now; but when by deep, daily meditation you become able to transfer your consciousness from the finite

* XVIII:25.
† Ibid. IV:38.

to the Infinite, you will be free. You are not meant to be a prisoner of the body. You are a child of God; you must live up to that divine birthright.

Give God First Place in Your Heart

Wherever your mind is, that is where you will spend your time. What if God had not given you the power to play or read or work? You could do nothing. So He should come first in your life. God knows what is in your heart; give Him first place there.

The only way to catch God is by love. Meditate upon Him, and then deeply pray: "Lord, I cannot live without You. You are the Power behind my consciousness. I love You. Reveal Yourself to me." When you give up sleep to meditate upon Him, when you forsake selfishness and cry because of His suffering in your brothers, He comes to you. When you actually sacrifice for Him, He is caught in the net of your love. Nothing else can capture Him.

Knowledge prepares the way to love. You cannot love that which you do not know. Knowledge of God must therefore precede love for Him. This knowledge comes with practice of *Kriya Yoga,* * the technique that Lahiri Mahasaya gave. When you know God, you will love Him; and when you love Him, you will surrender yourself to Him.

Until your devotion for God and awareness of Him become complete, don't rest; don't give in to sleep when you should be meditating. Never give anything preference before God! His love is the greatest love there is. So long as you let other things come first, He will wait. But your delay may be too long, and your suffering may be great. Don't procrastinate. Be certain in the sincerity of your conscience that you have made the effort to commune with Him. Don't rest, don't give up until you can see Him with your own eyes, or feel Him in your heart. Birth, play, marriage, children, old age—life is finished. That is not living! Life is much deeper and more wonderful than that, I have found. When you know God, there is no more sorrow.

* *Kriya Yoga* means union (*yoga*) with the Infinite through a certain action or rite (*kriya*). Specifically, it is a meditation technique through which the divine union can be realized. Lahiri Mahasaya, guru of Paramahansa Yogananda's guru, played a key role in the revival in this age of the ancient *Kriya Yoga* science. (See glossary; see also *Autobiography of a Yogi*, chapter 26.)

All those you loved and lost in death are with you again in the Eternal Life. You don't know whom to consider your "own" anymore, because everyone is yours.

The beauty of God is vast. To enjoy flowers for their loveliness is good, but far greater is to see behind their purity and beauty the face of God. To be carried away by music for its own sake cannot compare with hearing God's creative Voice in it. Though God is immanent in the finite beauties of creation, it is wisdom to realize one's eternal Self beyond form and finitude. You know how fond I am of our grounds at the Mount Washington and Encinitas *ashrams.** I never tire of their beauty. But the Lord gave me an awakening experience recently. I inwardly saw people sitting about and talking. One of them proposed some activity, but another said, "No, Paramahansaji taught that we must not do that." I suddenly realized that this was a vision of years to come, after I was no longer here in this body. For a moment I was shaken; then I came back to ordinary consciousness.

There is no use in becoming attached to anything in this world. So many things come and go in the Lord's cosmic drama. I see airfields destroyed, and the sea filled with dead, and many other things to come. In my heart I see a world without me. That freedom God gives ultimately to every soul.

One great saint said, "I care not where I may be, O Lord, but punish me not with obliviousness of Thee." There is no greater punishment. Jesus said: "It is better for thee to enter into life maimed."† All suffering can be taken away by the contact of God.

Awake from the Nightmare of Suffering

In a dream you may see yourself running down a street, pursued by an enemy. Suddenly you are shot, and you think, "Oh, how terrible! I am dying! I am sad to leave this world."

* An *ashram* is a spiritual hermitage; often a monastery. Mt. Washington Ashram Center is the international headquarters of Self-Realization Fellowship (Yogoda Satsanga Society of India), located on Mt. Washington in Los Angeles. The Ashram Center in Encinitas, California, is a branch of Self-Realization Fellowship.

† Mark 9:43. I.e., maimed of all desires and habits that prevent man from thinking of God.

Then you see yourself dead. The undertaker cremates your body, and your friends come to mourn when the ashes are laid away. But suddenly you wake up and see that it was only a dream. You are alive! This is similar to what happens at death.

God showed me in a vision that those who are dying in the fighting in Spain are only dreaming a terrible dream of death. As soon as their consciousness is lifted from the body, they awake as from a nightmare, and are glad to be free of it. Our life experiences are all part of a dream. Man himself has created the nightmare of war. But after its victims have been thrown from their bodies, they realize it was only a horrible dream from which they have awakened. They know they are not dead. This is a great metaphysical truth.

If you know you are dreaming, you don't suffer from your bad experiences in the dream. But if you are identified with the dream, and in it someone strikes your head and kills you, that dream death seems a true and terrible experience until you wake up and understand it was not real. It is the same after death. Once you are out of this body, you realize you are not dead; you are free of a nightmare. So death is not the end; it is a freeing of the consciousness from imprisonment in the physical dream-body. That release brings a sense of great freedom. We should never seek death. Rather, we should prepare our consciousness by meditation and God-communion, so that when death comes, in its own time, we are able to look upon it as a dream, nothing more. I can see the dream nature of life and death anytime I wish. Hence I attach little importance to this body.

In Oneness with God Know That Life Is a Dream

Live in the consciousness of Spirit, in that oneness with God wherein you know that life is a dream. It is very easy to do when you make the effort. When suffering comes it is more difficult to detach your consciousness from identification with the body; so be wise and make the effort now, while you have strength and health.

Material desires take away the desire for the Infinite. Every day or so someone tells me I need this or that. It seems ridiculous, because I know that thousands do not have what I am told

I "need." If they don't need it, why should I? Your only real need is God; there is no other necessity. Be not attached to possessions, music, books, food, or any other sense pleasures. In God you have eternal life. Become aware of this great truth; otherwise your appointments in life will take over, and you will die still bound by them. If you are one with Him, you are not compelled to return to this dream earth again. You are free to come and go as you like,* to serve God in His children on earth.

If you live in the joy of God, you will not know what death is. You do not get to that state when you pray mechanically. Become completely absorbed in your prayer, with faith that God is listening. If you thus fervently, lovingly pray to God, He will come to you at any time.

---

* The doctrine of reincarnation provides the only plausible explanation for the seeming injustices in inequalities among men—all of whom are God's beloved children. The soul, all-perfect and ever-perfect, is compelled by the law of evolution to incarnate repeatedly in progressively higher lives—retarded by wrong actions and desires and accelerated by spiritual endeavors—until Self-realization and God-union are attained. Having then transcended the Lord's delusion, the soul is forever freed. "Their thoughts immersed in That (Spirit), their souls one with Spirit, their sole allegiance and devotion given to Spirit, their beings purified from poisonous delusion by the antidote of wisdom—such men reach the state of nonreturn" (Bhagavad-Gita V:17). In the Bible it is similarly written: "Him that overcometh will I make a pillar in the temple of my God, and he shall go no more out" (Revelation 3:12). A soul who returns to earth after attaining liberation, incarnates of his own free will as a master, to help liberate others. Such voluntary returns are called *vyutthana,* reversion to earthly life after *maya* has ceased to blind. Such incarnations are rare in any age.

Answered Prayers

Self-Realization Fellowship international headquarters,
Los Angeles, California, October 19, 1939

Having come to this world from we know not where, we naturally wonder about the origin and purpose of life. We hear about a Creator, read about Him, but know not any way to contact Him. We only know that the entire universe depicts His intelligence. Just as the intricate works of a tiny watch arouse our admiration for the watchmaker, and the huge complicated machines in a factory cause us to marvel at their inventor, so when we see nature's wonders we feel awed by the hidden intelligence behind them. We ask ourselves: Who made the flower a living form, reaching out to the sun? Whence came its fragrance and beauty? How were its petals formed so perfectly, and tinged with lovely colors?

At night the stars and the moon, shedding silvery light around us, move us to reflection on the intelligence guiding these celestial bodies through the sky. The moon's soft light is insufficient for the activities of the day; thus a benign intelligence suggests to us that we rest at night. Then the sun comes up, and its bright light makes us look clearly and squarely at the world around us, and at our responsibility to satisfy the needs that beset us.

There are two ways in which our needs can be taken care of. One is the material. For example, when we have ill health we can go to a doctor for medical treatment. But a time comes when no human aid can help. Then we look to the other way, to the Spiritual Power, the Maker of our body, mind, and soul. Material power is limited, and when it fails, we turn to the unlimited Divine Power. Likewise with our financial needs; when we have done our best, and still it is inadequate, we turn to that other Power.

Everyone thinks that his problems are the worst. Some feel more oppressed than others because their resistance is weaker. Because of differences in their mental power, people put forth varying amounts of energy. If one has a very great difficulty and his mind is weak, he will not succeed in overcoming the problem. A man whose mind is powerful could break down the barriers of that difficulty. Even so, the mightiest men have sometimes met failure. When overwhelming material, mental, or spiritual troubles beset us, we realize how limited are the powers of life in this physical world.

Our endeavor must be not only to acquire financial security and good health, but to seek out the meaning of life. What is it all about? When we are hit with difficulties we react upon our environment first, making whatever material adjustments we believe may help. But when we come to the point of saying, "Everything I have tried so far has failed; what to do next?" we start to think hard about a solution. When we think deeply enough, we find an answer within. This is one form of *answered prayer*.

Prayer Is a Demand of the Soul

Prayer is a demand of the soul. God did not make us beggars; He created us in His image. The Bible and Hindu scriptures declare it. A beggar who goes to a rich home and asks for alms receives a beggar's share; but the son can have anything he asks from his wealthy father. Therefore we should not behave like beggars. Divine ones such as Christ, Krishna, and Buddha did not lie when they said we are made in the image of God.

Yet we see that some people have everything, seemingly born with a silver spoon in their mouth, whereas others seem to attract failure and troubles. Where is the image of God in them? The power of Spirit lies within each one of us; the question is how to develop it. If you will follow the lesson in my experiences with God, you are bound to find the result you are seeking. In the past you may have been disappointed that your prayers were not answered. But do not lose faith. In order to find out if prayers work or not, you must have in your mind an initial belief in the power of prayer.

Your prayers may have gone unanswered because you chose to be a beggar. Also, you should know what you may legitimately ask of your Heavenly Father. You may pray with all your heart and power to own the earth, but your prayer will not be granted, because all prayers connected with material life are limited; they have to be. God will not break His laws to satisfy whimsical desires. But there is a right way to pray. The cat is said to have nine lives; difficulties have ninety-nine! You have to find the one sure way of killing the cat of difficulties. The secret of effective prayer is to change your status from beggar to child of God; when you appeal to Him from that consciousness, your prayer will have both power and wisdom.

In Will Power Lies the Germ of Success

Most people become extremely nervous or tense when they are trying to accomplish something that means a great deal to them. Anxious, nervous actions do not draw the power of God; but continuous, calm, powerful use of the will shakes the forces of creation and brings a response from the Infinite. The germ of success in whatever you want to accomplish is in your will power. Will that has been badly battered by difficulties becomes temporarily paralyzed. The resolute man who says, "My body may be broken, but my head of will power remains unbowed," demonstrates the greatest expression of will.

Will power is what makes you divine. When you give up using that will, you become a mortal man. Many people say we should not exercise our will to change conditions, lest we interfere with God's plan. But why would God give us will if we are not to use it? I once met a fanatical man who said he did not believe in using will power because it developed the ego. "You are using a lot of will now to resist me!" I replied. "You are using it to talk, and you are obliged to use your will to stand, or walk, or eat, or go to the movies, or even to go to sleep. You *will* everything you do. Without will power you would be a mechanical man." Non-use of the will is not what Jesus meant when he said: "Not as I will, but as Thou wilt."* He was demonstrating that man must learn to bend his will, which is gov-

* Matthew 26:39.

erned by desires, to the will of God. Therefore right prayer, when it is persistent, is will.

You must believe in the possibility of what you are praying for. If you want a home, and the mind says, "You simpleton, you can't afford a house," you must make your will stronger. When the "can't" disappears from your mind, divine power comes. A home will not be dropped down to you from heaven; you have to pour forth will power continuously through constructive actions. When you persist, refusing to accept failure, the object of will must materialize. When you continuously work that will through your thoughts and activities, what you are wishing for has to come about. Even though there is nothing in the world to conform to your wish, when your will persists, the desired result will somehow manifest. In that kind of will lies God's answer; because will comes from God, and continuous will is divine will.

Cauterize the "Can'ts" in Your Brain

A weak will is a mortal will. As soon as trials and failure cut it off, it loses its connection with the dynamo of the Infinite. But behind human will is the divine will that can never fail. Even death has no power to deter divine will. The Lord will definitely answer that prayer behind which the will force is continuous. Most people are mentally or physically lazy, or both. When they want to pray, they think instead of sleep, and when the head nods they dive into bed and that is the end of prayer. The will is buried. Mortal man's brain is full of "can'ts." Being born in a family with certain characteristics and habits, he is influenced by these to think he can't do certain things; he can't walk much, he can't eat this, he can't stand that. Those "can'ts" have to be cauterized. You have within you the power to accomplish everything you want; that power lies in the will.

Whoever would develop will power must have good company. If your desire is to become a great mathematician, and your customary associates all dislike mathematics, you will certainly be discouraged. But when you mix with accomplished mathematicians, your will is reinforced; you think, "If others can do it, I can do it."

Don't immediately jump into big things in your eagerness

to develop your will. To succeed, first try out your will on some little thing you thought you could not do. If you work hard at it, you can be successful. I remember all the goals my friends and many others told me I could never accomplish, but I did. Such "well-wishers" can do much harm. God save us from their kind! Company has the greatest influence on will. If instead of coming here, you went to a drinking party every Thursday, you could not help but pick up something of that worldly vibration. Your will is definitely inspired or weakened by your company. To develop will by yourself is extremely difficult. You require an example before you. If you would be an artist, surround yourself with good paintings and artists. If you would be a divine man, surround yourself with spiritual company.

Belief and experience are quite different. A belief comes from what you have heard or read and accepted as fact, but experience is something you have actually perceived. The convictions of those who have experienced God cannot be shaken. If you had never tasted an orange, I could fool you about its characteristics; but if you had already eaten one, I could not deceive you. You would know; you would have had the experience of it.

Seek the Company of Those Who Strengthen Your Faith

Thoughts about God, success, healing, and so on lie in your brain in the form of tabloid tendencies. You should experience them. In order to experience your thoughts you must use will power to materialize them, and in order to develop the necessary strength of will, you must associate with those who have great will power. If you want healing by God's power, seek the company of those who strengthen your faith and your will.

I traveled throughout India trying to find someone who knew God. Such souls are rare. All the teachers I met told me about their beliefs. But in spiritual matters I was determined never to be satisfied with words about God. I wanted to experience Him. What I am told has no meaning for me unless I experience it.

Once I was talking with a friend of mine, a broker, about the saints of India. He did not share my enthusiasm. "All these so-called saints are fakes," he said. "They don't know God."

I didn't argue; I changed the subject, and we started to talk about the brokerage business. When he had told me quite a great deal about it, I said smoothly, "Do you know there is not a single reliable broker in Calcutta? They are all dishonest."

"What do you know about brokers?" he retorted angrily.

"Exactly," I replied. "What do you know about saints?" He couldn't answer. "Don't dispute what you don't know about," I went on good-naturedly. "I know nothing about the brokerage businesss, and you don't know anything about saints."

The practice of religion has come to a point where very few try to make their spiritual thoughts a matter of experience. I speak to you only about my experiences; I do not care to lecture on what I know only intellectually. Most persons become self-satisfied about what they have read of Truth, without ever having experienced it. In India we do not seek spiritual guidance from someone just because he has a theological degree, nor do we seek out those who have only studied the scriptures, without experiencing their truths. Spiritual victrolas who merely mouth truth do not impress us. We are taught to recognize the difference between a man's sermon and his life; he must demonstrate that he has experienced what he has learned.

Assure Your Ultimate Arrival in Heaven

When you try to experience your spiritual convictions another world begins to open up to you. Don't live in a false sense of security, believing that because you have joined a church you will be saved. You yourself have to make the effort to know God. Your mind may be satisfied that you are very religious, but unless your consciousness is satisfied with direct answers to your prayers, no amount of formal religion can save you. Of what benefit is praying to God if He does not answer? Difficult though it is to obtain His response, it can be done. To assure your ultimate arrival in heaven, you must test the power of your prayers until you have made them effective. When I was just a little child I made up my mind that when I prayed, my prayer had to be answered. That kind of determination is the way. Every test comes then, to break your will, but God's power to respond is unlimited; the persistent continuity of your will power will bring His answer.

You should learn to concentrate your thoughts. Therefore it is important to have time to be alone. Avoid the constant company of other people. Most of them are like sponges; they draw everything out of you, and you seldom receive anything in return. It is worthwhile to be with others only if they are sincere and strong, and if each one is conscious of the other's sincerity and strength, so that you exchange noble soul qualities.

Do not while away your time in idleness. A great many people occupy themselves with inconsequential activities. Ask them what they have been doing and they will usually say, "Oh, I have been busy every minute!" But they can scarcely remember what they were so busy about! Too many diversions, also, weaken your mental powers. If you go every day to the movies, they will lose their attraction, and you will become bored. Movies are all basically the same—lovers, heroes, and villains. We may enjoy a beautiful motion picture story, but life is seldom like that; if on the other hand it is too realistic, who wants to see more of life as it is, when he goes to be entertained?

Life is very tricky and we must deal with it as it is. If we do not first master it ourselves we cannot help anyone else. In the seclusion of concentrated thought lies hidden the factory of all accomplishment. Remember that. In this factory continuously weave your will pattern for attaining success over opposing difficulties. Exercise your will continuously. During the day and at night you have many opportunities to work in this factory, if you do not waste your time. At night I withdraw from the world's demands and am by myself, an absolute stranger to the world; it is a blank. Alone with my will power, I turn my thoughts in the desired direction until I have determined in my mind exactly what I wish to do and how to do it. Then I harness my will to the right activities and it creates success. In this way I have effectively used my will power many times. But it won't work unless the application of will power is continuous.

It is a wonderful feeling to be able to say, and know, "My will power, surcharged by the Divine Will, shall accomplish my aim." If you lazily leave everything to the Divine Power and neglect to use your God-given will, results will not be forthcoming. The Divine Power of Its own accord wants to help you; you don't have to coax. But you do have to use your will to demand as His child, and to behave as His child. You must banish the thought that the Lord with His wonderful power is far away in heaven, and that you are a helpless little worm buried in difficulties down here on earth. Remember that behind your will is the great Divine Will; but that oceanic Power cannot come to your aid unless you are receptive.

Surcharge Your Will Power Through Concentration

The way to become receptive is to sit quietly and concentrate your thoughts on a worthy wish until your mind and thought become completely dissolved in that idea. Then will power becomes divine—omniscient and omnipotent—and can be successfully applied toward realizing your goal. You can't just sit there and wait for success to fall into your lap; once your course is set and your will is firm, you have to make a practical effort. Then you will see that whatever you require for success starts coming to you. Everything will push you in the right direction. In your divinely surcharged will power is the answer to prayer. When you use that will, you open the way through which your prayers can be answered. This is my experience. I used to attempt certain things just to test my will power; but I don't do that anymore. I know it works.

Once, long ago, I saw that one of my students was going wrong. Foreseeing the impending tragic results, I brought out every possible reason that might dissuade him from the course his life was taking; but I saw that no amount of my will power helped him, because he had made up his mind to follow the way of evil. "All right," I told myself finally, "it is 'good-bye'; let him go." But soon my great love and concern for him came to the fore again. I sat under a banyan tree and began to visualize him. Fervently and repeatedly I broadcast to him a mental message: "God has told me to command you to return." By evening my body and mind were athrill with the intuition that he was coming.* At last, there he was at the gate; the "prodigal

---

* Great masters enjoy a divine awareness that permeates the entire body. For example, their intuitive perception of the wrong thoughts of a disciple may be felt physically, like sharp pinpricks. Similarly, harmonious, happy intuitions are sometimes accompanied by a pleasant tingling sensation. *(Publisher's Note)*

son" had come back to the fold. He *pronamed* * and said, "All day long, wherever I went and whatever I did, I beheld your image. What was it all about?"

"God was calling you through me," I replied. "It was His call, not mine. There was no selfish motive in my desire; but I had made up my mind I wouldn't stir from this place until you came." That kind of determination can change the world. A marvelous power!

So, deep prayer does work. The best time to pray is at night, when there are fewer distractions. If necessary, sleep a little in the evening so that you are wide awake when you have your prayers at night, and have it out with God. At first it will seem hard, but as you keep on trying it will become easier. You will be surprised at the results. As soon as your will becomes powerful, God begins to answer. And when the Infinite condescends to break His vow of silence, you will not be able to contain your joy. But if you have an egotistic desire to demonstrate to others the power of your prayers, or if you commercialize it, you will lose that power. God will respond to you no more; you will have frightened Him away. He comes only when you are sincere and when you love Him for His own sake. When you are impressed with yourself and want to show off, He sees that you seek, not Him, but fame and glorification of your ego, and He will not come.

Who Will Persist Until God Answers?

God is not a mute unfeeling Being. He is love itself. If you know how to meditate to make contact with Him, He will respond to your loving demands. You do not have to plead; you can demand as His child. But which of you will spend the necessary time? Which of you will persist until you become so concentrated that you receive an answer from Him?

Suppose you have a mortgage on your home and you cannot meet it. Or there is a certain job you want. In the silence that comes after meditating deeply, concentrate with unswerving will on the thought of your need. Do not keep looking for the result. If you sow a seed in the ground and then take it out

* "Bowed down." (See *pronam* in glossary.)

every once in a while to see if it is growing, it will never sprout. Similarly, if every time you pray you look for a sign that the Lord is granting your wish, nothing will happen. Never try to test God. Just go on praying unceasingly. Your duty is to bring your need to God's attention, and to do your part in helping God to bring that desire to fruition. For example, in chronic diseases, do your best to help promote healing, but know in your mind that ultimately God alone can help. Take that thought with you into meditation every night, and with all your determination pray; suddenly one day you will find the disease gone.

First, the mind receives the suggestion. Then the Divine impregnates the mind with His power. Finally the brain releases the life energy to heal. You do not realize the power of God that is in your mind. It controls all the bodily functions. You can promote any condition in the body if you exercise that power of your mind. It is necessary first to learn the right method of meditation; then you can apply its divinely empowered concentration to heal the body, or to help you in any other difficulty.

Every day undertake something that is difficult for you, and try to do it. Though you fail five times, keep on, and as soon as you have succeeded in that direction, apply your concentrated will on something else. You will thus be able to accomplish increasingly greater things. Will is the instrument of the image of God within you. In will lies His limitless power, the power that controls all the forces of nature. As you are made in His image, that power is yours to bring about whatever you desire: You can create prosperity; you can change hatred into love. Pray until body and mind are completely subjugated; then you will receive God's response. I constantly find that my slightest wish is answered.

Your Greatest Necessity Is God

Between the eyebrows is the door to heaven. This center* in the brain is the seat of will. When you concentrate deeply there and calmly will, whatever you are willing shall come about. So never use your will for evil purposes. To will harm to

* The seat of the "single" or spiritual eye; the *Kutastha*, or Christ Consciousness center.

someone intentionally is a grave misuse of your God-given power. If you find your will going in the wrong direction, stop! Not only is it a waste of your divine energy, it will be the cause of your losing that power; you will not be able to employ it even for good purposes.

Determine honestly whether or not your prayer is legitimate. Do not ask God for things that are quite impossible in the natural order of life. Ask only for true necessities. And know the difference between "necessary necessities" and "unnecessary necessities." The best way to cure yourself of desires for "unnecessary necessities" is to reason them away. Dreaming of big buildings used to be a hobby of mine, but that interest is gone now. I have plenty of them, and all the headaches that accompany their maintenance! Ownership is a worrisome responsibility. Cut out desires for needless possessions. Concentrate only on your real needs.

Your greatest necessity is God. He will give you not only your "necessary necessities," but your "unnecessary necessities" as well. He will satisfy your every desire when you are one with Him. Your wildest dreams will come true.

When I was a little boy in India I so much wanted a pony, but my mother wouldn't allow me to have one. Some years later, after I had started my school for boys in Ranchi, I brought home a horse for our use. One morning I found she had given birth to a colt. Just what I had wanted in my childhood! Many such experiences have come to me. Long ago, while I was traveling in Kashmir, I saw this building* in a vision. Years later, when I came to Los Angeles and saw this place, I recognized it as the building in my vision, and knew that God intended it to be ours.

Follow the Rules of Prayer

The first rule in prayer is to approach God only with legitimate desires. The second is to pray for their fulfillment, not as a beggar, but as a son: "I am Thy child. Thou art my Father. Thou and I are One." When you pray deeply and continuously you will feel a great joy welling up in your heart. Don't be satis-

---

* Self-Realization Fellowship international headquarters atop Mount Washington in Los Angeles. Paramahansaji's vision of it occurred around 1913.

fied until that joy manifests; for when you feel that all-satisfying joy in your heart, you will know that God has tuned in your
prayer broadcast. Then pray to your Father: "Lord, this is my
need. I am willing to work for it; please guide me and help me
to have the right thoughts and to do the right things to bring
about success. I will use my reason, and work with determination, but guide Thou my reason, will, and activity to the right
thing that I should do." This is how I have always prayed. Now,
as soon as I ask God about some undertaking, I know whether
I should do it or not, and I know what steps I should and should
not take.

Be practical and earnest about prayer. Concentrate deeply
on what you are praying. Before you seek a job, or sign a con-
tract, or do anything important, think of that Power. Think of
it continuously. Take time out of sleep. Your mind is habituated to resting at night from the day's duties, and keeps urging,
"Sleep." You must answer with all your divine power of will:
"Away with sleep! My engagement with God is more important." Then you will receive God's response.

Making Religion Scientific

First Self-Realization Fellowship Temple at
Encinitas, * *California, December 22, 1940*

God is approachable. Talking of Him and listening to His words in the scriptures, thinking of Him, feeling His presence in meditation, you will see that gradually the Unreal becomes real, and this world which you think is real will be seen as unreal. There is no joy like that realization.

The joy of God is boundless, unceasing, all the time new. Body, mind, nothing can disturb you when you are in that consciousness—such is the grace and glory of the Lord. And He will explain to you whatever you haven't been able to understand; everything you want to know.

There is no use trying to know too much now. How many incarnations would you have to spend to learn all that is written in the book of nature? Millions of lives would not be sufficient. So why bother? All things you will find and understand in God. The masters of India have always said, "First know Him." Then, whatever you desire to know, He will reveal to you. This is His kingdom; this is His knowledge.

As life goes on, its illusions fall away; you see what it is all about. And when the illusions of childhood and youth are gone, what is there left? Only in the divine consciousness behind this door [Paramahansaji here touched his forehead to indicate the location of the Christ center, seat of the spiritual eye†] can we find pure happiness. I cut the world out of my life

---

* The first temple on the grounds of the Self-Realization Fellowship Hermitage in Encinitas was built in 1938 on a bluff overlooking the Pacific Ocean. It was called the Golden Lotus Temple. Gradual erosion of the shoreline ultimately caused the structure to slip into the sea.

† The spiritual eye is the pranic star door through which man must enter to attain superconsciousness, Christ Consciousness, and Cosmic Consciousness. "I am the door: by me if any man enter in, he shall be saved, and shall go in and out, and find pasture" (John 10:9).

because of its delusive influence, which makes unimportant things seem important. We are all living in a land of make-believe, trying to "keep up with the Joneses"; yet it is only by remaining in the consciousness of Spirit that we can be happy. Try it!

God is eager to bring you to His kingdom, for He craves something too: that you spontaneously seek Him and cling to Him. Otherwise, He would not have created the universe and man. His perfection is not conditioned by this craving; but the one reason behind His creating us is His desire that we love Him and return to Him. He is looking forward to that time. In our love is His fulfillment.

The Father has given us freedom to jump into the fire of world illusion or to return to His home. It is a question of what you would like. Let us all go Home, that we need not come back into this terrible world. We do not know under what conditions we will incarnate again. Certainly we do not want to be reborn in times of suffering and depressions such as we are having now. These troubles are the result of man's selfishness and hate. The whole earth is groaning because God has been forgotten.

Resolve now to go home to your Father. You are fearfully wasting your time, and you can't afford to. You don't know how fortunate you are to have been born as a human being. In that you are blessed more than any other creature. The animal is not able to meditate and have God-communion. You have your freedom to seek Him and you don't use it. You sit a little while in meditation and your mind wanders away. But when the mind prays and prays, and prays again, heaven opens. Then you will be given all the convincing experiences by which you shall know that God *is*.

God Is Waiting for Your Invitation

I speak not from book learning, but from perceptions of God. I could not speak of Him this way if I didn't see or feel Him; He wouldn't let me. As I speak to you I see before me whatever I am talking about; many times I don't even see you. I wouldn't tell you anything at all if I didn't know Him. But I am here to tell you that the very joy you are seeking in sex, money, wine, love, fame—that joy is within yourself. You don't have to go elsewhere. You don't have to beg or flatter God; but you have to ask. You have to pray to Him sincerely and lovingly, "Come to me."

You are not determined enough. As the miser loves money, as the lover loves the beloved, so should you love God; then you will find Him, without fail. It is difficult, but if at night you sit long in meditation you won't know time. Even when I don't get any sleep, I never miss it. When God comes, where is sleep? where is the body? Nothing matters but His intoxicating presence. You read in novels of ideal love, but it is nothing compared to the love of God. Hasten to Him. To be ever conscious of Him is the most wonderful existence. As I am talking to you, again and again the whole world melts away and I feel only His Bliss.

Creation Is Meant to Disillusion You

Science devises methods for your physical comfort, stimulating and catering to endless desires. But after a while creature comforts become burdens, pleasures no longer, because you find it is hard work to take care of them. Thus you "pay" for everything you get except divine blessedness. For that you have only to sit still and ask your Heavenly Father. If I thought I had to earn God I wouldn't try; as a son I have a right to know Him. If you ask your right from the Father, He will give it to you. To those devotees who urge, He comes. That is what He wants. His whole creation is intended to disillusion you, and thus cause you to draw back to Him. You don't know when you will be taken away from this earth; there is no law that you will enjoy a long life. This proves how foolish it is to waste time. I live from minute to minute, day to day. I know only the joy of living; inside, complete resignation to Him.

A time will come when everything will be made or accomplished by will. Whatever you wish you will see done. This I have demonstrated again and again in my life. Development of the heavenly power of will for its divinely intended use—to know God—is the only purpose in human life. He has created each one of you, and He is throbbing in you, crying to enter your consciousness so that He may release you. I am sure He feels guilty for having created us! Every day I ask Him why He did it. (I talk to Him about anything that comes to my mind. He likes it, that I am "after" Him; He knows His creation is anything but perfect.) The Lord replies that you cannot make steel until you have made the iron white-hot in fire. It is not meant for harm. Trouble and disease have a lesson for us. Our painful experiences are not meant to destroy us, but to burn out our dross, to hurry us back Home. No one is more anxious for our release than God.

It is His voice that is speaking through me. If only one person responds and finds his freedom in Spirit, my task is done. The salvation of one life is worth more than the conversion of thousands. I tell you of one Master of this universe—one Beloved who is waiting for you, crying for you. You don't know how He rejoices when a soul enters His kingdom! He gathers all the angels together and they celebrate that soul's entrance into heaven. What joy there is!

For good reason you are not allowed to remember your past incarnations. Suppose you have been born ten times. You have therefore had ten mothers. How can you love them all the same? You are meant to learn that behind those ten mothers there is One Mother; behind all friends, One Friend; behind all fathers, One Father; behind all loves, One Love. How wonderful is that recognition! It is as if you had been playing hide-and-seek in the corridors of incarnations, and then you find Him! When I realized that One Love, I could not contain myself. My mind vanished into the Infinite Kingdom. It is so, even now. The joy of Spirit is endless.

Seek a Definite Understanding of Truth

In the physical sciences everything is systematized into definite conceptions: combine two particular substances, or two substances in a particular way, for a certain result. The great masters of Self-Realization Fellowship are telling you why you should seek God scientifically, and the scientific way to get to Him. Every effort you make to follow these instructions will bring to you a definite understanding. Some read a little about the spiritual laws, and then put the book aside.

That is not the way to Self-knowledge. You must make these truths a practical part of your life.

Most people don't take religion seriously. They keep it in the realm of imagination and fancy. In India we are taught the practical use of religion. We don't say, "Well, I shall find out all about God in the hereafter." We want to know God now.

Science and religion should go hand in hand. All the results of scientific investigation are definite and are connected by reason, whereas religion is often dogmatic. When Jesus urged his disciples to have faith, he didn't mean blind belief. It breaks my heart when I see blind dogmatism, for it is one reason why the majority of people have no real interest in God. Although there are nevertheless many who are interested in God, real seekers are few, because hardly anyone tries to understand his way out of this dream drama. Few of His children appreciate the gifts of the Heavenly Father, and of those who do, fewer still try deeply or scientifically enough to know Him. Those who want to seek Him earnestly should learn how to do so scientifically.

By Yoga, Religion Can Be Made Scientific

Yoga is definite and scientific. Yoga means union of soul and God, through step-by-step methods with specific and known results. It raises the practice of religion above the differences of dogma. My guru, Sri Yukteswar, extolled Yoga; he did not, however, indicate that realization of God thereby would be immediate. "You have to work hard for it," he told me. I did, and when the promised results came, I saw that Yoga was marvelous.*

Those who do not give time to their religion cannot expect to know all at once about God and the hereafter. Usually people don't make the effort, or if they do, the effort is not deep and sincere enough. Nighttime should be spent with God. You sleep more than necessary, and thus waste many valuable hours. Night was meant to screen all the attractions of

* "O Arjuna, I have informed thee about that same ancient (forgotten universal highway of) Yoga—for thou art My friend, devoted unto Me. This mystery (of Yoga) is the producer of supreme benefit (to mankind)" (Bhagavad-Gita IV:3).

the world, that you might the more intently explore the kingdom of God. He created darkness to obscure material objects, for He wants you to forget the world at night and seek Him. Read the scriptures, read the *Lessons,* * and meditate—the glory and the joy it brings! Nothing else can give you that experience. See if it isn't true.

Remember, if you don't find God, you are not making enough effort in your meditation. Should you not find the pearl after one or two divings, don't blame the ocean. Blame your diving; you are not going deep enough. If you dive really deep you will find the pearl of His presence. Unless we apply definite methods of science in practicing religion, it becomes little more than a salve for our conscience. "Oh yes, I go to church every Sunday," people say; but they don't know why they go. And once they have said "Amen" after the sermon, they forget all about church until the next Sunday. Isn't that foolish? If you do not commune with God there, why should you go?

The saints say that if you coax God earnestly enough, you can see Him. But you have to do it all yourself. It is good to meditate with a few others, but make the supreme effort alone at night, not just in church on Sundays. Get away from everyone. It is good for your health, your nerves, and your longevity not to mix too much with people. Most of them are thinking only of what you can give them. Hardly anyone thinks of your highest welfare except your spiritual teacher and God. The wise teacher will give you but one instruction: think of God.

And share Him; there is no form of service greater than to speak of God. If you convince someone that the path of error leads to the valley of death, and that the path of meditation leads to everlasting life, you have given him something of more value than a million dollars. Money is perishable, but realization of God will go with us beyond the portals of the grave. Therefore whenever I see anyone striving and struggling with great intensity to know God, it gives me great joy.

Although I am planning and doing things in the world, it is only to please the Lord. I test myself: even when I am work-

* Scientific principles of yoga meditation are taught in the *Self-Realization Fellowship Lessons,* available from the SRF international headquarters in Los Angeles.

ing I whisper within, "Where are You, Lord?" and the whole
world changes. There is nothing but a great Light, and I am a little bubble in that Ocean of Light. Such is the joy of existence
in God.

The experiences I have told you about are scientifically
attainable. If you follow the spiritual laws, the result is certain. If the result doesn't come, find fault with your effort. Intensity in all your religious practices is the only way. Those
who don't meditate regularly and deeply are restless whenever
they do meditate, and give up after a short effort. But if you
make a greater effort day by day, the ability to go deep will
come. I don't have to make any effort now; the whole world is
gone instantly when I close my eyes and gaze into the Christ
center. And I used to sit for hours trying to forget the body and
the thoughts! I came to a point where I thought it was no use.
But I saw it was my fault. Between the restless thoughts and
God there is a wall; the ordinary person doesn't try, so he
never gets over that wall. But the spiritual fighter goes on.
When the mind becomes still, you are in the kingdom of the Infinite. Those who have spent too much time on foolish things
remain fruitlessly knocking outside.

Communion with God is the only thing to live for. You
will have to come to that understanding eventually, often
after much suffering. Why not learn now? He is ready to welcome you. You can't fail to reach God ultimately. It is foolish
to ask, "Will I be able to get into the kingdom of heaven?"
There is no other place you can stay, for that is your real
home. You don't have to earn it. You are already God's child,
made in His image. You have only to tear away the mask of the
human being and realize your divine birthright.

Satan Makes Us Think God Is Unattainable

So never say that you won't be able to get into the kingdom of heaven. Satan drops that delusive thought in your
mind to keep you here. You are not a mortal being. When I
heard that from my guru I was overjoyed. Thereafter I refused
to consider myself a sinner. Nor should you call yourself a sinner; it is a desecration of the image of God within you. Nor
should you let anyone else call you a sinner. What does it mat-

ter, what you were yesterday? You are a child of God, now and evermore. Who can keep you away from the kingdom of God? That is how you should feel. But you must scientifically pursue Him. The science of religion is to make the effort in meditation until God becomes real to you, until you know that He alone is real. I used to go to the crematory grounds and pray to see through the delusion of the world; I cried in the woods, I closeted myself in the attic, praying unceasingly until that realization came. I beheld burning worlds steaming and fuming around the feet of my Divine Mother.* In the light of Her wisdom all my mortality was consumed.

Meditation Is the True Practice of Religion

The true practice of religion is to sit still in meditation and talk to God. But you don't get to that point of intensity, you don't concentrate enough, and that is why you remain in delusion. To teach the value of long, intense concentration on God, I instituted an all-day Christmas meditation just before Christmas each year.† At first the devotees feel only how long it is, but as they go deep they become oblivious of time. Most churchgoers can't sit still for an hour unless there is something going on all the while to divert their minds.

To be in the consciousness of God is entirely different; it comes when you sit quietly and say: "One by one I close the doors of the senses, lest the aroma of the rose or the song of the nightingale distract my love from Thee."‡ And as you go on saying that with deeper and deeper concentration and devotion, you will see after a little while that you have forgotten all distractions; before your inward gaze a light appears, or saints appear, or you are engulfed in a deep peace or divine joy.

---

* "That aspect of the Uncreated Infinite which is active in creation is referred to in Hindu scriptures as the Divine Mother. The Lord in the form of the Cosmic Mother appears in living tangibility before true *bhaktas* (devotees of a Personal God)."—Paramahansa Yogananda in *Autobiography of a Yogi*.

† A spiritual custom begun by Paramahansaji in 1931 and carried on by Self-Realizationists in their *ashrams*, temples, and centers throughout the world. Daylong meditations are also held at other times during the year, on days of special spiritual significance. *(Publisher's Note)*

‡ From "Prayer at Night" in Paramahansa Yogananda's *Whispers from Eternity*.

Any spiritual activity does good by keeping the thought of God alive, but what is ultimately necessary is this intensity of effort to know Him. There should be centers of meditation all over the world, where devotees come together to commune with God. When I come to the temple it is for one purpose: to be with God and to tell you of God. And you come here for my words and to try by meditation to feel His presence.

One moon dispels the darkness of the heavens. So is one soul who is trained to know God, a soul in whom there is true devotion and sincere seeking and intensity; and wherever he will go he will dispel the spiritual darkness of others. Those who are even thinking of God shine a little, but they are not able to give light to the world. Ordinary religious people are like stars, giving only a tiny light.

Meditation Provides the Proof of God's Existence

By scientific meditation become a true devotee, that like the moon you dispel the darkness around yourself and others. Without realization through meditation, religion is the most mysterious book of all; you will never be able to understand it. But by meditation you have the proof of God's existence.

Go to your room and shut the door—make no fuss. Sit down and talk to God. Practice meditation. Let your mind become so intense that the next time you sit to meditate you won't have to make the effort; your mind will be fixed immediately on Him. If you don't make a great effort to conquer physical and mental restlessness in the beginning, you will have difficulty every time you meditate throughout the years. But if you make that supreme effort at the start, you will soon be happy and free.

When I utter the name "God" my whole being melts away in His Joy. But that I had to work for. Make the effort. I was not at first the devotional kind. My mind used to be very restless. But now it is just like fire. As soon as I put my mind at the Christ center, all thoughts are gone—breath, heart, and mind are instantly still, and I am aware only of Spirit.

Make religion real by scientific methods. Science gives you definiteness and certainty. Sit quietly and practice the methods that have been given by great yogis of India: Mahavatar Babaji, Lahiri Mahasaya, Swami Sri Yukteswar.* Find in yourself that supreme blessedness of which I speak to you, and when you do you will see that religion is no longer a myth but a scientific certainty. Pray to Him, "Lord, You are the Master of creation, so I come to You. I will never give up until You talk to me and make me realize Your presence. I will not live without You."

Intensity, Secrecy, Devotion, and Constancy Are Necessary

The great Indian saint Sri Ramakrishna was worshiping a stone image of Kali, the Cosmic Mother, and praying for Her to appear to him in reality. His spiritual anguish became so intense that he felt life was no longer worth living. At this moment his eyes fell on a sword that was kept in the temple, and like a madman he seized it, with the intention of ending his life. In that moment the Mother revealed Herself in Her cosmic form. Her devotee was engulfed in an oceanic Bliss. In the very place where the saint had this experience, that same stone statue of the Divine Mother assumed a living form and spoke to me.†

If I hadn't spent hours seeking God in meditation I would not have known that religion is a science. Intensity, secrecy, devotion, and constancy are necessary. You don't know when death will come. Every minute keep your mind on God. Everything you want and need is right within you; seek long and seek deeply. I meditate for hours; I see no one until I am finished. You must make up your mind that you are not going to be bothered by anyone or anything. Then you won't know time.

In my Yogoda school in Ranchi,‡ India, I used to spend all my spare time roaming around the grounds, here and there sitting awhile to meditate, until my mind was drunk with God. That is the only way to find Him. Don't waste your time. When you are able to live in the divine consciousness, four to

* Including Paramahansa Yogananda, these are the Self-Realization Fellowship line of Gurus. (See *Gurus* in glossary.) *(Publisher's Note)*

† The experience is related in *Autobiography of a Yogi*, "The Heart of a Stone Image."

‡ See *Ranchi school* in glossary.

six hours of sleep are plenty; you will never feel tired, you will never miss sleep. Sleep is under my control; it is the same with eating. I have something infinitely greater, and God has proven that when He is with me all the "necessities of life" become unnecessary. In that consciousness you become more healthy than the average person, more joyous, more bountiful in every way. Don't seek little things; they will divert you from God. Start your experiment now: make life simple and be a king.

Understanding the Unreality
of Matter

Circa 1926

The Hindu scriptures point out that belief in the nonexistence of matter and the allness of Spirit should not be founded on dogmatic, illogical, unintelligible, or inexplicable theories, but on scientific inner investigation and exact understanding.

People generally identify themselves with the body, which is supported by food; but they fail to realize that the basic source of bodily existence is *prana* (life energy).* No food or other outer aid can revive a man from whom the cosmic current has withdrawn.

The link between man's material body and his immaterial mind is *prana*. The ancient Hindu sages discovered the existence of *prana* and formulated the science of *pranayama*,† life-energy control.

Lord Jesus fasted in the wilderness for forty days. He said: "Man shall not live by bread alone, but by every word that proceedeth out of the mouth of God."‡

The "word" is cosmic vibration; the "mouth of God" is the medulla oblongata in the posterior part of the brain, tapering off into the spinal cord. This, the most vital spot in the human body, is the divine entrance ("mouth of God") for the

---

* "Lifetrons," the finer-than-atomic energies that sustain life in all things in the universe. There are two kinds of *prana:* cosmic energy, the omnipresent source of life and vitality permeating and surrounding all living things; and the specific *prana* or energy pervading each human body.

† Through *pranayama* the adept is able to control the life energy in the sensory-motor nerves, and thus free his mind from body-consciousness during meditation. He is able also to use this life energy to heal or vitalize his body at will.

‡ Matthew 4:4.

"word" or *Aum*,* the cosmic vibratory energy by which man is sustained.

People who never fast do not know from experience that man can live, as Christ did for forty days, solely by the "word" of God.

In the early stages of a week's fasting, hunger is present; but as the days go by, less hunger and a sense of freedom are distinctly felt. Why? Because denial of gross food to the body compels it to depend on immaterial food: the life current.

Man's will power is the great generator of energy. Through will power and willingness one is able to draw quickly on the infinite store of inner strength. A person who is unwilling to perform his daily tasks experiences a lack of energy. A man who works hard but with willingness is borne up physically and mentally by the cosmic current.

One who learns and practices the metaphysical methods of living by will power and by consciously tapping the inexhaustible source of life energy is freed from many limitations of the body.

The Hindu sages and yogis say that matter is materialized mind-stuff; and some of them, like Jesus, have proved this truth by demonstrating the power to materialize and dematerialize their bodies and other physical objects.

The Chemical Elements of Matter Are Electronic Vibrations

Modern science shows that matter is composed of vibratory forces. The chemical elements, the structural factors responsible for all forms in the universe—from stones and stars to man—are nothing more than different forms of electronic vibrations. For example, in ice we find coldness, weight, form; it is visible. Melt the ice; it becomes water. Pass electricity through it; it becomes invisible hydrogen and oxygen, which, analyzed further, are forms of electronic vibrations. One may therefore say scientifically that ice does not exist, even though

---

* Gross matter emanates from and is sustained by the intelligent cosmic vibration of God, the subtle building material of the universe. The primal properties of this vibration are light and sound. *Aum* is the sound of God's creative vibration, referred to in Christian scriptures as the Amen, the Holy Ghost, and the Word. (See *Aum* in glossary.)

it is perceptible to our senses of sight, touch, and so on. In reality its essence is invisible electrons or forms of energy.

In other words, that which can be dissolved into invisibility cannot be said to have valid existence. In this sense, matter can be considered as not existing; but matter does have relative existence. Matter exists in relation to our mind and as an expression of invisible electronic forces that do exist, being unchangeable and immortal.

Both water and ice are manifestations of invisible gases and have only formal, transitory existence. Similarly, both mortal mind and matter are fleeting manifestations of Divine Consciousness, and possess merely formal existence; in reality only Cosmic Mind exists.

Just as a child is born through the instrumentality of parents, so matter is dependent on mind for its existence. Matter is born from Divine Mind and is perceptible to mortal mind; in itself and of itself, matter has no reality, no intrinsic existence.

The blind or nonintellectual electronic forces of creation are nevertheless creative teleological agents because they contain within themselves the vibrations of the universal, conscious-of-itself life force or *prana*, which in turn issued from the fiat of Divinity.

"God said, Let there be light: and there was light,"* that is, the projection of Divine Thought and Will became light or vibratory energy, the flowing forth of life current and electrons, which further vibrated more strongly and became the diverse subtle or unseen forces of nature, which in turn externalized themselves as the ninety-two principal elements of matter that constitute the universe.

To human consciousness, matter is both perceptible and real. But man has discovered through theoretical investigation, through logic, and through certain laboratory experiments (such as converting a visible piece of ice into invisible forces) that a permanent and unalterable creative power must underlie all the transitory and illusive forms of the phenomenal world.

This truth may be grasped just as we grasp the fact that the

* Genesis 1:3.

ocean exists though its waves have no permanent existence, being just passing, formal manifestations of one great substance. Waves cannot exist without the ocean, but the ocean exists with or without waves.

These concepts can be intellectually understood but cannot be *known* until one has learned the method of converting matter into life force, and life force into Cosmic Consciousness,* as Christ, Krishna, and other Self-realized masters were able to do. To such enlightened ones, matter *per se* does not exist, because they see that beneath the slight rippling waves of creation is the changeless Ocean of Spirit.

The Universe Is God's Dream

In the *Vedanta*† and *Yoga* philosophies the universe is spoken of as God's dream. Matter and mind—the cosmos with its stars and planets; the gross surface waves and the subtle undercurrents of the material creation; the human powers of feeling, will, and consciousness; and the states of life and death, day and night, health and disease, success and failure—are realities according to the law of relativity governing this dream of God's.

All the dualities perceived by the law of relativity are real to the dreamer, the mortal man who plays his little part in the great cosmic dream. To escape from *maya*, illusion, the law of relativity, one must awaken from the dream into eternal God-wakefulness. We cannot change the lawful dream by imagination or by denying its existence, or by accepting "life" but rejecting "death," or by recognizing health but ignoring sickness. One state is as much a part of its opposite state as are the two sides of a fabric. The dualities are inherently and essentially one. The truth seeker does not try to separate them in his mind, but to rise above them by wisdom.

The man who considers his body to be different from his mind, and who wants to accept as "real" only the positive,

---

* The essence of Spirit. (See glossary.)

† Literally, "end of the Vedas." *Vedanta* is the philosophy presented in the latter portion of the Vedas. This philosophy declares that God is the only reality and that creation is essentially an illusion. Man's duty therefore is to transcend the illusion by realization of God.

happy, and beneficial aspects of a universe unalterably dual in its nature, is a man deeply asleep in the delusions of the dream world.

Just as a person has dreams that seem real for a time but lose their validity when he emerges into the waking state of consciousness, so it is possible for man to awaken from the dream of matter-reality and to live in the changeless realm of Spirit.

Only the superman, who has learned to expand and transfer his consciousness to the Infinite, can realize creation as a dream of God's; he alone can say with true knowledge that matter has no existence. By means of a long series of self-disciplinary steps—through following the scientific yoga path or any other way of spiritual perfection, whether that of love, wisdom, service, or self-effacement—the God-seeker dissolves the dualities and discerns the Eternal Oneness. "He who, freed from delusion, knows Me as the Supreme Spirit obtains omniscience. He worships Me with his whole being."*

* Bhagavad-Gita XV:19.

Man's Greatest Adventure

Self-Realization Fellowship international headquarters,
Los Angeles, California, February 29, 1940

Life is the greatest adventure imaginable. Although some lives are without much interest and excitement, others are full of extraordinary experiences. I heard of a man who tried thirty-two times to commit suicide, and something happened every time to prevent him. Imagine what it would be like to know all about the lives of all the people who are now on earth, and those who are gone, and those who are yet to come! Such is God's power. Jesus said, "Are not two sparrows sold for a farthing? and one of them shall not fall on the ground without [the knowledge of] your Father."* The lifetimes of experiences of all men are in God's memory. It is difficult indeed to conceive of a consciousness that is aware of everything that has ever happened. Yet to fathom the nature of Spirit is the greatest adventure in this universe. I will give you a picture of it as it is coming at this moment before my spiritual eye.†

Truths are more than imagination; they are real. Yet their origin is a thought in the mind of God. All of the different forms of atomic matter, for example, are but materialized thoughts of God—they can be reconverted into thoughts, and the thoughts can again be materialized into objects. Man also has the power to conceive ideas, but his imagination is not very strong. If his imagination became powerful enough, man could create material objects on earth.‡ He has latent with-

---

* Matthew 10:29.

† The telescopic gaze of intuition. During deep meditation the single or spiritual eye becomes visible within the central part of the forehead. Great yogis who live unbrokenly in the state of God-consciousness are able to behold it whether meditating or carrying on ordinary activities.

‡ Jesus spoke of the divine potential in that man who realizes the presence of God within himself: "Believe me that I am in the Father, and the Father in

in him the same creative power by which God, even as He thought, materialized His mental creations in the world. But it has become next to impossible for man to materialize his thoughts because he has not utilized the free power, the divine power of thought, bestowed on him by God.

When we try to imagine the consciousness of God we wonder how He can remember all things, because we judge everything by the standard of our own mental capacity. We understand according to our own experience. A person whose memory is not strong tends to assume that everyone else's memory is the same way. Yet there are persons of exceptional memory who can recall a whole book, perhaps, just as easily as you can remember a few lines. Those who are forgetful find it difficult to realize that others can have an unfailing power of recollection.

A jeweler remembers his jewels, a bookkeeper the figures in his books; so God is able to remember everything that He has created in this universe. Being gifted with almighty power, He has instant recall of everything that has ever happened. God does not need a limited physical brain to remember what has passed. His limitless consciousness is all-knowing.

The Origin and Power of Memory

Memory is a wondrous power. All human memory comes from God's tremendous memory. For example, you cannot tell me about all the motion pictures you have seen since birth, but if I were to show you one of those films again, you would instantly recall it. The divine underlying memory is right there within you, ever recognizing experiences that have passed. As soon as you see the opening scene again, the whole story comes back to you. "Oh, I saw this picture before," you say. "I remember how it ended."

How is it that we can recognize a picture—every detail of it—that we have seen years ago? Because all happenings are recorded in the brain. As soon as you put the needle of attention on a certain record of experience, your memory begins to play back that experience. If I ask where you were sitting when we

me.... I say unto you, He that believeth on me, the works that I do shall he do also; and greater works than these shall he do..." (John 14:11–12).

were here together last Thursday, you recall it and begin to re-member other things as well. If I ask, "What did I say?" my words start coming back to you.

The inner power of memory comes from God and is per-fect. It never forgets. The ordinary man's memory cannot hold the consciousness of all experiences at one time, but the under-lying divine memory retains everything simultaneously and permanently. Therefore good or poor memory is a matter of conviction. You have convinced yourself that you have a weak memory and so you have a weak memory. However, it is not easy to jump from this belief to the opposite. Much effort is re-quired to convince yourself that your memory is in actuality a manifestation of the all-recalling divine memory of God.

The greatest human memory is naught but a borrowing from the unlimited consciousness of God, in which are record-ed all the adventures of all human beings and other life-forms.

Creation—Dual Adventure of God and Man

The story of God's creation is marvelous—how He pro-jected into existence all beings on this earth, and how He is working behind the scenes to bring us back to our real exis-tence in Him. It is almost impossible to describe in human lan-guage the cosmic adventure of God's creation and its subtle intertwining with the individual life-adventures of countless human beings.

We find that human beings live on the average sixty years, the crocodile from sixty to a hundred. The redwood tree lives for two thousand years, the dog only about fourteen, and the horse at most about thirty-six years. It is evident that Some-one has fixed these various life-spans. Yet we hear of some great yogis who have lived for hundreds of years.* I know definitely that Mahavatar Babaji† has lived for centuries and is still in

---

* "Great saints who have awakened from the cosmic mayic dream and have realized this world as an idea in the Divine Mind, can do as they wish with the body, knowing it to be only a manipulatable form of condensed or frozen en-ergy. Though physical scientists now understand that matter is nothing but congealed energy, illumined masters have passed victoriously from theory to practice in the field of matter control" (*Autobiography of a Yogi*, chapter 31).

† *Mahavatar*, "great or divine incarnation"; *Babaji*, "revered father." He is

his body in perfect youth. Trailanga Swami * is said to have lived for more than three hundred years. Truth is more fascinating than fiction.

It is possible to imagine that under favorable conditions (and if there is no waste of vital essence, † and there is proper food and right thinking) the human body could go on indefinitely. But the pressures on the body are terrific. When a mouse is caught in a trap, its heart beats many times faster than it does normally, and when you are unable to pay your bills, your heart does the same! Thus worry takes its toll. And there are other kinds of stress. I am told that the Police Commissioner of Chicago has demonstrated with instruments the possibility that if noise were taken away from the cities, their residents would live ten years longer.

We are living in a wonderful world nevertheless. Those who exist only to "eat, drink, and be merry," and to sleep, have no idea of the wonders of human life.

The adventure begins with the struggle the soul goes through to enter a womb at the time of conception. In the astral world‡ there are millions of souls struggling to return to earth, to enter the mated sperm and ovum cells at the time of conception. Saint or sinner, unless you have attained final re-

---

the guru of Lahiri Mahasaya, who in turn is the guru of Swami Sri Yukteswar, the guru of Paramahansa Yogananda. Babaji's transcendental life and powers are described in *Autobiography of a Yogi*.

* In addition to his extraordinary age, Trailanga Swami was noted for his many miracles. He weighed three hundred pounds, although he rarely ate. Often he would meditate for days, seated on top of the Ganges waters; or remain sometimes hidden for long periods under its waves. He was often seen at the Manikarnika Ghat, sitting motionless in the sun on the blistering stone slabs. His habitual disregard of nature's laws was a constant reminder to those who saw him that oneness with God is the highest law.

† The vital essence, or sexual fluid, contains a high concentration of *prana*. If not dissipated, the power therein can be used to enhance physical health, mental vitality and creativity, and spiritual development.

‡ "In my Father's house are many mansions..." (John 14:2). The high and low astral spheres, composed of subtle light and energies of lifetrons, are the heaven (or hell) to which souls go after death of the physical body. The length of stay there is karmically predetermined. So long as one has unfulfilled material desires or earthly *karma* (effects of past actions not yet worked out), he must reincarnate on earth to continue his evolution back to God.

demption there is a great desire to reincarnate again on earth.
At the time of conception there is a flash in the ether and one
soul enters as the sperm and ovum cells unite. You had to fight
to get into the womb. Not only you but many souls rushed to
enter, and the ones that won are you, and you, and I. It was not
an easy victory.

Prenatal Consciousness

After you have entered the womb you ask, "What have I
done? I have been free from the confining mortal body for so
long, gliding along in a weightless body of light, and now I am
caught again in a physical form." Nevertheless, you become accustomed to these new conditions during the nine months in
the womb. That is the punishment. It is nine months of living
in a dungeon in which you have to breathe through someone
else, eat through someone else, receive your blood, and the
power for its circulation, through someone else. You are dependent. Your soul cries to the Lord, "Let me out of this prison! I
can't see, I can't hear, I am bound."

If there is a hades or purgatory it is those nine months in
the mother's body—helpless, in darkness, bound to one spot
like a tree, with only occasional memories of the past coming
in, and then lapses into sleep. It is when memories of the past
life come that you struggle in the mother's body. I have trans-
ported my consciousness into these prenatal states and I know
what I am saying.* The baby's sleep and wakefulness in the
mother's body do not depend on her sleeping and waking. The
child's will to move is a memory coming from the soul's past.
So he stirs restlessly in the mother's body until he tires and
goes to sleep. Then he wakes up for a while and moves again.
He feels hunger, and, through the nourishment in the mother's
blood, the satisfaction of his hunger.

The infant slightly hears the vibrations of the mother's
heartbeat and circulation; by these sounds he is made conscious of his body and he wants to be free. Thus the soul's first
adventure is the fight between two ideas: the wish to return to
earth in a human form, and the desire to feel the freedom of
having no form.

* It is possible for the advanced yogi, through his interior union with omnipresent God, to perceive sympathetically the experiences of all beings.

The soul's human encasement starts out as a fishlike form with a tiny tail. That form grows into an animal form, curled up in the womb. There comes an occasional memory of the past life, and the embryo stirs. The struggle becomes greater as the embryo begins to grow into a human form in the mother's body. The soul cries, "Let me out!" When the will becomes very strong, the baby is born. Premature babies are souls who are very stubborn-willed. They don't want to remain nine months in the mother's body, and so they come early.

The Breath of Life

The infant arrives in this world crying; because, the saints say, the soul remembers its previous incarnations and does not like the thought of coming back to earth again to go through the struggle of life here. Related also to this memory is the attitude of supplication in which a baby usually holds its hands before it comes into the world. It is praying to God, "Please don't give me physical birth again."

The physiological explanation of the baby's crying is that the lungs must be opened up in order to start the breathing process, and the baby's first cry is an effort to activate the lungs and start the breath of life. When the baby is born, the breath goes in, and the soul that was semi-dormant becomes a living being with an independent life. "God breathed into his nostrils the breath of life; and man became a living soul."* Many persons mistakenly believe that the soul enters the body at birth, but if the soul were not already there, the body would not have developed from the original tiny cells. Should the soul leave the embryo before birth, the infant will be born dead.

Man's body is made of sixteen basic material elements supported and activated by nineteen elements† of subtle energy. These can be condensed into pure consciousness. "Man became a living soul" refers to the fact that the ordinary man's physical body, which is made of chemicals ("the dust of the

* Genesis 2:7.

† The essence of the astral body that dwells within man's physical form, activating and enlivening it. These nineteen elements are: intelligence, ego, feeling, mind (sense consciousness); the powers behind the five senses and five instruments of action; and the five *pranas*, or life forces.

ground"), must breathe oxygen in order to be sustained on earth, as ordained by God when He first "breathed into his nostrils the breath of life."

When the baby is born, he blinks at the light, he hears sounds, he smells and tastes, and he breathes. He sees that conditions seem to be normal—he has a physical body again. His prenatal resistance to birth ends with his first breath, when *maya* (the cosmic delusion that "existence" depends on body and breath) comes over him. He feels once more attracted to the physical world.

As time goes on the baby struggles for control over his body. How often you see him repeatedly thrusting his hands and feet up in the air in an attempt at coordination! All these actions are directed by the subconscious mind through the soul's memory of the past. That memory is always there. You instinctively fear death because you remember the many times you have been through that experience. You are also afraid of pain because you have suffered many times before.

When the baby grows into a little child he is surrounded by the influences of the mother's and father's guiding will, and the wills of other relatives as well. Each one wants him to be something different, and his naughty friends want him to be still something else!

The child has a great many struggles with these conflicting pressures. This is a miserable life, so it is good to give your children a little freedom. Young ones who are given too much freedom, however, may later lament, "I wish I had been told long ago not to do this; then I would not be what I am today." Think of all the struggles, physiological and mental, one has to go through until be becomes a youth. At that time of life the senses become more active and the youth has a great inner battle with himself. The struggle with the senses is a tremendous contest. To conquer in this adventure of youth, to go victoriously through this thrill of living, is a great experience.

Man Should Befriend Himself

It is wonderful to be alive, but there are many agents waiting to kill us. An adventure with wild animals in South Africa is nothing compared to the adventure of life itself. No other tale in history is as interesting. Man with his intelligence knows how to protect himself against animals, but he doesn't know how to protect himself against his own bad habits and evil ways. The greatest of all enemies of man is himself. More than personal or national enemies, more than germs, bombs, or any other threat, man should fear himself when he is wrong. To remain in ignorance of your divine nature and to be overpowered by bad habits is to make an enemy of your own self. The best way to be successful in this adventure of life is to be your own friend. Krishna said: "The Self is the Friend of the (transformed) self, but the Enemy of the unregenerate self."*

The Subtle Enemies

It is easy to picture ourselves starting off to explore some wild and unknown country. If we are going by ship we want a lifeboat with us; should the steamer sink, we know we can get into the boat and save ourselves. But in so many of life's experiences there seems to be a leak in our lifeboat, no matter what precautions we have taken.

In a jungle infested with animals you can take reasonable care against them, but subtle dangers are more difficult to overcome. How to protect oneself against a barrage of germs? Millions are floating around us all the time. We think we are safe when we take precautions against dangers we can see and hear, but we have only inadequate means to protect ourselves against germs. In your own bloodstream the white corpuscles are constantly fighting these organisms. Drugs only numb them; the white corpuscles are the soldiers who move in and destroy them. If your blood is weak, the soldiers will not be able to help you. In the lungs of many unsuspecting persons lurk fierce tuberculosis bacilli, ready to destroy their host. Nature forms a restraining wall of cells around them, but it is effective only so long as the body can keep up its resistance. This struggle of life goes on constantly in the unseen jungle of life within! If you could examine your food under a microscope you would not eat it. Germs are having a feast thereon, and you are swallowing them whole. The water you drink is alive with such organisms. There is no true vegetarian be-

* Bhagavad-Gita VI:6.

cause everyone eats millions of germs each day. Shall man then stop eating?

Prepare for Every Kind of Battle

In order to go safely through this jungle of life you must equip yourself with the proper weapons. You have to be a well-trained soldier. The layman who doesn't know how to protect himself is soon killed. The wise man who is armed against all forms of warfare—against disease, against destiny and *karma*, against all evil thoughts and habits—becomes the victor in this adventure. It requires carefulness and, in addition, the adoption of certain methods by which we can overcome our enemies.

As we progress we learn better methods of vanquishing the causes of our physical, mental, moral, and spiritual disasters. When you have gone successfully through physical illnesses and accidents and inner struggles, then you can say that life was a sweet adventure. Jesus could say this. But before you have similarly conquered, it is premature to say that life is sweet. Until you have attained final ascension, liberation of the soul in God, life is not yet finished for you. You have not overcome the desire to be adventurous until you have ascended consciously in Spirit.

Seeing someone who is suffering, you feel thankful that you are not going through that particular adventure. But you may be next. The possibilities of harm to the body are numerous. So be equipped. The scientist says, "Eat nourishing food and follow health laws to protect yourself from germs." The politician says, "Be good soldiers to protect yourselves from outside enemies." We are living in strange times. Even women, the proverbial saviors of the world, are being trained as soldiers to kill others' children. Horrible! But once in a while some good comes from war—it removes cowardice from us.

The Importance of Mind Power

In this jungle of life, surrounded by enemies—disease, poverty, suffering, bad habits, and wrong desires—there are so many rules to be observed that life becomes intolerable when you try to keep them all in mind. You tire of them because each department of life is limitless in its potential for diversity. When you attempt to apply health rules you are nearly overwhelmed—there is no time to think about anything else! And everyone has a different set of health precepts for you to follow. We are under a great hypnosis. As I tried different methods, this truth dawned on me: *mind controls the effectiveness of them all.*

God has given us one tremendous instrument of protection—more powerful than machine guns, electricity, poison gas, or any medicine—the mind. It is the mind that must be strengthened. As for the body, I will do only the will of God. If He tells me to go to a doctor, it is all right; and if He tells me to suffer, it is all right. Whatever is His will is my will. An important part of the adventure of life is to get hold of the mind, and to keep that controlled mind constantly attuned to the Lord. This is the secret of a happy, successful existence.

The Ultimate Protection Is God-Communion

Even though you adopt physical methods of healing, do not put all your faith in the methods, but in the power of God behind them. If you have cut your finger, put iodine on it, but inwardly pray: "Lord, help me not to be dependent on medicine, but to rely on mind power alone." You have not been taught how to attain that mental state. It comes by exercising mind power and by attuning the mind to God through meditation. In this way you should gain complete power over the mind before you try to deny matter and material remedies. Until then it is best to take common-sense steps to help the body. When you can drink poison and remain unaffected by it, you can rightfully deny matter and say mind is everything. You must arrive at that consciousness first.

God offers you an invincible weapon by which you can eradicate all your sorrows and suffering: wisdom, which comes through God-communion. The easiest way to overcome disease, disappointments, and disasters is to be in constant attunement with God.

We are babes in the woods of life, forced to learn by our own experiences and troubles, stumbling into pitfalls of sickness and wrong habits. Again and again we have to raise our voices for help. But the Supreme Help comes from tuning in with Spirit.

Whenever you are in trouble, pray: "Lord, You are within me and all around me. I am in the castle of Thy presence. I have been struggling through life, surrounded by many kinds of deadly enemies. I now see that they are not really agents for my destruction; You have put me on earth to test my power. I am going through these tests only to prove myself. I am game to fight the evils that surround me; I will vanquish them by the almightiness of Your presence. And when I shall have passed through the adventure of this life I will say: 'Lord, it was hard to be brave and fight; but the greater my terror, the greater was the strength within me, given by You, by which I conquered and realized that I am made in Your image. You are the King of this universe and I am Your child, a prince of the universe. What have I to fear?'"

As soon as you realize you have been born a human being you have everything to fear. There seems to be no escape. No matter what precautions you take, there is always a misstep somewhere. Your only security is in God. Whether you are in the African jungle or at war or racked by disease and poverty, just say to the Lord, and believe: "I am in the armored car of Your presence, moving across the battlefield of life. I am protected."

There is no other way to be safe. Use common sense and trust fully in God. I am not suggesting something eccentric; I am urging you to affirm and believe, no matter what happens, in this truth: "Lord, it is You alone who can help me."* So many have fallen into ruts of disease and wrong habits and have not pulled themselves out. Never say you cannot escape. Your misfortune is only for a time. The failure of one life is not the measure of whether or not you are a success. The attitude of the conquering man is unafraid: "I am a child of God. I have nothing to fear." So fear nothing. Life and death are only different processes of your consciousness.

* "To men who meditate on Me as their Very Own, ever united to Me by incessant worship, I supply their deficiencies and make permanent their gains" (Bhagavad-Gita IX:22).

Everything the Lord has created is to try us, to bring out the buried soul immortality within us. That is the adventure of life, the one purpose of life. And everyone's adventure is different, unique. You should be prepared to deal with all problems of health, mind, and soul by common-sense methods and faith in God, knowing that in life or death your soul remains unconquered. You can never die. "No weapon can pierce the soul; no fire can burn it; no water can moisten it; nor can any wind wither it....The soul is immutable, all-permeating, calm, and immovable."* You are eternally the image of Spirit.

Is it not freeing to the mind to know that death cannot kill us? When disease comes and the body stops working, the soul thinks, "I am dead!" But the Lord shakes the soul and says: "What is the matter with you? You are not dead. Are you not still thinking?" A soldier is walking along and a bomb shatters his body. His soul cries, "Oh, I am killed, Lord!" And God says, "Of course not! Are you not talking to Me? Nothing can destroy you, My child. You are dreaming." Then the soul realizes: "This is not so terrible. It was only my temporary earth-life consciousness of being a physical body that made losing it seem the end of me. I had forgotten that I am the eternal soul."

The Goal of Our Life-Adventure

True yogis are able to control the mind under all circumstances. When that perfection is reached, you are free. Then you know life is a divine adventure. Jesus and other great souls have proved this. Nothing could touch them. They enjoyed uninterruptedly the sweet romance with God. It is the only part of the adventure that has any purpose.

Human love is meaningless unless anchored in the unconditional love of God. A boy and a girl fall in love, and after a time they fall out of love. Romance with human beings is imperfect. The romance with God is perfect and everlasting.

You will finish this life-adventure only when you conquer its dangers by your will power and mind power, as did the Great Ones. Then you will look back and say: "Lord, it was a pretty bad experience. I came near failing, but now I am in the safety of Your presence forever."

* Bhagavad-Gita II:23–24.

We can see life as a wonderful adventure when the Lord finally says, "All those terrifying experiences are over. I am with you evermore. Nothing can harm you."

Man is playing at life like a child, but his mind grows stronger through fighting sickness and troubles. Anything that weakens your mind is your greatest enemy, and whatever strengthens your mind is your haven. Laugh at any trouble that comes. The Lord has shown me that this life is but a dream. When you wake up, you will remember it only as a dream of joy and sorrow that has passed. You will know you are everlasting in the Lord.

Self-Analysis: Key to the Mastery of Life

First Self-Realization Fellowship Temple at Encinitas, California, November 6, 1938

Let us leave the confines of ego and wander in the vast fields of soul progress. As time is marching on, so must your souls march on to a greater expansion of your life in Spirit. The initiative to undertake your most important duty in life is often buried beneath the accumulated debris of human habits. You must free yourselves from their stultifying influence and start to sow the seeds of the success that you desire. Life is worthwhile when you are accomplishing the most essential work, which is to find out the meaning and true values of your existence.

Man should be instructed by this cosmic motion picture of life. It is not being shown without a reason. Each day we behold different scenes, and each day has a lesson to teach. You are meant to learn the lesson by concentrating on the supreme purpose of human existence: to know Who is behind your life.

Without Self-Analysis, Man Leads Robotlike Life

Millions of people never analyze themselves. Mentally they are mechanical products of the factory of their environment, preoccupied with breakfast, lunch, and dinner, working and sleeping, and going here and there to be entertained. They don't know what or why they are seeking, nor why they never realize complete happiness and lasting satisfaction. By evading self-analysis, people go on being robots, conditioned by their environment. True self-analysis is the greatest art of progress.

Everyone should learn to analyze himself dispassionately. Write down your thoughts and aspirations daily. Find out what you are—not what you imagine you are!—because you want

73

to make yourself what you ought to be. Most people don't change because they don't see their own faults.

Everyone is the product of his heredity and environment. If you were born in America you reflect distinctive American characteristics. If you were born in China or England, you are likely to reflect the interests of those nationalities. Your environment is the result of your true heredity—the traits and desires acquired by you in past lives. This heredity of past incarnations has led to your being born in the particular family and environment in which you now find yourself.

When we read about the families of important people, we often note that sons of great men are not necessarily of the same mental caliber as their fathers. This failure of biological heredity in man raises a great doubt in our minds: why don't we find the same results in human life that we observe in the plant and animal kingdoms, where good pedigree usually produces good offspring? We must probe the inner life of man for an answer.

Traits from Past Lives Influence Us Now

In a literary family it is not unusual to find a boy who doesn't like literature at all. He has been brought up with literature-loving companions, yet has no affinity for it. Why? Environment or heredity in the ordinary sense does not explain it. But beyond these factors is reincarnation. We are born into a particular family because of certain characteristics that are similar. But every person in a family is an individual soul who brings his own distinctive traits from his past lives. Hence there are always some biological hereditary resemblances in families, yet each person is different in character.

A man takes birth in a certain family, a particular social and national environment, owing to specific causes—his own past actions. Therefore man is the architect of his own destiny. One can almost predict what he will be in his next life by analyzing his dominant interests and habits in this one.

Whatever You Have Done, You Can Undo

So self-analysis is important for the progress of the soul. Let us suppose that tragedies have been your favorite reading for many years, and that you naturally feel you will continue to enjoy them for the rest of your life. But if you analyze yourself and see that you are becoming morose from constant reading of this type of literature, you will wish to form a new habit of perusing inspiring spiritual books. By doing so you will change the course of your life. We can alter ourselves very quickly with strong determination; but without it, one does not change effortlessly or in a minute the habit patterns of years. To eradicate a habit of long standing you must apply the full strength of your determination in counteractivity until the bad habit is worn out. Most persons don't have the necessary patience. But everyone should feel encouraged by this truth: whatever you have created or done, you can undo.

When you analyze what you are, have a firm desire to banish your weaknesses and to make yourself what you ought to be. Don't allow yourself to be overwhelmed with discouragement at the revelation of your shortcomings that honest self-analysis usually brings.

Thought Produces Everything in the Universe

A theory has been advanced that thought is a product of the endocrine glands. Such a conception is unfounded. Flesh cannot produce thought. Mind is the architect of the microcosm and the macrocosm. As water by cooling and condensation becomes ice, so thought by condensation assumes physical form. Everything in the universe is thought in material form. The endocrine organ is just a physical structurization of a microcosmic thought-blueprint.

The physical and mental aspects of man are closely interrelated; it is commonly observed that a person whose liver is out of order becomes cranky. When you are bilious, you don't feel like smiling and saying "Peace" to everyone! You feel unamiable. Your thoughts and emotions are affected by your physical state.

A weakening of the organs has a corresponding weakening effect on mental power. Those who eat a great deal of meat are often surly and full of vexation. If I were to put you on a grape-juice diet for a week, it is likely you would feel uplifted and harmoniously disposed toward all.*

I recently met a man who was wearing just a lightweight suit and no overcoat, although it was terribly cold. He said he was seventy years old, and that he never feels cold. He didn't even wear socks! He had accustomed his body to chilly weather. Mind influences body more than vice versa, but the bodily chemicals do exercise a constant influence on the mind.† Body and mind are interdependent.

Dreams Reveal the Omnipotence of Mind

For example, suppose I am dreaming that I am awake and in the kitchen, and very hungry. I eat something and drink a glass of milk. My hunger and thirst are gone, and I feel satisfied. What was the cause of my satisfaction? Was it the food? Remember, I am dreaming. Is it not simply a change of thought that made me feel satisfied? Since I am dreaming, it is my mind that thought it had taken food. The hunger and the food and the milk were only ideas in my dream. All were made of the same mind-stuff. When I wake up I realize that my experiences were nothing but a series of ideas. A mere change of thought removed the unpleasant sensation of hunger and substituted the pleasant sensation of eating food and drinking milk. So you see, thought by itself can do anything.

Once I was traveling by train when the weather was extremely hot; the air felt as if it were coming from a furnace.

---

* Overeating and improper eating create in the body excessive toxins that have a definite negative effect on the mind, making it both sluggish and irritable. Occasional fasting on grape or orange juice has a cleansing effect on the system, which in turn vitalizes the brain. Such fasts, undertaken one day a week, or occasionally for three days at a time, have been found effective in helping to keep the body properly cleansed of impurities. Fasting for longer than three days at a time should be under the supervision of someone well trained in the science of fasting.

† Serious research on the effect of diet and nutrition on mental health was begun many years after Paramahansa Yogananda had made this observation. Persons from poverty areas who were denied proper nourishment showed decidedly slower mental development and responses. In addition, science has shown that some forms of insanity (heretofore considered incurable) improved remarkably with the simple administration of vitamins, and that the causes of certain forms of depression, anxiety, and other emotions can be traced to chemical imbalances in the system. *(Publisher's Note)*

Everyone around me was suffering, but I was smiling within because my mind was dissociated from the thought of the heat. I had said to myself: "Lord, the same electricity that makes heat in a furnace makes ice in a refrigerator. Therefore why shouldn't I be able to redirect that electricity of Yours to produce cold right now?" In that instant I felt as if a sheet of ice had enveloped me.

Change Your Mental Attitude

We should bear in mind, however, that it is not wise to disregard the body wholly. One should eat proper foods in preference to wrong foods. And if you must live with people who make you nervous, then once in a while you should change your surroundings. But it is better still if you can change your *mental* environment, so that you won't be disturbed by others' actions. Change yourself, and you can then live anywhere in peace and happiness.

Most of the world is like a mental hospital. Some people are sick with jealousy, others with anger, hatred, passion. They are victims of their habits and emotions. But you can make your home a place of peace. Analyze yourself. All emotions are reflected in the body and mind. Envy and fear cause the face to pale, and love makes it glow. Learn to be calm and you will always be happy.

So remember, whatever type of ego you have, whatever personality you are trying to express, you should make an effort to analyze your true nature and to develop its best qualities. One may have a moral ego or a patriotic ego or an artistic ego or a businessman's ego, and so on. If morality is your ideal, live uprightly and express your goodwill to all. That is real morality. It is pride that makes self-righteous persons so ready to judge those about them who are weak. True morality includes compassion for others in their ignorant wrongdoings.

Those who are products of the material ego suffer much and needlessly. Such persons should learn self-control; otherwise they are just like pieces of matter in action—they have to smoke so many times a day, they must eat certain foods, they always get a headache if they miss their lunch, they can sleep only in a particular kind of bed. It is all right to utilize creature comforts, but never be enslaved by them.

If you are a cross between an intellectual and a materialistic ego, that is better. But unless you develop and maintain a balanced nature—intellectually, materially, and spiritually— you are not going to be happy. Your spiritual intuition tells you how to control your life, so that you are not mastered by it. It is unwise to let the materialistic ego govern your judgment; your conscience and intuition should decide.

The Conditions of Happiness: Plain Living, High Thinking

Plain living and high thinking should be your goal. Learn to carry all the conditions of happiness within yourself by meditating and attuning your consciousness to the ever-existing, ever-conscious, ever-new Joy, which is God. Your happiness should never be subject to any outside influence. Whatever your environment is, don't allow your inner peace to be touched by it. Analyze yourself; make yourself what you should be and what you want to be. People seldom learn true self-control; they do things that are detrimental to their highest welfare and think they are making themselves happy; but they are not. To be able to do things when and because you ought to do them, and to refrain from doing what you know is injurious—these are keys to real success and happiness.

Don't keep your mind engaged in too many activities. Analyze what you get from them, and see if they are really important. Don't waste your time. To read a good book improves you much more than seeing movies. I often say, "If you read for one hour, write in your spiritual diary for two hours; and if you write for two hours, think for three hours; and if you think for three hours, meditate all the time." No matter where I go, I keep my mind continuously on my soul peace. You too should always point the needle of your attention toward the North Pole of spiritual joy. Then no one can ever disturb your equilibrium.

Remember, if each day does not find you a better person than you were the day before, you are going backward—in health, in mental peace, and in soul joy. Why? Because you don't exercise enough control over your actions. You yourself made your habits, and you can change them. If you have been thinking wrongly, make up your mind to be with good company and to study and meditate. A change of company can make a great difference to you. When you come here, even for these few hours, your mentality changes; you feel a refreshing peace. When you go to a dance or a party your mind is often restless, nervous, and excited. Afterward, if you enter a different, calmer atmosphere, you feel more peaceful again. The greatest influence in your life, stronger even than your will power, is your environment. Change that, if necessary. Until you are mentally strong, you can never be what you want to be without a good environment to help you. When you are having difficulty in trying to change for the better, spiritual company and other uplifting influences are essential.

Self-analysis is also essential to help you better yourself. If you can analyze yourself fearlessly, you will be able to stand the critical analysis of others without flinching.

Those who like to dwell on the faults of others are human vultures. There is already too much evil in the world. Don't talk of evil, don't think of evil, and don't do evil. Be like a rose, wafting to all the sweet fragrance of soul goodness. Make everyone feel that you are a friend; that you are a helper, not a destroyer. If you want to be good, analyze yourself and develop the virtues in you. Banish the thought that evil has any part in your nature, and it will drop off. Make everyone else feel that you are an image of God, not by your words but by your behavior. Emphasize the light, and darkness will be no more. Study, meditate, and do good to others.

Seclusion Is the Price of Greatness

Seclusion is the price of greatness. Be alone within. Don't lead the aimless life that so many persons follow. Meditate and read good books more. There are so many inspiring things to know, and yet man spends his time foolishly. Happiness will never come if you don't concentrate and act on the wisdom of great men. Their thoughts are there to help you, in the scriptures and other truthful books.

So don't waste time, constantly seeking new excitement. Once in a while it is all right to go to the movies and have a little social life, but mostly remain apart and live within yourself. Happiness depends on meditation, on knowing great minds through their thoughts in books, and on surrounding yourself with people who are noble and kind. Enjoy solitude; but when you want to mix with others, do so with all your love and friendship, so that those persons cannot forget you, but remember always that they met someone who inspired them and turned their minds toward God.

Healing by God's Unlimited Power

Self-Realization Fellowship Temple,
Hollywood, California, August 31, 1947

There are three kinds of illness: physical, mental, and spiritual. Physical sickness is due to different forms of toxic conditions, infectious disease, and accidents. Mental sickness is caused by fear, worry, anger, and other emotional inharmonies. Soul sickness is due to man's ignorance of his true relationship with God.

Ignorance is the supreme disease. When one banishes ignorance he also banishes the causes of all physical, mental, and spiritual disease. My guru, Sri Yukteswarji, often said, "Wisdom is the greatest cleanser."

Trying to overcome various kinds of suffering by the limited power of material curative methods is often disappointing. Only in the unlimited power of spiritual methods may man find a permanent cure for the "dis-ease" of body, mind, and soul. That boundless power of healing is to be sought in God. If you have suffered mentally over the loss of loved ones, you can find them again in God. All things are possible with His help.

Unless one really knows God, he is not justified in saying that only mind exists, and that one does not need to obey health laws or to use any physical aids for healing. Until actual realization is attained, one should use his common sense in all he does. At the same time one should never doubt God, but should constantly affirm his faith in God's omnipresent divine power.

Doctors try to learn the causes of disease and to remove those causes so that the illnesses do not recur. In their use of many specific material methods of cure, doctors are often very skillful. However, not every disease responds to medicine and surgery, and therein lies the essential limitation of these methods.

Chemicals and medicines affect only the outer physical composition of the bodily cells and do not alter the inner atomic structure or life principle of the cells. In many cases no cure of disease is possible until the healing power of God has corrected, from within, the imbalance of "lifetrons" or intelligent life energy in the body. The two basic causes of disease are underactivity and overactivity of the life energy, *prana*, that structures and sustains the body. The improper functioning of any one (or more) of the five governing pranic currents—*vyana*, circulation; *udana*, metabolism; *samana*, assimilation; *prana*, crystallization; and *apana*, elimination—adversely affects bodily health. When the natural harmonious balance of these subtle energies is restored by God's divine power, the atomic balance of the physical cells they nourish is restored; the healing is perfect, and often instantaneous. So long as balanced vitality is maintained by right living, proper diet, and *pranayama* meditation (life-energy control techniques), the body's own life energy "electrocutes" disease before it can develop.

Balanced Development Is Essential

Injury and disease are more often the cause of death than is old age. Most people die before true old age has set in. In some cases, and they are exceptional, all parts of the body grow weak at once; such persons die, without pain, like ripe fruit that falls in due time from the tree. But the majority are plucked from the tree of life before they are really ripe for death.

In most cases of death, one bodily part had ceased functioning before the rest. It may also happen that if one part is stronger or more developed than another, the resulting imbalance of the life force in the body may cause suffering and even death. For example, someone with a weak heart in a strong-muscled body may injure his heart by overuse of his muscular strength. Sandow,* "the strong man," died at fifty-eight when a

---

* Eugene Sandow (1867–1925), advocate of physical culture and wrestling, noted for his physique and physical prowess. The famous athlete traveled widely to expound his ideas on physical fitness.

blood vessel in his brain burst as a result of his having raised a car singlehanded. Overexercise that leads to unbalanced development may thus have harmful consequences.

The Self-Realization Fellowship Energization Exercises* place the least strain on the heart and provide for a uniform development of the body. Simple outdoor exercise, such as walking; balanced diet and moderation in eating; and quiet meditation are all conducive to health.

Obey Nature's Laws and Have More Faith in God

A master may ignore, without ill effect, dietary and other rules for health. The ordinary individual, however, should be careful to maintain physical well-being by right observance of the laws of nature.

One's diet should be wisely chosen. The body requires for health certain amounts of starch, protein, and fat, but in excess they can be harmful. Very little starch is necessary; bread is no longer held to be the "staff of life." Too much starch in the diet, especially from white flour, causes an over-accumulation of mucus in the body. (A certain amount of mucus is necessary, of course, to prevent the entry of harmful microbes into the mucous membranes.) Eat abundantly of foods that contain a high proportion of mineral salts, such as fruits and vegetables. This type of diet prevents constipation, which, when present, predisposes the body to many diseases.

Nature tries by reflex action to remove causes of physical distress. When dust gets into the eye, we involuntarily try to wink the dust away. When dirt or dust enters the nose, we sneeze. If we eat something unwholesome, we get rid of it by regurgitation. When disease attacks any internal organ of the body, nature provides many means by which the organ may protect, defend, and renew itself. However, owing to various habits of living that alienate most men from nature, their innate powers of recuperation and rejuvenation become impaired and are prematurely lost.

Harmful microbes are ceaselessly attacking the body;

---

* These exercises, for energizing the body through conscious direction of *prana* by will power, were developed by Paramahansa Yogananda in 1916. They are taught in the *Self-Realization Fellowship Lessons. (Publisher's Note)*

good ones are ceaselessly defending it, aided sometimes by diet, herbs, medicines, and other health measures. *But an unlimited source of protection for man lies in his strong thought that, as a child of God, he cannot be affected by disease.*

Mind has much greater power than medicine. But to deny any power to medicine is unreasonable, because if drugs have no power, a man could take poison and not die. While one should not deny the potency of medicines and drugs, one should understand that continuous dependence on them will prove their limitations; a time will come when they will lose their former efficacy in restoring the body to health. The only infinite power of healing lies in man's mind and soul. The body cannot be healed by spiritual means if the mental power and faith are weak. Permanent healing comes through the boundless power of the mind and through God's grace.

Fruits, Vegetables, and Nuts Superior to Meat

According to one school of thought, some diseases may be cured by eating the organs of animals. A savage devours the heart of a lion in the belief that his own heart will thus be invigorated. The tissues of chicken hearts are known to have a strengthening effect on the heart of man; and the liver helps those who are anemic. However, many health authorities state that iron- and vitamin-rich foods such as eggs, cashew nuts, soybeans, molasses, dried apricots, dried lima beans, dried peas parsnips, spinach, and parsley may successfully be substituted for liver in overcoming anemia. Pepsin taken from animal organs is useful in cases of stomach ulcers; but pepsin is also present in the fruit of the papaya, which is a valuable healing aid to those who suffer from any form of impaired digestion.

When man is sick he may feel justified in eating anything that has healing value, but animal flesh is not actually necessary for this purpose; indeed, it may increase the bodily burden by contributing toxins to the bloodstream. Thus, while flesh foods may aid in healing one illness, they sometimes create a condition whereby another disease may develop elsewhere in the body. That is why the safest diet for man is fresh fruits, vegetables, finely ground nuts, and vegetable and dairy proteins. In certain cases the system may not tolerate raw fruits and vegetables, but the average person will benefit by including them daily in his diet.

In vegetables and fruits God has infused medicinal power to help in overcoming disease. Even these, however, have but a limited potency. The organs of the body are essentially sustained by the energy of God, and the person who employs various methods to increase this energy will have at his command a greater power for healing than is afforded by any medicine or diet.

Purify the Body of Harmful Toxins

Three-fourths of the body consists of water; hence the bodily demand for water is much greater than that for food. (Death by thirst is a suffering more acute than death by starvation.) It is important to give the body plenty of water. Drinking unsweetened fruit juices also is good. In localities where water has a calcium content high enough to dispose toward hardening of the arteries in man, he should take, instead, fruit juices and watermelons, cantaloupes, and similar juicy fruits. Some health researchers say, however, that persons who have sinus trouble should not take citrus juices.

Make it a point to drink plenty of liquids (and I do not mean soda-water beverages!) to wash away toxins in the body. But avoid drinking liquids with meals, as this can be injurious to digestion. One tends to wash down the food without chewing it properly. If starches are not partially digested in the mouth, they often do not digest fully in the stomach. To chew food well is important—the stomach has no teeth. Hasty eating is harmful; particularly if large amounts of liquid are taken with the meal, thus diluting the gastric juices. Also, drinking liquids with meals gives a tendency to obesity.

It is important to keep the bloodstream healthy. Beef and pork may release into the bloodstream toxic poisons and microbes. The white corpuscles try to destroy the microbes, but if the latter are strong and if the white corpuscles are insufficient to resist them, toxic reactions set in. Fish, chicken, and lamb are preferable to beef and pork, which are highly acid-producing.

The most important principle in connection with eating

is to avoid any form of overindulgence. As one learns to re-
strain himself he becomes healthier. It may often happen that
one's desire for a certain food is so great that he thinks he cannot resist it. His senses dictate to him, saying that he must eat
that food, even when he knows it may be harmful to him. If he
refuses to perpetuate his bad habits, he will find that he comes
to dislike what is injurious and to like what is beneficial.
Greedy people fill themselves and still they are looking for
more food. By overeating, they dare to strain a heart-pump that
has been overworked for perhaps forty years!

Many persons thoughtlessly eat late at night. Usually
sleep soon follows, during which man's internal machinery
slows down. The food may lie in the stomach without being
properly digested. Eating shortly before the nightly rest is
therefore unwise.

There is nothing worse for body and mind, however, than
drinking intoxicating liquors. Under their influence a man
may do things that in his right mind he would be ashamed to
do. Violence, greed, lust for money and sex, even murder, may
result from drunkenness. The belief that wine, sex experiences, and money will bring happiness is said by the sages to
be the chief delusion that man must overcome in order to realize his true nature.

Liquor increases man's desires for money and sex, and it is
therefore the worst evil of the three. It is an unnecessary and
extremely dangerous indulgence, because it stifles reason. A
drunken man is no longer a true man. It is wisdom to strive to
maintain only normal appetites.

Increase Your Natural Resistance to Disease

Fasting is a natural method of healing. When animals or
savages are sick, they fast. The bodily machinery thus has an
opportunity to cleanse itself and to obtain a much-needed rest.
Most diseases can be cured by judicious fasting.* Unless one
has a weak heart, regular short fasts have been recommended

* In Armenia, Dr. Grant Sarkisyan has successfully used fasting to treat patients for a variety of disorders, including bronchial asthma, skin diseases, the
initial state of arteriosclerosis, hypertension, stenocardia, and digestive tract
diseases. A selective diet is to be followed after discharge from the hospital, the

by the yogis as an excellent health measure. Another good method of physical healing is through suitable herbs or herb extracts.

In using medicines, one often finds that they are not powerful enough to bring about a healing, or that they are so powerful that they irritate the bodily tissues instead of healing them. Similarly, exposure to certain types of "healing rays" will burn the tissues. There are so many limitations in physical methods of healing!

Better than medicines are the rays of the sun. In them is a wonderful healing power. One should take a ten-minute sunbath every day; and on weekends a total of three hours' sunbathing, taken in periods of from ten to thirty minutes (provided one is used to exposure to the sun). The healing current thus absorbed is said to remain in the body for three months. Ten minutes a day is better than only occasional exposure for longer periods. A short sunbath daily, reinforced by good health habits, will keep the body supplied with sufficient life energy to destroy all harmful microbes.

Healthy persons possess a natural resistance to disease, and particularly to infections. Illness comes when the resisting power of the blood has been diminished by wrong eating or by overeating, or when overindulgence in sex has depleted the vital energy. To conserve the physical creative energy is to supply all the cells with vibrant life energy; the body then pos-

---

preference being for vegetable and fruit dishes, which Dr. Sarkisyan feels are important for longevity.

In the Soviet Union, Dr. Uri Nicholayev has given fasting therapy during the past twenty-three years. He states that sixty-four percent of his patients have been helped. Their illness is mental: schizophrenia.

At George Air Force Base, Victorville, California, twenty-five patients underwent fasting treatment for up to eighty-four days for obesity. Sixteen completed the program, with weight losses of forty to one hundred pounds. Dr. Robert M. Karns, who conducted the experiment, also reported that a forty-eight-year-old diabetic patient, who was receiving twenty-five units of insulin daily before the fast, was able to discontinue the insulin treatment after the fast. A sixty-year-old patient reported improvement of an arthritic and heart condition.

In experiments with mice, which are often the testing ground for treatment of man's disorders, it was demonstrated that the life-span could be increased by fifty percent. The treatment? Fasting. *(Publisher's Note)*

sesses a tremendous resistance to disease. Sexual overindulgence weakens the body and renders it vulnerable to illness.

You Can Increase Your Life-Span

One naturally has a better chance to overcome sickness in youth than in old age. (There are always exceptions, however, owing to karmic conditions.) The average length of life today* is sixty years. Many doctors agree that it is easily possible to increase one's life-span by careful living.

Mahavatar Babaji and a number of other great masters have lived for several hundred years. Life may be prolonged indefinitely—not by food, medicine, exercise, sunbathing, and other limited means, but by contact with the immeasurable power of God. We should think not only of the body but also of the Spirit. If we attain perfection in oneness with Spirit, we shall find perfection in body also.†

Many persons are continually busy looking after their physical welfare but neglect the development of their minds. The key to all power lies in the mind. If one fails to cultivate that power, when serious disease comes he may die without making any resistance, regardless of his age.

The Power of a Smile

Conserve the vital energy, follow a balanced diet, and always smile and be happy. He who finds joy within himself discovers that his body is charged with electric current, life energy, not from food but from God. If you feel that you can't smile, stand before a mirror and with your fingers pull your mouth into a smile. It is that important!

The healing methods I have touched on briefly in connection with food and the cleansing of the body by herbs or fasting are limited in their effectiveness; but when one is joyful within, he invites the help of the inexhaustible power of God. I mean a sincere joyfulness, not that which you feign outwardly

---

* I.e., in 1947, when this talk was given.

† Great ones who have attained the perfection of oneness with Spirit may nevertheless endure intense bodily suffering—not because of any failure on the part of Spirit, but because they choose, with divine permission, to work out on their own bodies some of the karmic effects of others' wrong actions, in order to help those persons.

but do not feel within. When your joy is sincere you are a smile-millionaire. A genuine smile distributes the cosmic current, *prana*, to every body cell. The happy man is less subject to disease, for happiness actually attracts into the body a greater supply of the universal life energy.

There are many things to talk about on this subject of healing. The main idea is that we should depend more on mind power, which is illimitable. The rules for guarding against disease should be: self-control, exercise, proper eating, drinking plenty of fruit juices, occasional fasting, and smiling all the time—from within. Those smiles come from meditation. You will find then the eternal power of God. When you are in ecstasy with Him you consciously bring His healing presence into your body.

Permanent Healing Comes from God

Mind power carries with it the unfailing energy of God; that is the power you want in your body. And there is a way to bring in that power. The way is communion with God by meditation. When your communion with Him is perfect, the healing is permanent. When the causative power of God comes, the healing effect is instantaneous; no time is required for cause to ripen into effect.

Many people in distress try to evoke that power, but when they are not healed at once they lose faith in the Lord instead of continuing to try to enlist His aid. The man who clings to the Divine is bound to be healed; because God knows that the devotee is praying, and He cannot but respond. But when you give up, the Father says, "All right. I see that you can do without Me. I shall wait for you."

The Supreme Power may be invoked by continuous faith and unceasing prayer. You should eat rightly and do whatever else is necessary for the body, but continuously pray to Him: "Lord, Thou canst heal me because Thou dost control the life atoms and subtle conditions of the body that doctors cannot reach with medicines." The external factors of medicines and fasting have a certain beneficial effect on the physical body, but they do not affect the inner force that sustains the cells. It is only when you go to God and receive His healing power that the life energy is directed into the atoms of the bodily cells and produces instantaneous healing. Wouldn't you rather depend more on God?

But the attempt to change one's dependence from physical to spiritual methods should be gradual. If a man accustomed to overeating falls sick and, with the intention of trying to achieve a mental healing, abruptly starts fasting, he may be discouraged if success is not forthcoming. It takes time to change one's way of thinking from dependence on food to dependence on mind. To be responsive to the healing power of God, the mind must be trained to *believe* in divine aid.

Out of that Great Power all atomic energy is throbbing, manifesting and sustaining every cell of the physical universe. As moving pictures are sustained by a beam of light coming from the projection booth of a movie house, so are all of us sustained by the Cosmic Beam, the Divine Light pouring from the projection booth of Eternity. When you look to, and find that Beam, you will behold Its unlimited power to rebuild the atoms and electrons and lifetrons in all body cells that may be "out of order." Commune with the Great Healer!

Eliminating the Static of Fear from the Mind Radio

First Self-Realization Fellowship Temple at Encinitas, California, October 16, 1938

Everything in the universe is composed of energy, or vibration. The vibration of words is, by extension, a grosser expression of the vibration of thoughts. The thoughts of all men are vibrating in the ether.* Because thoughts have such a high vibratory rate, they have not yet been detected there; but it is fortunate that we do not know the thoughts of all men.

Through the instrumentality of radio, you can push a button and lo, you hear music and voices! If it were not for the intelligence in the ether, through which the radio waves travel to your receiving set, you might hear all the different broadcasts at once. God created the ether, and He planned that man would create radio and radio-wave vibrations which could be transmitted and received through this medium. Radio waves depend on the ether for transmission, and on electricity for amplification in broadcasting and receiving. The sounds of radio broadcasting are always present in the ether, but are inaudible to us without a radio instrument. The vibratory radio-waves represent thoughts that are being transmitted through space into any receiving set that is tuned in.

When you are near and dear to someone, you can feel the thoughts of that person; but you are probably not able to do this with anyone as far away as India unless you have developed range. Those of you who practice regularly the *Self-Realization*

---

* The hypothetical ether is not considered necessary to present scientific theory on the nature of the material universe. But Hindu scriptures refer to ether as a fine vibratory "background" on which creation is superimposed. It fills all interstices of space, and is the vibratory force that separates all images, one from the other. (See *ether* and *elements* in glossary.) *(Publisher's Note)*

Fellowship Lessons on concentration and meditation, and are very calm, will be able to feel the thoughts of others, even from a distance. Your mind will become more sensitive.

We are all human radios: you receive the thought messages of others through your heart,* the center of feeling, and broadcast your own thought messages through the spiritual eye, the center of concentration and will. Your antenna is in the medulla, the center of intuitive superconsciousness. Suppose you are away from home and you wish to perceive what is happening there. If your feelings are very calm and your mind quiet, you will be able to intuit the feelings and thoughts of your family at home. When you become capable of great concentration, your feeling can penetrate everywhere; your perception becomes charged with energy, with electricity.

The World Is Only a Thought in the Mind of God

There is in reality no space† between India and here. But we are in America and we think we have to allow twenty-five days for a steamer trip before we can reach India. According to material consciousness time is required to traverse such a distance. But energy cuts down space. If we go by airplane, the trip takes but seven days.‡ The distance is decreased by the increased energy of flight—the more energy, the more reduction of space or distance. Suppose you are sleeping and you dream that you are going to India. You take the train to New York, board the boat, stop at various ports of call, and arrive in Bombay. All this can be done in minutes in the dream, because in thought there is no space. Or suppose I am dreaming that I am dialing a radio and I tune in India. There is no space; it is all an idea in my brain.

The whole world exists only in thought, such is the power

---

* The occult seat, in man, of *chitta*, intuitive feeling.

† Space and time are a part of the delusion of *maya*, which, to the perception of mortals, divides and measures the indivisible Infinite. In God's consciousness, which is untouched by *maya*, and to the devotee united with God in divine awakening, near and far, past, present, and future, all dissolve in the eternal omnipresent Now.

‡ Seven days in 1938, and today a complete earth orbit in a matter of minutes by a spaceship! Time and space already have been greatly bent to the will of man. "Tomorrow" he may conquer them. *(Publisher's Note)*

of mind. Space is a mental concept. I can close my eyes and think of things that are two thousand miles away, and yet all those miles are a mere expansion of thought. Space and time are merely differentiations of thought. What is the difference between ice cream and hot coffee in a dream experience? When you awaken, you realize that in the dreamland ice cream was one thought and hot coffee another; they were merely two different ideas.

Thought has omniscient power. The kind of thought I am speaking of is the thought of God. As He is omnipresent through thought, so are we. Are we not already connecting the thought of America and the thought of India by radio? There is no space there.

Often when you are trying to tune in a radio station, static comes in and disturbs the program you are trying to hear. Likewise, when you are trying to accomplish some personal transformation in your heart, "static" may interrupt your progress. That static is your bad habits.

Fear Cannot Enter a Quiet Heart

Fear is another form of static that affects your mind-radio. Like good and bad habits, fear can be both constructive and destructive. For example, when a wife says, "My husband will be displeased if I go out this evening; therefore I won't go," she is motivated by loving fear, which is constructive. Loving fear and slavish fear are different. I am speaking of loving fear, which makes one cautious lest he hurt someone unnecessarily. Slavish fear paralyzes the will. Family members should entertain only loving fear, and never be afraid to speak truth to one another. To perform dutiful actions or sacrifice your own wishes out of love for another person is much better than to do so out of fear. And when you refrain from breaking divine laws, it should be out of love for God, not from fear of punishment.

Fear comes from the heart. If ever you feel overcome by dread of some illness or accident, you should inhale and exhale deeply, slowly, and rhythmically several times, relaxing with each exhalation. This helps the circulation to become normal. If your heart is truly quiet you cannot feel fear at all.

Anxieties are awakened in the heart through the con-

sciousness of pain; hence fear is dependent on some prior experience—perhaps you once fell and broke your leg, and so
you learned to dread a repetition of that experience. When you
dwell on such an apprehension your will is paralyzed, and
your nerves also, and you may indeed fall again and break your
leg. Furthermore, when your heart becomes paralyzed by fear,
your vitality is low and disease germs get a chance to invade
your body.

Be Cautious But Not Fearful

There is hardly anyone who does not fear disease. Fear was
given to man as a cautionary device to spare him pain; it is not
meant to be cultivated and abused. Overindulgence in fear only
cripples our efforts to ward off difficulties. Cautious fear is
wise, as when, knowing the principles of right diet, you reason,
"I won't eat that cake, because it is not good for me." But unreasoning apprehension is a cause of disease; it is the real germ
of all sickness. Dread of disease precipitates disease. Through
the very thought of sickness you bring it on yourself. If you are
constantly afraid of catching a cold, you will be more suscep-
tible to it, no matter what you do to prevent it. Do not paralyze
your will and nerves with fear. When anxiety persists in spite
of your will, you are helping to create the very experience you
are dreading. Also, it is unwise to associate more than is necessary and considerate with people who constantly discuss their
own and others' ailments and infirmities; this dwelling on the
subject may sow seeds of apprehension in your mind. Those
who are worried they are going to succumb to tuberculosis,
cancer, heart trouble, should cast out this fear, lest it bring
about the unwelcome condition. Those who are already sick
and infirm need as pleasant an environment as possible, among
people who have a strong and positive nature, to encourage
them in positive thoughts and feelings. Thought has great
power. Those who serve in hospitals seldom fall ill, because of
their confident attitude. They are vitalized by their energy and
strong thoughts.

For this reason, as you get older, it is best not to tell others
your age. As soon as you do, they see that age in you and associate it with diminishing health and vitality. The thought of
advancing age creates anxiety, and thus you devitalize yourself.

So keep your age private. Say to God: "I am immortal. I am blessed with the privilege of good health, and I thank Thee."

Therefore be cautious, but not fearful. Take the precaution of going on a purifying diet now and then, so that any conditions of illness that may be present in the body will be eliminated. Do your best to remove the causes of illness and then be absolutely unafraid. There are so many germs everywhere that if you began to fear them you would not be able to enjoy life at all. Even with all your sanitary precautions, if you could look at your home through a microscope you would lose all desire to eat!

Techniques of Tuning Out Fear

Whatever it is that you fear, take your mind away from it and leave it to God. Have faith in Him. Much suffering is due simply to worry. Why suffer now when the malady has not yet come? Since most of our ills come through fear, if you give up fear you will be free at once. The healing will be instant. Every night, before you sleep, affirm: "The Heavenly Father is with me; I am protected." Mentally surround yourself with Spirit and His cosmic energy and think: "Any germ that attacks me will be electrocuted." Chant *"Aum"* three times, or the word "God." This will shield you. You will feel His wonderful protection. Be fearless. It is the only way to be healthy. If you commune with God His truth will flow to you. You will know that you are the imperishable soul.

Whenever you feel afraid, put your hand over your heart, next to the skin; rub from left to right, and say, "Father, I am free. Tune out this fear from my heart-radio." Just as you tune out static on an ordinary radio, so if you continuously rub the heart from left to right, and continuously concentrate on the thought that you want to tune out fear from your heart, it will go; and the joy of God will be perceived.

Fear Ceases with the Contact of God

Fear is constantly haunting you. Cessation of fear comes with the contact of God, nothing else. Why wait? Through Yoga you can have that communion with Him. India has something to give you that no other nation has ever given. I owe

everything to my guru, Swami Sri Yukteswar; he was a master
in every way. It was by following his wisdom that I was able to
succeed in my mission in the West. He said, "Whatever you
do, try to do it as nobody else has done it before." If you remember that thought, you will succeed. Most people imitate
others. You should be original, and whatever you do, do well.
All nature consciously communes with you when you are in
tune with God.

We often consider ourselves first, but we should always include others in our happiness. When we do that from the goodness of our hearts, we spread abroad a spirit of mutual consideration. If everyone in a community of one thousand persons
behaved this way, each one would have nine hundred and
ninety-nine friends. But if everyone in that community behaved like an enemy to the other, each one would have nine
hundred and ninety-nine enemies.

Conquering the hearts of others by the power of love is
the greatest victory you can win in life. Always try to consider
others first and you will find the whole world at your feet.
That was the greatness of Jesus. He lived and died for all. Men
of great material power who live only for themselves are soon
forgotten, but those who live completely for others are remembered forever. The King of Kings had no throne of gold during
his brief span on earth; but he has reigned for twenty centuries
on a throne of love in the hearts of millions of people. That is
the best throne to have.

A Single Thought May Lead to Redemption

When you came into this world you cried, whereas everyone else rejoiced. During your lifetime, work and serve in such
a way that when it is time for you to leave this world, you will
smile at parting while the world cries for you. Hold this
thought and you will always remember to consider others before yourself.

This vast world was made that you might use your intelligence to acquire knowledge of the Spirit, knowledge about
your Self. *Just one thought may redeem you.* You don't realize
how effectively your thoughts work in the ether.

How would you know human love if God Himself didn't

give it to you by planting His love in the heart of each being? And since God is so kind and so loving, then He should be the object of your search. He doesn't want to impose Himself on you. But the mysterious working of your body, the intelligence He has given you, and every other wonder in life should be sufficient stimulus to make you determine to find God. Every human being would be redeemed if he would try. You must try!

When I started in this path, my life at first was chaotic; but as I kept on trying, things began to clear up for me in a marvelous way. Everything that happened showed me that God *is*, and that He can be known in this life. When you find God, what assurance and fearlessness you will have! Then nothing else matters at all, nothing can ever make you afraid. Thus did Krishna exhort Arjuna to face fearlessly the battle of life and become spiritually victorious: "Surrender not to unmanliness. It is unbecoming of thee. O scorcher of foes, forsake this small weak-heartedness and arise!"*

* Bhagavad-Gita II:3.

Nervousness—Cause and Cure

Circa 1927

Nervousness is a malady that can be overcome by a specific medicine: calmness. The disturbance of mental equilibrium, which results in nervous disorders, is caused by continuous states of excitement or excessive stimulation of the senses. Indulgence in constant thoughts of fear, anger, melancholy, remorse, envy, sorrow, hatred, discontent, or worry; and lack of the necessities for normal and happy living, such as right food, proper exercise, fresh air, sunshine, agreeable work and a purpose in life, all are causes of nervous disease.

Any violent or persistent mental, emotional, or physical excitement greatly disturbs and unbalances the flow of life force throughout the sensory-motor mechanism and the lamps of the senses. If we connect a fifty-watt bulb with a two-thousand-volt source, it would burn out the bulb. Similarly, the nervous system was not made to withstand the destructive force of intense emotion or persistent negative thoughts and feelings.

Far-Reaching Effects of Nervousness

Nervousness is no simple problem; it is a deadly enemy with far-reaching effects. Physically, it is difficult to heal any disease so long as it is aggravated by nervousness. Spiritually, an imbalance of life force in the body makes it extremely hard for the devotee to concentrate or meditate deeply enough to acquire peace and wisdom. But nervousness can be cured. The sufferer must be willing to analyze his condition and remove the disintegrating emotions and negative thoughts that are little by little destroying him. Objective analysis of one's problems, and maintaining calmness in all situations of life will heal the most persistent case of nervousness.

Realization that all power to think, speak, feel, and act comes from God, and that He is ever with us, inspiring and guiding us, brings an instant freedom from nervousness. Flashes of divine joy will come with this realization; sometimes a deep illumination will pervade one's being, banishing the very concept of fear. Like an ocean, the power of God sweeps in, surging through the heart in a cleansing flood, removing all obstructions of delusive doubt, nervousness, and fear. The delusion of matter, the consciousness of being only a mortal body, is overcome by contacting the sweet serenity of Spirit, attainable by daily meditation. Then you know that the body is a little bubble of energy in His cosmic sea.

The victim of nervousness must understand his case, and must reflect on those continual mistakes of thinking which are responsible for his maladjustment to life. When the nervous man once admits to himself that his disease is not mysterious in its cause, but the logical outcome of his own habits, he is already half cured.

The Nervous System

The nervous system is the telephonic outlet and inlet of the body, providing man with his response to outer and inner stimuli. Excitement upsets the nervous balance, sending too much energy to some parts and depriving others of their normal share. This lack of proper distribution of nerve force is the sole cause of nervousness. The calm man—he who avoids excitement because he is not overly attached to his ego and is aware that God, and not he, is running this universe—is always able to meet any situation in life because his nerve force is equilibrated. Lord Krishna said: "With unwavering discrimination, free from delusion, neither jubilant at pleasant experiences nor downcast by unpleasant experiences, the sage becomes established in God."* This is the goal we must strive for and attain.

The nervous system supplies life current to the brain, heart, and other parts of the body. It distributes energy to the five senses of sight, sound, touch, taste, and feeling. Nerves are our medium of contact with the outer world and the

* Bhagavad-Gita V:20.

source of all our sensory reactions. How important it is, therefore, to keep the nerves in a state of perfect balance, not shocking one part of the body with too much energy and consequently limiting the supply to other regions. Not by restlessness or emotional reactions, but by calmness, by deep trust in God, we reach the yogic state of an equilibrated being.

The yogis have special techniques by which one can revive tissues burned out by nervousness, by sending life energy into nerves partially destroyed by mistreatment. Each cell and tissue in the nervous system is a living, intelligent structure. Life energy can always renew it.

Overcome Nervousness by Good Company

Nervousness is of two kinds—psychological and mechanical, or superficial and organic. The psychological or most common variety is due to mind excitement. This condition, long continued in, and accompanied by association with uninspiring people and wrong diet and health habits, causes the chronic or organic manifestations of nervous diseases.

The diet should be simple, balanced, and not too plentiful. Exercise should be regular. Too much sleep drugs the nerves, and too little sleep is hurtful to them. But all-important is the choice of company. Tell me what kind of friends a man has and I will tell you what he is. Flatterers do not help us. We should seek the society of superior men—those who tell us the truth and help us to improve ourselves. He is our best friend who humbly suggests how we may benefit our life by worthwhile changes.

Strong criticism, delivered in a mean or heartless way, is like hitting a man on the head with a hammer. The power of love is infinitely more effective. Kind suggestions, given with love and understanding, can accomplish wonders; mere fault-finding accomplishes nothing. One is fit to judge others only after he has perfected his own nature. Till then, judging oneself is the only profitable analysis.

Association with calm, wise people is one of the quickest ways to banish nervousness and realize our innate divinity. Nervous people should stay away from those suffering from similar troubles.

Calmness Is the Best Cure

The best cure for nervousness is the cultivation of calmness. One who is naturally calm does not lose his sense of reason, justice, or humor under any circumstances. He can always separate sentiment or wishful thinking from fact. He is not led astray by the honeyed tongues of dishonest men with improbable schemes for acquiring unearned wealth. He does not poison his bodily tissues with anger or fear, which adversely affect circulation. It is a well-proven fact that the milk of an angry mother can have a harmful effect on her child. What more striking proof can we ask for, that violent emotions will finally reduce the body to an ignominious wreck?

Poise is a beautiful quality. We should pattern our life by a triangular guide: calmness and sweetness are the two sides; the base is happiness. Every day, one should remind himself: "I am a prince of peace, sitting on the throne of poise, directing my kingdom of activity." Whether one acts quickly or slowly, in solitude or in the busy marts of men, his center should be peaceful, poised. Christ has given us the ideal. Everywhere, he demonstrated peace. He passed through every conceivable test without losing his poise.

God is everywhere, controlling planets, galaxies; yet He is not disturbed. Though He is in this world, yet He is above this world. We must reflect His image and likeness. We must meditate often and hold on to the peaceful aftereffects. We must send out thoughts of love, goodwill, harmony. In the temple of meditation, with the light of intuition burning on the altar, there is no restlessness, no nervous striving or searching. Man is truly home at last, in a sanctuary not made with hands, but with God-peace.

The Physical and Spiritual
Rewards of Fasting

*Self-Realization Fellowship international headquarters,
Los Angeles, California, March 9, 1939*

The physical results and spiritual experiences of fasting are wonderful. The spirit within becomes disassociated from the demands of the body as the body itself is freed from gross habits. I have just passed my thirtieth day of dieting and fasting, and it seems as natural as if I had never eaten. All of you who are able should go on a three-day fast; if possible, a longer one.* You would begin to discover that you can live without food.

Pains or aches in the body indicate that something is going wrong with its machinery; repairs are needed. Think how conscientiously you keep your auto clean and in good repair. Much more complex than any car is the human body; and the Lord wants you to keep it clean and in good running order, also, while at the same time depending more on Him. The secret of good health does not lie only in chemicals; one should rely even more on God's energy within.

This life force within our bodies is, in fact, the source of life. It is a conscious power: the creator of the organs, and the supplier of their vitality as well. Ordinarily, life force is continually reinforced by mind power and food. But if it has been too much misused, it gives up and refuses to work anymore. Its power may grow dim in the eyes, for example, and then you cannot see well. No food gives strength, no change of air invigorates, nothing can restore energy to the body when its life force begins to diminish.

---

* Persons in good health should experience no difficulty in fasting for three days; longer fasts should be undertaken only under experienced supervision. Anyone suffering from a chronic ailment or an organic defect should fast only upon the advice of a physician experienced in fasting procedures.

102

Fasting gives rest to the overworked organs, the bodily engines; and also to the life force itself, relieving it of extra work. When you cease to make the life force feel it has to depend for its existence on external sources—food, water, oxygen, sunshine—it becomes self-supporting, independent.

It is overeating for three hundred and sixty-five days of the year that creates many kinds of disease. Undeviating regularity in eating, whether the system actually needs food or not, is also a curse to the body. The more you concentrate on the palate, the more disease you will have. To enjoy food is all right, but to be a slave to it is the bane of life. Why should you let nature hurt you? Nature cannot punish you if you are not attached to the body or bound by food. You must recognize that life force is the sustainer of the body.

Without being fanatic, place the greatest emphasis on the mind, with the object of making its power more and more dependable. If you insist on making your mind a slave to your body, the mind will take revenge. It will relinquish its power, so that you will have to depend on someone or something else to help you; and no doctor or medicine can help any patient if the patient's mind has become so weakened that the disease has become chronic. Three-fourths of the cure lies in the mind.

In India, we teach how to conquer the body so that one can rely to a greater degree on the mind. Those who constantly look to physical means for health and healing will be dependent on them always. But mental power is superior. One should learn gradually to make greater use of the mind. By doing so, you will realize that the mind is a superb instrument. Whatever you command, it will do. This I have seen in my own life.

One day when I was giving a lecture in Milwaukee, it was terribly hot; my face was streaming perspiration, but I couldn't find my handkerchief. For a moment I didn't know what to do. Then I put my consciousness at the Christ center and inwardly said, "Lord, my body is cool." At once all perspiration disappeared, and my body felt cool as could be! So it is good to try to depend more on mind. However, you cannot deny the body entirely; if you truly did so, you wouldn't think or eat or move.

Some are interested in the power of mind over body principally to demonstrate health. But health is not the purpose of life. Communion with God is the purpose of life. You may feel well for a while, but a time comes when nothing avails. Then who will help you? God. Fasting is one of the great ways of approaching God: it releases the life force from enslavement to food, showing you that it is God who really sustains the life in your body.

But the temptation of Satan is that as soon as the mind thinks "food," you want to eat. Once, as a little boy in India, I had a cold and I wanted to eat some tamarind, which is considered very bad for colds. My sister strongly disapproved, but because of my insistence she grudgingly brought me some of the fruit. I took one piece, chewed it, and spit it out. Without my swallowing the tamarind, the desire for its taste was satisfied. Since man all too often acquires the habit of greed, it is unfortunate for him that God didn't create the body in such a way that he could enjoy the sense of taste and let damaging excess or unhealthful food bypass the organs of digestion and assimilation!

Self-Control—the Sanest Way to Health and Happiness

But in truth the only way to health and happiness, and the sanest way, is self-control. To be master of yourself, so that you are not overpowered by your senses, is one of the greatest blessings you can have. If you overload a wiring system with too much electricity, it burns out. And every time you load your digestive system with too much food, the life force burns out. When you refrain from overeating, and when you fast, the life force takes rest and becomes recharged.

If your auto is not working properly, you send it to a garage. It runs better for a while, and then something else goes wrong and you send it back for further repairs. The same must be done for the body. The physical effects of fasting are remarkable. A fast of three days on orange juice will repair the body temporarily, but a long fast will completely overhaul it.* Your body will feel as strong as steel. But if you want a permanent overhaul, then you must also watch at all times what, and how

* See footnote on page 86.

much, food you take into your body.

Know the Right Way to Fast

In fasting you must know what to do. That is why proper supervision is necessary for a fast longer than three days. I don't advise anyone to make his first fast a long one, for he will become weak. A one-day fast on fruit each week, or a three-day fast on orange juice each month, are good ways to accustom oneself to fasting. The faster must be mentally prepared for those who will immediately begin to sympathize and tell him that he will become sick and die if he doesn't eat. It is true that on a longer fast you may feel weak during the first few days, because the life force has been accustomed to dependence on food. But gradually, as the days pass, you no longer feel any weakness. Your life force and spirit become detached from food. You see that the body is sustained by life force alone.

I know the secret by which one can fast and still not lose weight. The life force, when under one's conscious control, may be utilized to take off flesh or to keep the body at normal weight. Either way, it is effective. When this principle is applied, the normal temperature of the body does not go down, no matter how long one fasts. Drawing energy from the medulla, the "mouth of God,"* the life force begins to rely more and more on its innate regenerative power instead of depending on outside sources.

Human beings in a perfect state of suspended animation can be buried for five thousand years or unto eternity and remain alive. Life is eternal. It depends not on breath, nor on food, water, or sunshine. Remember always that you are the Imperishable Spirit. This is the way to live.

Our consciousness survives after death, but the ordinary man loses that feeling of continuity and so thinks he is dead.

---

* Matthew 4:4: "Man shall not live by bread alone, but by every word (*prana*, life energy) that proceedeth out of the mouth of God (that flows forth from the medulla into the body)." It is through the center of superconsciousness in the medulla that God breathes His "word"—cosmic intelligent vibration, or energy—into man. A reservoir of this energy accumulates in the brain. Thence it flows down from the medulla into the five spiritual centers (*chakras*) in the spine, which act as distributors, feeding this life energy to all parts of the body.

Every one of us is going to die someday, so there is no use in being afraid of death. You don't feel miserable at the prospect of losing consciousness of your body in sleep; you accept sleep as a state of freedom to look forward to. So is death; it is a state of rest, a pension from this life. There is nothing to fear. When death comes, laugh at it. Death is only an experience through which you are meant to learn a great lesson: you cannot die. Why wait for death when you can realize this now? The first lesson you have to learn is that life is not dependent on food. By fasting you can prove it to yourself.

Function Well Under All Circumstances

Everyone should develop his mental power, so that he is able to function well under all circumstances—sleep or no sleep, food or no food, vacation or no vacation. Regularity is admirable and necessary; we must acquire the habit of regularity in order to obey the laws of God. But to be unable to deviate from that habit without ill effect is wrong.

All the fundamental habits of a child are formed between the ages of three and seven. Good environment will help to guide his development, but to change (if desirable) the salient tendencies of a child, special training is required. In my school in Ranchi, India, I gave the boys rigid training of the body. They fasted often, and slept on a blanket on the floor, never using pillows. Sometimes they meditated for hours. To help children by rigid discipline to be free from the tyranny of the body is to confer on them a lifelong blessing. One of the schoolboys sat for twelve hours in meditation without winking his eyes. If you had such poise, how much happier you would be! How much more peace you would have! The greatest training lies in scientific, balanced discipline of the body, mind, and spirit. And in that lies the heart of fasting.

The Metaphysical Science Behind Fasting

There is a great metaphysical science behind fasting. Jesus reminded us of this truth when he said: "Man shall not live by bread alone...." Two things keep you bound to earth: breath and "bread." In sleep, however, you are peacefully unaware of any need for either breath or food; your spirit is detached from body-consciousness. Fasting uplifts the mind in the same way.

Through fasting, let your mind depend on its own power. When that power manifests, the life force in the body becomes increasingly reinforced with the eternal energy continually flowing into the brain and spine from the cosmic energy around the body, entering through the medulla. Becoming detached from dependence on outer physical sources of bodily sustenance, the life force sees that it is being supported from within, and wonders how this is so. The mind then says: "The solids on which the body used to depend are nothing more than gross condensations of energy. You are pure energy. And you are pure consciousness." Then, whatever command the mind impinges on the consciousness of the life force, it will manifest accordingly.

Anything can be done by mind power. That is how Jesus was able to change stones into bread. So you see how unjust it is to the mind and to the all-powerful life force within you, to say you can't live without food. Make your life and body impervious to suffering. Conquer yourself. By long fasting you realize that everything is mind.

Every force and object in this universe is a product of the Divine Mind, in the same way that all the things you perceive in a dream are creations of your own mind. On the conscious plane also, if your mind creates the thought that the body will be weak from fasting, it will be weak; or if you have been fasting, and momentarily think it is making you weak, the body will actually feel weak. But if you make up your mind that the body is strong, it will not feel any weakness; rather, it will feel great power. Most people do not know this because they have never tried it. The mind will not show its miracles unless you make it work. And it will not work so long as you continue to depend more and more on material things. That is why its marvels remain hidden from ordinary vision. But when, through fasting, you learn how to depend on mind, it will work in everything, whether conquering disease, or creating prosperity, or realizing the supreme goal of life—finding God. "The self-governed yogi whose mind is under ceaseless control attains the peace of My being—the final Nirvana (deliverance)."*

* Bhagavad-Gita VI: 15.

Self-realization:
Criterion of Religion

Self-Realization Fellowship Temple,
Los Angeles, California, August 22, 1933
First Self-Realization Fellowship Temple,
Encinitas, California, August 27, 1939
(Compilation)

The temple God loves most is the temple of His devotee's inner silence and peace. Whenever you enter this beautiful temple here,* leave restlessness and worries behind. If you do not let go of them, God will not be able to come to you. First establish in yourself a temple of beauty and peace; there you will find Him, on the altar of your soul.

Sometimes one feels discouraged, thinking it is too late to find God. It is never too late. The Bhagavad-Gita teaches that if one realizes that this world is false and only Spirit is real, though it be in the last moment before death, he will enter a better world after his earth-exit.†

Sooner or later each one of us will be taken away from this earth. Find out now what life is all about. The great purpose of your experiences here is to stimulate you to search out their meaning. Don't give importance to this procession of humanity. As time marches on, you must eventually realize that you are a part of the great One. Make God-realization your goal. Mahavatar Babaji said that even a little bit of this *dharma*— righteous action, seeking to know God—will save you from

---

* Golden Lotus Temple formerly at Encinitas, California.

† "O Arjuna! this is spoken of as the 'established in Brahma (Spirit)' state. Anyone entering this state is never deluded. Even at the very moment of transition (from the physical to the astral), if one becomes anchored therein, he attains the final state of Spirit-communion from which he goes no more out" (Bhagavad-Gita II:72).

dire fears.* The prospect of death, or of failure or other grievous troubles, awakens in man a great dread. When you are helpless to help yourself, when your family cannot do anything for you, when no one else can give you aid, what then is the state of your mind? Why allow yourself to be put in such a position? Find God, and anchor yourself in Him. Before anyone else was with you, who was with you? God. And when you leave this earth, who will be with you? Only God. But you won't be able to know Him then unless you make friends with Him now. If you deeply seek God, you will find Him.

Everything in creation is a temptation to lure you from God. But He is more tempting than any earthly temptation. If you attain even a glimpse of Him you will realize this; and you can find Him by inner prayer and meditation and by strong determination. Your resolutions with God must be firm; He will not come so long as your mind is roaming elsewhere. He wants to come to you but you don't let Him; you would rather seek a little sense pleasure or spend your time on books or cocktail parties. So God says, "All right, My child, play on."

If God is seeking anything, it is our love. He knocks at every heart and asks us to come unto Him, but most persons don't want to go. Yet when they get into trouble or become sick, they are quick to call for Him. He who makes friends with the Lord while he is prosperous and happy will always find God near when he needs Him. But he who procrastinates in forming that relationship will have to fight his tests alone until, through wisdom and unconditional surrender, he finds the Eternal Friend.

Out of this great mass of humanity only a few are deeply seeking God. Where are they who thought this earth was theirs two hundred years ago? All are gone—and from among them perhaps only a few understood the truth about life and became Self-realized devotees of the Lord. Nevertheless, each succeeding generation thinks this life is real! For the little while you are here you make much of this show. Don't become too involved in it. Find God! He is trying to draw us with His love. He is showing us all the miracles we could want to see—the

* Paraphrasing the Bhagavad-Gita, II:40.

wonders of growing things and the perfect routine in nature. He is right there behind the flowers. Seek Him out. The scientist didn't make his discoveries by the use of blind prayer; he followed the laws of science. If you apply scientific spiritual laws with sincere devotion, God will be with you automatically. Open your eyes of devotion, for by continuous ardor plus application of spiritual law you will find Him.

Spiritual Development Must Balance Material Advancement

Different nations have specialized in different arts and sciences; India mastered the scientific art of God-realization. I have come to teach you India's spiritual science. Unless a balance is created by developing spiritual realization along with advancement of the physical sciences, individuals and nations will be lost in misery and destruction. If today's world leaders were illumined by Self-realization, and worked together, they could within a few years banish war and poverty from the earth. Only spiritual consciousness—realization of God's presence in oneself and in every other living being—can save the world. I see no chance for peace without it. Begin with yourself. There is no time to waste. It is your duty to do your part to bring God's kingdom on earth.

Many persons hesitate to seek God, imagining that life will then have to be gloomy. Not so! The unalloyed happiness I find in communing with the Lord no words can describe. Night and day I am in a state of joy. That joy is God. To know Him is to perform the funeral rites for all your sorrows. He does not require you to be stoic and morose. This is not the right concept of God, nor the way to please Him. Without being happy you will not even be able to find Him. The more peaceful you are, the more you will be able to feel His presence. The happier you are, the greater will be your attunement with Him. Those who know Him are always happy, because God is joy itself.

People try to find happiness in drink, sex, and money, but the pages of history are filled with tales of their disillusionment. The time I have spent in meditation has made my life unimaginably fruitful. A thousand bottles of wine could not produce the joy it has given me. In that joy is the conscious guidance of God's wisdom. When you are attuned with Him in this way, even though you unwittingly do wrong it will be righted by the Lord's omniscient direction; if you make a poor judgment it will be corrected by Him.

Wait no longer! Whoever hears this message, know that I am speaking truth. It is His voice, His power, His authority. If I were to display all the powers that God has given to me, throngs would come. But I do not seek that kind of following. Not powers, but the love of God must attract you; for only then will you change and make an effort to know Him. That is my aim.

I could not preach about God in this way if I did not know Him. In the same way you can know Him. That is why I stress Self-realization, which means you can know within your own consciousness that what I am saying is true. You don't have to believe; you can *know*. If I had a thousand mouths, I would speak through them all to convince you.

My Only Wish Is to Give You a Glimpse of God

You don't realize how much you miss God, because you have never known Him. Once you do contact Him, no power on earth will be able to turn you away from Him. My only wish is to give you a glimpse of God, because having Him, no other gain is greater. Satan tempted Jesus with dominion over the whole world; but he said, "Get thee behind me, Satan."* Jesus had that Something which is infinitely greater. Knowing God is more satisfying than the fulfillment of any earthly desire. Every lesser wish of your heart will be taken care of when you have Him who is your greatest Treasure. This is my own true testimony. He fulfilled my every desire. I do not seek things now; they seek me. When God gives Himself to you, He will fulfill your slightest wish. It is not necessary to ask. That is the state you want. But first you have to prove that you desire the Lord Himself more than His gifts.

Out of the abundance God has given me I have kept nothing for myself. I am always free, for nothing belongs to me. I am working only for Him and for all of you. Because of this,

* Luke 4:8.

anytime the thought of some need crosses my mind, God fulfills it. I have to take care what I mentally tell the Lord, for it is sure to materialize! This state of satisfaction no worldly prosperity can give.

God is seeking you; you must seek Him. Follow this Self-Realization way. It will bring you to Him more quickly than any other path. I have tried all methods; and I entered this path on the basis of reason, not emotion. Through the demonstration of their own realization, the great masters of Self-Realization Fellowship have shown that by following their way you can find the Lord, you can be among the greatest of the spiritually great, just as by learning from a great scientist you can become a great scientist, if you apply yourself. Charcoal does not receive and reflect the sunlight, but the diamond does. Charcoal mentalities, full of doubts and negation and spiritual slothfulness, cannot receive God. But diamond mentalities, sincere and full of faith and perseverance, receive and reflect the wisdom of the Divine Consciousness.

It Is Necessary to Understand the Meaning of Religion

To most persons religion is a matter of family tradition or social benefit or moral habit. They have no conception of the importance of religion. When I asked one man what religion he followed, he replied: "Nothing in particular. I change churches according to convenience."

Those who are not seeking God as the paramount necessity of life do not understand the meaning of religion. Why do all people seek money? Because they are conditioned to the thought that money is essential to supply the things they need for their well-being. They don't have to be told this; they simply know it. Why then do most people not understand the necessity of knowing God? Because they lack imagination and discrimination. Very early in life I saw that theological and even scriptural answers to certain questions could never fully satisfy the soul, unless their truth were experienced through realization and God-communion. For example, when my mother died and when other loved ones began to be taken away from me, I rebelled inwardly against it; but no one could give me an explanation that satisfied me. I decided I had to find the answer myself, through my own effort. "I am not going to accept this blindly," I vowed. "I am going to find the answer from Him who is the Maker of this universe." I sought directly from God the understanding of life's mysteries that I could not find in the teachings in the churches and temples. If religion could not satisfy me as to why some persons are born poor and some rich, some blind and some healthy, how could it convince me of the justice of God? The masters of India, by attaining God-communion, found the answers to life's riddles through inner realization, and showed us how we can do likewise.

There are many kinds of religionists in the world, and each religion has its own cross-section of this diversity. There are those whose approach to religion is wholly emotional. When their feelings are played upon too much they become hysterical with religion. But in an extreme display of emotion one loses touch with God. Emotionally excitable types want "pep" in religion; when you lecture from the intellectual plane they fall asleep. It is too dull, they say. But playing upon others' emotions is simply juggling with their minds; it is not giving them Truth, or God.

The intellectual religionist delights in hearing about various theological or philosophical concepts, flattering himself that he is on a higher rung of divine understanding than the emotional religionist. But intellectual stimulation, also, is only another kind of "drug," a different form of mental juggling that does not give the seeker what he really needs, any more than does over-stirring of the emotions.

Religionists who cling blindly to dogma will often parrot what they do not really understand or have not realized. When you ask them questions, they quote scriptures and tenets like spiritual victrolas. It is useless to reason with them because they are so sure they know it all.

True Religion Satisfies the Demands of Your Soul

Dogmatic religionists are convinced that if you do not believe in a certain way you are doomed. Science does not teach you in that way; it proves its points. And true religion satisfies the demands of your soul, not by words but by proof. I wanted never to be so dogmatic that I would stop using my reason and common sense. When I met my guru, Sri Yukteswar, he said: "Many teachers will tell you to believe; then they put out your eyes of reason and instruct you to follow only their logic. But I want you to keep your eyes of reason open; in addition, I will open in you another eye, the eye of wisdom."* Sri Yukteswarji gave me a teaching whose truth I could realize for myself. That is why I followed this path. No one can shake me from it.

The liberalist is the other extreme of the dogmatist. He follows everything! In the belief that he is being broadminded he says, "All spiritual paths are good; therefore I will not bind myself to any one of them." While respecting all, it is better to adhere to one path than to be a religious butterfly, flitting everywhere. Avoid both false liberality and blind dogmatism. Cling dogmatically only to wisdom, and you will find God.

Every effort one makes for God will be noticed by Him. However, if one doesn't follow a proven scientific way to God, his progress is comparable to riding in an old bullock cart. Sincere seekers will receive some realization, no matter what path they follow; but with only blind belief and mechanical prayers it could take them incarnations to reach the Lord.

Whatever Religion You Choose, Give It a Good Test

Seek until you find the path most suited to the spiritual inclination of your heart and mind, and then be steadfast. Whatever you take up, give it a good test. In the same way give the Self-Realization teachings a chance. Jewelers can tell a good gem from a fake, and the genuine spiritual teacher can differentiate between sincere and idle seekers. There are some who take the *Self-Realization Fellowship Lessons* but do not study or practice them. Ask them what the teaching is about, and they reply vaguely, "Oh, it is grand!" If you ask what they have learned, they go on about what a good teaching it is, "but

* The eye of intuition, or divine wisdom; the omniscient spiritual eye. "The deluded do not perceive Him staying or departing or experiencing the world of the *gunas* (qualities). Those whose eye of wisdom is open see Him" (Bhagavad-Gita XV:10). "When thine eye is single, thy whole body also is full of light.... Take heed, therefore, that the light which is in thee be not darkness" (Luke 11:34-35).

I haven't practiced it." Those who practice know the blessings of this path.

Seekers should be taught to find God first. To concentrate on money or health as primary objectives in following a religion is to become sidetracked. True, it is through God that one receives everything else; but he who seeks other things first will feel the bonds of limitations. A qualified spiritual teacher knows and loves the Lord; his supreme interest is in God. One teacher tried to persuade me to accept his spiritual guidance with the promise that I would have a great many followers. His offer did not attract me, because I wanted God alone. Great teachers will always seek to interest you in knowing the Lord. They will not take you up a blind alley.

Without God-communion, the lifeblood of religion is missing. Church is not the place for dances, movies, and frequent social gatherings. These divert people from God. One can find sufficient worldly entertainment in town. Go to church for one reason: communion with God. Divine communion is the criterion of religion. That is what my guru taught me, and that is why I have followed him unconditionally and wholeheartedly. As a result of his teaching I am enjoying that sacred communion with the Lord every moment of my existence. That is what religion must be.

If I tell you of a wonderful fruit I have found, and describe it to you in detail every day for a year without ever giving you a taste of it, you won't be satisfied. Hearing about truth cannot relieve the soul's hunger; if you are content to hear truth without making any effort to know God, it has falsely satisfied you. You must hunger so deeply for God that you will seek Him out in earnest. The purpose of religious lectures and sermons is to awaken in you that irresistible soul-longing for Him.

Realizing God Requires Self-Disciplinary Effort

Once in a while I meet someone in whom I see a little bit of real devotion for the Lord. But God-realization is so much greater than that! The God-knowing devotee sometimes sees the whole world filled with His light—a wonderful experience. But it can't come to you in one minute. Realizing God requires long perseverance in the practice of those methods that lead to Self-realization.

The desire for happiness is the strongest desire of all. True and lasting happiness is found in God. When you discover Him, a great joy will come over you, a joy you will find nowhere else. Sri Yukteswarji said to me: "When your joy in meditation and communion becomes greater than any other joy, you have found God.* If the whole world were given to you, you would not know what to do with it; you would only feel burdened, worrying about everything. Study the lives of princes and men of the world; see how they were vexed." We are like puppets in the hands of destiny; but the man who is one with the Light of the world, who has nothing and yet has everything, is a happy man. He who is one with God is not afraid of anything, even annihilation of the body. Jesus said: "Destroy this temple, and in three days I will raise it up."†

The church has become a beggar. Ironically, money is needed in the development of all good works, including those performed by the church. The dollar itself has no brains; it can serve both good and evil schemes. To seek money to spread God's work is righteous action. Money thus used is doing good. And the more one sacrifices for God's work, the greater will be his reward.

All Churches Should Be Hives of God-Communion

Every church does good, and for that I love them all. They will truly fulfill their high calling when they become places of God-communion. They should be like hives, filled with the honey of God-realization. Unless this truth becomes more manifest in religion, you will see that the church as such will gradually disappear. Religion will be practiced in secluded spots out-of-doors, where God can come to those few devoted souls who really want to know Him. This has happened in India. Some of her temples have become not so much places of meditation for divine communion as mere gathering places for

* "Only that yogi who possesses the inner Bliss, who rests on the inner Foundation, who is one with the inner Light, becomes one with Spirit. He attains complete liberation even while living in the body" (Bhagavad-Gita V:24).

† John 2:19.

pigeons and people. Real seekers in India gather under the trees to meditate on God. More and more this will happen in churches everywhere. The dissatisfaction of real truth seekers with dogmatism, and the emptiness of organization without individual Self-realization, will force a great world change in the concept of religion.

Scientific Methods Needed to Follow the First Commandment

*"Thou shalt love the Lord thy God with all thy heart, and with all thy soul, and with all thy strength, and with all thy mind; and thy neighbor as thyself."** These two commandments sum up the whole purpose of religion. If you sincerely love God you will do only what is based upon truth. Your love will not allow you to err against Him. Bring in the light, and darkness will vanish as though it had never been. Bring in love of God and the darkness of ignorance flies away. The science of yoga explains the truth behind the first commandment, and gives definite scientific techniques that enable the devotee to attain the divine communion necessary in order to love God so completely. Behind each part of these commandments is a deep metaphysical truth:

"Love the Lord...with all thy heart": It is God who has given you the power to love your family and friends. Why should you not use that power to love Him as you love your dearest ones on earth? You should be able to say: "My Lord, I love You as the father loves the child, as the lover loves the beloved, as the friend loves the friend, as the master loves the servant. I love You with the strength of all human loves, for Thou art my Father, my Mother, my Friend, my Master, my Beloved." When you truly love God with all your heart, you feel that love for Him day and night.

As I was leaving home to seek God I was inwardly torn by the conflict of loyalties. My father had done everything for me, and the whole family was crying over my imminent departure; but the love of God was stronger, and I was able to overcome the limitations of familial love.

Many human beings say "I love you" one day and reject you the next. That is not love. One whose heart is filled with

* Luke 10:27.

the love of God cannot willfully hurt anyone. When you love God without reservation, He fills your heart with His unconditional love for all. That love no human tongue can describe.

"...and with all thy soul": You cannot fulfill this part of the commandment unless you know your soul. You know it in an unconscious way each night, for in deep sleep you are aware only of existing; you have no consciousness of being either man or woman. You are soul. You can consciously know your soul—your true self—by meditation. And when you know yourself as soul you will have discovered the presence of God within you. The moon's reflection cannot be seen clearly in ruffled water, but when the water's surface is calm a perfect reflection of the moon appears. So with the mind: when it is calm you see clearly reflected the moonèd face of the soul. As souls we are reflections of God. When by meditation techniques we withdraw restless thoughts from the lake of the mind, we behold our soul, a perfect reflection of Spirit, and realize that the soul and God are One.

"...and with all thy strength": This aspect of the commandment is highly scientific. It means withdrawing all your strength—all your energies and consciousness—into their source, which is God. Yoga teaches you how to control your life energies and transmute them from body-consciousness into God-consciousness.

"...and with all thy mind": When you are praying to God, your attention and concentration should be wholly on Him. You should not be thinking about your Sunday dinner or your work or any other worries and desires. The Lord knows your thoughts. Krishna said: "Whenever the fickle and restless mind wanders away—for some reason or for no reason!—let the yogi withdraw it from distractions and return it to the sole control of the Self."* When I pray to God, my mind stays riveted on Him. If you develop that calm intensity of concentration you will find that a time comes when no matter what else you are doing, days and nights pass with your mind inwardly absorbed in God.

"...and thy neighbor as thyself": The ordinary man is inca-

---

* Bhagavad-Gita VI:26.

pable of loving others in this way. Self-centered in the consciousness of "I, me, and mine," he has not yet discovered the
omnipresent God who resides in him and in all other beings. To
me there is no difference between one person and another; I behold all as soul-reflections of the one God.* I can't think of
anyone as a stranger, for I know that we are all part of the One
Spirit. When you experience the true meaning of religion, which
is to know God, you will realize that He is your Self, and that
He exists equally and impartially in all beings. Then you will
be able to love others as your own Self.

Self-realization Converts Conviction into Experience

Truth alone should be the binding force of religion. Truth I
have brought to you through Self-Realization Fellowship. This
work is spreading because of the wisdom and blessings of the
God-realized masters behind it. All over the country I have seen
wonderful students who are held to this spiritual path for one
reason: Self-realization. My only plan to hold people is by their
own Self-realization. That is the only way I wish to hold them.
If there are hundreds in my classes, all right; if there are empty
seats, it is all right. I never wish for anything. I would rather
have a few real souls than hundreds without sincerity. The
great purpose behind this movement is to give people their own
Self-realization. When people will realize that it is their duty
and privilege to know God, then a new era will come on earth.
Scriptures, sermons, and lectures eventually cease to satisfy
the seeker who truly longs to feel the presence of God; but
when he *realizes* truth, he knows life as it should be.

Practice the truth you hear and read about, so that it is not
just an idea but a conviction born of experience. If reading
books on theology satisfies your desire for God, you have not
grasped the purpose of religion. Do not settle for intellectual
satisfaction about truth. Convert truth into experience, and
you will know God through your own Self-realization.

---

* The experience of Paramahansa Yogananda here described is spoken of in the
Bhagavad-Gita (VI:9): "He is a supreme yogi who regards with equal-mindedness
all men—patrons, friends, enemies, strangers, mediators, hateful beings, relatives, the virtuous and the ungodly."

Practice Truth—Meditate—for God-Communion

What is needed is spiritual experience. Only divine communion can remove the great boredom that exists when one is not following the spiritual path scientifically. What is necessary in order to have that spiritual experience? The habit of daily meditation. God is realizable. You can know Him *now*, through meditation. Then without any question, without any doubt, without a speck of mental reservation you can say: "I am with God." Why not? He is your own.

The time has come for man to know truth for himself. That which I am giving to you is self-realizable. To some the *Self-Realization Fellowship Lessons* may seem just another course of philosophical study, to be added to one's library; but those who practice them know their value. With every new spiritual instruction I received from Sri Yukteswarji he said, "You must know this truth." And I did. In the beginning of my spiritual search in India I had steadfastly refused to join any society because I didn't find in them demonstrable truth. But when I found my guru and this path, and saw through my own experience that it worked, I gave my life to this cause.

The Desire That Satisfies All Desires

Self-Realization Fellowship international headquarters,
Los Angeles, California, October 26, 1939

The glory of God is great. He is real, and He can be found in this life. In men's hearts there are many prayers—for money, fame, health—prayers for all manner of things. But the prayer that should be first in every heart is the prayer for God's presence. Silently and surely, as you walk on the path of life, you must come to the realization that God is the only object, the only goal that will satisfy you; for in God lies the answer to every desire of the heart.

When you have found it impossible to fulfill some urgent wish by your own effort, you turn to God in prayer. Thus every prayer that you utter represents a desire. But when you find God, all desires vanish, and there is no need for prayer. I don't pray. That may seem a strange thing to say, but when the Object of your prayer is with you all the time, you no longer have need to pray. In fulfillment of the wish or prayer for Him lies joy eternal.

Material desires come through certain mistaken conceptions about the purpose of life. This earth is not our home. The scriptures have told us we are children of God, made in His image, and that it is the will of the Divine that we return to our Source. What man does not realize is that unless and until he goes back to the Source, back to God, he will have to struggle to fulfill endless desires. Reflect on that. Man cannot help having desires, and it is not a sin to have them; but most human longings hamper fulfillment of the supreme desire to return to God, hence they are detrimental to man's happiness. Until he wants and has God, man will continue to long for whatever else he believes will make him happy. But to him who has God, instant fulfillment of all desires comes automatically.

There are two classes of desires: those that help us to find God, and those that obstruct our finding Him. For example, if someone hits you, you want to retaliate; but if you overcome that desire by using the superior power of love, you have applied the action that will help you to find God. All desires should be satisfied in the divine way. When you try to satisfy them in the worldly way, you only multiply your difficulties. If you learn to give every desire to God, He will see to it that your good desires are fulfilled and the harmful ones are overcome. There is no protection greater than your conscience, and the divine quality of your good desires. If you but *looked* at your soul, the all-perfect reflection of God within you, you would find all your desires satisfied! In that divine consciousness, having which, no other gain is greater, you would be unmoved even if the whole world were given to you; neither would praise elate you, nor blame hurt. You would feel only the great joy of God within.

God's Children Should Not Beg

Always seek the guidance of the Divine in trying to fulfill your legitimate desires, because that is the supreme way to receive the answers to all your prayers. But one thing you must remember: cut out begging from your prayer! Change your old attitude of supplication. You should pray to God intimately, as His child, which you are. God does not object when you pray from your ego,* as a stranger and a beggar, but you will find that your efforts are limited by that consciousness. God does not want you to give up your own will power, which is your divine birthright as His child.

Naturally, one should distinguish between reasonable and unreasonable prayers or desires. And bear in mind that, once you have made this discrimination, whatever good or bad desires you hold on to are bound to be fulfilled. If you cling to any evil desires, they will be granted; and you will find out what harm and unhappiness they cause. As time goes on, you will realize that even though your wish was fulfilled, your

---

* The ego consciousness; identification with the mortal body, which creates a feeling of separateness from God, and hence a feeling of limitation.

heart is still not satisfied; you will feel something within you rebelling. For example, suppose you have weak digestion, yet you want to eat fried foods. Not surprisingly, you suffer every time you do. Although you feel delight while fulfilling that desire, the aftereffect is pain; thus you are made aware that you have done wrong. It is wiser to use discrimination to separate your evil desires from your good ones and, having done so, to avoid the fulfillment of those wrong desires. Learn to be guided by your conscience, the divine discriminative power within you.

The Danger of Unfulfilled Desires

Unfulfilled desires remain in the heart. And what is the harm in harboring them? It is this: Every desire consists of specific forces, either good or evil, or a mixture of both. And when you die, though your body is gone, those forces do not die. As mental tabloids they follow your soul wherever it goes, and when you are reborn, these tabloids manifest as behavioral tendencies. Thus, a person who has died an alcoholic brings with him the tendency to alcoholism when he is reborn; and it remains with him until he overcomes desire for alcohol.

The behavior of even the smallest child reveals certain characteristics of past lives. Some children have terrible temper tantrums; others are moody. God did not make them that way. Unfulfilled desires of past lives fashioned those psychological tendencies; and, because of them, the soul, even though made in the image of God, appears as something different. If the image of God within you is distorted in this life by anger or fear, and you do not conquer such uncharacteristic qualities now, you will be reborn with them; and you will have the burden of these misery-creating tendencies until you overcome them in some future incarnation.

It is better, therefore, to work out or overcome all your desires now. They would be finished immediately and for all time in the supreme joy of God's presence; but until you know Him, your unconquered desires will remain to hound you.

There are two ways of finishing your desires—by realizing, through reason and discrimination, or wisdom, that only

God can give permanent unalloyed happiness; and by fulfillment. In many cases desires lie hidden within the subconscious. You think they are finished, but they are not. Life is indeed a great mystery; but the mystery clears away when you dissect life with the scalpel of reason. If every day you sit quietly for a little while and analyze yourself, you will discover that you have many unsatisfied desires. They are like dangerous germs that you carry through life, and wherever you go, in this life or the next, they will go with you.

The best course is to do away with all dangerous desires in this life, by discrimination, and to concentrate on fulfilling your good desires. If you feel drawn to commit suicide, or to do something evil, get rid of such desires now. Convince yourself, by reason and by good actions, that you are a child of God, made in His image, and rise above your moods and bodily habits. Be more detached. In this way you will conquer. If you suffer from a chronic ailment, try mentally to separate yourself from the consciousness of the body. By discrimination you can conquer the senses. Discrimination is the fire that burns up desire.

It is a general practice to store in the attic all of one's unwanted, unnecessary "junk," and once in a while to have a good housecleaning. Similarly, hidden away in the attic of your subconscious mind are many potentially harmful desires that one day may give you great trouble. It is important, therefore, to analyze yourself. Perhaps you are a hateful or moody or angry type of person. If so, these stored traits are the result of your own past behavior. In order to clean out your mental attic of such unwanted furnishings, you must vigorously employ constructive, positive, loving action.

Love Thine Enemies

Suppose that even though an old enemy dies, you continue to feel hatred toward him. In time that bitterness will produce ill effects in your own body and mind. It is better to concentrate on trying to behold God in your enemy; for by doing so you release yourself from evil vengeful desires that destroy your peace of mind. By heaping hatred upon hatred, or giving hate in return for hate, you not only increase your enemy's hostility toward you; you poison your system, physically as well as emotionally, with your own venom.

Conscience Will Tell You What You Are

Sometimes one feels a desire to "take it easy." This is not wrong; to get away from everything now and then gives a person a chance to think what life is all about. Most people are floating along on the current of custom and fashion. They have never actually lived their own life; they have lived the life of the world, and where has it gotten them? So it is wise now and then to remove yourself from everyday considerations; to calm your mind and try to understand what kind of person you are and what kind of person you want to be. And remember, the truest testimony you can find is the testimony of your own conscience, the discriminative voice of the soul. Whatever your conscience says, that is what you are. Think of the power of the conscience of Jesus. His accusers spat upon him and crucified him and yet he said, "Father, forgive them." That kind of discrimination is the only power that will bring light on your path. Whenever there is an overwhelming desire in your heart to pray for a certain thing, use your discrimination. Ask yourself, "Is it a good desire or a bad desire for which I seek fulfillment?"

Man's Lost Treasure Is God

There are many influences that nourish desires in you. When you see a new model car, you want one. When you see a new model house, you want one. Some new style of apparel comes out and immediately you yearn to wear that fashion. Whence do these desires come? I used to sit for hours pondering this. Can you classify all your desires? I sorted mine, and kept only the good ones; and when I had the contact of God, I found all those good desires at once fulfilled. Today you wish for one thing and tomorrow you hanker after something else. Your mind, having descended from almighty God, is not satisfied with the offerings of this world; and it will never be satisfied, because you have lost your soul's richest treasure, which alone can satisfy all your desires, and that is God.

It is true there are some good and necessary desires, and

you should strive to fulfill them. But never forget, while pursuing your little desires, to satisfy first your supreme desire—for God. Belief in the necessity of fulfilling lesser desires and duties first is man's greatest delusion. I well remember that during my training as a young disciple of my guru, Swami Sri Yukteswarji, I kept promising myself daily, "I will meditate longer tomorrow." A whole year slipped by before I realized that I was still putting it off. At once I made a resolution that first thing in the morning I would clean my body and then meditate long. But even then, as soon as I stirred about I became caught up in my daily duties and activities. Thereupon I resolved to have my meditation first. Thus I learned a great lesson: First comes my duty to God, and then I take care of all lesser duties. Why not? God says, "Why should I open the doors of eternity to you, when you put other duties before Me?" If you are not soaring to the heights of Spirit, of what account are you? You have nothing to offer God or man.

So seek Him first. To give more importance to your earthly duties is false reasoning, because at any moment the angel Gabriel may call you—at any moment you may be taken away from here. Why then give so much importance to life? for life is very peculiar. You think you are quite secure. Suddenly a loved one dies, or you lose your health, and all security vanishes. How I loved my mother and thought she would be with me always, and suddenly I found she was gone!* Don't be afraid of death, but be prepared for it.

Life is not what it seems to be. Don't trust it, for it is very tricky, and full of disappointments. Perfection was not meant to be found here. I am not giving you a false picture of life. This is not the kingdom of God; it is God's laboratory, where He is testing souls to see if they will overcome evil desires by good ones, and make Him their supreme desire, so they can return home to His kingdom.

Take God, Not Life, Seriously

Life is full of tragedy and comedy, a kaleidoscope of infinite variety. No two things are the same. Everyone's life is in-

* Paramahansa Yogananda was not yet eleven when his mother died. (Publisher's Note)

dividual. Each person has a different kind of face, a different kind of mind and desires. We would become bored if we had exactly the same experiences every day; we would soon tire of life. Were heaven itself the same every day, we wouldn't want it. We enjoy variety. The stereotyped conception of heaven is all wrong. If it were boring, all the saints would pray to come back to earth for a little change! Heaven is something infinitely different, ever pleasantly new, whereas earth is often unpleasantly new!

Yet, no matter how trying life is, most people become accustomed to it and assume there is no other way to live. Not being able to compare this life with the spiritual life, they do not realize how painful and boring earthly living is.

Actually, life is not real; it is only an entertainment. And just as old movies are shown over and over, so basically the same old incidents occur and recur in life. And although life will go on eternally, the same themes depicted in past films will be portrayed again and again. It is true that history repeats itself. We are all museum pieces!

Whatever comes in life, just take it joyfully, impersonally, as you would a motion picture. Life is entertaining when we do not take it too seriously. A good laugh is an excellent remedy for human ills. One of the best characteristics of the American people is their ability to laugh. To be able to laugh at life is marvelous. This my master [Swami Sri Yukteswar] taught me. In the beginning of my training in his hermitage, I went about with a solemn face, never smiling. One day Master pointedly remarked, "What is this? Are you attending a funeral ceremony? Don't you know that finding God is the funeral of all sorrows? Then why so glum? Don't take this life too seriously." He taught me that one must be mentally above every crucifixion of earthly experience in order to find complete happiness in God.

Krishna taught: "Even-minded during happiness and sorrow, profit and loss, triumph and failure—so encounter the battle of life! Thus thou wilt not acquire sin."* To remain even-minded, no matter what comes, is one of the best ways to

* Bhagavad-Gita II:38.

conquer delusive desires. This I learned from the example of my great master—even to the last, changeless. Christ also demonstrated that spirit. And God's love was not taken away; even though Jesus was tortured, he did not lose his divine consciousness. God's protection of our joy and peace is the greatest fortress possible. Throughout all trials and sufferings, remember the good things that God has given you. Your soul is a divine temple of God. The darkness of mortal ignorance and limitations must be driven out of that temple. It is wonderful to be in the consciousness of the soul—fortified, strong!

Be afraid of nothing. Hating none, giving love to all, feeling the love of God, seeing His presence in everyone, and having but one desire—for His constant presence in the temple of your consciousness—that is the way to live in this world. Those who have other desires will not know true satisfaction.

Environment Shapes Our Desires

Desires are formed according to one's environment; they are created by, and therefore limited by, your sense perceptions. Attending a country fair satisfies a desire for a little excitement; but after you have been to a world fair and viewed all the different exhibits, a small fair no longer holds any attraction. This illustrates the importance of having communion with God now, for the comparison with inferior earthly joys; then your desires will be of a much higher and more advanced nature. The desire to be one with God is the greatest of all. When you are through with any lesser desire, you soon pick up another, but when you have God, all other desires are satisfied completely. "Seek ye *first* the kingdom of God, and his righteousness; and all these things shall be added unto you."* Why not fulfill first this highest desire? for when He answers your prayer to know Him, all other desires will be instantly fulfilled throughout eternity.

Perhaps you feel that you have no desires. Well, I have often noticed what happens when people go shopping. They may have no particular desire to buy, but suddenly something catches their eye and they think, "I must have it!" Day and night that object is on their mind, and finally they buy it,

* Matthew 6:33.

even if they have to borrow the money. Then, after having it for a while, their happiness in it grows stale, and they want something else. We meet people who say, "If only I could have a thousand dollars (or a car, or a swimming pool)," and when that wish is satisfied, they yearn for something different. Human desires are not perfect, hence their fulfillment does not lead to perfect happiness.

The world environment will try to prevent you from remembering that the only worthwhile desire is to have God. But every day you should remind yourself of this. And when you have made up your mind not to smoke, or eat unwisely, or lie or cheat, be firm in these good desires; don't weaken. Wrong environment saps your will and invites wrong desires. Live with thieves and you think that is the only life. But live with divine persons, and after having divine communion, no other desires can tempt you. All become stale. Therefore even a few moments of deep meditation, or the company of a saint, will be a raft of inspiration to carry you across this ocean of delusion to the shores of God.

Be Safe in the Castle of God's Presence

Joy lies in continually thinking of God. The longing for Him should be constant. A time comes when your mind never wanders away, when not even the greatest affliction of body, mind, and soul can take your consciousness from the living presence of God. Is that not wonderful? to live and think and feel God all the time? to remain in the castle of His presence, whence death nor aught else can take you away? "On Me fix thy mind, be thou My devotee, with ceaseless worship bow reverently before Me. Having thus united thyself to Me as thy Highest Goal, thou shalt be Mine own."* When you are proof against all desires, you are enjoying the Presence Eternal.

This life is strange. Everything is subject to change. That is why one should not anchor his happiness on this life. Our time will pass on; what you are seeing now will be gone one day. Change is good if you don't let it hurt you. When it does hurt, the rebellion you feel is meant to show you that you should not have any desires. When you are anchored in that

* Bhagavad-Gita IX:34.

great Spirit you are enjoying everything, but without attachment. Therefore it is worthwhile to make the effort to know Him. Otherwise life can horribly disillusion you.

When I went back to India in 1935, I was looking forward to visiting some of the places I had enjoyed as a child, but upon my arrival I saw everything had changed. The stage was differently set. The greatest disillusionment came to me when I visited my old home in Ichapur, where I used to play and watch the birds. I was shocked. Only one remembered tree was left. That is the way life is; one by one, things familiar and dear vanish from our sight. I would have given anything then to have seen our home as it was in my childhood. Nevertheless I did see it later, materialized in a vision: we swam in the pond, and I went upstairs in the house and lay on the bed and ate mangoes, as I had done so many years before.

Scrutinize your desires carefully now. Sort them and keep only good ones; and let not even those good desires choke off the one important desire, for God. That must not be stifled. You are in great delusion when you ask God for fulfillment of your earthly desires and never ask Him to make a gift of Himself to you. What would you think of a son who says, "Mother, write a check for me," whenever he wants anything, but otherwise gives no thought to her? Don't be like that; never be ungrateful.

When this book of life shall be closed, there will remain with you only the realization gained from those desires you have fulfilled in connection with God. So read from *Whispers* *
and then meditate before you go to bed each night. When you wake up, think of God. Pray not only before taking food, but when you are eating, and afterward. When you are working, weave the thought of God around that activity. When you are in touch with God, you will see all your desires mysteriously fulfilled. But you must seek Him first. He has given you everything; but only if you forsake all His gifts, preferring Him, will He surrender Himself. When you show God that you are will-

* *Whispers from Eternity*, a book of spiritualized prayers by Paramahansa Yogananda. A spiritualized prayer is one to which God has responded. Any devotee praying deeply and sincerely to Him in those same words will receive a similar blessing. *(Publisher's Note)*

ing to sacrifice everything to know Him, He will come to you.

Carry a Portable Heaven Within

The hardest obstacle to overcome is yourself. When you sit to meditate at night, your nervousness and restlessness are still with you. Learn to control your mind and body. Be king of yourself. Carry within you a portable heaven, and in life or in death, in heaven or in hades, that inner heaven will be with you. Pray deeply, sincerely, "O God, I yearn to know You. You must answer me!" and next morning pray again, "Lord, You must come to me!" and pray again the next night in the same way, in the language of your heart; if you keep on, He must respond. But when you pray halfheartedly, while thinking in the back of your mind about something else, He knows He is not first with you, and He does not respond.

Have God first. Have God now. Don't wait, because delusion is very strong. Before you know it, the time will have come for you to quit this world. Whenever you have a moment, sit down and meditate. No matter how many times your prayers have not been answered, don't worry; keep on praying. Pray with sincerity. Believe that your prayer is answered.

In my life I have seen the most wonderful demonstrations of God's response to prayer. I urge you to pray not for little things, but for His presence. Only that prayer is worthwhile. If you are willing to sacrifice an hour or two of sleep for meditation every night, you will enter the kingdom of God. Don't watch the time. With deep sincerity pray, "Lord, I want You alone." Bad habits and restlessness will try to shake you from your effort, but keep your mind on God and you will find His presence with you.

Desires for worldly joys create the magnetic attraction that draws man back to earth, life after life. Reincarnation is no longer necessary for those who have fulfilled their desires in God. Whenever they want to fulfill any wish, they simply think of that object and it is materialized before them. My mother appeared before me in flesh and blood, just as I see you here. How kind is God, how marvelous is God! that He materealizes the objects of our desires to show us His love and gratefulness when we have given Him first place in our hearts.

To be able to demonstrate health or wealth or power or friends with God's help is fine, but if you can coax God Himself to respond to your prayers, you are a man of destiny. So don't rest until you demonstrate God in your life. He will give you everything you ever wished for; and He will test you. The tests in the spiritual life are greater than in any other. But you who pass His tests shall say: "Lord, my greatest prayer has been answered. What else could my heart want or need, but You?"

In God Is All Happiness

Self-Realization Fellowship Hermitage,
Encinitas, California, June 10, 1937

God in His infinite mercy gives to us His joy, His inspiration, true life, true wisdom, true happiness, and true understanding through all the various experiences of our lives. But the glory of God is revealed only in the quietness of the soul, in the intensity of the inner effort of the mind to commune with Him. It is there that we find truth. Outside, delusion is very strong; very few people can get away from the influences of outer environment. The world goes on with its infinite complexities and diverse experiences. Each life is new and each life has to be lived differently. Yet underlying all life is the silent voice of God, ever calling to us through flowers, through scriptures, and through our conscience—through all things that are beautiful and that make life worth living.

The more you concentrate on the outside, the less you will know of the inner glory of the everlasting joy of Spirit. The more you concentrate within, the less you will have of difficulties without. But most people do not understand this truth because of the influence of worldly company and environment, and bad habits. Environment keeps you more or less engrossed; it never allows you to think of deeper realities. Even in this beautiful place in Encinitas I have seen that some students came without the pure intention of seeking spiritual development. If you choose to see God you can see Him everywhere. Habits are predatory; they destroy. You should learn to be happy with what you have. Don't wish for anything more than what is already coming to you. The Father knows what you need.

The best way to be unendingly happy is to be conscious of the Father. Your paramount desire should be God-realization;

the determination to be with Him should be supreme in your consciousness.

I have given everything to God. There is nothing else that I can give anymore. And I have already realized that the only purpose of life is to know God. Many people may doubt that finding God is the purpose of life; but everyone can accept the idea that the purpose of life is to find happiness. I say that God is Happiness. He is Bliss. He is Love. He is Joy that will never go away from your soul. So why shouldn't you try to acquire that Happiness? No one else can give it to you. You must continuously cultivate it yourself. The forces of nature are constantly trying to give you the pleasures of the world, but such transitory satisfactions only end in sorrow and bitterness. Even the most favored person, one who appears to have everything, may not be happy. And you will never be satisfied for long with earthly things. They give only a false peace and contentment. The whole world has been plunged into chaos through greedy desires. Greed is creating war. Nothing else is causing it.

He who conquers himself is the greatest victor in this battle of life. Money, fame, desires—everything that goes against this ideal is a detriment to our peace and happiness. If people would only learn to concentrate on the real values of life, they would find true happiness; but they are carried away by earthly desires. I find that no temptation can make me deviate from the path I have chosen. I could enthrall thousands with the powers God has given me, but that course would be a detriment to me, and in any case I do not seek to enthrall thousands. I love to see true devotees—those who are anchored in God. Souls who love God will come here, and those whose enthusiasm will last to the end of life will find Him.

God Must Come to Those Who Truly Want Him

It is impossible to deceive the Lord because He is sitting right behind your thoughts, and knows what you are thinking and desiring. If in your heart you truly renounce the world and seek inner communion with Him, He will come to you. But you must know that you want Him and nothing else. Once that desire for Him is established in your heart, He must come.

The only thing to live for is the contact of the Divine, the communion with God. That is why Jesus said, "The harvest truly is plenteous but the laborers are few."* Believe the words of Jesus, who lived truth. Has there ever been a greater example of godliness for us than when he said, "Father, forgive them, for they know not what they do"?†

Everybody wants to have more money than the next person, and when he has it he is not satisfied, because he finds there is still someone else who has more than he. People live in a bedlam of misery, created by their own desires. Learn to be satisfied with what you have. The average person in America has much more than the average person in Europe or India, or in any other land. But still he is not happy! He is burning with anxieties and worries.

God's way is the easiest way. It is best to go to the Father first and ask Him what is best for you. When you know that He is, and that He awaits you, why should you waste your time on lesser things? Have you ever tried sincerely to see if the Father talks to you or not? The Lord is speaking to all human beings. What more can He do to attract your attention?

I don't want people to think that they can attain realization simply by listening to others or by reading books. They must practice what they read and hear. It is better to go to church than to stay at home and listen to idle chatter, but even in church you must feel Him within, and you must know the technique by which you can realize His presence. Emotionalism and intellectualism cannot give realization.

When you resign yourself completely to God, when you are never tempted to pray for selfish ends, and when you are sure that God is your spirit, that He is your soul and everything else—then you are free.

Think! A few decades hence, this existence of ours will have become a dream; and my sitting here and talking with you will have become part of that dream. All the great masters of the past have become dreams in the consciousness of mankind. But those great ones have attained. They are always conscious of what is going on.

* Matthew 9:37.   † Luke 23:34.

What a dream this life is! And yet, when you look at your body now and see how it throbs with life, you become fully convinced again of the reality of this dream. You think you must have this or that and then you can be happy. But no matter how many of your desires are satisfied, you will never find happiness through them. The more you have, the more you want. Learn to live simply. "His mind is full with contentment whose desires ever flow inward. That man is like a changeless ocean which is kept brimful with constantly entering waters. He is not a *muni* who bores holes of desires in his reservoir of peace and lets the waters escape."*

Seek God in Solitude

You need to be guided by those who know God, those who commune with Him. Jesus taught us to seek God in solitude.† In the solitude of inner silence you learn about the Holy Ghost. The great masters of India also speak of this divine power. The true meaning of the Holy Ghost has first come in this land through Self-Realization Fellowship. Everything in creation is vibration, which is guided by the intelligence of God. That intelligent vibration is the Holy Ghost.‡ Everyone should learn how to contact the Holy Ghost through meditation; Self-Realization teaches you how.

In the silence of your soul, in the bower of your concentra-

---

* Bhagavad-Gita II:70. The true *muni* is a monk who observes spiritual silence (*mauna*), by controlling the waves of thoughts and feelings that are ceaselessly in motion during ordinary consciousness.

† "But thou, when thou prayest, enter into thy closet (the inner silence of meditation), and when thou hast shut thy door (to the noisy senses), pray to thy Father which is in secret (within you); and thy Father which seeth in secret shall reward thee openly" (Matthew 6:6).

‡ The outward, active manifestation of the omnipresent Christ Consciousness, its "witness" in creation (Revelation 3:14). Holy Ghost is also referred to in the Bible as "the Word" (John 1:1) and "the Comforter" (John 14:26), and in Hindu scriptures as "*Aum*." This invisible divine power is the only doer, the sole causative and activating force that upholds all creation through vibration. Through a special yoga meditation technique, taught by Self-Realization Fellowship, the adept communes with the Holy Ghost, the blissful Comforter: "The Comforter, which is the Holy Ghost, whom the Father will send in my name, he shall teach you all things, and bring all things to your remembrance, whatsoever I have said unto you" (John 14:26).

tion, the romance with the Infinite is endless. But you cannot have God and mammon* together. You must give yourself to God wholly. He is the Eternal Lover, and He is begging for the love of you all.

You must learn to use your will and concentration in order to seek God wholeheartedly. Your actions are dictated by your habits. You are always being forced by habits to do things that you don't want to do. You are your own enemy and you don't know it. You don't learn to sit quietly. You don't learn to give time to God. And you are impatient and expect to attain heaven all at once. You cannot get it by reading books or by listening to sermons or by doing charitable works. You can get Him only by giving your time to Him in deep meditation.

Look to God Alone

You must make the effort to please God first. It is impossible to please all. I try never to displease anybody. I do my best and that is all I can do. My first aim is to please God. I use my hands to pray in adoration before Him, my feet to seek Him everywhere, my mind to think of Him as always present. Every throne of thought must be occupied by God—God as peace, God as love, God as kindness, God as understanding, God as compassion, God as wisdom. This is the only thing that I have come to tell you. Naught else.

Learn the Self-Realization technique of meditation. Keep good company. Don't look to others, but to God alone. And every day speak of this work to others. Every day do good to some people. As long as there is money in my pocket I never cease to give. My bank is God.

Last of all, you must know God, just as the great ones know Him. If you follow the technique, you will find Him through your own efforts.

One day I was walking outside the hermitage, thinking of my great guru, Sri Yukteswarji, and wondering about him. I felt sad that I was enjoying this beautiful *ashram* and that he could not be here to share it with me. Suddenly he appeared to me in the sky and said, "You think you are the only one enjoying this place! I am enjoying it from all space."

* Matthew 6:24.

You must strive to be one with God. Practice meditation every day and learn to love Him deeply, and to love your neighbors as yourself. This is the only way to avoid war. There must be spiritual cooperation. Without spirituality there cannot be happiness, either national or individual. And happiness must start with the individual. God-communion is the only answer to all problems, whether they be physical, financial, matrimonial, moral, or spiritual.

Happiness comes by feeling that you are one with God— that you are the child of God—a prince child of the King of the Universe. You are not a beggar child. You have jailed yourself in the body because of ignorance of your Father. You must free yourself from this jail. You must keep your mind riveted to God no matter what comes. Then you will find great peace and joy. "Their thoughts fully on Me, their beings surrendered to Me, enlightening one another, proclaiming Me always, My devotees are contented and joyful."*

* Bhagavad-Gita X:9.

How to Be More Likable

*First Self-Realization Fellowship Temple at
Encinitas, California, August 20, 1939*

Some persons are born with a likable nature; everyone is
attracted to them. Some are never liked. Others are neither
liked nor disliked; they are just ignored. Why? Impartial God
is not responsible for the uneven distribution of attractive
qualities. The differences in each man's character are of his
own cultivation. He himself has created those pleasant or unpleasant qualities, in this or in past lives. It would be a great injustice if God were responsible for starting off some children
with the advantage of likable good qualities and others with a
handicap of obnoxious bad qualities. But it is not He who has
established bad tendencies in some children and good in others;
therefore we cannot hold God accountable.

God creates all men equal, made in His image. In order to
see the justification of man's seeming inequalities, we must understand the law of reincarnation. Knowledge of this law was
buried and forgotten during the Dark Ages. Jesus spoke of reincarnation when he said: "Elias is come already, and they knew
him not.... Then the disciples understood that he spake unto
them of John the Baptist."* The soul appearing in one incarnation as Elias (Elijah) had returned in another incarnation as
John the Baptist.

There would be no meaning to life if it did not afford us
sufficient opportunities to develop our potentials and satisfy
our desires. Without reincarnation, how does the divine justice operate for those souls who have no chance to express
themselves because they are encased in the body of a baby that
is born dead, or of one that perhaps lives only to the age of six?
Those souls could hardly be condemned to Hades, because

---

* Matthew 17:12-13.

they have done nothing to deserve punishment; nor could they go to heaven, having had no opportunity to earn it. The answer is that this earth is a vast schoolhouse, and the law of reincarnation is the justice that brings each man here again and again until he has learned all of life's lessons. Lord Krishna referred to this truth: "Diligently following his path, purging himself of sin, attaining perfection by the efforts of many births, the yogi finally enters the Supreme Beatitude."*

Man himself has cultivated his bright and dark qualities. Somewhere, sometime, in this or other lives, the seeds were planted by his own actions. If he permits the seeds of harmful acts to grow, they will crowd out the seeds of good that he has sown. The wise cast out the seeds of evil from the garden of life.

Attractiveness Comes from Within

One should learn to analyze himself and others to determine why some persons are liked by all and others are not. Even among children we find some whom everyone regards affectionately and others whom everyone avoids. One of the first conclusions from such analysis is that if a person is to become likable, he must make himself more attractive from within. Sometimes even the most physically attractive person may be repellent because of the inner ugliness reflected in his speech and actions.

At one time the secret of popularity was supposed to be "it," a kind of physical appeal and magnetism. But having "it" does not necessarily make one likable. Our good or bad traits determine whether, and by whom, we are liked or disliked. Evil attracts evil; good attracts good. "It" is not what we should want, but the kind of magnetism that will draw good to us, that will bring sincere friends and merited admiration. Can externals such as clothes and a pretty or handsome face give us this kind of attractiveness? No. It has to be created within.

Avoid moodiness. There is no unpleasantness in being grave; but your expression is quite different when you are indulging in a dark mood. Your face is a mirror that reveals every

* Bhagavad-Gita VI:45.

change of feeling. Your thoughts and emotions, like waves, ebb and flow in the facial muscles, continuously altering your appearance. Everyone you meet sees and reacts to these facial expressions of what you are inwardly thinking and feeling. You can fairly well control your eyes and your smile, and thus conceal your feelings from some; but not from all. Lincoln rightly said, "It is true that you may fool all the people some of the time; you can even fool some of the people all the time; but you can't fool all of the people all the time."

In our eyes is the entire history of our life. It cannot be concealed from those who know how to read it. There are spiritual eyes, half-spiritual eyes, dishonest eyes, sensual eyes. What one does is written there. If I were to analyze what I see in a person's eyes, he would be astonished at my accuracy.

Never do anything that taints your mind. Wrong actions cause negative or evil mental vibrations that are reflected in your whole appearance and personality. Engage in those actions and thoughts that nurture the good qualities you want to have. If you conduct yourself in accord with the truths I am telling you, you will find your life beautifully different.

You Are Judged Largely by the Way You Conduct Yourself

One is judged somewhat by his dress, but largely by the way he conducts himself. Always be clean and trim in appearance. Avoid overdressing: fussy clothes and accessories make one look like a museum piece! Clothe yourself simply and neatly, and as befits your personality. But first of all learn good behavior. Once you have developed your mind and cultivated appealing inner virtues, dress becomes less important.

Mahatma Gandhi has proved that clothes alone do not "make the man." He wears* only a loincloth, by way of identifying himself with the simple masses of India. There he once arrived thus clad for a party that was being given by an English governor. The servants would not let him in. He returned home and sent a package by messenger to the governor. It contained a suit. The governor called him at his home and asked the meaning of the package. The great man replied: "I was in-

---

* Gandhi was still living when Paramahansaji gave this talk. *(Publisher's Note)*

vited to your party, but I wasn't allowed entrance because of my dress; therefore I have sent my suit instead." The governor of course insisted that he come. Even in London Gandhi went to call on the King and Queen of England clad only in his loincloth. He had transcended the clothes personality. Now I am not recommending this mode of dress! Gandhi has a mission to fulfill, and this is a part of his role. If one becomes as great as Gandhi, he also may do as he sees fit.

The point is, one should not think all the time about the body; nor should he be careless of it. To give the body too little or too much attention makes one become unbalanced, fanatical. Look after the body in a reasonable way, and remember always what is most important—your mentality, your behavior. Give more attention to the mind, the springboard of your behavior, for that is what most persons respond to.

When with Others, Be Sincere and Thoughtful

Be interested in others. When you are by yourself you have a right to think and do what you want to; but when you are with others, you should not be absentminded or uninterested. The company of a corpse would be preferable to that of an absentminded person; the indifference of a corpse bears no insult. When you are in the company of others, be with them wholeheartedly; but when your interest in being with them lags, make a polite excuse and withdraw. You have no right to remain while your mind is absent.

Be genuinely amiable when you are with others. Never be a "sourpuss." You don't have to laugh boisterously, like a hyena, but don't wear a long face either. Just be smiling, congenial, and kind. Smiling on the outside when you are angry or resentful inside, however, is hypocrisy. If you want to be likable, be sincere. Sincerity is a soul quality that God has given to every human being, but not all express it. Above all, be humble. Though you may have admirable inner strength, don't overwhelm others with your strong nature. Be calm and considerate of them. This is the way to develop likable magnetism.

Strive always to be understanding. Some people choose to be quarrelsome and to misunderstand us no matter what we say or do. They go about with a chip on their shoulder. To draw real friends, one must cultivate understanding. True friends understand one another no matter what they do. You should be like that.

What is life unless you have the right kind of friends around you? There is a magnet in your heart that will attract true friends. That magnet is unselfishness, thinking of others first. Very few persons are free from self-centeredness. Yet one can develop the quality of unselfishness very easily if he practices thinking of others first. A mother usually has this quality. Her life is service. She gives to her husband and children first. Because she always thinks of others before herself, others think of her. That is the tradition in the homes in India. We are taught the same spirit in the *ashrams* of real spiritual teachers.

Consideration for others is a most wonderful quality. It is the greatest attractiveness you can have. Practice it! If someone is thirsty, a thoughtful person anticipates his need and offers him a drink. Consideration means awareness of and attentiveness to others. A considerate person, when in the company of others, will have an intuitive awareness of their needs.

Live for Others and They Will Live for You

There are those who would say, "I am a devout man." Yet if someone else sat in their church pew they would be ready to take off the intruder's head! Once in a while I see this sort of incident in my classes. If another person wants your seat, give it, even though you must stand. By your exemplary behavior you will have someone else thinking considerately of you every day. When you learn to live for others, they will live for you. When you live for yourself, no one is interested in you. You can best attract others by your good actions.

If you look around, when you attend a party, you will almost always notice some guests who are openly envious of what others have. No one wants to be with thoughtless, selfish people. But everyone is glad to be with a tactful, considerate person.

Practice consideration in your speech as well as in your actions; and when you feel tempted to speak harshly, control that impulse and talk calmly instead. Let no one hear harsh words from you. Be not afraid to speak truth when you are asked to do so; but do not force your thoughts on others. Remember also, it may be truth to speak of the blind man as a blind man, or the sick man as a sick man, but it is better to avoid such bluntness. By the kindness and consideration of your speech you help to uplift others and make them better.

It isn't always your words that others listen to, however, but the strength and sincerity behind them. When a sincere man speaks, the world moves. When he says something, others listen. Some persons talk on and on, hoping to convince the hearer by the steady barrage of words. But the captive listener is only thinking, "Please let me go!" When you talk, don't talk too much about yourself. Try to speak on a subject that interests the other person. And listen. That is the way to be attractive. You will see how your presence is in demand.

My mother was considerate in that way. Fathers and mothers should never talk against one another to the children. They should keep their troubles completely to themselves. My parents had that self-control; they were really like gods. Only once did I see trouble between my father and mother. All that we children knew was that a carriage was at the door and our mother was going away. Uncle came in and asked Father, "What is the matter?" Father said, "I have no objection to her spending money for her charities; I only ask that she not spend beyond my income." Uncle whispered something in Father's ear. After a few conciliatory words from Father, Mother sent the carriage away. She never said a word against Father. She was always thinking of others.

It is a joy to live for others. When I am alone I have hardly any impulse to eat, but when I am with others I like to fix appetizing dishes for them. I saw that same characteristic in my guru, Swami Sri Yukteswarji. During my first visits to his *ashram*, I gained the impression that he always had savory food to eat. But once I went there when he didn't expect me, and I saw he was having the plainest meal imaginable. I questioned him about it. "I don't have special dishes except when you come," he replied. "I like to prepare them for you."

Once a fellow college student accompanied me to the market to buy some pineapples. There were only two; one was larger than the other. I bought both of them and handed the

large one to my friend. He was so surprised! He thought I had
intended to keep that one for myself. A wonderful feeling
arises within a person when he is considerate of others, thinking first of them. As soon as you are concerned for someone
else, not only does he think of you, but God thinks of you too.
If you are thoughtful, doing for others all the time, then even if
you part with your last penny to help them, God will return
even more blessings to you.

Another thing to remember: Each one of you has some
special quality, a uniqueness, that others have not. Also, each
one is richer or poorer in some way than others are. If you are
unselfish, good-tempered, understanding, you are richer than
those who are selfish and angry and jealous.

Perfect Balance Is the Altar of God

Mankind is like a large zoo—so many people behaving so
differently, most of them having no real control over themselves. But before one can realize the true Goal of life, he has
to have that self-control. He must seek balance. Perfect balance is the altar of God. Strive for this; and once you have attained it, never lose it. Christ did not lose it when he was being nailed to the cross. He said, "Father, forgive them, for they
know not what they do." The ordinary person cannot bear his
tests.

When I started on the spiritual path I supposed that only
good would happen to me; but I found that many difficult experiences also came. Then I reasoned: "Because I love God so
deeply, I have expected too much from Him. From now on I
will say, 'Lord, let Thy will be done.'" Severe trials came. But I
held to the thought, "Let Thy will be done." I wanted to accept whatever He sent my way. And He always showed me
how to be victorious in every test.

Even death is nothing to the spiritually strong. I once
dreamed I was dying. Nevertheless I was praying to Him: "Lord
it is all right; whatever is Thy will." Then He touched me and
I realized the truth: "How can I die? The wave cannot die; it
sinks back into the ocean and comes forth again. The wave
never dies; and I can never die."

When you go to a clothing store, you try to find a garment

that is suited to you, that brings out the best in you. You should do the same for your soul. The soul has no particular apparel; it can don any style it wants to. The body is limited, but the soul can put on any kind of mental dress, any kind of personality.

If you think deeply about any person, study his history, and consciously imitate his personality, you will begin to be like him; you will establish your identity with that personality. I have practiced this, and I can take on any personality I wish. When I put on the personality of wisdom I can talk of nothing but wisdom. When I adopt the personality of Sri Chaitanya,* a great devotee of God, I can speak of nothing but devotion. And when I attune myself to the personality of Jesus, I cannot speak of God as Mother—only as the Father, as he did. The soul can adopt any mental dress it admires or desires, and change that dress as often as it pleases.

When you meet a wonderful person, don't you wish you were like him? Think of all the noble qualities that are in the hearts of great men and women; you can have them all in your own heart. You can be humble and strong, or brave like a general fighting for a righteous cause. You can have the conquering will of Genghis Khan or the divine will and love and surrender of St. Francis.

Seek God, and Be Victorious in Life

Above all, develop the will to seek God, no matter what the obstacles. Then you will be victorious in life. When I am trying to do something for the work, and many trials come, I sometimes think: "Why should I have to go through this? I have found God. I don't need these things for myself."† But then I tell Him: "I will accept whatever comes to me. I care

---

* Sri Chaitanya's fame as a *bhakta* (devotee of God) spread throughout India in the 16th century. When in Gaya, in 1508, he had a spiritual awakening and became inflamed with love for God, whom he worshiped as the *avatar* Lord Krishna.

† In the Bhagavad-Gita, III:1, the devotee Arjuna similarly lamented to the Lord: "If Thou dost consider understanding [realization of truth] to be superior to action, why then dost Thou counsel this awful activity?" And when facing his test on the cross, Jesus cried to God: "If it be possible, let this cup pass from me: nevertheless not as I will, but as thou wilt" (Matthew 26:39).

not what people think of me, because one day they are with me, the next day they are against me. Your pleasure is my pleasure. Your assurance is my assurance."

Emulate the consciousness of the great ones such as Christ. Realize his omnipresence. The Father gave Jesus that universal consciousness by which he knows all things. Even as I am talking, he knows what I am saying. Though you don't see him, I see him. He is right here—a great light, transforming this temple. Everyone here is within that light which I see. We are like waves in the ocean of that light—the light of Christ Consciousness, the light of God. When you see His light and His presence, then you know that this life is nothing more than a test that everyone must go through to reach God. If Satan's tests are conquered, then even Satan becomes the tool of God. Every trial is a blessing if it brings us nearer to God. This is what you should remember. And whatever you do on earth, do it for God.

Each human being is unique; no two can be exactly the same. Think of yourself in this way: "My personality is the gift of God. What I am, no one else is. I shall be very proud of my divine individuality. I shall improve myself and don a personality of goodness." If you play your part well, you are just as good as the soul who plays the part of a king or a queen. And so long as you play your role well, you will be attractive and loved by all. Your part well-played is your passport to God.

Abraham Lincoln was an accomplished actor on this stage of life. He was not afraid to play his difficult role. He was working for God and for what he believed to be right: the equality of man. That is why he is remembered and loved today. If you strive to serve God, you have served everyone. Seek to please Him, not man.

What you expect others to be, you be first. Practice these suggestions. Take one quality at a time and work at developing it. From today, for instance, practice peace. Then take cheerfulness; try to smile even when you are unhappy. Then work at cultivating courage and fearlessness. Some persons are terrified of the dark. If you are one of these, practice going into a dark room until you get over this fear. Develop the consciousness that God is with you. You can be in an impregnable castle and still disease can get at you there. Yet you can be on the battlefield with bullets flying all around you, and if your time to leave the body has not come, nothing will hurt you. Practice perfecting sincerity, unselfishness, business ability, and so on. Work at it like the strong-minded martyr who never compromises his ideals. No matter what comes, do not let it bother or deter you. Be like that.

Practice consideration and goodness until you are like a beautiful flower that everyone loves to see. Be the beauty that is in a flower, and the attractiveness that is in a pure mind. When you are attractive in that way, you will always have true friends. You will be loved by both man and God.

Developing Personality

Self-Realization Fellowship international headquarters,
Los Angeles, California, October 28, 1938

Personality and its development are generally considered only in the light of realizing some material goal, such as increasing one's business or social opportunities. The real nature of personality is rarely analyzed.

What, essentially, *is* personality? It is the ego consciousness; not ego in the sense of inflated pride, but as the consciousness of existence. Each one of us knows: "I exist."

Further, we are conscious of existing in a certain way, as a man or a woman, and with certain characteristic qualities. We think about ourselves in terms of our individual background, experiences, and environment. A housekeeper thinks of herself as a housekeeper, a lecturer thinks of himself as a lecturer, a scientist thinks of himself as a scientist. Yet when they are asleep they forget their daytime activities. In sleep the consciousness of existence remains, though the egoistic concept of the wakeful personality may fade away entirely. But as soon as one awakens he remembers and becomes reassociated with his environmental identity. Therefore the personality a man displays in his wakeful hours is merely a cultivated and partial individuality.

The consciousness of existence is fundamentally a universal, unlimited state; but it becomes more or less bound by the personality traits that we hold to from day to day. Eventually we forget that our individual qualities can be expanded or contracted, according to our behavior.

Whence does our true personality derive? It comes from God. He is Absolute Consciousness, Absolute Existence, and Absolute Bliss. The Creator knows that He exists; He also knows that His existence is eternal, and that His nature is ever-new Bliss.

With the human mind we cannot know the Infinite Mind or perceive what ineffable Spirit is; but through the superconsciousness of the soul we can taste the Divine Presence as Bliss. The joy we receive from any experience flows from God, even though it may have been roused by some outward circumstance.

By concentrating within, you can directly feel the divine bliss of your soul within and also without. If you can stabilize yourself in that consciousness, your outer personality will develop and become attractive to all beings. The soul is made in God's image, and when we become established in soul awareness, our personality begins to reflect His goodness and beauty. That is your real personality. Any other characteristics you display are more or less a graft—they are not the real "you." The divine man, living in the cosmic consciousness of God, can assume any kind of outer personality he wishes.

When I am conscious of my human personality I have limitations, but as soon as I change my consciousness to the soul sphere I see everything just as if it were a motion picture. A person concentrating on the beam by which images are shown on a movie screen can see that all those figures are scintillating by the current of light emanating from the projector. In the same way, I see the world and all its creatures solely as projected thoughts of God. Concentrate on matter and you see everything in terms of matter. But as soon as you lift up your consciousness to the state of divine awareness, you see the oceanic current of God's light flowing behind all matter. You see everything in terms of Spirit.

Though the unity of God is reflected in everything, it appears diversified in cosmic nature. His creative life flows throughout the earth; put a seed in the ground and it begins to grow. Metals express a certain power and beauty of God. In the vegetable kingdom He changes His personality again; the active expression of life is more visible in plants. Still, a study of creation reveals that every metal, every plant, every animal has a distinctive personality; and in man we find an even more expanded individuality, for man *knows* that he is a living, conscious being. But all these different personalities have been borrowed from God; He is the only Life. "O Arjuna! I am the Self in the heart of all creatures; I am their Origin, Existence, and Finality." Thus the Lord describes Himself in the Gita.* And in the Bible we read this declaration: "I am Alpha and Omega, the beginning and the ending, saith the Lord, which is and which was, and which is to come, the Almighty."†

Intuition Develops One's True Personality

Our soul intuition is a faculty of God. He has no mouth, yet He tastes everything. He has no hands or feet, yet He feels the whole universe. How? By intuition, by His omnipresence.

Man ordinarily relies upon his senses to supply him with information about himself and the world in which he lives. His mind doesn't know anything except what his five senses tell him. But the superman relies upon intuition, his "sixth sense," for knowledge. Intuition doesn't depend on the senses or the power of inference for its data. For example, you feel certain that something is going to happen, and it does happen, exactly as you foresaw it. Each one of you has probably had some such experience. How did you know without any inferential or sense data? That direct knowing is the soul's power of intuition.

The ancient Indian sage Patanjali tells us that scriptural authority is not in itself proof of truth. How then can you know that the Bible and the Gita are true? The data relayed by the senses and the power of inference cannot give final proof. Truth is ultimately understood or "proved" solely by intuition, soul realization.

Your true personality begins to develop when you are able, by deep intuition, to feel that you are not this solid body but are the divine eternal current of Life and Consciousness within the body. That is how Jesus could walk on the water. He realized that everything is composed of the consciousness of God.

Human personality can be changed to divine personality. Banish the consciousness that you are a bundle of flesh and bones. Every night God makes you forget that delusion. But as

---

* Bhagavad-Gita X:20.   † Revelation 1:8.

soon as you wake up you are back again in the seeming confinements of the body.

Man Can Be Whatever He Wants to Be

Man can change his outer and inner nature by concentration. A person of strong mind can be whatever he wants to be. The limited human personality can be greatly expanded by meditation. When you close your eyes and feel the vastness of the soul within you, and when you can make that consciousness enduring, then you will have the personality that God intended you should have. The experience of the wakeful state has become predominant in your consciousness. But at the time of deep sleep, when man is granted freedom from the limitations of the flesh, you are in touch with Truth, with your real personality. Your attitude changes with the subconscious and superconscious realization: "I am infinite. I am a part of everything."

As your consciousness expands with divine understanding, your personality becomes increasingly attractive and powerful. When your character grows in a spiritual way, you can assume almost any shade of personality you desire. Mind is illimitable; and as you develop spiritually and your inner life becomes separate from body consciousness, you no longer feel any egoistic attachment to the flesh; you are aware of ineffable freedom.

You shouldn't identify yourself as any particular type of individual. Rather be able to change your personality whenever you want to. I have done many different things in my life, just for the fun of it. I have invested money, I have done the work of a musician, of a contractor, of a cook. Truly, you can accomplish anything if you do not accept limitations by identifying yourself with your present personality. When you say to me that you can't do this or that, I don't believe it. Whatever you make up your mind to do, you can do. God is the sum total of everything, and His image is within you. He can do anything, and so can you, if you learn to identify yourself with His inexhaustible nature.

No matter if you have health and wealth and everything else you want of the world, still there will always be some disillusion that will bring grief. Nothing of the earth is lasting; only God is lasting. When you develop the individuality that is an expression of His presence within you, which is your true Self, you will be able to attract anything you want. Any other personality you try to develop—whether that of an artist or a businessman or a writer—will bring disenchantment in its wake, because all human expressions have their limitations. You may go after success or money or fame, and achieve it; but always some flaw—lack of health or insufficient love or something else—will hurt you. The best course is to pray: "Lord, make me happy with awareness of Thee. Give me freedom from all earthly desires, and above all give me Thy joy that outlasts all the happy and sad experiences of life."

Never Forget Your True Nature!

Remember that as a child of God you are endowed with greater strength than you will ever need to overcome all the trials that God may send you.

Often we continue to suffer without making an effort to change; that is why we don't find lasting peace and contentment. If we would persevere we would certainly be able to conquer all difficulties. We must make the effort, that we may go from misery to happiness, from despondency to courage.

It is necessary first to feel the importance of changing our condition. This attitude stimulates our will to action. Let us resolve that we will always make an effort to improve our Self-knowledge and thus continuously better our existence.

India's spiritual scientists explored the kingdom of the soul. They have given to mankind for its benefit certain universal laws of meditation by which real seekers—those who wish to find a good life by changing themselves—may scientifically control their minds and attain Self-realization.

When you develop your divine nature you become completely detached about the body; you no longer feel identified with it. You look after it as you would attend to a little child. As you realize your true Self more and more, by meditation, you become freed from mental and physical pains. You cast off your lifelong limitations. That is the best way to live out your days on earth.

Awaken Your Divine Personality

Remember that it is not harmful to own things, but it is harmful to be owned by them. It is difficult to have the right balance. Struggling too hard for money, you may neglect your health. You will find that everything will betray you if you betray your loyalty to God. So let not one drop of oil fall from the lamp of your attention in the sanctuary of inner silence as you meditate each day, and as you carefully perform your duties in the world.* That is the personality you want to develop—dutiful in carrying out your obligations in life, but aware that your real Home lies within. What is the use of developing a personality based on worldly values, which are ever changeful and fleeting? Rather strive for a personality that is derived from your living in the continuous consciousness of God. Bhagavan Krishna said: "When a man completely relinquishes all desires of the mind, and when his Ego (self) is entirely contented in the true Self, he is then considered to be one who is settled in wisdom."†

Awaken that meek yet thunderous divine personality—strong as the lion, gentle as the dove. When you make up your mind that you will meditate and follow this path, nothing will be able to take you away from it. Perform your worldly tasks faithfully, without forgetting for a moment your highest duty, to God.

---

* A story oft-related in India tells of the spiritual test given by the great saint, King Janaka, to his would-be disciple, Sukadeva. To test the young devotee before accepting him for spiritual training, Janaka required Sukadeva to tour the royal palace while carrying in the palm of his hand an oil lamp filled to the brim. The condition of passing the test was that Sukadeva was to observe minutely (and subsequently report to the King) every item and detail in each palatial room, without spilling one drop of oil from the brimful lamp. The meaning of the test is that the spiritual aspirant must learn to keep his attention centered in God, not allowing his thoughts to wander from Him for a moment, lest the oil of divine communion be spilled, while at the same time he performs accurately to the last detail his duties in the world.

† Bhagavad-Gita II:55.

The Divine Art of Making Friends

*First Self-Realization Fellowship Temple at
Encinitas, California, January 22, 1939*

Friendship is the noblest human expression of God's desire to show His love to man. God showers affection on the baby through the father and mother; their feeling for the infant is inborn, because our Creator has ordained that our parents can't help but love us. But friendship comes to us as a free, impartial expression of His love.*

Two strangers meet, and by an instantaneous choice of their hearts they wish to help each other. Have you ever analyzed how this happens? The spontaneous mutual desire to be friends comes directly from God's divine law of attraction; cumulative mutual acts of friendship between two souls in past lives gradually create a karmic bond that irresistibly attracts them to each other in this life.

So long as it is uncontaminated by selfishness or attraction to the opposite sex, this impulse is pure. But often it is tainted. Friendship grows on the tree of our innermost feelings; it is desecrated by unwholesome desires and selfish actions. If you put the wrong kind of fertilizer on the roots of a tree, the fruit that develops will be poor; and when you feed the tree of human feeling with the emotion of selfishness, your unworthy motives will blemish the fruit of friendship. To feel interested in someone just because he is rich or influential and can do something for you is not friendship. And to be attracted to someone primarily because that person has a beautiful face is not friendship. When that face loses its youthful attractiveness, the "friendship" will evaporate.

* "He finds peace who knows Me...as the Infinite Lord of Creation, and as the Good Friend of all creatures" (Bhagavad-Gita V:29).

Develop Friendships from the Past

It is true that you cannot find friendship everywhere. Some persons you see every day and never know, and others you feel you have known always. You should learn to recognize that inner cue. Wherever you are, always keep your eyes open, and if you feel divinely attracted to someone, you should develop friendship with that person because he has been your friend in some life before. There are many friends whom we have known in past lives, but those friendships have not yet been perfected. It is better to start building on a foundation that has already been laid than to dig for a foundation on the sands of temporary acquaintances. It is easy for one to think he has many friends, until they do something hurtful to him, and then he feels deeply disillusioned.

Many people make mistakes in choosing friends because they are deluded by outer appearances. The only way to recognize real friends is to meditate more. You should try to find friends the divine way, and that is to purge your consciousness of all thought of facial or other appearances as factors in determining your feelings about others. If you do this, one day you will be able to discover true friends all around you. You will feel God's friendship through those humble human channels that do not resist Him. Through the pure of heart the divine light of friendship will flow to you.

To Attract Friends, Improve Your Character

You cannot attract true friends without removing from your own character the stains of selfishness and other unlovely qualities. The greatest art of making friends is to behave divinely yourself—to be spiritual, to be pure, to be unselfish—and to start friendship where the foundation of friendship has already been laid in a past life.

Friendship should exist in all human relations: between parents and children, between husbands and wives, between men and men, between women and women, and between men and women. It is unconditional. When you have the impulse to befriend others, it is the presence of God that you feel. Friendship is a divine impulse. God is not satisfied to look after His human children only in the guise of parents and other relatives. He comes as friends to give us opportunities to express unconditional love from our hearts.

The more your human shortcomings drop away and divine qualities come into your life, the more friends you will have. Was not Lord Jesus a great friend to all, and Lord Buddha, and Lord Krishna? To be like them you must perfect your love for others. When you can convince others of your friendship; when you are sure, through the tests of time and many shared experiences, that a person really feels for you from the soul, and you feel for that person in the same way—not for any gain, but solely because of the divine impulse of friendship—you will behold in that relationship the reflection of God.

Give Friendship to All, As God Does

Do not allow your friendship to remain locked up in one person, but gradually establish this divine relationship with others of noble ideals. If you try to build friendship with a wrong-minded person you will be disillusioned. Be friends first with the truly good, then go on being a friend to others until you can feel friendship toward everyone, until you can say: "I am a friend to all, even my enemies." Even toward those who were crucifying him, Jesus felt only friendship, exemplifying in his final ordeal that which he had always taught: "...Love your enemies, bless them that curse you, do good to them that hate you, and pray for them which despitefully use you, and persecute you."*

True friendship is divine love, for it is unconditional and it is real and lasting. Emerson beautifully expressed this ideal in one of his essays:† "The highest compact we can make with our fellow is—'Let there be truth between us two forevermore.' ...It is sublime to feel and say of another, I need never meet or speak or write to him, we need not reinforce ourselves or send tokens of remembrance; I rely on him as on myself, if he did thus or thus, I know it was right." You can talk freely with a friend without being misunderstood. But friendship can never develop if there is any hint of demand of one on the other. Friendship can be built only on a basis of freedom and spiritual

* Matthew 5:44.

† *Conduct of Life: Behavior.*

equality. Therefore you should treat everyone in that divine light, in the consciousness that each person is an image of God. If you mistreat someone you will never know friendship with him.

Many people go through life without friends. I can't imagine how they are able to carry on. Real friends seldom misunderstand us, and if they do it is only for a little while. Should someone abuse your trust, go on giving love and understanding just the same, as you would hope to receive it. But if that person continues to behave spitefully, and goes on slapping the extended hand of friendship, then it is better to withhold your hand for a time.

Universal Friendship Starts at Home

Friendship should start at home. If in your family there is one who is particularly in harmony with you, develop friendship with that person first. Then, if you feel drawn to someone of similar ideals among your acquaintances, develop that relationship. Banish all desires born of selfishness or sex compulsion. In giving pure friendship you will see the guidance of God. Develop friendship with good people, and the more you meditate the more you will recognize friends of the past. Meditation awakens "sleeping memories of friends once more to be." Many persons whom I had seen in vision, I later met; and here in America I have found many whom I saw in vision on the ship as I was first coming to this country in 1920.

Friendship is a great universal force. When your desire for friendship is strong enough, though an unknown person who is spiritually attuned to you be living at the South Pole, the magnetism of friendship will nevertheless draw you together. Only selfishness can destroy this magnetism within us. He who thinks of himself all the time wrecks friendship. Such persons cannot attract friends, because they are unable to expand and receive the good in life.

God gave you a family so that you may learn how to love others, and then give that kind of love to all. Our dear ones are taken away from us by death and other circumstances that we may learn not to love persons in merely human relationships, but to be in love with Love Itself, which is God, the Being be-

hind all human masks. "When a man beholds all separate beings as existent in the One that has expanded Itself into the
many, he merges with Brahma."*

Friendship means investing your love where there is no
prejudice of human relations. In married life there is the compulsion of sex, and in family life there is the compulsion of hereditary instincts. But in friendship there is no compulsion.

Let us give our love to all. Let us pray that we meet our
friends of the past and prove our friendship with them, so that
we can finally understand and merit the friendship of God. Unless we are united with all of His children through a spirit of
friendliness, we will not be united with God.

I know no strangers. What a great state of happiness and
joy! Even the worst enemy cannot make me feel that I am not
his friend. When that awakening comes, you are in love with
all. You see that everyone is your Father's child, and the love
you feel for all beings never dies. It grows, increasing until you
realize, in the love of friends, the divine love of God.

* Bhagavad-Gita XIII:31.

The True Experience
of Spiritual Ecstasy

Self-Realization Fellowship international headquarters,
Los Angeles, California, December 16, 1934

God has given us the power of spiritual inspiration—realization of the pure bliss of His presence within us. But the evil force in creation has invented spurious imitations. The temporarily exhilarating effects of alcohol and drugs are counterfeits of true spiritual experiences. The use of alcohol and drugs frequently leads to overindulgence in sex, which shuts out the power of spiritual inspiration by tying the mind to intense body-consciousness.

Many people take wine to banish sad or unpleasant memories and worries, but that kind of forgetfulness robs man of his native soul wisdom—the very power by which he was meant to overcome his trials and to find lasting happiness. God, being Joy Itself, wants us to seek and to find, within our souls, His ever-new bliss.

The counterfeits are harmful, for they are the lures of *maya,* the cosmic delusive force that is ever trying to mar all the beautiful expressions of God in this universe. Throughout creation we see the dual forces of good and evil opposing each other: God created love, the satanic force created hate; God created kindness, the satanic force created selfishness; God created peace, the satanic force created disharmony.

Knowing this, you should realize that alcohol and drugs are detrimental to your happiness; they obliterate the real joy and intelligence of your soul. Even one drink, or one indulgence in drugs* may start a permanent habit, because there

* Except when prescribed as necessary by a reputable medical doctor, and taken under his supervision.

may be such a tendency already imbedded in your subconsciousness from past lives. What is evil should always be shunned as evil.

The Wine of Spiritual Ecstasy Is Incomparable

Once you have tasted the wine of spiritual ecstasy, you will find that no other experience can compare with it. Ever strive to establish the divine consciousness in your children by teaching them to meditate, that they be not tempted to play with the fire of delusive counterfeit joys. Sacred bliss is never-ending, but the pleasures that come from alcohol and drugs are short-lasting and ultimately bring misery.

Every night in sleep you have a taste of peace and joy. While you are in deep slumber, God makes you live in the tranquil superconsciousness, in which all the fears and worries of this existence are forgotten. By meditation you can experience that holy state of mind when you are awake, and be constantly immersed in healing peace.

When the divine joy comes, immediately my breath is still and I am lifted into the Spirit. I feel the bliss of a thousand sleeps rolled into one, and yet I don't lose my ordinary awareness. This is universally the experience of those who go deep in the superconscious state. When the profound ecstasy of God falls over you, the body becomes absolutely still, the breath ceases to flow, and the thoughts are quiet—banished, every one, by the magic command of the soul. Then you drink of God's bliss and experience an intoxication of joy that not a thousand draughts of wine could give you.

As the ordinary person drowses on the borderline of sleep, he feels a little happiness, but he quickly loses that awareness and is fast asleep. Sleep is not total unconsciousness, for when you awaken, you always know whether you slept well or not.

There are various kinds of sleep—some light and some deep. But more intoxicating than even the most blissful slumber are those spiritual experiences one may have consciously with God. Beyond the mysteries of the sleepland lie all these divine joys. I can remain in any state I wish to. Often I stay between the sleepland and the awareness of the world—in the superconscious state.

Consciousness Has a Limitless Span

Your mind has a vast, a limitless, span; but you do not realize it. I can go into the depths of sleep and enjoy the sleep state and at the same time be with the world. Or I can sleep and dream, and at the same time also hear everything that is going on around me. Sometimes I sleep just as the ordinary person does, and again I can sleep and consciously watch myself sleeping. In the superconscious state you can see that your body and mind are sleeping and yet have total awareness of all happenings. This is possible only when you have developed the ability to enter at will the superconsciousness, and return at will to the ordinary state of mind.

You need never worry that by meditation (or by imagination or by the practice of inner silence) you may go out of the body and fail to return. That idea is entirely false. The *maya*-induced attachment to the body is so powerful that you can't escape from it that easily! Even if your ordinary waking awareness is obliterated, so long as your subconscious mind remains tied to the body you cannot leave it permanently.

What Is the Proof of Self-realization?

If you imagine something very strongly, it becomes visible as a hallucination, having no intrinsic reality. You should understand the difference between imagination and Self-realization. *The essential proof of Self-realization—of God's consciousness in you—is to be truly and unconditionally happy.* If you are receiving more and more joy in meditation, without cessation, you may know that God is making manifest His presence in you. If there is a break in the flow of divine happiness, then there is something wrong in your consciousness, some kink that needs to be removed with the help of your guru. By maintaining steady communion with him, through daily meditation and by following his precepts—the *sadhana** he has given you—he will straighten out that kink for you.

You cannot be with the Lord just by thinking you are divinely enlightened. You must improve yourself—you must

* The path of spiritual discipline and instruction given to one by his guru. (See glossary.)

perfect yourself. There is a lot of difference between the potential realization of God and the actual realization of God. You can never know Him except through humbleness, wisdom, and devotion. The humble man is the one who will know God.

Those who go deep in the superconsciousness automatically develop unusual spiritual powers, and control over natural forces. But no man of true God-consciousness ever uses his powers unwisely, for egotistical display. Sages realize that the Lord is the Sole Doer, and humbly return to Him the extraordinary gifts He has bestowed on them. Is not everything in the universe a miracle? By his mere existence is not man a miracle? If human beings are not satisfied with all the wonders that God has created, why should His saints perform further miracles? They never do, unless—for some special reason, often an unfathomable one—the Lord so commands them.

Beyond the Kaleidoscope of Subconsciousness

I will illustrate how the superconsciousness differs from the subconsciousness. The superconscious is that state in which you can *consciously*, during wakefulness or sleep, produce any sensation in your body at will, without any external stimulus. That is the proof. In the subconscious dreamland you can drink a glass of hot milk, but this experience comes to you unbidden; in the superconscious state you can create that or any other experience consciously and at will. Unless you are able to do this, do not delude yourself that you have reached superconsciousness.

Millions of devotees never get beyond the kaleidoscope of the subconscious mind, which manifests its wonders mostly during sleep. But in the superconscious state you can see or know anything that you wish to—not by imagination but in reality. I can sit in this chair and transfer my mind to India and see exactly what is going on in my old home there.

The advancing devotee progresses through three stages of spiritual awareness, the Sacred Trinity: First he experiences superconsciousness, oneness with the creative power in creation: *Aum*, "God the Holy Ghost." Next comes Christ Consciousness, merging in the Infinite Intelligence within creation: *Tat*, "God the Son." Finally, he attains the highest, Cosmic

Consciousness, the Truth beyond creation, the ineffable Absolute: *Sat,* "God the Father."

Sometimes a devotee dwells in the subconsciousness, sometimes he is lifted to superconsciousness and to Christ Consciousness, and a few great souls are able to go beyond Christ Consciousness into Cosmic Consciousness, the realm of Causeless Spirit.

In the Christ-conscious state you don't have to visualize things first in order to experience them. You don't have to picture India—you are there; you are aware of all creation. That experience is an endless expansion of consciousness. You are *in* the blade of grass and *on* the mountaintop; and you can feel every cell of your body and every atom of space.

But Cosmic Consciousness is beyond even that. When you can feel your presence in all creation, and also know the Joy that is beyond creation, then you are a Godlike being.

Three Paths to
Cosmic Consciousness

Trinity Auditorium, Los Angeles, California, February 9, 1934

So long as even a little tremor of thought and mental rest-lessness is present, you cannot reach cosmic consciousness. The Self-Realization Technique of Concentration* helps great-ly to improve the quality and power of one's concentration. Its practice will save the earnest seeker from years of fruitless wandering on the subconscious plane. That land you want to avoid; it is full of illusory and imaginative spiritual expe-riences. One must reach the superconscious state to have real spiritual experiences and realizations of truth.†

The world has a habit of much teaching and little practic-ing. You may hear a lecture on sugar a hundred times, but you will not know its flavor until you have tasted it. Neither can the glory of any true teaching be known except by practice. You have to live the teachings of the prophets and the great ones. Then their truths become your own, and you realize that truth is demonstrable, and universal. When you practice truth—

---

* Concentration is a state of complete one-pointedness and stillness of con-sciousness. The nature of creation is motion; the nature of Spirit is motion-lessness. "Be still, and know that I am God" (Psalms 46:10). Concentration is therefore essential to divine communion. The techniques of concentration and meditation taught in *Self-Realization Fellowship Lessons* lead to perfect at-tunement of human consciousness to divine consciousness. (See *Concentration Technique* in glossary.)

† The subconscious level of man's awareness has its usefulness as the reposi-tory of memory and as the land of sleep and dream. But in meditation it can be a real deterrent, luring the absentminded, imaginative, or psychically inclined aspirant into a realm of fanciful hallucinations that have no more reality or spir-itual value than one's ordinary dreams at night. Scientific meditation tech-niques, and the devotee's own effort to practice them correctly, draw the mind instead to the superconscious state of Self-realization and God-communion.

whether you call yourself a Christian, a Hindu, a Buddhist, or a devotee of any other religion—Christ will claim you, and so will Krishna, Buddha, and all other divine incarnations of Truth.

Follow the path of truth steadfastly. Remember that out of thousands, only a few seek God; and out of those seekers, perhaps only one really knows Him.* He who is persistent will realize God. So try your best to make meditation a regular experience in your life. May you never forget God and never be satisfied until you have Him! Be able to say, "Behind this finite frame I feel the Infinite." I never come to class until I know He is with me. I never teach unless I have made that complete communion. And I know that when I talk from that plane students will not forget what they have learned.

Concentration—a Requisite for Finding God

To be able to concentrate is essential for spiritual progress; without concentration you shall never find God. Learn how to shut out of your consciousness all sounds and other earthly distractions. As soon as your consciousness is right, God is there. He isn't hiding from you; you are hiding from Him. When in deep meditation you see any inner light,† try to hold it, and to feel you are inside it, one with it. That is where God is. Try to realize you are that light of God.

The more peace you feel during concentration and the longer you concentrate, the deeper you will go in God. If the time given to reading books about spiritual truth were spent in meditation, you would have far greater advancement both mentally and spiritually. Sleep less, and give more hours to meditation; the rest you will enjoy is a hundred times more refreshing than sleep.

Unless you can cut off sounds from your consciousness you cannot reach God. That is why saints have sought the seclusion of caves and forests. Plunge into the inner silence again and again by practicing the methods of concentration and medi-

* "Only one among thousands of men strives for salvation; and, among those exalted seekers, perhaps only one will perceive Me as I am" (Bhagavad-Gita VII:3).

† The light of God or the spiritual eye.

tation I have given you, and you will find great peace and happiness. The Gita says: "Free from ever-hoping desires and from cravings for possessions, with the heart and mind controlled (by yoga concentration), retiring alone to a quiet place, the yogi should constantly try to unite with the soul." *

The silence of deep meditation should be practiced more in all churches and temples. Everyone should talk less. During my hermitage training in India my guru, Swami Sri Yukteswar, would lecture to us only once in a while. Most of the time we sat around him without any talking, and concentrated within. If we even stirred, he would reprove us. A real teacher possesses more than book knowledge, and in spiritual life it is necessary to learn wisdom from such a teacher; one who knows, and knows that he knows, because he has experienced— not merely read about—truth.

The Invisible Source of Visible Worlds

Space is divided into two parts or aspects. On one side of space is creation. On the other side is God alone; creation is completely absent. That is the world of the "darkless dark" and the "lightless light." In the Gita the Lord says: "Where no sun or moon or fire shines, that is My Supreme Abode...."†

The same duality is true of human consciousness. Your being has two sides—one visible, the other invisible. With open eyes you behold objective creation, and yourself in it. With closed eyes you see nothing, a dark void; yet your consciousness, even when dissociated from form, is still keenly aware and operative. If in deep meditation you penetrate the darkness behind closed eyes, you behold the Light from which all creation emerges. By deeper *samadhi*, your experience transcends even the manifested Light and enters the All-Blissful Consciousness—beyond all form, yet infinitely more real, tangible, and joyous than any sensory or supersensory perception.

God has given you the opportunity to observe in your own consciousness the operation of the same laws that govern the universe. The state of consciousness without form that is experienced with closed eyes may be compared to the endless re-

* Bhagavad-Gita VI:10.   † Bhagavad-Gita XV:6.

gion of "darkless dark" and "lightless light," where God exists without any of the forms, qualities, and dualities that characterize the sphere of His material creation. In this boundless stretch of eternity behind creation, God alone lives in the unqualified consciousness of ever-existing, ever-conscious, ever-new Bliss. No world or any other created thing exists in His consciousness in that part of infinity where He reigns as the Absolute. But on the other side of space He is aware of everything—all creation—in Himself.

In the Invisible is the factory of the universe. Einstein said that space looks very suspicious, because everything comes out of it and everything disappears into it. Whither do electrons vanish, and whole worlds?

Any time you become fascinated by some material creation, close your eyes, look within, and contemplate its Source. You see nothing, feel nothing. Yet all visible objects have come out of that Invisible. "The light shineth in darkness."* If you keep peering into the darkness you will find that great Light. Behind the darkness is the Christ Consciousness. Behind the darkness is the teeming life of other worlds. "In my Father's house are many mansions."†

Right behind space is Intelligence. And right behind you is God. Live no longer in ignorance of His presence. Churn the darkness with your meditation. Don't stop until you find Him. There is so much to know! so much to see within! The answer to every problem will come to you straight from the Infinite. The truths that I perceive within by meditation reveal the basis of physiological laws that science is discovering by other methods. When I close my eyes, I can see the subtle life currents flowing in my body.

In the quietness you experience when your eyes are closed, don't feel you are alone. God is with you. Why should you think He is not? The ether is filled with music that is caught by the radio—music that otherwise you would not know about. And so it is with God. He is with you every minute of your existence, yet the only way to realize this is to meditate. And those of you who do meditate should go deeper!

* John 1:5.   † John 14:2

Don't fall asleep at night until you actually feel some expression of the presence of God within you. Peer into that darkness until you discover its wondrous secrets.

For your encouragement I tell you of an experience I had today in the superconscious state. I was sitting in the library at Mt. Washington. It was about four o'clock. Suddenly my breath disappeared. My limbs became rigid. I found myself watching the process of death. Breath and movement had left my body, yet I was conscious. This experience of death was wonderful. I saw my body and all nature as a cosmic motion picture, created from God's light. Joyously I cried, "There is no death, Lord! This whole world is nothing but a movie!"

A ruler on his throne may say, "Ah, I am king!" but let death give one knock and he is gone. He is a real king who feels God in all forms in creation. Death shall not frighten him, because he beholds it as a portal to the divine kingdom.

The First Path to Cosmic Consciousness

Of the three ways to expand human consciousness into cosmic consciousness, the first is the social way, wherein you shut out "self" and live for all. Be loyal to your friends, and feel love for everyone. God gave you a family that you might expand your consciousness by caring and doing for others. In family life we learn love and self-sacrifice for our loved ones, and thus attain some expansion of consciousness. But this is not enough. Love that becomes personal is exclusive, confined; when love becomes impersonal, it expands. Develop impersonal love; be able to give everyone the same love that you bestow on your family, and to do for others exactly as you would for yourself. The social way to cosmic consciousness is to behave toward everyone in this way.

God loves all His children alike—they are all His divine family, and His love is impersonal. His children should give that same kind of love to one another. This is the divine plan. To forget it is to suffer. The whole world-attitude should change. You *are* everyone, because your true nature is omnipresence.

I enjoy giving things to others; I feel the greatest happiness in seeing their joy. When we feel for and love others, we find that all of creation responds to us. Jesus, who gave up his body "as a ransom for many,"* showed us the social way of attaining cosmic consciousness. Christlike, you too should serve all men as your Self.

The man of cosmic consciousness is a happy man. He doesn't limit his love to a few, excluding everyone else. So should you make the whole world your own family. Will you remember? This consciousness is with me every moment. I have no caste, no country—I feel that all are mine. Love all men as your brothers, love all women as your sisters, and all older people as your parents. Love all human beings as your friends.

The Second Path

The second way to cosmic consciousness is the way of self-discipline. Do not be a victim of immoderation. Enjoy things, but don't be attached to them. Be free. Be pleasant and self-controlled. Avoid becoming a slave to wrong habits, and act only according to your righteous convictions. To attain cosmic consciousness it is necessary to possess self-control and to rise above dualities—heat and cold, pleasure and sorrow, health and sickness. Learn to endure all things without any excitement or disturbance of mind. "He who is everywhere nonattached—neither joyously excited by good, nor disturbed by evil—has an established wisdom."†

The Third and Highest Path

Lastly is the way of meditation—the metaphysical path. If while meditating you are still conscious of the breath, you are tied to body awareness. To enter cosmic consciousness one must free himself from the bonds of the body through guru-given meditation methods.

If you put a sealed jar of water in a tank of water, that which is in the jar is separated from that which surrounds the jar; but if you remove the lid, the water in the jar and the water in the tank can mingle. Similarly, ordinary people shut out God because their consciousness is sealed in by the lid of ignorance. When that lid is removed by right methods of medita-

* Matthew 20:28.
† Bhagavad-Gita II:57.

tion, one feels the peace of God inside and outside the body. As you increase the length and depth of your meditations you will find more and more peace, and an ever-new joy. Whatever else you may try, it will not produce the divine consciousness that comes from meditation.

The Lord is all around, but you don't feel Him. And you cannot feel Him, within or without, until you remove the lid of ignorance and merge your consciousness with His, to discover Him within yourself. If you sink in material desire you will suffocate. If you sink in the ocean of God you will live forevermore.

Once you have found God, you experience real and lasting satisfaction. Human friendships may be severed, but God will never leave you. Though everyone else forsake you, if you have Him, you have everything.

Be a Smile Millionaire

Self-Realization Fellowship Temple,
Hollywood, California, June 5, 1949

The real smile is the smile of bliss that comes when you meditate, when you feel the joy of God's presence. That is the smile on Lahiri Mahasaya's* face. He is seeing the world partially, but seeing God fully. My smile comes from a joy deep within my being, a joy that you also may attain. Like a fragrance it oozes out from the core of the blossoming soul. This joy calls others to bathe in its waters of divine bliss.

The average man is familiar with four states of mind. When a desire is fulfilled, he is happy. When a desire is denied, he is unhappy. When he is neither glad nor sorrowful, he is bored. When these three emotions, these three states of mind—pleasure, pain, and boredom—are sloughed off, he has peace.

Beyond Peace Is Bliss

Peace is the absence of the alternations of sorrow and pleasure, and the absence of boredom. It is a very desirable state. After a tumultuous ride on the crests of pain and pleasure, with frequent dips into the troughs of boredom, you enjoy floating on the calm sea of peace. But greater than peace is bliss—bliss of the soul. It is an ever-new joy that never disappears, but remains with your soul through eternity. That joy can be attained only by perceiving God.

If you place a pot of water under the rays of the moon and then agitate the water, you create a distorted reflection of the moon. When you still the waves in the pot, the reflection be-

---

* A reference to the photograph of Lahiri Mahasaya, the guru of Paramahansa Yogananda's guru. The unusual circumstances surrounding the taking of this photograph are described in *Autobiography of a Yogi,* chapter 1.

comes clear. The time when the water in the pot is quiet and clearly reflecting the moon, is comparable to the meditative state of peace, and the still deeper state of calmness. In the peace of meditation all waves of sensations and thoughts are absent from the mind. In the deeper state of calmness, one perceives in that stillness the moonèd reflection of God's presence. Peace is a negative state, being merely the absence of the waves of pleasure, pain, and indifference; and so after a little while the meditator is attracted once more by the desire to experience the waves of motion. But as meditative peace deepens into calmness and the ultimate positive state of bliss, the meditator experiences a joy that is ever new and all-satisfying.

When you sleep, you still thoughts and sensations passively. When by meditation you still thoughts and sensations consciously, you experience first the state of peace; and the muscles of your face will form a smile that reflects the peace of your heart. But you must look beyond peace in order to behold, undistorted by sensory stimuli and motor reflexes from sense-associated thoughts, the purity of your soul. The state you feel then is ever-new bliss. Saints always have this joy in their hearts. Secure in the divine inner assurance, they are unshaken by anger or fear. Using the scalpel of reason or intuition, they can dissect their own or others' thoughts on the operating table of the mind and remain unmoved. "In soul bliss, all grief is annihilated. The discrimination of the blissful man soon firmly establishes him in the Self."*

Smile with the Love of God

Most smiles are born of good emotions arising out of doing good, or out of feeling sympathy, love, kindness, or mercy. But the most wonderful way to smile is to fill your heart with the love of God. Then you will be able to love everybody; you will be able to smile all the time. All other forms of smiles are evanescent because emotions flicker and pass away, no matter how good they are. The only thing that can last is the joy of God. When you have that, you can smile all the time. Other-

---

* Bhagavad-Gita II:65.

wise, when you are feeling merciful toward someone and he returns your kindness with a slap, you won't be able to feel mercy toward him any longer.

A man I knew made a great show of his distress when his wife died. I saw through his emotionalism. "You will marry within a month," I told him. He was so angry at me he would not see me after that, but he did remarry within a month. He thought his love for the first wife was so great, but you see how quickly he forgot her.

I shall never forget how much my guru, Sri Yukteswarji, taught me when he told me this little story about his life: "When I was a little boy I took a notion that I wanted an ugly little dog belonging to a neighbor. I kept my household in turmoil for weeks to get that dog. My ears were deaf to offers of pets with more prepossessing appearance. I wanted only *that* dog."

The same sort of fixation seizes people in so-called romance. Lovers become hypnotized by a face; they can't forget it. But the real beauty we should seek in others is not outward, but inward.

When your soul is filled with joy you are attractive. I like only divine smiles, because without them, human beings are like puppets—today they are saying they will love you forever; tomorrow they are in the grave. Where is their great love then? Where is the promise, "I'll love you forever?" But if you can make God say even once to you, "I love you," it is for eternity. Why do you waste your time for a little human love, and money, and this and that, when in God you can find everything— all the love that is in the whole world, all the power in creation? But don't seek Him for power; seek Him for love. Then you will discover the chink in His armor. When you give Him your unconditional love, He can no longer refuse you Himself.

To Find Bliss, Meditate

Meditate more. You do not know how wonderful it is. It is much greater to meditate than to spend hours seeking money or human love or anything else that you can think of. The more you meditate, and the more your mind stays centered in the spiritual state during activity, the more you will be able to smile. I am always there now, in that bliss-consciousness of God. Nothing affects me; whether I am alone or with people, that joy of the Lord is always there. I have retained my smile—but to win it permanently was hard work! The same smiles are there within you; the same joy and bliss of the soul is there. You don't have to acquire them, but rather regain them. You have merely lost them temporarily by identifying yourself with the senses.

If you think that objects of sight, hearing, taste, smell, and touch will give you supreme joy, you are mightily mistaken. They will only take it away. If you put conditions around your joy—"without the sight of that face I cannot be happy"—you will never find unalloyed bliss. Because no sense-produced pleasure is permanent. Time relentlessly works its havoc on physical beauty; everything in the material world is subject to change. Therefore if you could see all the beautiful faces in the world; if you were to hear all the music and touch everything that you desire to, you would still not have found real happiness. You may imagine you are happy, however. Sometimes, after you have dug and dug to get at some object of desire, you find no happiness in the object itself, yet you derive a certain satisfaction from the labor you have put into getting it, and you therefore think you are happy. But such satisfactions are short-lived.

So do not seek your happiness in the senses. Find joy within and express it in your face. When you do that, wherever you go a little smile will surcharge everyone with your divine magnetism. Everybody will be happy!

But remember it is the Lord alone who changes each heart; we must not at all ascribe to ourselves the power to do good. The only one who does good is God. It is His world. If you feel Him as the Indweller of this body—that it is He who works in everything; and if you give everything—both good and bad actions—to Him, you will be surprised to see how all your actions gradually will be changed to good. You will not be able to do anything wrong when the consciousness of God is with you. Give your life to Him. In all you do, say, "It's You, Lord, not I! Not I, Lord!" Destroy ego; it is a great obstruction to this liberating realization. You are not the Doer; can you lift your hand if the Lord quenches the little beam of life in your medulla oblongata?*

How to Banish External Impressions

Once I was sitting outdoors at Encinitas, and it was very cold. I turned my consciousness within, and in a twinkling I couldn't feel the cold at all. Joy came over me; once in a while I saw my surroundings melt into one light, like the beam of a motion picture. If I concentrated on the picture, I saw the picture. If I concentrated on the beam, the world vanished. You cannot see anything without your consciousness. So if you have full mastery over your mind, and you look within at your soul, even though your eyes are open you will see only that great light of God, and feel His great joy. Only as you look outward through the eyes will your consciousness perceive the outer world. It is all God's motion picture. I could see, that day in Encinitas, on one side the sensations and thoughts that were dreams of my consciousness which came from God, and on the other side, as I retired within, no sensations at all—just pure joy. And though I was sitting in that extreme cold, clad only in swim trunks, I could feel the cold and the scenery disappear and joy alone come; later I felt the slight impressions of sensations together with that great joy.

Practice this—practice the presence of God. Don't be satisfied with a little prayer, or seeing a little light, and then going to bed. Sleep is a drug. If you can fairly control sex; if you can fairly control all the senses; and if you go after God with all the power of your soul, He will come to you. Even if you are a great moralist and a spiritually inclined person, without the perception of God you have very little.

So do not deceive yourself. Meditate more—unceasingly and sincerely. Tell God, "I know my weaknesses. But Lord, they belong to You, because You created me. I have no wish for anything except to be with You, because You are the One who is showing this movie. You are free from its dual aspects of comedy and tragedy. So am I free, because I am Your child."

Don't call yourself a sinner; nor call yourself righteous and

---

* The medulla center (or *chakra*) is the principal point at which life force enters into the body.

be proud. Say rather that the Lord is with you, and that He—no one else!—is working through you. Then you will see a different world. Without the consciousness of God this world appears full of struggle, violence, and terrible disappointments. But with Him it is a haven of happiness.

When I was watching the motion picture, *Song of Bernadette,* I was so deeply touched by some of the events in the saint's life that I cried. At last I said: "What's the matter with me?" I looked at the picture again and saw only shadows and light; I lost the consciousness of drama. I couldn't cry anymore; a great joyous state came over me.

The Motion Picture of Creation

In a second, God can duplicate the form of any person who has gone out of the world; He wants you to know that. He wants you to understand that this creation is a show. If you take the show seriously, you are going to get hurt, and you won't like it; you won't be able to stand life, with its sorrow and disease and pain. Whenever anything hurts the body, I put my mind at the seat of spiritual awareness at the point between the eyebrows; then I feel no pain at all. But when I concentrate on the hurt, I feel the delusion of pain. If you can keep your mind centered in the spiritual consciousness of your soul you will not suffer when the delusive shadows of sorrow appear on your mental screen. Pray to God unceasingly to reveal Himself as the sole joyous Reality.

You have already lost so much time—death may take you away at any moment, and then you won't have time to know Him. You must realize Him before you go out of the body cage. Tell Him, "I want to feel Your presence." But He won't let you out of this hospital of delusion permanently until you cure yourself of the disease of desires. Do everything for God. Working for Him is just as important to your spiritual progress as meditation.

Meditate on the Lord at night until you are uplifted in Him and feel locked in His joy; and when you come down to perform activities during the day, bring and keep with you the remembrance of that state. Then you will be all the time with God. And you will always be able to smile and say, "A little bit of sorrow or a little bit of pleasure or a little bit of peace cannot create any tumult in the ocean of ever-new bliss that fills my soul."

Laugh at *maya*, delusion. Watch life as a cosmic motion picture, then it cannot work its delusive magic on you anymore. Be in God-bliss. When you can stand unshaken 'midst the crash of breaking worlds, you shall know that God is real. He doesn't mean to hurt you. He has made you in His image. He has made you already what He is. That is what you don't realize, because you acknowledge only that you are a human being; you do not know that this thought is a delusion.

When you are suffering from cancer it is not fun. Yet St. Francis suffered from diseases and at the same time he was healing the sick and raising the dead. His divine joy could not be taken away. So by all means get to God. But He won't receive you until you prove to Him that you do want Him and that you have no desire to get mixed up in His show.

Don't Question God—Love Him

Nor should you question God. You will reap only doubt. You will not be able to understand His laws until you become one with Him. So why waste time trying to understand them by an intellectual approach? If you are reading a novel in which the hero is being mistreated, the villain is winning, and each chapter seems to contradict the preceding one, you will feel frustrated and angry with the author. But when you read the last chapter you are satisfied, and you think how wonderful that novel was because it was so complex. So God is the Master-Novelist, and one is wonderstruck at the paradoxes and intricate plot of His creation. Don't try to solve these riddles; you will be lost. When you find Him, in that last chapter, He will give you the solutions to all the enigmas of human life. And you won't be able to question His wisdom when you hear His replies. That I know!

Live with God in your heart and have no fear in the world—fear will be afraid of you! You will be free from this cosmic delusion. Then you will smile, "I know at last the mystery of it all." But don't try to know first; love God first. Then He will tell you everything. And you can smile an eternal smile. Your thoughts, your words, your writings, and everything you do will be impregnated with the joy shining in that smile. Wherever you meditate you will leave behind a fragrance of smiles, and whoever will come there will also be moved to smile with God. You can smile all the time when you dwell in His ineffable bliss.

Lord, Possess Us with Thy Love

Self-Realization Fellowship international headquarters, Los Angeles, California, on Paramahansaji's birthday, January 5, 1945, following traditional Indian ceremonies honoring the Guru's birth

Each of us is a child of God. We are born of His spirit, in all its purity and glory and joy. That heritage is unassailable. To condemn oneself as a sinner, committed to the path of error, is the greatest of all sins. The Bible says: "Know ye not that ye are the temple of God, and that the Spirit of God dwelleth in you?"*

Always remember: your Father loves you unconditionally. But because He has given you freedom to go away from Him or to approach Him, He is waiting for you to express your desire for His love before He comes to you.

Once when I was meditating I heard His voice, whispering: "Thou dost say I am away, *but thou didst not come in.* That is why thou dost say I am away. I am always in. Come in and thou wilt see Me. I am always here, ready to greet thee."

Deep sincerity is necessary in the spiritual path. In guilelessness comes the birth of Spirit. Jesus said: "Thou hast hid these things from the wise and prudent, and hast revealed them unto babes."† Before God our human wisdom is nothing. The only way we can coax Him to surrender Himself to us is by offering to Him the same unconditional love that He gives to us.

Everyone will eventually find salvation, but those who tarry on the way fall into the ditch of indifference. Indifference prevents man from realizing how important it is to find God now, in this moment. Our great whirling planet, our human individuality, were not given to us merely that we might exist for a time and then vanish into nothingness, but that we

* I Corinthians 3:16.   † Matthew 11:25.

might question what it is all about. To live without under-standing the purpose of life is foolish, a waste of time. The mystery of life surrounds us; we were given intelligence in order to solve it.

God Is the Lover Behind All Love

I have realized, by searching for lasting love, that it was Someone Else who cared for me through all human loves. The Divine has loved me as mother, as father, and as friends. I searched for that one Friend behind all friends, that one Lover whom I now see glimmering in all your faces. And that Friend never fails me.

God is behind everything. "Honor thy father and thy mother,"* but "love the Lord thy God with all thine heart, and with all thy soul, and with all thy might."† You should under-stand the importance of cultivating divine friendship with Him, and of not wasting any more time. How do you know, when you go to sleep, whether or not you will wake up? One by one we leave this earth. But there is nothing to grieve about. When we die, we are required to be reborn on earth, starting another life where we left off in this one.

I behold life and death like the rise and fall of waves on the sea. At birth a wave rises from the surface, and at death it sinks into sleep in the bosom of God. I have realized this. I know I can never die; for whether I am sleeping in the ocean of Spirit or awake in a physical body, I am ever with Him. That supreme happiness cannot be found in the world; but we need not run away to the jungle to seek Him. We can find Him in this jungle of daily life, in the cave of inner silence.

It doesn't matter how many mistakes you have made; they are only temporary. You are formed in the image of Spirit. The Lord created this delusory motion picture of earth and all its pleasures for but one purpose: that perchance you would see through His play of *maya* and forsake it to love Him alone. This is the truth; it cannot be otherwise. Why are we made to feel love for our family members, only to watch them slip away, one by one? These events take place to help us realize that it is He who is loving us behind all loved ones.

* Matthew 19:19.   † Deuteronomy 6:5.

The difficulty about this motion picture of life is that all unrealities seem real, and all realities seem unreal. Each night in sleep the world is made to disappear from our consciousness, so we might understand that the material universe is not real. This lesson of sleep comes not to frighten us, but to make us seek the reality of God. The soul can never be satisfied with anything but Him and His love. His spirit is the reality that nothing else can match.*

Don't Waste Time

So many years are gone from our lives already. And only so many years, weeks, days, and hours are left. Don't waste time. In your heart, tell Him night and day, "Lord, I want Thee." Never be insincere about that. Never reason, "Tomorrow I will seek God. Today let me have a good time." Always say, "Today, my Lord, *today* I want Thee."

Just now I see the great light of God spread everywhere— such joy, such light! "Lord, I bow to Thee on this beautiful occasion in which Thou art born in us in new glory. May I always be blessed with awareness of Thy presence, and may each one of us here be thus blessed, that we may all know Thou art seeking to be born anew in our consciousness."

Love Him, talk to Him every second of your life, in activity and in silence, with deep prayer, with the unceasing desire of your heart; and you shall see the screen of delusion melt away. He who is playing hide-and-seek in the beauty of flowers, in souls, in noble passions, in dreams, shall come forth and say: "You and I have been apart for a long time, because I desired that you give Me your love willingly. You are made in My image, and I wanted to see if you would use your freedom to give Me your love."

I pray that God give you the imperishable gift of His love. But without effort you won't find Him. If you make twenty-five percent of the effort, the rest of it will come through God and guru. This evening has passed like a moment, for He has been with me every second. This is what I wanted to feel, that

---

* "That which is unreal is nonexistent. That which is real cannot be nonexistent. Men possessed of wisdom know the final truth about reality" (Bhagavad-Gita II:16).

you are showing appreciation to me merely to express your appreciation of Him who sent me. May His blessings be ever with you; may His consciousness never leave you. May you realize, within and without, the fullness of His presence.

Call God Your Own

God doesn't readily respond to us, because we are shy before Him; we fail to show how much we want Him. Don't be afraid of Him. Call Him your own and pursue Him unceasingly, in thought and in action, and you shall find Him to be the greatest haven of safety.

"I offer the bouquet of these souls to Thee, O Father, that they may adorn the altar of Thy presence. Be Thou unceasingly with them. Father, Thou art the head of this family. We are Thy children, gathered together to sing the glory of Thy name. Banish the darkness of ignorance with Thy light; drive away all gloom from the shores of our minds with the expanding light of Thy presence. Naughty or good, we are Thy children. Reveal Thyself unto us. Bless everyone here. I feel their kind thoughts for me. All kindness, honor, respect, and love given to me, I offer to Thee, O Father! Thou art my love, my all.

"Bless us with Thy grace. Destroy our desire for anything but Thee. Be Thou the King sitting on the throne of all our ambitions. Let the light of Thy glory spread over the vast world. Bless us all, saturate us with Thy presence. May we realize more and more that Thou hast always been ours. Thou art ours now; Thou wilt ever be ours. We thank Thee for the benediction and love Thou hast bestowed upon Thy family assembled here. May we all someday celebrate Thy birth in us in eternity, in immortality, and in unceasing joy."

Pray with me: "Our Father, bless us that when we are free, we may gather in heaven to celebrate Thy birth within us. Manifest Thyself within and without. Unite us all; in the light of that union may we find Thy One Presence. With all the devotion of our merged hearts, of our united souls, we fall at Thy feet of omnipresence. Bless us that we never be indifferent to Thee. May an undying fire of love possess our hearts. We bow to Thee, our Father, our very own. Thy presence be with us now and forever."

Controlling Your
New Year's Destiny

Self-Realization Fellowship Temple,
Hollywood, California, January 2, 1944

If you saturate with devotion a thought of God, and by your concentration impress that thought deep within you, then in the temple of superconsciousness the Lord of the universe will come to receive that loving thought.

Ask God to help you fulfill all the good thoughts and resolutions that you are making now for the New Year. Resolve that you are going to do just what you think you should do, and that under no circumstances are you going to be cowed into doing otherwise by your old bad habits.

There was a great lesson for me in the book I have been writing. I used to write without ever reading over the manuscript—a task I always avoided. But I had to go over and over every bit of my autobiography.* The Lord disciplined me, yet in a noble way, because I have enjoyed reliving those wondrous experiences as I read the account again.

I have ventured many projects in this life. I have lectured, designed and built buildings, done artwork, played musical instruments, planted gardens, founded a school, but always the secret of my success was will power. I can truthfully say that destiny is what you make it.

Analyze yourself. What happened to your good intentions and noble ambitions of the past year? Did you let them die for want of dynamic will-to-accomplish? Make a strong determination to avoid repetition of old errors in this New Year. Plan your time. Resolve that you are not going to be an automaton run by the world and by your own habits; that is not the way to

---

* *Autobiography of a Yogi.*

true happiness. You must change; you must *be able to change.*
Vague desire to improve is not enough. You have made yourself
what you are now, and you can become whatever you want to
be, but you have to use will power.

More confining than stone walls are the prison bars of
habit. You carry this invisible prison with you wherever you go.
But you can be free! Determine now to break out of the jail of
habits and race for freedom. How frightful life is, that from the
age of three we are limited by habit. As soon as I realized I was
caged in by habit I broke through all the bars. I would not
permit myself to be bound by habits that made me say, "I can't
do that," or, "I have to do this," or, "Don't do that to me, it
makes me nervous," or, "I can't stand the cold," and so on.

Why are these habits so strong from early childhood? Because they have been carried over from previous-life experiences. Our moods are inkmarks traced on the graph of life by
the *karma* of the past. Wrong habits and moods are more offen-
sive than the odor of the skunk. Why behave like a human
polecat, making everyone else uncomfortable and punishing
yourself as well? At one time or another we all have done so,
because we all have carried with us obnoxious peculiarities.

Reclaim Your Lost Divinity

But we can overcome undesirable traits. The human mind
is elastic. If you pull it gradually, it will yield to your tugs. Yet
you don't even try. God has given us more than enough power
to overcome all the trials and shortcomings of our lives. Saint
Francis, though ill and sightless, could heal the sick and raise
the dead. Outwardly blind, inwardly he beheld the great Light
of the universe. God puts His true children such as Saint
Francis to greater tests than He gives to ordinary people. But no
one passes through the gates of freedom until he has passed all
God's tests, until he has learned to live like a true son of God.
Why should you think of yourself as a weak mortal? You are
potentially a son of God. You do not have to acquire anything;
you have only to *know*.

To try to be a millionaire in this incarnation is really
much more difficult than to be a true son of God. Earthly environment is so limited that many people die without having be-

come what they want to be. But to know God is possible in one lifetime, because you don't have to acquire Him; He is already your own.

Even if everyone were to pray day and night to become as rich as Henry Ford, their prayers could not be granted because earth is not a place where everybody can be a Henry Ford. But everyone can be rich in Spirit, for God has given everyone equal power to become like Him. When you claim your divinity, everything belongs to you. A Henry Ford might lose his wealth or his health, but a Jesus Christ can create health or wealth or anything else he wants, at will. So don't long to be as rich or as healthy as someone else; have only one desire: to be like God. Jesus never claimed that he was the only son of God. The Father loves you, His child, just as much as He loves Jesus. And God won't deny you anything if, like Jesus, you establish your true status with Him. Meditation is the way to reclaim your lost divinity.

Habits are grafts on our real nature, which is ever-free Spirit. In my childhood I used to get very angry, but when I made up my mind not to, I never again gave in to anger. If I hadn't used my will I wouldn't have been able to accomplish that, or anything else in this life. You too can use your will. The errors of a lifetime can be corrected *today*. Make a resolution in this New Year to realize the truth that although as a mortal man you have certain habits, as a divine being you are free. Why should you lie to yourself? Why should you ascribe to yourself the faults of the past? You must destroy them. Otherwise they will become grafts on your tree of life. You must not allow that. Affirm again and again: "I am a child of God. I am one with God."

Apply Will and Discrimination to Resolution

Every strong resolution you make with great determination can become a habit at once. Why should you not be able to do what you wish, guided by reason? You must try. Away with all your faults! Review your actions of the past year. See what troublesome habits you may have displayed: perhaps you fight with people, or you eat too much, or you are jealous. Make up your mind today, and *know* that you are never going to do those things again. Just say to yourself, "Paramahansaji said he had an aversion to editing, but he became an editor; and if he could make himself an editor, I can do this." Why couldn't you? Everything I have tried to do with will power has worked. And I give you hope that if you make up your mind, you too will succeed. God has given you the power to dynamite your troubles. "Beware, O ye mountains, stand not in my way! Your ribs will be shattered and tattered today!" Those words are from a song by a great swami.* In another part he sang, "I hitch to my chariot the fates and the gods!"

The Romans used to tie prisoners to chariots and drag them on the ground—a terrible practice! Yet in it is a lesson for us, for we allow our habits to treat us in the same way. We should make habits our prisoners rather than our captors; hitching them to the chariot of our will, we should drive them instead of letting them drag us. To be able to do whatever we know we should do, not merely that which we whimsically want to do, is to be really free.

Learn to discriminate in this New Year: examine every impulse that comes, to see if it is the right thing for you to act on. And when your reason tells you to do a certain thing, let neither the fates nor the gods stand in your way. But if you find out that you are wrong, be able to change your mind. Some people are so stubborn, they do not want to admit they are wrong. But one should be guided by reason, not by blind will. If, after calmly reasoning, you make up your mind that what you have set out to do is right, then nobody should be able to stop you. If I had no job I would shake up the whole world until people would say, "Give him a job to keep him quiet!" (I do not say these things out of personal pride, but that you may learn from my experiences.)

Work of any kind, if done in the right spirit, gives you victory over yourself. You may clean bathrooms, but if you do it with the thought of serving and helping people, you are showing the right spirit of a man of God. The attitude with which you work is what counts. Mental laziness and working unwillingly spoil one. People often ask me, "How do you do so many

* Swami Ram Tirtha.

things?" It is because I do everything with the greatest pleasure and spirit of service. Inwardly I am all the time with God.
And though I sleep very little I always feel fresh, because I perform my duties with the right attitude: that it is a privilege
to serve.

You must realize that you are a child of God. Make up your
mind that you are not going to be run by that old habit-bound
self. The temporary limitations and imperfections of the body
and brain cannot hold you back; as soon as you give the verdict
and strongly will to be a new person, you will change.

You have been a prisoner of your habits and it has not
been good for you. It is because of wrong habits of thinking
and acting in this and in other lives that your bodily kingdom
yields now to invasions of disease, troubles, moods, and ignorance. From now on you must say: "I am not the slave of the
body. I am the dictator of my own kingdom. My thoughts are
going to be exactly as I wish them to be." Once you have
changed your habits, you will say to yourself, "How simple it
was to do it! How unkind I have been to myself by not exchanging my soul-stultifying habits for those that bring happiness."

Are You a Psychological Antique?

Habit-bound people can best be described as psychological
antiques. They are the same, year in and year out. They say the
same old things, do the same old things. Converse with them
just a little while and you can anticipate exactly what their
next remark will be. Take a look in the mirror of introspection
and see if you are a psychological antique. Most people are.

But why should you be one? Change your habits. Cast out
moods. Try to be better every day. Let people be able to say,
"What a wonderful change has come over him!"

The man of Self-realization has achieved mastery over the
old habit-dulled self. Recognizing such mastery in Jesus, the of-
ficers who had been sent by the Pharisees to arrest him came
away marveling instead at his assurance, saying, "Never man
spake like this man."* A master's nature is infinite; it cannot
be contained in the narrow confines of human conceptions.
Every time I thought I had succeeded in categorizing my guru,

* John 7:46.

Swami Sri Yukteswarji, I found him to be different, greater, nonclassifiable.

Sometime you have to break the habit of attachment to the mortal body and get back to God. There is no alternative. You are a prodigal son here on earth. Your infinite nature must be rediscovered. You will never be happy so long as you remain habit-mired in ignorance of your eternal soul-nature. It does not matter who you are; the only way you can find lasting joy is to go back to God. You do not have to leave earth's shores and put on wings; you must learn rather to be happy here and now, under all conditions; and to include others' happiness in your own joy. Go out of your way to make others happy. You cannot please everybody, but to those souls who cross your path, give kindness and love. There is no more liberating action than sincerely to give people kindness in return for unkindness. Why not be like a flower that gives fragrance even when crushed in the hand? The Gita teaches: "He who is free from hatred toward all creatures, is friendly and kind to all...is dear to Me."*

If people criticize you, do not ignore them. See if you have the fault they ascribe to you, and if you do, silently correct your error. But it is seldom necessary to confess your faults to others; often it is unwise. Should they become angry with you, they might unkindly hold your confession over your head as a threat. To a God-realized spiritual teacher or guru you can tell your faults, but not to someone who cannot help you, and who might instead hurt you by broadcasting your flaws to others.

A Stream of Divine Power

Learn to mix with good people. The faces of many of you who come here have become more spiritual. And the more you are in tune with me and refrain from fussing about little things, the better you will be. A steady stream of divine power will flow to you, for the Great Ones sent me here. When I am gone you will realize this truth with greater impact. I am here only to deliver their message. Little by little a spiritual change will come to the true followers of this path, and their influence will spread over the world. Self-Realization is one of

* Bhagavad-Gita XII:13.

the greatest spiritual movements ever sent to help mankind. It has been blessed by the Great Ones—Mahavatar Babaji, Lahiri Mahasaya, Sri Yukteswar—in communion with Christ and Krishna. The grace of these masters is not gone from the earth. They are waiting to help you and to help the world, but they can work only through the free choice of man. The world has gone mad with hate and war, but Jesus' way of brotherly love is the solution to the world's problems. We can make this world proof against war by following his teachings as he meant us to.

On this last meditation day,* Christ came to me several times: first as a little child, then as a grown man, and finally as he looked before his crucifixion. I had been thinking that I would have to meditate long, before he would come to me. And he surprised me! God was showing me through this experience that no further effort is needed once you have convinced Him that you want Him more than all the gifts of the world. Then He takes away the screen of mystery and comes to you as Christ or Krishna, or Babaji, or as any great incarnation in whose form you desire to behold Him.

Make up your mind that in this New Year you are going to be more Christlike in your behavior. You must make the effort now. You must meditate more. Self-Realization Fellowship was not brought into existence merely to give glimpses of God through words, but that you might know Him through your own experience. We teach that true fellowship with man can come only after one has gained experience of God. If you contact God within yourself, you will know that He is in everyone, that He has become the children of all races. Then you cannot be an enemy to anyone. If the whole world could love with that universal love there would be no need for men to arm themselves against one another. By our own Christlike example we must bring unity among all religions, all nations, all races.

We must train ourselves to plain living and high thinking. It would be good if each family had a small garden in which to grow some of their food. Live more simply, so that you can find

* The annual Self-Realization Fellowship all-day Christmas meditation. (See footnote on page 51.)

time to enjoy the little pleasures of life. Man races through his span, working, eating, sleeping; and that is about all he accomplishes. Eliminate any habit or activity that disturbs your mental peace and happiness.

In this New Year, resolve to cast out from the temple of your mind all the devils of bad habits; to plan your life so that you can do all the things you want to do. If it is happiness you want, have it! There is nothing that can stop you. You are an immortal child of God, and all the difficulties that visit you are meant only to stimulate you to higher achievements.

The Best Resolution—Give More Time to God

Choose which habits you are going to destroy in the New Year. Make up your mind about them and stick to your decision. Resolve to give more time to God: to meditate regularly every day, and on one night each week to meditate several hours, so that you can feel your spiritual progress in God. Resolve that you are going to practice *Kriya Yoga* regularly and that you are going to control your appetites and emotions. Be a master! Make up your mind strongly now.

Think of the good resolutions you have made in the past— that you were not going to be dictated to by your old habits and thoughts. But have you kept them? It is an insult to your soul and to God to give in to your weaknesses. Be master of yourself, captain of your destiny. Danger and you were born together, and you are the elder brother, more dangerous than danger! Do not lose the courage and determination that you feel as you listen to me now. Pray with me:

"Heavenly Father, give us the strength to carry out all our good resolutions in the New Year. May we always please Thee by our actions. Our spirits are willing. Help us to materialize all our worthy wishes in the New Year. We will reason, we will will, we will act; but guide Thou our reason, will, and activity to the right thing that we should do in everything. *Aum.* Peace. Amen."

How to Outwit Temptation

Self-Realization Fellowship international headquarters,
Los Angeles, California, November 15, 1934

Satan, or cosmic delusion, is always snaring us through our ignorance. That is how he obstructs God. The Lord could easily destroy Satan, but prefers to overcome him by love. Whenever we choose the divine offerings of eternal joy instead of the passing pleasures of the senses, the Adversary is robbed of his dark power. So it is up to us to cooperate with our Heavenly Father, that the Devil may be vanquished.

Whenever you are slothful and careless, you help Satan to pull you toward his side. Jesus prayed: "Lead us not into temptation, but deliver us from evil."* Temptation is not our own creation; it belongs to the world of *maya*, and all men are subject to it. But to enable us to free ourselves, God gave us reason, conscience, and will power.

To give our approval to sinful activities is to find ourselves in trouble. When by our wrong thoughts we fall into the pit of error, we should pray: "Father, leave us not here, but pull us out through the force of our reason and will. And when we are out, if it is Thy will to test us further, first make Thyself known to us—that we may realize that Thou art more tempting than temptation."

So long as you feel unwilling to deny yourself some particular pleasure that is detrimental to your welfare, you are in the region of Satan; the evil results of succumbing to harmful sense lures will at one time or another overtake you. But if you are convinced that temptation is dangerous to you because it promises happiness and in the end gives sorrow, you can outwit the Devil.

* Matthew 6:13.

Why Sense Experiences Are Alluring

Temptations are alluring; there is no doubt about that. Our sensory powers are all directed to the outer world. There is a current of life energy flowing from the brain through the nerves into the eyes, ears, nose, tongue, and skin. The sensations we experience through these instruments are the result of this outward-flowing current, and we tend to like the feeling. That is the appeal of the senses. Overindulging them is dangerous; until a man is established in wisdom, the outgoing energy leads him into sense bondage.

By the five-rayed searchlight of the senses, we perceive and explore the world of matter. Through the senses we learn to like things that are pleasing to see, hear, smell, taste, and touch. The desire for a particular sensation becomes a habit. The trouble is, most people have not had any experience of the Spirit, which is hidden behind matter; hence they have no standard of comparison between the exciting, pleasurable perceptions of the senses and the unknown ineffable bliss of the soul. And there is no chance to compare until one has renounced or become mentally insusceptible to all sense enticements. The only way to avoid the trap is to realize by reason or experience that there are higher joys.

Habit Is a Pitiless Dictator

Commandments to refrain from harmful experiences are generally futile. Whenever you order a person not to do something, he immediately wants to do it. The taste of forbidden fruits is sweet in the beginning, but in the end, bitter. Yet no matter how much suffering people experience, they go on doing the same self-harming things. Once you have established a liking for a certain sensory experience, the habit sits like a dictator in the brain and commands you to indulge yourself, even though it is against your best interests. You don't want to repeat an act, and yet you do it. Try never to let yourself reach a point where you become such a victim of wrong habits. You must be the master of yourself; do not let any habit control you. Whenever the desire for a particular sensory experience becomes habitual, it is time to stop that practice.

I used to be fond of ginger ale because it reminded me of

our lemonade in India. Some students arranged to have this beverage on hand for me wherever I went. One day I found my supply was all gone, and I missed it. "Mr. Ginger Ale," I said, "you have gone too far, and I hadn't even realized it! Goodbye." The next day I purposely drank a little ginger ale as a test, and it tasted terrible. My thought of the previous day had been so strong that the desire was banished immediately.

I never miss anything that is taken away from me or that I voluntarily give up. No physical comfort can bind me. I have tried it out. You must be able to pass through all experiences of life without attachment. Lord Krishna said: "The man of self-control, roaming among material objects with subjugated senses, and devoid of attraction and repulsion, attains an unshakable inner calmness."* Any time you *have* to have something—a soft bed, a pillow, or whatever—remember that you are putting yourself into slavery; and when your will and discrimination are held captive by binding sense attachments, you will lose the infinite kingdom of God. Jesus is still enjoying the transcendental ecstasy that he experienced when he resurrected himself in the Lord. But those who exist in ignorance, subject to the pressures of desires, will continue that way life after life until they resist worldly seductions.

You should be careful not to let anything hurt your true happiness. Corroding emotions of anger, greed, and jealousy, and overstimulation by sex, alcohol, or drugs are extremely detrimental to you, for they prevent the realization of soul joy. Never abuse the sensory powers by overindulgence, if you would be really happy. "Ever fed, never satisfied; never fed, ever satisfied" is a true axiom about unwholesome sense experiences.

Wisdom Is Man's Best Protection

Protect yourself within the fortress of wisdom. There is no greater safety. Complete understanding will bring you to a point where nothing can hurt you. But until you have attained wisdom, when temptation comes you must first stop the action or urge, and *then* reason. If you try to reason first, you will be compelled in spite of yourself to do the thing that

* Bhagavad-Gita II:64.

you don't want to do, because temptation will overcome all reason. Just say "No!" and get up and go away. That is the surest way to escape the Devil. The more you develop this "won't" power during the intrusion of temptation, the happier you will be; for all joy depends on the ability to do that which conscience tells you you *should* do.

Don't let your environment and sensory desires control you. Virtue and spiritual living are far more charming than sensual indulgence, but the habit chains of temptation hold people fast. If the Lord once tempted you with His love, you would want nothing more. Nothing else would interest you. When you are convinced that He is the most desirable Treasure, nothing on the material plane can ever again tempt you and overcome your power of discrimination.

To know God is the only worthwhile ambition to have, because He is happiness everlasting. We should want Him because He is the panacea for all our suffering. He is the answer to all our needs. The very things that our hearts cry for—love, fame, wisdom, everything else—we find in communion with that Complete One. Even if you are the most famous man in the world, death will be the end of your awareness of fame; you will not know then that people adore you. But Jesus is aware that his devotees love him; because his consciousness is one with the consciousness of God manifesting throughout creation, the Christ Intelligence, omnipresent, omniscient, ever living.

So why strive hard to have something you will lose just as you cross the portals of the grave? Money, fame, prestige, sense indulgence, material comfort—these are all pseudo pleasures, offered by Satan in place of the real joy of divine communion. Remember that temptation is powerful only because you have no sense of comparison with anything better. When you are strongly tempted, your wisdom is momentarily a prisoner of your desires and habits. But the highest way to freedom is to be so merged in the inexhaustible joy of God that you are able to relinquish all worldly pleasures in an instant.

If you find true joy in this life, you will have it now and in the afterlife too. Which do you want: God's eternal bliss, which may be yours by denying yourself a few pleasures now? or worldly happiness now, which will not last? Convince your heart by comparison. Every effort that you make to climb upward will be recognized by God.

Even If You Are the Greatest Sinner, Forget It

Don't think of yourself as a sinner. You are a child of the Heavenly Father. No matter if you are the greatest sinner, forget it. If you have made up your mind to be good, then you are no longer a sinner. "Even an evildoer who turns away from all else to worship Me exclusively may be counted among the good, because of his righteous resolve. He will fast become a virtuous man and obtain unending peace. Tell all, O Arjuna, that My devotee never perishes!"* Start with a clean slate and say: "I have always been good; I was only dreaming that I was bad." It is true: evil is a nightmare and does not belong to the soul.

Temptation is sugarcoated poison; it tastes delicious, but death is certain. The happiness that people look for in this world does not endure. Divine joy is eternal. Yearn for that which is lasting, and be hardhearted about rejecting the impermanent pleasures of life. You have to be that way. Don't let the world rule you. Never forget that the Lord is the only reality. The real love of your Cosmic Father is playing hide-and-seek with you in your heart. Your true happiness lies in your experience of Him.

Man is sunk in a dream of ignorance, imagining that he is suffering with illness and sorrow and poverty. Once when King Janaka, a great Indian saint, was deep in prayer, he suddenly exclaimed, "Who is in my temple today? I thought it was myself, but I see the Eternal is there. And the little self, this body-bundle of bones, is not I. It is the Infinite that is in my body. I bow to Myself. I offer flowers to Myself." Someday that realization will come to you, and you will no longer think you are a mortal, a man or a woman; you will know that you are a soul, made in the divine image, "and that the Spirit of God dwelleth in you." †

* Bhagavad-Gita IX:30–31.

† I Corinthians 3:16.

The soul is bound to the body by a chain of desires, temptations, troubles, and worries, and it is trying to free itself. If you keep tugging at that chain which is holding you to mortal consciousness, someday an invisible Divine Hand will intervene and snap it apart, and you will be free.

Protect yourself against temptation and sorrow by reason and by communion with God. In the Bhagavad-Gita the Lord says: "The ignorant, oblivious of Me as the Maker of all creatures, are blind to My presence within the human form."* Meditation is simply reminding yourself again and again that you are not the limited physical body, but the Infinite Spirit. Meditation is arousing the memory of your real Self and forgetting what you imagine you are. If a drunken prince goes into the slums and, forgetting entirely his true identity, begins lamenting, "How poor I am," his friends will laugh at him and say, "Wake up, and remember that you are a prince."

You have been likewise in a state of hallucination, thinking you are a helpless mortal, struggling and miserable. Every day you should sit quietly and affirm, with deep conviction: "No birth, no death, no caste have I; father, mother, have I none. Blessed Spirit, I am He. † I am the Infinite Happiness." If you again and again repeat these thoughts, day and night, you will eventually realize what you really are: an immortal soul.

Fix Your Mind in the Divine Consciousness of Meditation

Temptation, greed, attachment to people and possessions, slavery to the senses, ignorance of your Spirit-nature, idleness, and mechanical living are the worst enemies of your happiness. Be busy working, with your mind fixed in the divine consciousness that is cultivated by meditation, for then you will be really happy and you will be really living.

When I started meditating, I could not imagine that I would ever find such joy in it. But as time went on, the more I meditated, the greater became my peace and bliss.

If you are getting tired of the life you are leading, and yet you go on filling it with more possessions and more desires for

* IX:11.

† From a famous song by Swami Shankara, peerless exponent of Vedic monism. (See glossary.)

new experiences, you are on the wrong road. The surest way to
avoid temptation is to lead a natural life: a life in harmony
with God. Don't lead an unnatural existence, restlessly seeking happiness from a world that is powerless to bestow it. Life
is too precious. Every day I pray to Him: "Take everything
away from me if it is Your desire. I am trying to do my best,
Father, but know this for certain: above all I want to please
You. I will try to please others, too, but more than anything
else I want to please You." When you pray like that you may
suffer many tests of desires. But as you go on fighting wrong
habits and tendencies, He begins gradually to come upon you;
finally you will see that like a great flood He has swept away
all your undesirable traits.

Krishna said: "The man who physically fasts from sense
objects finds the sense objects fall away for a little while, leaving behind only the longing for them. But he who beholds the
Supreme is freed even from longings."* Banish all darkness by
His light, and evil thoughts by good thoughts. Eliminate temptation by discovering God's superior attraction in meditation.
That is the best weapon against temptation. Any time you
feel that your will is being overpowered, meditate until you
feel the Divine Presence.

* Bhagavad-Gita II:59.

Curing Mental Alcoholics

Circa 1949

The individual who drinks too much forms a pernicious habit. If he makes no effort to curb his indulgence in liquors, he may become an alcoholic and helplessly suffer from an overwhelming desire to drink without any limit, without rhyme or reason. Such unfortunate people often spend all their money on drink; they eat very little and seem to get some nourishment from the liquor itself. The normal sense of responsibility toward maintaining good health and an honorable standing in the family, society, and the world is lost. They may eventually lose all sense of pride and be picked up dead drunk anywhere— in a ditch, or in the middle of the street—exposed meanwhile to the dangers of being robbed or run over.

The foregoing description of liquor alcoholics serves to illustrate what I mean by "mental alcoholics." The latter may be individually classified according to their particular psychological extreme, which might be chronic anger, fear, sex, sadism, gambling, stealing, jealousy, hate, greed, moods, craftiness, or stupidity.

When from the very beginning of life a person displays extraordinary tantrums of anger, fear, jealousy—or any other of the aforementioned characteristics—then one may know that he has acquired those abnormal mental habits in a previous existence.

Parents who notice any such evil psychological tendencies in their child, even in its infancy, should get busy and take some steps to prevent the child from becoming a psychological alcoholic; if possible, by placing him in another environment under the good care of spiritual teachers.

Through continued good company and proper environment for many years, a mental alcoholic may become free from the octopus grip of the inborn evil. While the mental alcoholic is receiving thoughtful care in a good environment, the evil consequences of his bad habits should be explained to him, and he should be encouraged to reason with himself about them and to make a distinct effort not to display them under any circumstances. Each indulgence in a prenatally acquired mental habit makes it stronger and stronger, until the possessor becomes literally a slave to it.

A False Conception

The angry man, the sexual man, the greedy man forgets his own position, and his relations with society, and commits great blunders that ruin his life and the lives of others. Many of these mental alcoholics think that if they give expression to their psychological habits, they will feel somewhat relieved. But the self-indulgent habit of giving in to harmful impulses is extremely pernicious, for it is by repetition of such evil expressions that a person becomes a chronic mental alcoholic, making a fool of himself anytime and anywhere.

If children are exposed to an evil environment while their minds are in a plastic state, they will develop wrong habits that, unchecked, may lead to chronic mental alcoholism. Parents who notice a sudden change in a child—perhaps a calm-natured boy suddenly turns into a repeatedly angry boy—should immediately take care of this. The causes of his frustrations should be determined and removed, and new avenues for constructive use of his energies sought.

Those who habitually display any of the foregoing traits are mental alcoholics. They recklessly ride down the Niagara Falls of continuous bad habits, smashing their happiness to pieces as they helplessly but willingly indulge in uncontrolled expression of their worst traits. It is not good to remonstrate with mental alcoholics who frequently display violent moods of disgust and boredom with the world. Their attitude is a result of their continuous repetition of wrong habits. They should be treated as psychological patients suffering from chronic mental diseases.

Counteractive Influences

A change of company is the best remedy for acute mental alcoholism of any kind, for the will of the mental alcoholic has become a slave to habit; hence he has no resistance whatsoever to evil. The most effective cure is to move him immediately to an environment that will be a specific antidote to his toxic mental condition.

If possible, the angry mental alcoholic should be placed with one or more individuals who do not become angry, even under irritating circumstances. The sexual person ought to be surrounded by self-controlled people; the habitual thief needs the society of honest people. The chronically timid can be helped by association with the brave, and by reading stories of men who were heroes. Moody or scornful or "sourpuss" types should have the companionship of habitually cheerful people.

A mental alcoholic should remember that poor elimination, and eating meat (beef and pork especially), will aggravate his psychological malady, fixing it even more firmly in his brain. An abundance of fruits and vegetables in the daily diet, and each week a one-day fast on fruit juices—with a longer fast occasionally—will greatly help to change the cerebral grooves that entrench the pernicious habits.

Sexual excess impairs the nervous system and the brain cells, which in turn aggravates anger in a mental alcoholic. Overindulgence in sex destroys will power, also. Hence all mental alcoholics should learn control over the sex impulse, that they may practice moderation in marital relations, as nature intended.

Petty Dictators

Often we find that the breadwinners in a family—father or son or, sometimes, mother or daughter—display a tendency toward mental alcoholism because of the consciousness that they are in a position to dictate. Such little dictators in families should not freely unload their moods on innocent, harmless dependents, and thus lose the inner respect of those around them. When a family dictator thinks he can get away with doing what he pleases at home, he gradually begins to do what he pleases in expressing unpleasant moods or evil traits outside the family. Eventually he does this anytime and anywhere. If petty family tyrants don't check their indulgence in these sadistic habits, they gradually become mental alcoholics, behaving immaturely and causing untold trouble to those who are closely or even casually associated with them, as well as to themselves.

If you are a mental alcoholic, try to cure yourself; but meanwhile refrain at least from trying to infect or influence others. For whether or not you succeed, you will probably cause yourself added trouble. Think what pandemonium would break loose if suddenly somebody dropped a skunk in your peaceful home, where you had been sitting quietly meditating or reading a book by the fireplace. You and those around you would no doubt try to evict the skunk, and in so doing be drenched with its malodorous chemicals. Both the family and the skunk would suffer.

So it is not wise for a human skunk to enter an environment where he is unwanted. He is likely to cause trouble for everyone around him, and in the end may suffer harsh treatment. Please remember that a human skunk carrying a mental vibration of terrible moods, and the reflection of it on his face, creates incalculable harm in peaceful environments; this biped is unwanted anywhere.

It is better even to hide mental alcoholism than to give in to its influence in public. Continued shameless indulgence is the soil in which prenatal or postnatal tendencies thrive. The individual who is prenatally disposed to mental alcoholism must be doubly careful not to live in an environment that waters the innate psychological seeds of his bad habits or moods.

Of course, when you meet a person who treats you formally, and with a galvanized smile says, "How do you do, I am awfully delighted to see you," while inside he is thinking, "I could cheerfully chop off your head for disturbing me," you sense his inner feeling and you don't like it. I myself like to know where I stand with people. I prefer blunt treatment to hypocritical behavior. No one likes to risk having the snake of insincerity dart out at him from under a rosebush of smiles.

However, it is better for a mental alcoholic to be friendly toward people, even if hypocritically, than to vent on them his evil moods. Self-control practiced daily, even in insignificant matters, will help the mental alcoholic to come out of his drunken indulgences little by little.

Overcoming Malignant Moods

*First Self-Realization Fellowship Temple at
Encinitas, California, March 5, 1939*

Moods are not easily defined; but you know what they are. When you are in a mood, your behavior is not natural; you are not the person you should be. The end result is that you feel wretched. And how foolish it is to be unhappy through your own doing! Nobody *likes* misery. Why not analyze yourself next time you are in a mood? You will see how you are willingly, willfully making yourself miserable. And while you are doing so, others around you feel the unpleasantness of your state of mind. Wherever you go, you tell about yourself without speaking, because your whole mood carries its vibrations in your eyes, and anyone looking at you is aware of the negativity recorded there. Seeing the dark feelings reflected in your eyes, others are repelled; they want to stay away from those discomforting vibrations. You must remove moods from your mental mirror before you can remove their reflection from your eyes.

We Live in a Glass House

You are living in the glass house of this world, and everyone else is watching you. You cannot pose; you have to live a natural life. So why not behave in such a way that others will look up to you? Why should they not see joy in your face? All your good qualities are covered up inside by your moodiness.

Not only are others observing how you conduct yourself; you also are studying how they behave. Because you tend to make comparisons as a result of constantly watching those around you, you fall into moods. Or you may become moody over the endless difficulties one encounters in this world.

Moods are often a result of environmental influences. Each one of us is affected in different ways by the world about us. But you should not allow yourself to indulge in moods over external conditions. Why should you take on the effects of your environment? There are people who resort to moods in an attempt to avoid facing some problem. But moodiness is neither an escape nor an emotional safety valve. It is natural now and then to fall momentarily into a mood; but don't hold on to it!

Each type of mood has a specific cause, and it lies within your own mind. To remove a mood you must remove its cause. One should introspect each day in order to understand the nature of his mood, and how to correct it, if it is a harmful one. Perhaps you find yourself in an indifferent state of mind. No matter what is suggested, you are not interested. It is necessary then to make a conscious effort to create some positive interest. Beware of indifference, which ossifies your progress in life by paralyzing your will power.

Perhaps your mood is discouragement over sickness; a feeling that you will never regain health. You must try to apply the laws of right living that lead to a healthy, active, and moral life, and pray for greater faith in the healing power of God.

Or suppose your mood is a conviction that you are a failure, and can never succeed at anything. Analyze the problem and see if you have really made all the effort you could have. Consider the hard work of the president of the United States. He has to try to please all the forty-eight states,* and other nations as well. We have to marvel that it is possible for a man to understand so much and undertake so much. And as there is such a difference between the working capacity of the ordinary man and that of the president, how much greater the difference between that of the president and God, who is infinitely busier! God is managing the whole universe, down to the most minute detail—*and we are made in His image.* Therefore we cannot make excuses for failure to succeed. Don't be afraid of hard work; it has never hurt anyone. However, one should learn to work—and to think—calmly. When you are

---

* Alaska and Hawaii were not yet states at the time Paramahansaji made this observation. *(Publisher's Note)*

calmly active you can accomplish anything you set out to do, for the mind is clear.

In addition to not working hard enough for success, most people are not mentally active enough. They spend too much time not thinking. It is considered to be relaxation. However, in true relaxation one is calmly active mentally; he may reflect about God, or about a beautiful peaceful scene, or about some pleasant experience. Calm, positive mental activity is revivifying. Yet many people wrongly associate creative effort with strain, and go about it with a tense, nervous attitude.

Moods Get Their Grip on a Vacant Mind

Creative thinking is the best antidote for moods. Moods get their grip on your consciousness when you are in a negative or passive state of mind. The time when your mind is vacant is just the time it can become moody; and when you are moody, the devil comes and wields his influence on you. Therefore, develop creative thinking. Whenever you are not active physically, do something creative in your mind. Keep it so busy that you have no time to indulge in moodiness.

Creative thinking is marvelous—like living in another world. Everyone should develop this power. I think hardly a word of my lecture before I come here; but I get into the consciousness of my subject, and my soul begins to tell me wonderful things. When you are thinking creatively, you don't feel the body or moods; you become attuned with Spirit. Our human intelligence is made in the image of His creative intelligence, through which all things are possible; and if we don't live in that consciousness, we become a bundle of moods. By thinking creatively we destroy those moods; and by thinking creatively we will find all the answers to our problems, and to the problems of others.

Moods are like cancer—they eat into the peace of the soul. That is why the moody man cannot rid himself of his troubles. Remember: no matter how wrong everything has gone for you, you have no right to be moody. In your *mind* you can be a conqueror. When bested, the moody man admits defeat. But the man whose mind remains unconquered, though the world be in cinders at his feet, is yet the victor.

Do you want to be a prisoner or a conqueror? By binding yourself so tightly in moods, you render yourself incapable of going on with the battle of life. As soon as you allow a mood to enwrap your mind, your will becomes paralyzed. Moods befog the brain, and hence impair judgment, so that your efforts are wasted.

Moods Are the Brakes on Your Wheels of Progress

You can conquer your moods, no matter how terrible they seem. Make up your mind that you are not going to be moody anymore; and if a mood comes in spite of your resolve, analyze the cause that brought it on, and do something constructive about it. Don't go on doing things in a state of indifference, if that is your attitude, for indifference is the worst of all moods. At such times, remind yourself that you are not your own creator; God created you, and He is running this universe for you. Whatever your work, do it enthusiastically, for Him. Busy yourself in creative activities, for He has given you infinite power. How dare you make yourself a mental failure by indulgence in the intoxicant of moodiness! Free yourself from these devastating mental states. They are the real brakes on the wheels of your progress. Until you release them, you cannot move on. Every morning, remind yourself that you are God's child, and that no matter what the difficulties, you have the power to overcome them. Heir to the cosmic power of Spirit, you are more dangerous than danger!

An intelligent boy does not care to work on simple problems; he enjoys the challenge of difficult ones. But many people are afraid of life's problems. I have never feared them, for I have always prayed: "Lord, may Thy power increase in me. Keep me in the positive consciousness that with Thy help I can always overcome my difficulties." Think constructively about a problem till you cannot think anymore. When I am solving a problem, I go to the nth degree to cover all possible steps toward its solution, until I can honestly say: "I have done my best, and that is all I can do." Then I forget it.

A person who keeps the worry of a problem in his consciousness becomes moody. Avoid that. When a problem comes up, instead of dwelling on it, think of every possible avenue of action to rid yourself of it. If you are unable to think, compare your particular trouble with others' similar troubles, and from their experiences learn which ways lead to failure and which ways lead to success. Choose those steps that seem logical and practical, and then get busy implementing them. The whole library of the universe is hidden within you. All the things you want to know are within yourself. To bring them out, think creatively.

Magical Effect of Sincere Love

Moods blunt one's feelings and understanding, making it impossible to get along with others. Domestic life should be a temple of heaven, but moods can make it a hades. A husband comes home and finds his wife in a sullen mood, and he can't reason with her. Or he returns from work in a nasty mood, and she can't reason with him. So much trouble comes to people because of moods!

When someone else in your family is seething with anger, or is wholly indifferent, you are affected immediately by his mood. Or perhaps you go to someone in great joy, but he is moody and quarrelsome, and finally he gives you a slap. Immediately your joy vanishes, and you want to retaliate. Do not put on the mood of another. The Bible tells us that if anyone smites us on the left cheek, we should turn the right cheek. How many do that? More often, the person slapped wants to give his assailant twelve slaps in reprisal—and perhaps a kick, or even a bullet! It is easy to strike back, but to give love is the highest way to try to disarm your persecutor. Even if it doesn't work at the time, he will never be able to forget that when he gave you a slap, you gave love in return. That love must be sincere; when it comes from the heart, love is magical. You should not look for the effects; even if your love is spurned, pay no attention. Give love and forget. Don't expect anything; then you will see the magical result.

Do you realize that within you, in your soul, is a superb garden? a wondrous garden of thoughts, fragrant with love, goodness, understanding, and peace, and more beautiful than any earthly flowers that grow. You cultivated a fragrant blossom whenever someone in anger misunderstood you and you continuously gave love to him. Isn't the aroma of that love and understanding more lasting than that of any rose? So always think of your mind as a garden, and keep it beautiful and fragrant with divine thoughts; let it not become a mud pond, rank with malodorous hateful moods. If you cultivate the heavenly scented blooms of peace and love, the bee of Christ Consciousness* will steal into your garden. As the bee seeks out only those flowers that are sweet with honey, so God comes only when your life is sweet with honeyed thoughts. Resolve that in your garden of good soul qualities you will not allow the evil stinkweed of anger to grow. The more you develop flowerlike divine qualities, the more God will reveal to you His secret omnipresence in your soul.

"He who is tranquil before friend and foe alike, and in (encountering) adoration and insult, and during the experiences of warmth and chill and of pleasure and suffering...that person is very dear to Me."† By continuously giving love to those who are unkind, peace to those who are harassed by worries, sweetness to those who are bitter, joy to those who are laden with miseries; and by constantly setting a better example for those who follow the path of error, you destroy moods by keeping the mind creatively busy. If you can't be busy outwardly, be constructively busy inwardly.

Live in a World of Wonder

I often say: If you read for one hour, write for two hours; and if you write for two hours, think for three hours; and if you think for three hours, meditate all the time. God is the repository of all happiness; and you can contact Him in everyday life. Yet man mostly occupies himself in pursuits that lead to unhappiness. Meditation is the best way to destroy moods and live in a world of wonder—a world such as Narada, a great *rishi*, knew when he said: "Lord, I was singing Thy praises, and became lost in Thee. When I came back to this consciousness, I saw that I had slipped from my old body, and You had given me a new one!"

---

* God's omnipresent intelligence, and the attractive force of His love, manifested in creation.

† Bhagavad-Gita XII:18-19.

A similar story is told in India about another saint. A young man had just died. His body had been carried to the cremation grounds and the mourners were preparing to light the fire, when suddenly an old man came running, crying out, "Stop! Don't do it, I will use that body." As soon as he said this, the man's aged body dropped lifeless to the ground, and the young man got up from the pyre and ran off toward the forest. The old man was a great saint; he had simply not wished to interrupt his devotions by taking rebirth in an infant's helpless body.

Fear Enters When God Is Shut Out of Life

There are so many wondrous things to know about life and death, and meditation is the way. Learn to live in this world as a son of God. Death holds terror for man because he has left God out of his life. All painful things frighten us, because we love the world without understanding its mystery and purpose. But when we behold everything as God, we have nothing to fear. We are constantly "born" in life as well as death. The word "death" is a great misnomer, for there is no death; when you are tired of life, you simply take off the overcoat of flesh and go back to the astral world. *

Death means an end. A car whose parts are worn out is dead; it has come to an end. And so at death the physical body comes to an end. But the immortal soul cannot be dead. Every night, in sleep, the soul lives without any consciousness of the physical body; but it is not dead. Death is only a greater sleep, wherein the soul lives in the astral body without the consciousness of the physical body. If loss of physical-body consciousness signified death for man, then the soul would die when we go to sleep. But we are not dead when we are asleep; nor are we completely unconscious, because when we awaken, we remember whether we slept well or not. So, in the after-state of death we do not die.

* The Hindu scriptures state that the soul of man is encased successively in three bodies: the idea or causal body, a subtle astral body, and a gross physical body. The astral world is the subtle realm of finer forces to which the soul, still encased in its causal and astral bodies, retires at physical death to continue its spiritual education and evolution until it incarnates again on earth. (See glossary.)

Those who allow their minds to ossify are truly dying. To solve the mystery of life you must be born anew every day. This means you must strive daily to improve yourself in some way. Above all, pray for wisdom, because with wisdom everything else comes. Be controlled not by moods, but by wisdom. And with that wisdom, develop creative thinking and activity. Keep busy doing constructive things for your own self-improvement and for the benefit of others, for whoever would enter God's kingdom must try also to do good for others every day. If you follow this pattern, you will feel the mood-dispelling joy of knowing you are advancing, mentally, physically, and spiritually. You will surely reach God, for that way leads to the kingdom of heaven.

Strive continuously to overcome moods; for as soon as you feel moody, you are cultivating seeds of error in the soil of your soul. To indulge in moods is to die gradually; but if you try daily to be cheerful in spite of any upsetting experiences, you will have a new birth. Until this human birth becomes transmuted into a highly spiritual birth, you cannot be "born again"* in God.

Moods are "catching," and at times of general depression can affect large numbers of people. Man should not take life's unhappy incidents so seriously. It is better to laugh a little than to make a tragedy of every misfortune. The Gita teaches: "He is dear to me who feels no distinction between the glad and the sad (aspects of phenomenal life), who is free from grief and cravings, and who has banished (the relative consciousness of) good and evil."† To have an optimistic disposition and try to smile is constructive and worthwhile; for whenever you express divine qualities, such as courage and joy, you are being born again; your consciousness is being made new by the manifestation of your true soul nature. This is the spiritual rebirth that enables you to "see the kingdom of God."

---

* "Except a man be born again, he cannot see the kingdom of God.... Ye must be born again" (John 3:3, 7).

† Bhagavad-Gita XII:17.

Reincarnation Can Be Scientifically Proven

Circa 1937

If one believes in the existence of a just God, then a belief in reincarnation can follow very readily, as the two concepts are really dependent on one another. But what about the skeptics and the atheists? Can the truth of reincarnation be scientifically proven to their satisfaction? Can the theory of reincarnation be in any way scientifically experimented with, so as to furnish not only hope, but actual proof, of its reality?

Material scientists claim that they have not found any actual proof of the existence of a God, and hence cannot offer any proof of the existence of His just law, giving equal opportunity to all life to improve through reincarnation. To such scientists, the sufferings of innocent babies and other inequities of life seem inexplicable, and point to the absence of a just Creator.

Scientific Law

On the other hand, most of those who do believe in a just God base their convictions on belief only, and have no scientific proof to offer to unbelievers. They do not dare, for the most part, to scrutinize or deeply question their faith, for fear of losing it or of creating some social inharmony. They are not aware, in other words, of the existence of a scientific spiritual law that can prove their beliefs to be truth.

But why should not spiritual law be investigated by the same methods of experimentation used by the material scientist to discover physical truths? This question was asked centuries ago by the Hindu savants, and they set about the task of answering it. Their experiments resulted in scientific methods that can be followed by anyone to discover the reality of spiritual law, and hence of reincarnation and every other great cosmic truth.

Since the means of proof do exist, no one has a right to say that reincarnation and other spiritual laws do not operate, until he has tried the methods and seen the results for himself. A doubting physical scientist is entitled to express his opinion, but it remains an opinion only, not a fact. In physical science, certain procedures must be adopted and followed in order to prove the truth of any given theory. Germs are not visible to the naked eye; one must use a microscope to detect their presence. If a person refuses to look through the microscope, he cannot be said to have scientifically tested the theory that germs are present. His opinion is therefore valueless, since he has not followed the prescribed rules for arriving at the truth of the theory. So it is in spiritual matters. The method has been discovered, the rules laid down, and the result is open to anyone who is interested enough to experiment. In the Western world, owing to lack of this scientific approach to spiritual law, the value of religion has been greatly diminished as a vital factor in the life of man, and spiritual doctrines are believed in or rejected simply on the grounds of personal bias, rather than as a result of scientific investigation.

How Were the Spiritual Laws Discovered?

How did the spiritual scientists (*rishis*) of ancient India discover these unalterable cosmic laws? Through experiment on the life and thought of man, in the laboratories of their hermitages. To find the truth of physical things, we must experiment with physical substances. So, to find the truth of reincarnation, or the passage of the same soul through many bodies, it is necessary to experiment upon the consciousness of man. These scientists of old found that the human ego persists through all changes of experience and thought during the states of wakefulness, dream, and dreamless sleep during one's lifetime. The cognitive experiences changed, the environment, sensations, thoughts, and bodily states changed, but the sense of identity, of "I," did not change from birth to death. The Hindu experimentalists argued that through concentration on the self, through a constant, conscious, aloof, unidentified introspection or watching of the various changing states of life—of wakefulness, dreaming, or dreamless sleep—that one could perceive the changeless and eternal nature of the self. Ordinarily, one is conscious of his waking state, and sometimes he is conscious also of his dreaming state. It is not uncommon, during a dream, for a person to be aware that he is dreaming. Through certain methods and practices, one can maintain conscious awareness during every state of his being: wakefulness, dreaming, dreamless sleep, and *turiya*, "deep sleep," the ever-awake superconsciousness (the unrestricted region of mind) beyond dreamless subconsciousness.

Relaxation in Sleep

During sleep, there is involuntary relaxation of energy from the motor and sensory nerves. Through practice, one can produce this relaxation during the waking state also, at will. In the big sleep of death, there is total relaxation—the retirement of energy from the heart and cerebrospinal axis. By deep meditation, this complete relaxation may be produced consciously in the waking state. In other words, every involuntary function may be accomplished voluntarily and consciously by practice.

The *rishis* of ancient India analyzed death as the withdrawal of the electricity of life from the bulb of human flesh with its wires of sensory and motor nerves that lead to the different channels of outward expression. Just as electricity does not die when it is withdrawn from a broken bulb, so life energy is not annihilated when it retires from the involuntary nerves. Energy cannot die. It withdraws, upon the occasion of death, into the Cosmic Energy.

Current Withdrawn

In sleep, the conscious mind ceases to operate—the current is temporarily withdrawn from the nerves. In death, the human consciousness permanently ceases to express itself through the body; it is as though one had a paralyzed arm—he is mentally conscious of that arm, but cannot function through it. Medical records describe the case of a clergyman who once fell into a state of suspended animation. He heard everyone around bewailing his apparent death, but could not express his awareness through his physical organs. His body motor had "stalled" and refused to respond to his mental commands. After he had passed twenty-four hours in this state, and was about to be taken away for burial, he made a supreme effort and was able to move. This instance illustrates the constancy of the awareness of "I-ness" or personal identity, even though the body is seemingly lifeless.

The *rishis* taught that one must learn to separate the energy and consciousness from the body, consciously. One must consciously watch the state of sleep, and must practice conscious voluntary withdrawal of energy from the heart and spinal regions. Thus he learns to do consciously what death will otherwise force upon him unconsciously and unwillingly.*

An Amazing Case

There is a case on record, in the files of French and other European doctors, of a man named Sadhu Haridas—in the court of Emperor Ranjit Singh of India—who was able to separate his energy and consciousness from his body and then connect the two again after several months. His body was buried underground and watch was kept over the spot, day and night, for months. At the end of this time, his body was exhumed and examined by the European doctors, who pronounced him dead. After a few minutes, however, he opened his eyes and regained control over all the functions of his body; and lived for many years more. He had learned, by practice, how to control all the involuntary functions of his body and mind. He was a spiritual scientist who experimented with prescribed methods for learning the truth of cosmic law. As a result he was in a position to demonstrate the truth of the theory of the changelessness of personal identity and the eternal nature of the life principle.

* The life energy enters the body at the medulla, is stored in the reservoir of the cerebrum, and then descends into five other centers of life and consciousness in the spine, whence it is distributed to the organs of sensory perceptions and to all other parts of the body. At death, the life energy retires irrevocably into the spine and leaves the body through the medulla. The accomplished yogi can voluntarily and consciously withdraw the life energy from the body and senses into the spine, directing it upward to the highest centers of divine perceptions, where he is joyously aware of being "dead"—freed from sensory delusions of being limited to a purely physical existence.

Those who want to prove for themselves the scientific truth of the doctrine of reincarnation should first prove the principle of continuity of consciousness after death by learning the art of consciously separating the soul from the body.* This can be done by following the rules laid down many centuries ago by the Hindu savants: Learn (1) to be conscious during sleep, (2) to be able to produce dreams at will, (3) to disconnect the five senses consciously, not passively as during sleep, and (4) to control the action of the heart, which is to experience conscious death, or the suspended animation of the body (but not of the consciousness) that occurs during the higher states of superconsciousness.

Follow the Practices

Bhagavan Krishna taught: "The ego is continuously conscious of itself in childhood, youth, and old age; the embodied soul is uninterruptedly conscious not only of these states but also of attaining another body after death (in the long series of 'lives' and 'deaths' that are the ego's alternations between the physical and astral worlds)." †

By following the practices that lead to the four states outlined above, we can follow the ego in all states of existence—we can follow it consciously through death, through space, to other bodies or other worlds. Those who do not learn these things cannot retain their sense of personal identity, of awareness or consciousness, during the big sleep of death, and hence cannot remember any previous state, or even the "deep sleep" states during one life.

By adopting the methods of the ancient Hindu scientists who experimented with such laws, and who thereby gave the world a knowledge that is priceless and demonstrable, one may come to know the scientific truth of reincarnation and all other eternal verities.

* The Christian mystic St. Paul understood and demonstrated this mastery of life and death; he declared: "...I die daily" (I Corinthians 15:31).
† Bhagavad-Gita II:13.

Reincarnation: The Soul's Journey to Perfection

*Self-Realization Fellowship Temple,
Hollywood, California, February 20, 1944*

Reincarnation is the progress of a soul through many lives on the earth plane, as through so many grades in a school, before it "graduates" to the immortal perfection of oneness with God. Souls that are living in an imperfect state (unaware of their divine identity with Spirit) do not, upon the death of the physical body, automatically enter a state of God-realization. We are made in the image of God, but by identification with the physical body, we have put on its imperfections and limitations. Until this imperfect human consciousness of mortality is removed, we cannot become gods again.

A prince ran away from his palatial home and sought shelter in a slum. As a result of intoxication and of mixing with persons of bad character, he gradually lost sight of his true identity. Not until his father found him and took him home to the palace did he remember that he was actually a prince.

Similarly, we are all children of the King of the Universe who have run away from our spiritual home. We have kept ourselves locked up in human bodies for so long that we have forgotten our divine heritage. As often as we have come on earth we have developed new imperfections and new desires. So we come back here again and again until we fulfill all desires; or until, through increase of wisdom, we banish those desires. We must satisfy our desires, or, by cultivating wisdom, do away with them altogether. Very few persons get off the wheel of birth and death by trying to satisfy their desires, however; it is the nature of desire that each time one "satisfies" it, the craving to repeat the experience simply increases its hold, unless one's mind is very strong.*

It is better to satisfy small or unimportant desires, because in that way we can get rid of them. But it is necessary to do so with wisdom and discrimination; otherwise even small desires may come back in a stronger way, reinforced by experience. People who feel a desire to drink, for example, often "reason" thus: "I will have all I want today, and tomorrow I will do without." After several repetitions of this experience, the usual result is that they find they have instilled a habit, and then it is difficult to get rid of it. The same thing may happen with any other desire.

God is not a dictator who has sent us here and is telling us what to do. He has given us free will to do as we please. We hear a great deal about the importance of being good. But if we all go straight to heaven when we die (as some claim), what is the point in trying to do good while we are here? If there is the same reward for everyone at the end of life, why not be a greedy, selfish person, since the path of evil is often the easiest one to take? There would be no use in emulating the lives of great saints if when we die we all—the good and the bad alike—become angels.

On the other hand, if God has it in His plan for us all to go to Hades, again there would be no use in worrying about how we behave in this life. And would there be any value in watching one's actions if our lives are like automobiles—once they become old they are cast on the junk pile and that is the end of them? If that is all there is to man's life, there is no point in reading the scriptures or in exercising self-control.

The Importance of Time

If, however, there is a lofty purpose in living, how may we explain the seeming injustice in a baby's being born dead? What about those who are born blind or dumb or crippled; or who live only a few years and then die? Only the one who lives

---

* "The God-united yogi, abandoning (attachment to) fruits of actions, attains the peace unshakable (because rooted in self-discipline). The man who is not united to God is ruled by desires; through such attachment he remains in bondage" (Bhagavad-Gita V:12).

long has time to struggle against innate wrong tendencies and desires, and to try to be good. If there is no other chance (in a future life) for the little child who dies at six months, why did God give that child a mind and no time in which to develop the potentialities of that mind? The time element is most important in our progress. One life-span only may not afford sufficient time.

If a child dies early in life, there is a reason for that death; and because he did not have enough time in which to express his potential, human or divine, he will be given another opportunity in which to do so. Such a person is like a boy who is sick and cannot go to school. The boy does not leave school forever; as soon as he is well he goes back to school to start his lessons where he left off. So it is with life. If we don't have a chance to learn our lessons in this life, we shall have opportunities to learn them in some other.

When you can see "behind the scenes" you will realize that life on earth is a puppet show. It seems real to us now, but what we are experiencing at this moment will have a dream-like unreality to us a few years hence. And what we are experiencing now would have seemed unreal to us five years ago, had it been described to us then. Last Sunday most of you sat in other seats in the temple, and had other thoughts in your mind. Today we are seeing a different "picture show." Reflect on how many people you have known who are now vanished from this earthly stage.

The concept of life as a changing, passing show is not pessimistic; it should teach us not to take life seriously at all. *Maya*, cosmic delusion, makes us feel that the body is so real, such a necessary part of our being. Yet in a moment the body may be taken away from the soul by death, and the separation is not painful at all. When that "operation" is over, you have no need of time, dress, food, or shelter, for you no longer have to carry this bodily bundle of flesh. You are free of it. And you are still you. Have you ever sought to reason out why this truth is hidden? Or where may be now the millions of people who have gone away from our earth? Have you ever wondered if we are like so many chickens in a coop—when we are gone from the coop we are replaced by another flock? Is there no way to find out?

How We Live This Life Determines What We Are in the Next

We have been given the power to reason out where we go and whence we have come. But we don't take enough pains to analyze ourselves and our lives. Otherwise our common sense would tell us that whatever our character is today it will continue to be after death—perhaps a little better or a little worse, depending on how much effort we are making to improve ourselves. You go along 365 days a year, year after year, and perhaps you have made some progress; but your nature will be the same after death as it was before death. You will not become an angel just because you die! Only the body changes. Death makes no difference, otherwise. Death is like a gate you will pass through. Your body will be gone but you will be in every other respect the same. If you have a violent temper, you will not leave it behind, at death, with your physical body. Your violent temper will remain with you until you conquer it. If in your present life you have observed the laws of healthful living, in your next incarnation you will possess a healthy body. The last portion of life is more important than the first, because what you are at the end of this life is what you will be at the beginning of the next.

The first part of life is usually stupidly misspent, in a sort of bewildered state. Then romance comes, and finally disease and old age; the struggle with the body starts. I have coined a phrase, "patchwork living," to describe how one has to keep on patching and repatching the body to keep it going. The body is a trouble most of the time: a "spark plug" is missing, or the "tires" give out; you have headaches or a cold, or the stomach goes wrong; there is difficulty with the teeth, and so on. Always trouble, trouble! That is why it is so necessary to your happiness that you realize you are not the body, with all its aches and pains, but an immortal soul.

I don't take life seriously at all. I say, "Lord, anytime you want to remove this body from the soul, it is all right. So long as you keep me here, all right; but if I am to be free of the body, that is all right too." It is not necessary to die in order to claim freedom from attachment to the body. If you commune with God you will see that you are already free. You are not the body. You are eternal Spirit.

Is there any way to find out what we were in our last incarnation? Most certainly we can detect basic tendencies of thought and capabilities, by analyzing what we are now. The Hindu scriptures say that it takes a million years of harmonious, disease-free living for the soul to be liberated. Therefore, comparatively little change is to be expected in the ordinary man from life to life. But one's spiritual evolution may definitely be hastened by determined effort in right living and by the help of a true guru.

The sages of India have analyzed mankind as belonging to four basic types: the *Sudras*, those capable of offering service to society through bodily labor; the *Vaisyas*, those who serve through mentality, skill, agriculture, trade, commerce, business life in general; the *Kshatriyas*, those whose talents are administrative, executive, and protective—rulers and warriors; and the *Brahmins*, those of contemplative nature, spiritually inspired and inspiring.

Qualitatively, *Sudras* are those who see in life no greater purpose than the satisfaction of wants and desires of the body; such persons eat, sleep, work, multiply, and finally die. Millions today live in the *Sudra* or "laborer" state—concerned merely with the comfort and pleasure of the body.

The man in the *Vaisya* or mentally active state is always busy getting things done. Some people of this class think of nothing else but business; they live only to earn money, which they usually squander on sense enjoyments. But the best *Vaisya* type of businessman is much more evolved and creative in nature.

The third or *Kshatriya* class are those who, after having had the experience of earning money and of creating something along business lines, begin to understand what life is all about; they strive by self-control to win the battle with the senses. (The *Vaisya* man doesn't engage himself in such effort for inner improvement. He simply earns money and produces children and seldom thinks about the meaning of life except in terms of business.) But the third or *Kshatriya* class takes life more seriously. Such a man asks himself, "Should I not struggle with and destroy my bad habits?" He feels a desire to overcome evil tendencies and to do what is right.

The last and highest state is that of the *Brahmin:* knower of Brahma or God.*

Analyze Yourself to See How You Should Change

To recapitulate the four basic types of consciousness in man: *Sudra* is the sense-bound state of existence; *Vaisya* is the business or creative stage of man. *Kshatriya* is the warrior state, when man desires to do battle with his senses and to conquer his attachment to them. *Brahmin* is the wisdom state, attained by man when he has overcome all attachment to the senses and remains consciously immersed in Brahma, God.

Every human being fits into one of these four classifications, and if you analyze yourself you can find your class. Think over your life from childhood days and try to reason out in which of the four classifications you belong. Reflect on whether you have been living for sense pleasures, only catering to the senses and earning money; or perhaps just working without thinking or acting creatively.

Analyze yourself and see if you have been creative from your childhood. Some children, for example, think readily along mechanical lines, and want to open up and take apart things so that they can put them together again. Others show the greatest pleasure in drawing, or in playing or listening to music. It is not necessary to be an expert or a prima donna in order to consider that one has shown signs of creativity in this life. Even a nonsensical song such as "Yes, We Have No Bananas" is a product of a creative mind.

Anything one creates, whether it is expertly done or not, is an expression of creative talent. A flair for writing novels or for acting or for woodcarving or for painting or for music or for working with machinery, if exhibited early in life, indicates that you were probably in the *Vaisya* state in your past life.

Husbands and wives should not ridicule each other's or their children's creative tendencies. It is a sin against the evo-

* See *caste* in glossary.

lutionary process of God to try to suppress another's creative spirit.

Ask yourself if from childhood you have always tried to perform actions in accordance with the guidance of your conscience. Were you constantly watching your actions and trying to correct yourself when you were wrong? Did you have that struggle within from childhood? That reflects the third or *Kshatriya* state. But if from childhood your thoughts have always been of God, you have entered the fourth or spiritual state of the *Brahmin*.

Recognition of your belonging to one of the less advanced of these four types of mental attitude should not discourage, but encourage you. If upon self-analysis you find that you have not yet attained to the highest state, do not think yourself helplessly unfortunate. The idea is that if you haven't changed yet, it is now time that you should. Otherwise you will carry your present state into the next life too. When death comes you want to feel that you have passed that particular "grade" of life, and that you are free to go on to higher grades. Therefore you should change your life now. Analyze yourself and learn what you were before. Then you can begin to remold your life more ideally.

Learn to check your moods. The violent feelings you may experience in the present were all created in the past. If it were not so, why is it that some children are jealous from the very beginning, while others in the same family are calm and loving? There are children who would strike you if you were to tell them not to do a thing; others are quietly obedient. Another child may steal. Why? These traits are simply outcroppings of prenatal tendencies created in former lives.

I was once given a little baby to hold. I almost dropped it, for God suddenly revealed to me that that baby had been a cruel murderer in a previous life. But ordinarily, the past is a closely guarded secret. You may discover the true details only if the Lord wishes you to know them.

Discern Between Inner Worth and Outer Position

Once, in New York, a woman who was helping with Self-Realization Fellowship office work confided to me that she had met a marvelous man, a "psychic," who had told her wonderful things about herself, including the revelation that in a former life she had been Mary, Queen of Scots. I did not believe she had been that queen, and I silently uttered a little prayer that God would banish her delusion.

A few days later a student came to see me and, with great excitement, said, "I have just met a famous psychic (the same one the office worker had mentioned), who told me that in a past life I was Mary, Queen of Scots." I asked the office worker to come into the room; and, placing the two "queens" face to face, I asked, "Which one of you is the *real* Mary, Queen of Scots?" The ladies, happily, realized their mistake—which was one of undiscriminating credulity and of readiness to confuse true inner worth with conspicuous outer position.

The truth is, we love to be flattered. Unscrupulous persons thus may take advantage of us now and then. But who you were in a previous life and whether or not you were important in the eyes of the world is of little consequence. It is best to be born as a divine or *Brahmin* type, regardless of worldly position. All of you have something of that divine type in you; otherwise you would not be here this morning.

Exchange of Souls Between East and West

Out of millions of people, you have been drawn to this temple, because you have had something to do with the Orient and its spiritual teachings before. Now that you are an Occidental, outwardly, other Occidentals may laugh at you for going to what may seem to them a "heathen" church. Those who feel a prejudice against the East did not recently come from there; but those who feel a leaning toward the East were probably born there in a recent past life. By such indications one can distinguish Oriental and Occidental souls. Did you from early childhood enjoy the fragrance of incense, and stories and pictures of the East? Such inclinations would show that you had been quite recently in contact with the Orient.

Many souls from the East have reincarnated now in America. Desiring material perfection, they have been born here to enjoy the fulfillment of that desire and to help encourage American spiritual ideals. Similarly, many souls that for-

merly were born in America have since reincarnated in India in
order to benefit from her spiritual riches and to help India in
the development of the material side of her civilization. I hope
that many of you may go there to help India, and that many in
India will come here to serve in America. This world is God's
family. He is trying to improve all nations. He has no preference for one over another.

Another test of your past is your preference for certain
sensations. Some people like heat all the time. They have become accustomed, in other lives, to warm climates. Others
like cold better, which shows that they had been born in cold
climates before. If you have always had a special feeling for
the mountains, or the sea, you may be certain you brought that
attachment from another life. There are people who become
lonely if they are out of the city, and cannot stand quiet places.
That attitude too was cultivated in the past.

Those who have a driving ambition throughout life were
important men before. To have that tendency and not develop
it is to suppress oneself. In the proper environment such a person could become a great man. There are others who remain
unsuccessful, no matter what they do to get ahead. This indicates they have carried a failure tendency from the past. But
they should not give up the battle to overcome it. Such persons
must conquer wrong tendencies now or they will manifest
those faults in the next incarnation.

George Eastman once told me that in the early years of his
Kodak company he offered stock for twenty-five cents a share;
still it wouldn't sell. The family of the girl he wished to marry
objected to the match. The adverse circumstances were such
that it seemed he would never become a success; yet, after a
while, everything opened up for him. Why? Because he had
been creative and ambitious before, and he kept on cultivating
those tendencies in this life.

From childhood I wished for large buildings and many
people about me, and for shady trees and water wherever I
might go. And these are what I attract. I also knew from childhood that I would have such things; that when I wished and
worked for it, these places would come easily to me. When I
talked about it, people sometimes laughed skeptically. Never-

theless, such environments have materialized. At our Ranchi school we have a big pond; our Dakshineswar headquarters faces the Ganges River; our Encinitas hermitage overlooks the Pacific Ocean.*

So, through analysis of your present strong tendencies you can pretty accurately surmise what kind of life you led before.

Past Associations Influence Present Affinities

You may find that you have a strong affinity to certain foreign languages and that you are able to learn them quickly. Madame Galli-Curci, for example, amazed me by the ease with which she learned many phrases in Bengali. A love of certain languages is the result of past-life associations. You are attracted to German or French or Chinese or Bengali because you have spoken them before.

Recently I met a young American girl who told me, "I have never studied any Oriental language, but lots of times I hear strange words in my mind. I can say them, but I don't know what they mean." She forthwith said about nine words in Bengali. She had never in this life studied the language, nor had she known anyone who spoke Bengali. Yet she knew these words and pronounced them correctly.

In traveling, you begin to like certain scenes more than others. If some place stands out above all the rest in its attraction for you, you have probably been in that vicinity before.

So by these various clues you may discover certain general ideas about your past lives. From this point on, meditation can bring about a deeper knowledge of what you were before.

Occasionally it happens that you go for the first time to a certain place where you seem to recognize certain scenes; but

---

* The school in Ranchi, Bihar, India, was founded in 1918 on the estate property of the generous-hearted Maharaja of Kasimbazar. The India headquarters of Self-Realization Fellowship—Yogoda Satsanga Society of India—was founded at Dakshineswar, Calcutta, in 1938. The Hermitage overlooking the Pacific Ocean in Encinitas, California, was a gift to Paramahansa Yogananda from Rajarsi Janakananda (James J. Lynn) in 1937. Rajarsi Janakananda, a spiritually exalted disciple of Paramahansa Yogananda, succeeded Paramahansaji as president of Self-Realization Fellowship (Yogoda Satsanga Society of India) in 1952. *(Publisher's Note)*

the people whom you once associated with those scenes are gone. And sometimes you meet people you feel you knew before. With me, recognition has always been instant, especially of those who had been disciples before.*

The following authentic case of remembrance of a past-life experience became world famous. A little girl, born in a small village in India, began inexplicably to pine away for a village in another part of India. Her condition became so serious that a doctor advised that she be taken to the distant village. This was done, and to the amazement of her companions, from the moment she entered the outskirts of the village she began to describe in detail everything in it. She knew people by their names (although she had never before been to this village), and went directly to a certain home where she called a man by name, saying that he had been her brother in her previous life. Nor did she stop there. She explained that in her past incarnation she had hidden some gold pieces in a brick wall of the same house, but that she had died without ever having told anyone about it. The little girl went to the place in the wall, and lo! the gold pieces were there still. She described her clothes and how they had been packed away, and they were found to be exactly as she had said. In the face of such evidence, we are not justified in doubting the genuineness and significance of her experience.

There is another case of a saint in India who went to a certain temple on a riverbank and said: "My temple was near here. It is now in the river." Divers went down, and found under the water a very old temple. This man had been, in a previous life, the saint to whom the now submerged temple had been dedicated.

A Pure Heart—A Clear Insight

If you keep above the consciousness of sex, and make your heart pure, so that when you look at others you will not be conscious of whether they are men or women, you will be able always to recognize at once those souls you have known before. If you have cultivated that impersonal consciousness you

---

* Those who received spiritual initiation from Paramahansa Yogananda in past incarnations. *(Publisher's Note)*

can instantly recognize people you knew before. Suppose you see a six-month-old baby, and then do not see it again until many years have gone by and the baby has become a man. You probably do not recognize that baby in the man. Yet certain features are the same, you would discover, if you had known that baby long enough to fix those features firmly in your mind. So, certain features of our past life remain with us. The eyes especially will be like they were before. Eyes hardly change because they are the windows of the soul. Those whose eyes reflect anger or fear or wickedness should try to change, to remove unlovely qualities that hide and hinder the expression of the beauty of the soul. Owing to the change of environment and company, your mind and body change somewhat. But the eyes change little. You are reborn with the same expression in them.

You can also tell by your inclinations if you were a man or a woman in your past existence. Many women are mannish, and many men want to be like women.

Both man and woman are equal in importance. Reason and feeling are present in both men and women. But in man reason predominates, and in woman feeling predominates. It is easier to influence a man by appealing to his reason than to his feeling; a woman responds more readily to an appeal to her emotions.

By God-communion you bring about the harmony or balance of these two qualities within yourself. I never acknowledge myself to be either man or woman. I feel for others with the love of a mother, but no one can dissuade me by an appeal to my emotions if my reason, or fatherly nature, does not concur. To achieve a divine balance of reason and feeling should be the purpose of both man and woman. Man usually has to cultivate more feeling, and woman has to cultivate more logic.

We Must Perfect Love in at Least One Relationship

There is a deep reason why God does not usually allow us to recall our previous lives. It is because we would be very clannish with those we knew before, instead of expanding our love to encompass others. God wants us to give friendship and love to all, but we must *perfect* it in at least one relationship.

When you meet old friends again, you can perfect your love in relationships with them. A disciple means one in whom the guru perfects the state of divine friendship. Those who follow the guru's wishes are his disciples. The wishes of a true guru are guided by divine wisdom, and if you tune in with his wishes you will become free, as he himself is free.*

Above all, you should learn the most you can from this life, and strive to pass to the highest grade of spiritual development in the school of life. Commune with God. When you can do that, the deficiencies of all lesser grades of living are forgiven. To free yourself from *karma* that binds you to the lesser duties of life, develop wisdom and God-consciousness.

* "If ye continue in my words, then are ye my disciples indeed, and ye shall know the truth, and the truth shall make you free" (John 8:31–32). "Men, devotion-filled, who ceaselessly practice My precepts, without faultfinding, become free from (all) *karma*" (Bhagavad-Gita III:31).

Will Jesus Reincarnate Again?

First Self-Realization Fellowship Temple at
Encinitas, California, November 26, 1939

Many persons predict a second coming of Christ. Others think that the real Christ has yet to come a first time. But Jesus did come on earth, and he went away. These are facts. Had his life been only a myth, as some say, his influence would not have survived for so many centuries. Even though he was crucified, his mission was taken up by people all over the world, because he lived for God.

"Behold, he cometh with clouds; and every eye shall see him."* Because of this passage in the Bible, many sincere persons believe that Christ is literally going to descend out of the clouds to us. The real explanation is metaphysical. When you close your eyes you behold darkness, but behind that darkness is the inner light. The contrast epitomizes the difference between this world and the kingdom of God.

When I close my eyes and concentrate my will, I see Christ in that light;† and every true devotee who is able to penetrate the spiritual eye shall see him. In that inner light I behold Jesus just as clearly as I see another person in this world. Everything perceived in that light is much finer. Wonderful visions of saints come—if you are in earnest, and if you have developed spiritually. Such experiences are not given to those who meditate just for a few minutes and then concentrate on something else. When you really "mean business" with God, and above all, love Him; when you willingly lose sleep in order to persist in your search for Him, then you begin to see divine

---

* Revelation 1:7.

† The light of the spiritual eye between the eyebrows. "The light of the body is the eye: if therefore thine eye be single, thy whole body shall be full of light" (Matthew 6:22).

visions. They are not hallucinations. True visions are emanations of reality.

Divine Justice and the Law of Reincarnation

You may or may not believe in the law of reincarnation; but if this life is the beginning and the end of human existence, it is impossible to reconcile the inequalities of life with a divine justice. Why is one man born in a rich family, whereas another child arrives in a poverty-stricken home, only to die of starvation? Why is one person healthy enough to live 100 years, and someone else sick all the time? Why are Eskimos born in the cold north and other peoples in moderate climates, where the struggle to survive is easier? Why are some babies born blind, or dead? Why? Why? Why? If you were God, would you do such unjust things? What is the use of reading and living according to the scriptures, if life is predestined by a whimsical God who deliberately creates beings with bodies or brains that are imperfect?

According to the law of cause and effect, every action creates a commensurate reaction. Therefore whatever is happening to us now must be a result of something we have done previously. If there is nothing in this life to account for present circumstances, the inescapable conclusion is that the cause was set in motion at some prior time; that is, in some past human existence. Your strongest moods and character tendencies did not begin with this birth; they were established in your consciousness long before. Thus we may understand how some persons show from early childhood certain definite talents, or weaknesses, and so on.

We may understand, too, how the perfect life of Jesus on earth was the result of several previous incarnations in which he had developed self-mastery. His miraculous life as Christ was the result of many past lives of spiritual schooling. He became an *avatar,* * a divine incarnation, because in previous lives as an ordinary human being he fought the temptations of the flesh and conquered. His example gives the rest of mankind definite hope. Otherwise, what chance have we? If God had sent angels to teach us I would say, "Lord, why didn't You

* See glossary.

create me as an angel? How can I emulate beings who were created perfect and who have had no experience with the tests and temptations that You have given me?"

We need for our ideal a being who is essentially like us. Jesus *had* temptations to face. "Get thee behind me, Satan," he said. And he conquered. Had he never known temptation, his saying, "Get thee behind me, Satan," would have been play-acting, and how could that inspire us? Although he had already conquered the flesh in other lives, he had to feel its weaknesses again in his incarnation as Jesus, to show humanity by his mastery how high he had grown spiritually, and to give heart to all men by his example.

Jesus Was Eliseus in His Former Life

Jesus attained most of his perfection in his former incarnation as Eliseus (Elisha). I know for certain that he was Eliseus in a past life, and that Jesus' guru, John the Baptist, was Elijah (Elias), in his former life.* Eliseus' later incarnation as Jesus was foretold several hundred years before the event, because he was destined to fulfill a divine plan of God's. That prophecy is told in the Book of Isaiah (7:14), eight centuries before Christ: "Therefore the Lord himself shall give you a sign: Behold, a virgin shall conceive, and bear a son, and shall call his name Immanuel." St. Matthew, recording the event of Christ's birth, stated: "Now all this was done, that it might be fulfilled which was spoken of the Lord by the prophet, saying, Behold, a virgin shall be with child, and shall bring forth a son, and they shall call his name Emmanuel, which being interpreted is, God with us."†

Jesus had learned all of life's lessons in this school of many incarnations, and had demonstrated his complete victory over material consciousness. That is why the Heavenly Father said of him, "This is my beloved Son, in whom I am well pleased."‡

Jesus was sent on earth as an example, that God's other children might know one who had overcome the delusions of this world. Great as he was, Jesus nonetheless said humbly: "I

---

* Referring to John the Baptist, Jesus said, "And if ye will receive it, this is Elias, which was for to come" (Matthew 11:14).

† Matt. 1:22–23.   ‡ Matt. 3:17.

do nothing of myself; but as my Father hath taught me."* His entire love was for God. His whole consciousness was absorbed in the Father.

We are all children of God. Many incarnations ago He created us as He created Jesus. In the Gospel of St. John we find Jesus himself declaring: "Is it not written in your law, I said, Ye are gods?"† Jesus was made in the image of God, as are we; and he conquered delusion, showing us how to do likewise. If you conquer delusion in this life you will go back to God and reincarnate no more. "Him that overcometh will I make a pillar in the temple of my God, and he shall go no more out."‡

But will Jesus come again? Metaphysically, he is already omnipresent. He smiles at you through every flower. He feels his cosmic body in every speck of space. Every movement of the wind breathes the breath of Jesus. Through his oneness with the divine Christ Consciousness he is incarnate in all that lives. If you have eyes to behold, you can see him enthroned throughout creation.

One who is liberated, as Jesus is, becomes one with Spirit. Yet he retains his individuality; for once God has created a human being, He keeps in His cosmic consciousness a permanent record of that creation. Every thought and action of every creature is recorded in the consciousness of God. Jesus referred to this when he said, "Are not five sparrows sold for two farthings, and not one of them is forgotten before God?"§

Christ Comes in Vision and in the Flesh to His Devotees

Jesus as an individual personality can reincarnate in two ways: in vision and in the flesh. If you have great devotion you can see him inwardly exactly as he appeared when he lived on earth. A number of saints have thus beheld him and have relived with him various events of his life.

Jesus can reincarnate again at any time, in the physical body or in the inner light, according to your devotion and power of concentration. Reincarnation is forced upon most of humanity, but because Jesus has freed himself he can come or not, as he wishes. He can appear to you in flesh and blood right now if you have that complete devotion which is necessary to

* John 8:28. † John 10:34. ‡ Rev. 3:12. § Luke 12:6.

attract him; but he will not come so long as your devotion is even one percent less than that.

Years ago, when I was living and teaching in Boston, I once became so busy that I forgot God for three days. The thought of continuing like that was intolerable; I was preparing to pack up everything and leave America. But just then a student of this path came by and asked to meditate with me. As we sat there in meditation I began to pray: "Lord, I love Your work here in America, but I love You more than the work, and if I am going to forget You in this country I will leave." Inwardly I heard the voice of God: "What do you want?"

Impulsively I said, "I would like to see Krishna and Christ with all their disciples." Instantly I beheld them, on a sea of gold, just as clearly as I am seeing you; and I worshiped them.

But in a little while my mind began to doubt. "This is not real," I thought. So I prayed again: "Lord, if the vision is true, let the other devotee in this room also see it." My friend suddenly cried out, "Oh! Krishna and Christ, on a sea of gold!"

Then a new doubt arose: was it only thought transference? But even as this idea crossed my mind, the voice of God said: "When I leave, the room will become filled with the fragrance of the lotus, and whoever comes shall notice it." Each person who later visited me in that room unfailingly asked, "What is this strange fragrance of flowers that I smell?"

For most of his followers Christ exists as an ideal personage they have read about in the Bible. But to me he is much more than that. He is real. Once, eight years ago, he came alone and meditated with me all night long. During that time I saw a vision of the Hermitage.* Many other times I have seen him in visions, and talked with him. And that same Christ you too can see.

You must be prepared to give up everything for communion with God. He will test you. When you pray and pray and meditate and still you don't see Him, but say, "Lord, it doesn't matter, You know that I am praying and I am not going to stop

---

* This talk was given in 1939; the Hermitage in Encinitas was built in 1936. Here Paramahansaji tells us that he saw the Hermitage in a vision in 1931. *(Publisher's Note)*

until You come"—then He will respond. One saint said, "I don't care when He comes—I know He *will* come." That is the attitude one must have.

When you make up your mind to work to attain the Christ consciousness that Jesus had, God will help you to fulfill that desire. But first you must attain self-mastery, even as Jesus did. God does not bestow great spiritual powers on devotees until they show Him they have conquered their human weaknesses. Otherwise they might hurt other persons, even destroy whole nations, by misuse of the divine might.

Jesus had sovereign power; he could easily have saved himself from crucifixion, but during the agony in the Garden he only said, "Father, not my will, but thine, be done,"* and on the Cross, "Father, forgive them; for they know not what they do."† In those final tests he showed he had wholly conquered all ego-impulses. When you have unlimited power, as Jesus did, and when everyone spurns you and still you do not retaliate, you are a conqueror indeed.

All Great Avatars Will Come Again

Every saint who has come on earth has contributed toward the fulfillment of God's desire for the spiritual upliftment of all His human children. The great ones come with two purposes: to inspire and enlighten a certain number or a large mass of people; and to train real disciples, those who pattern their lives after the master's. The latter are the members of the saint's true "family," constituting an inner group in whom he plants his spiritual life. Jesus had twelve such disciples—and others too—but one of the twelve betrayed his love and trust. The most difficult task for every God-ordained spiritual teacher is to produce others like himself, but Jesus made genuinely Christlike disciples.

Every spiritually enlightened teacher tries to enable many devotees to commune with God. Yet each great master nevertheless leaves some "unfinished symphony." Because it remains unfinished, that teacher has to come back again; but the time depends on God's will. What I am telling you is not in any book, nor is it anyone else's idea; but it is true.

* Luke 22:42.   † Luke 23:34.

Jesus often healed others, but they didn't always appreciate it. And he tired of healing their physical ills; he wanted men to know God. He sought only their highest good, but they crucified him; and so not all of his desire for their spiritual development was fulfilled. That is why he has to come back again. Great ones such as he return to earth to take more souls to God. Even though they have attained their own perfection, their desire for others' happiness and perfection has not been fulfilled. They want to bring their lost brothers back to God.

When you pray to Jesus he feels your prayer. Free souls such as Jesus are aware of the calls of their devotees. You may not know they are receiving the vibrations of your feelings, but they are. And when your loving demand is very strong, the great ones come to you.

Their desire is to redeem the whole earth, because every saint of God-realization knows there is no death for him. He is living in that Eternal Joy. Yet such saints are aware of the world's grief. They say to the Heavenly Father, "People are killing one another and suffering in many other ways. Why must this be?" And God says: "I will send you back sometime to help them."

The God-ordained saviors of mankind have to return to earth again, but when they will come, no one can say. Thus many people believe in Christ's second coming; but when it may happen depends on the will of God. The great ones come only with the permission of the Heavenly Father. In some cases, when the time is set, the prophets speak of it; but other *avatars* come unannounced. Just the same, they come. I too wish to come, again and again.

> I want to ply my boat, many times,
> Across the gulf-after-death,
> And return to earth's shores from my home in Heaven.
> I want to load my boat
> With those waiting, thirsty ones who are left behind,
> And carry them by the opal pool of iridescent joy
> Where my Father distributes
> His all-desire-quenching liquid peace.*

* From Paramahansa Yogananda's poem, *God's Boatman.*

It will be a wonderful thing to come to help all, and that is the way everyone should want to live on this earth. Why seek selfish gain? If we are known to God, we become known to His children, for in God we are all one. It is so important that we find Him! For our own sake we must know His love and be immersed in Him—night and day one continuous joy, unending happiness.

Great souls will reincarnate again. God gave them individuality and a divine role to play for Him. They have to do their work because they love God. They will come, because there are hosts of brothers in this world who are stumbling in the mud of delusion and suffering. The great ones have to come again, as Jesus too will come again, to take more souls to the kingdom of Heaven.

The Dream Nature of the World

Self-Realization Fellowship international headquarters,
Los Angeles, California, December 23, 1937

It is only when we wake from dreams that we know we have been dreaming. Similarly, this life may be realized as a dream only when we awake in Cosmic Consciousness.

During waking consciousness, the thought of a beautiful landscape does not carry with it an immediate power of materialization. But in sleep we have a heightened creative power of visualization and manifestation; our thoughts swiftly erect the various structures of a dream. The projection of dream images requires both thought and energy, just as the projection of moving pictures requires both film and the electrical energy of light.

In sleep, life energy is released from various bodily demands and retires to the brain cells, in which are stored the thought films of all past experiences. The enlivening action of the energy on the stored-up thought films in the subconscious mind results in the projection of the mental motion pictures we call dreams. Dreams are actually lessons in the working of Cosmic Consciousness. They come to man for a reason; their purpose is to awaken in him a realization of the dream nature of the universe and of the method of its operation.

The sages of India since ancient times have spoken of the universe as a materialization of the thought of God. It is easy to say, of course, that this universe is a dream. But the verisimilitude of "life" in our everyday experiences makes it nearly impossible for us to believe that the world is nothing more than a cosmic dream. It is necessary that we first develop mind power in order to be able to realize that the universe is actually made out of the thought of God and that, like a dream, it is structurally evanescent.

We know that thoughts are invisible. But in dreamland they may be made visible by the force of energy. So originally this whole universe—in the form of God's thoughts—was invisible, hidden within the cosmic stream of consciousness. Only when those thoughts were crystallized by God's cosmic intelligent vibration, or energy, did they become visible to us as the material universe.

So, although it is difficult to realize that this cosmic dream universe *is* merely a dream, we should endeavor to think along this line. Many practical benefits will come to us from such a true understanding of the physical world.

To illustrate, let us say that a sleeping man dreams he is a great and powerful warrior; that he goes to war, is shot, and lies dying. Just as he is feeling very sad, he suddenly wakes up. He laughs at his dream fears as he realizes he is not really a warrior, nor is he dying.

In "real" life one may have the same kind of experience. A soldier who goes to war and is mortally wounded suddenly wakes up in the astral world and realizes that the war experience was all a bad dream—that he has neither broken bones nor a physical body. Nevertheless, he is still conscious of life and of his individuality.

In order to realize that all the happenings of this world are dream experiences, we should learn how to visualize our thoughts—how to recharge them with the energy of concentration until they become visible manifestations. Proper visualization by the exercise of concentration and will power enables us to materialize thoughts, not only as dreams or visions in the mental realm, but also as experiences in the material realm.

Matter Originates in Thought

Starting with the power of his creative imagination, man has built wonderful scientific devices and a marvelous material civilization. Inventions are the result of the materialization of human thought. Many people try to achieve something in the realm of thought, but they give up when difficulties arise. Only those persons who have visualized their thoughts very strongly have been able to manifest them in outward form. Everything on earth had its birth in the factory of the mind—either in God's mind or in man's mind. Actually, man cannot think an "original" thought. He can only borrow God's thoughts and become an instrument to materialize them.

Experiment with your thoughts. Try out your strongest thoughts on your body. See if you cannot overcome undesirable habits and persistent ailments. When you are successful you may apply your thought to make changes in the world around you.

The relationship between thought and matter is very subtle. Suppose you see a wooden pillar, and try, by the power of thought, to remove the pillar. You cannot do that. In spite of what you think, the pillar is still there. It is a materialization of someone's previous thought. It will not go away merely by your thinking it is not there. Only when you *realize* it as a materialization of thought may you dematerialize it to your consciousness. As you learn by experimenting with overcoming habits, pain, and so on, you will begin to understand that the entire design of the body and all its processes are controlled by thought.

One may gather great wisdom by cultivating the consciousness that this world and everything in it is only a dream. First of all, do not take your earth experiences too seriously. The root-cause of sorrow is in viewing the passing show with emotional involvement. If you continually think to yourself, "I haven't lived as I ought to have lived," you only make yourself miserable. Rather, do your best to be better; and no matter what difficulties come, ever affirm, "It is all a dream. It will soon pass." Then no trouble can be a great trial to you. No happenings of this earth can in any way torture you.

The consciousness of pain also has to be overcome if you are to know that the world is only a dream. When I was a child I was hurt frequently when playing football, and whenever I dreamed of playing football I always dreamed that I was hurt. That fear-thought of being hurt had become rooted in my subconscious mind, so that I suffered dream injuries even in sleep!

So one should not take his troubles too seriously, lest they darken the subconscious mind. Difficulties come to us in order to awaken us to the realization that this life is a dream. This lesson we all have to learn. Then we can understand why there is so much difference in everything in the world: some people are poor, some are rich; some are healthy and some are sick. Although it may seem to be a terrible and cruel game, the justification of the complications of life is that all of it is only a dream. Take it as such.

Think of the many aspirations and hopes you entertained as a child and as a youth. They have gradually left you, but do not be discouraged; always believe that, whatever is coming, it will simply be another scene in the dream movie of God that is being shown in the playhouse of our minds. We have to behold dream tragedies and dream comedies that we may be variously entertained. If you can go to a movie and see a picture of war and suffering, and afterward say, "What a wonderful picture!" so may you take this life as a cosmic picture-show. Be prepared for every kind of experience that may come to you, realizing that all are but dreams.

Each human life constitutes a drama; and the events of each day represent a drama. You are living a fresh one each of the year's 365 days. The thought that you are merely a player in these dramas is very comforting. Realize that the acting out of whatever part you are called upon to play does not affect your real being. At the end of every earthly incarnation you are the same—the immortal soul—untouched by sickness, sorrow, or death. "The man who is calm and even-minded during pain and pleasure, the one whom these cannot ruffle, he alone is fit to attain everlastingness."*

Pride Is the Greatest Barrier to Wisdom

The experiences of my life have intensified my conviction that human pride is the greatest barrier to wisdom. Egotistical pride must go. It is a blind that prevents our seeing God as the sole Doer, the Director of the Cosmic Drama. You are playing different parts in this cosmic movie-house, and you may not foresee what part will be assigned to you tomorrow. You should be prepared for anything. Such is the law of life. Why sorrow, then, over life's experiences? If you take every happen-

* Bhagavad-Gita II:15.

ing as you would if you were seeing someone else playing it in a motion picture, you will not grieve. Play your 365 roles each year with an inward smile and with the remembrance that you are only dreaming. Then you will never again be hurt by life.

You have played many roles through many incarnations. But they were all given to entertain you—not to frighten you. Your immortal soul cannot be touched. In the motion picture of life you may cry, you may laugh, you may play many parts; but inwardly you should ever say, "I am Spirit." Great consolation comes from realization of that wisdom.

You cannot expect to wake up from the delusion that earth life is real merely by running away into the forest. You have to play out to the end the part that is given you. Each human being is contributing to the enactment of the motion picture of the cosmos. If you want to be happy you should play out your part with dignity, assurance, and happiness. When you are awake in God He will show you that you are unchanged, even though you have played countless parts in His earth drama.

Dissociate Yourself from Your Experiences

Think of it! Of the fifteen hundred million people who have died every hundred years, each one has played a definite part in this cosmic motion picture. In fact, each human being has played in addition a separate "home movie," his own private motion picture. If you were to multiply all the motion-picture lives portrayed by those millions of beings, you wouldn't be able to count them. But this show has a purpose: that you learn how to play the various parts of the life movie without identifying your Self with your role. It is important to avoid identification with pain or anger or any kind of mental or physical suffering that comes. The best way to dissociate yourself from your difficulty is to be mentally detached, as if you were merely a spectator, while at the same time seeking a remedy.

Don't expect to attain unalloyed peace and happiness from earthly life. This should be your new attitude: no matter what your experiences are, enjoy them in an objective way, as you would a movie. You have to find true peace and happiness within yourself. Your outer experiences should be only fun. You can convert all of them into miserable ones if you allow your mind to do so. You may have good health and not appreciate it at all. But if you become unwell, then you will appreciate what it is to have health. Show gratitude to God for what He bestows on you, without waiting for reverses to make you grateful.

You are a child immortal. You have come on earth to entertain and to be entertained. This is why life should be a combination of both meditation and activity. If you lose your inner balance, that is just the time when you are vulnerable to worldly suffering. Don't disgrace the name of God, the One in whose image you are made. Awaken the innate fortitude of the mind by affirming, "No matter what experiences come, they cannot touch me. I am always happy."

When I look back and compare, I find that life was much simpler at the time we started our first hermitage (in a little mud hut in India that we had rented for one rupee) than it is now, when we have the responsibility of maintaining this large institution. Yet I preserve my mental balance no matter what trials come. Learn to laugh at difficulties by remembering that you are immortal: "Killed many times, I yet live; born many times, I am yet changeless." Whether you are suffering in this life, or smiling with opulence and power, your consciousness should remain unchanged. If you can accomplish even-mindedness, nothing can ever hurt you. The lives of all great masters show that they have achieved this blessed state.

In order to be able to say with realization that all things are in the mind, you must first develop an inner consciousness of divine peace that remains unruffled by the experiences of this earth. Accept them as you would dreams; and the time will come when you will find that, just by the power of your strong thought, whatever you think will materialize. This is very difficult to do, but it can be done.

A scientist must busy himself with going through several experiments in order to arrive at one fact. But the spiritually developed man is able to perceive the fact without going through a physical process. If you first become one with God, then whatever you think can be materialized. This truth was demonstrated many times by Jesus. He had realized his unity with God.

Concentrate First on God

One's first concentration should be on union with God. Every day as you go through various earthly situations, mentally practice your oneness with God. If a pain comes along to disturb that consciousness you should reason, "Well, if I were asleep I wouldn't feel this pain; why should I be aware of it now? All experiences are fleeting dreams." Practice overcoming all trials in this manner.

The first state of concentration is to be able to see in your mind's eye anything that you wish. For example, I can keep looking at this room and concentrating upon it until, when I close my eyes, I can still see the room exactly as it is. This is the first step in deep concentration, but most people haven't the patience to practice it. I had the patience.

As you continue to practice visualization you will find that your thoughts become materialized. The cosmic law will so arrange it that whatsoever you are thinking of will be produced in actuality, if you command it to be so.

Suppose I am thinking of an apple, and the apple appears in my hand. That would be a demonstration of the highest power of concentration. The great ones can materialize anything right before your eyes, as did Babaji when he materialized a palace at the time of Lahiri Mahasaya's initiation in the Himalayas.* That was an expression of the power of concentration in its highest form. Nothing worthwhile may be gained without effort and without concentration.

* See *Autobiography of a Yogi*, chapter 34. Nikola Tesla, renowned electrical scientist and inventor, understood the possibility of direct materialization. He wrote:

"Long ago he (man) recognized that all perceptible matter comes from a primary substance, or a tenuity beyond conception, filling all space, the *Akasa* or luminiferous ether, which is acted upon by the life-giving *Prana*, or creative force, calling into existence, in never-ending cycles, all things and phenomena.

"Can man control this grandest, most awe-inspiring of all processes in nature? Can he harness her inexhaustible energies to perform all their functions at his bidding, more still cause them to operate simply by the force of his will?

"If he could do this, he would have powers almost unlimited and supernatural. At his command, with but a slight effort on his part, old worlds would disappear and new ones of his planning would spring into being. He could fix,

Don't be sensitive about the body and material concerns, nor let anyone hurt you. Keep your consciousness aloof. Give goodwill to all, but develop a state of consciousness wherein nobody can ruffle you. Try to make others happy every day. Share your wisdom with others. Do not permit yourself to lose interest in life. Learn everything about one thing, and something about everything. Realize that the more you seek, the more you will find; the realms of thought are infinite. The moment you think you have attained everything, you have circumscribed yourself. Search on and on, continuously, and in the valley of your humbleness will gather the ocean of God's wisdom.

The greatest thing you can do to cultivate true wisdom is to practice the consciousness of the world as a dream. If failure comes, say, "It is a dream." Then shut off the thought of failure from your mind. In the midst of negative conditions, practice "opposition" by thinking and acting in a positive, constructive way. Practice *titiksha*, which means not to give in to unpleasant experiences, but to resist them without becoming upset mentally. When sickness comes, follow hygienic laws of living, without permitting your mind to be disturbed. Be unruffled in everything you do. If you try hard to cultivate the dream-opposite of whatever trials you may be going through, you will be able to change a nightmarish situation into a beautiful experience. This freedom of mind will come when you realize that solids, liquids, and all other forms of matter are expressions of God's thought.

The best way to find true freedom is to meditate deeply. You can learn how to meditate by studying the truths in the

---

solidify, and preserve the ethereal shapes of his imagining, the fleeting visions of his dreams. He could express all the creations of his mind on any scale, in forms concrete and imperishable.

"To create and to annihilate material substance, cause it to aggregate in forms according to his desire, would be the supreme manifestation of the power of Man's mind, his most complete triumph over the physical world, his crowning achievement, which would place him beside his Creator, make him fulfill his ultimate destiny."—Copyright 1944 by J. J. O'Neill. From the book, *Prodigal Genius*, published by Ives Washburn Inc. Reprinted with permission of the David McKay Company Inc., New York.

Self-Realization Fellowship Lessons. No one else can convey to you the taste of sugar; you have to taste it yourself.

Yesterday I was sitting in my room, looking back over my life, and I realized that everything in the outer world that had promised great happiness had deceived me; but one thing has never deceived me—my inner peace. Indescribable billows of happiness surge over my soul. As I passed through various experiences over the years, that unchanging inner peace has been proof to me of the existence of God.

I was just thinking this when suddenly I saw a great Light. Everything else vanished. There was feeling—that was all. My hand was not a hand, but a feeling. When I touched my hands together there was no flesh there, only feeling. Then I understood that I had become thoughts; everything around me, the light and the room and the weight of the body—all were nothing but thoughts.

It was a delightful experience. Gone were the sorrow and sadness I had felt for things past, and in their place a great sense of freedom.

That consciousness of God-peace is never-ending. It is the only real state of happiness. Everything else will fail you. Nothing else can make you happy because only the joy of His presence is real.

It is not necessary to go through every kind of human experience in order to attain this ultimate wisdom. You should be able to learn by studying the lives of others. Why become helplessly involved in an endless panorama of events in order to discover that nothing in this world can ever make you happy?

One may learn the truth in two ways: by undergoing many good and bad experiences, or by cultivating wisdom. Choose which you prefer. Krishna said: "The attainment of wisdom immediately bestows supreme peace."* Jesus said: "Seek ye first the kingdom of God."† If you are seeking something else first, you will surely be disillusioned. Each man rationalizes, "Well, others have been deceived, but I won't be." Nevertheless, he will be deceived. The only experience that is real, the only experience that brings happiness, is awareness of the presence of God.

* Bhagavad-Gita IV:39.   † Matthew 6:33.

God's Nature in the Mother and the Father

PART ONE: THE MOTHER

*Self-Realization Fellowship Temple, San Diego, California,
Mother's Day, May 11, 1941*

Today let us hold a grateful thought for all good mothers who have nurtured their children with affection. If children would reflect on the love shown them by the mother, they would feel a desire to give similar affection to all the children of the world. May all sons and daughters who have been nurtured by a mother's love be themselves filled with a mother's affection, which is unconditional love, and express it toward others. Thus shall they solace the world with peace and bring heaven on earth.

The mother's love is not given to us to spoil us with indulgence, but to soften our hearts, that we may in turn soften others with kindness, and free struggling souls from the hard knots of bondage to the world. Those who are helplessly shackled by sin and dire difficulties need our tenderness and love.

My sincere and complete devotion to my earthly mother was the first cause of my love for the Divine Mother. Thus it was my great love for my mother that led to my illumination.

In India we like to speak of God as Mother Divine, because a true mother is more tender and forgiving than a father. The mother is an expression of the unconditional love of God. Mothers were created by God to show us that He loves us with or without cause. Every woman is to me a representative of the Mother. I see the Cosmic Mother in all. That which I find most admirable in woman is her mother love. Those who think of woman as an object of lust perish in that fire; but those who look upon all women as incarnations of the Mother Divine find

246

in them a sacredness that is inviolable. When you can see every woman as your mother, as some of our God-realized masters in India did, universal love comes into your heart.

Certain skeptical followers of a great saint wanted to test him, and sent to him some beautiful prostitutes. He quickly jumped up and cried: "Mother Divine, in these forms You have come to me. I bow to you all." The women knelt before him and were ashamed. From that moment they were spiritually changed.

Every man who looks upon woman as an incarnation of the Immortal Mother will find salvation. A husband should see in his wife the pure beauty of the Mother Divine. Looking upon the wife as the Mother, he will find in her a holy essence not discerned before.

Mothers would not be able to love their children if God hadn't implanted that love in them. Yet credit belongs to the instrument also, because the flood of divine love passes through the human mother. All the great masters have shown honor to their mothers. *Swami Shankara,* * after the death of his mother, disregarded the monastic injunctions against performing ceremonial family rites and cremated her body in a divine flame that he caused to emanate from his hand.

A home is made gracious by the presence of the Divine Mother in the form of the human mother. Isn't that a thought to remember? Do not forget it. Love for the Mother must be constantly cultivated in your heart, so that whenever you see a woman, you behold her as your mother. If you look upon woman without lust of the eyes, you will be able to draw from her store of spiritual treasures.

Why was the mother given such love? That she might love her child unconditionally. Loving one's own child is only a practice of the love divine. The mother thinks it is her own child, but it is the child of God. The child will be taken away as soon as the Divine Spirit calls. So every mother should extend that love she feels for her child unto all the children of the earth.

* Lord Shankara's *Prayer to the Divine Mother for Forgiveness of Sins* bears the refrain: "Though bad sons are many, never has there been a bad mother."

A mother is expected to look after her son, and a son is told to honor his mother; but I say that a son should not only love his mother but should look on all women as expressions of the Divine Mother.

Each mother should remember that the divine unconditional love is passing through her and she is blessed. She should realize that it is not her own love she gives, but the love of the Mother Divine in her. She should be proud of her children, but should not limit herself by bestowing love only on her own sons and daughters. A mother should give divine unconditional love to all. This is my message for you today.

Mothers, be proud that the Divine Mother took your form to give love tangibly to the world, not only to your children but unto all children of the earth. Then you will be really blessed; and instead of thinking that you have one child, or five children, you will realize, "I have many children all over the earth." In that awareness you are one with the Divine Mother.

The mother who looks upon all God's children as her own is no longer a mortal mother. She becomes the Mother Immortal. This is what all women saints are. One day they realize: "The great love that I feel for my child I now feel for all. Now I know that I am not this body, but an expression of the Cosmic Mother." Think what you can do! From an ordinary woman to Divine Mother! And why not? The Universal Mother made you in Her image and you should manifest that image by bestowing on all beings Her illimitable love.

PART TWO: THE FATHER

Self-Realization Fellowship Temple, Hollywood, California, Father's Day, June 18, 1944

On this Father's Day we affirm our fealty to the Heavenly Father. While the human father's love is not always unconditional, still his love is guided by wisdom, regard for law, and the will to protect others. The Divine Father of wisdom, law, and protection, who is represented in all good human fathers, we honor today.

A father should remember he is not just a human parent; he is a representative of the Heavenly Father. To that Cosmic Father I pay tribute. It is He who is behind all fathers. Each father should therefore realize that he has a responsibility to behave properly, for the transparent light of Spirit cannot flow through him if his mind is darkened with delusion and erroneous thoughts. He must keep himself pure, for it is through him and through all other fathers that the Heavenly Father looks after the children of earth.

A human father's body and mind ought to be a temple of the Divine Father. As an instrument of the Divine Being, the father plays his greatest creative role when he implants in his children thoughts that will lead to God-realization.

To produce offspring is not a unique accomplishment; the animals do that. But to produce children on the plane of divine love and in a spiritual consciousness is an important achievement. Even animals may be bred to order; yet many human children are born out of passion and accident, emotion and evil. How can they be pure and perfect? The perpetrators of thefts and other crimes are usually children who were born out of passion, although sometimes there is a good soul here and there.

Example Is the Best Teacher

Character building should be taught in schools and colleges, but fathers should realize that example is more important than schooling. One should not tell his children, "Do not do as I do, but do as I say." If you do not want a child to smoke, you yourself should not smoke. If you want a child to be mild and noble of speech, you should not talk to your wife impatiently, because the child notices your example. Be kind in word and thought because it is the Heavenly Father who has taken your form to look after the child.

Let every father remember, when tempted to speak to a child with dictatorial harshness, "Because my voice is meant to be used by the Cosmic Father, I should never allow Satan, the father of ignorance, to speak through me with mean, unreasoning sternness. I should always guide my children with the loving persuasiveness of truth. My mind should be a transparent glass through which shines the Heavenly Father's light of wisdom."

We should use the wisdom of the Father-God and the love of the Mother-God to bring peace on earth. A good father could never bring himself to kill his children; and if all fathers filled their hearts with the love of the Divine Father, who cares for His children of all nations, how could there be any war? Love is the spiritual weapon with which to end all war.

To the Lord I have dedicated my voice, my eyes, my hands, my feet, my heart, my body, my feelings, my will—my being. I say to all fathers: "When you destroy the ego, you will realize the protecting nature and wisdom of the Heavenly Father working through you."

Looking at Creation
with Seeing Eyes

Self-Realization Fellowship international headquarters,
Los Angeles, California, August 17, 1939

Marvelous indeed is the Lord's universe. Within it He is working all His wonders of creation. Do not be a walking "dead man" in this world; observe, analyze, and appreciate what God and His agent, man, have wrought here. How intricate is the universal mechanism! Reflect on the way we are made, and in what orderly fashion the whole machinery of creation runs according to cosmic law.

We all see the flowers and enjoy their beauty, but who knows what is causing the flowers? Anything one uses or sees every day—be it a handkerchief, a musical instrument, a house, or a tree—he should question and ponder by what means, of what substance, it is made. Cars are taken for granted; but if you were to visit the factories in which they are produced, you would realize how complicated automobiles are. Consider too what went into making the paper for the daily news, and the intricate machinery that imprints it—no human hand could operate so fast.

And if the creation of everyday man-made objects can be so complex, how vastly more complicated the creation of plants, animals, and human beings! It takes ten years' study of medical science to understand the composition, functions, and requirements of the seemingly simple human body. Even a casual analysis reveals much to wonder at—though I sometimes think God could have made a few improvements!

When a plant is growing in water in a glass jar, one can see that its roots are like hairs. Through the God-given intelligent energy in the roots the plant draws from soil and water the food it requires for growth. Like an upturned plant, man similarly absorbs through his hair electric currents helpful to the body.*

Is it not amazing that the sap which feeds the leaves of the plant flows upward against the pull of gravity? When the skin of the plant is removed, one can see the intricate network of tubes that channel this sap. That which carries on this process of sustenance and growth is the mystery called life. When I am in the ecstasy of God-consciousness, I behold this life in even a blade of grass. Little did I dream that I would be able to see such hidden marvels of creation! To concentrate on these marvels is to stand in awe of what the Lord has done.

With calculated precision God has ordained the structural form of each living thing, and the requirements for maintaining that form in good working order. If there is any deficiency in those requirements—food, for example—plants, animals, and human beings suffer. The average person draws from his food all the various chemical elements his body needs; but there are many dietary transgressors whose meals do not contain all the required elements, or the correct balance of them. Improper nourishment is one of the main causes of all sickness in man. The effects of dietary deficiency can be seen almost immediately in a plant when some necessary chemical is omitted from its food.

There are vital exchanges between man and all other living things. For eons India has had the custom of cremation and scattering the ashes of the dead. In this and other ways man feeds Mother Earth, and her plants in turn feed man.

The reciprocity between man and trees is well known. Man inhales oxygen and exhales carbon dioxide.† Trees absorb

---

* "The physical body, with roots of hair, cerebrospinal trunk, nerve branches, and boughs of hands and feet, bears a resemblance to an inverted tree....Some yogis do not cut their hair but keep it long, to draw from the ether a greater quantity of cosmic rays. The reason for Samson's having lost his superhuman strength when his hair was shorn by Delilah may well be that he had practiced certain yogic exercises that transform one's hair into sensitive antennae to draw cosmic energy from the ether."—Paramahansa Yogananda, *Self-Realization Magazine*, May–June 1963.

† An excess of carbon dioxide is poisonous to the body. However, a small amount of carbon dioxide is retained in the blood, and is vital to life as a regulator of the bodily chemistry. *(Publisher's Note)*

and store carbon dioxide and water, which they break down by photosynthesis to create carbohydrates (food). In the process they give off oxygen, essential to man.* Photosynthesis, being dependent on sunlight, stops at night. However, through another process called respiration, trees continuously release carbon dioxide into the atmosphere, particularly at night when the counteracting influence of carbon-absorbing, oxygen-producing photosynthesis is not present. As night air is usually still, the heavy carbon dioxide gas settles near the ground. In part for this reason, the custom of sleeping on beds—that is, above ground level—came about.

The Limitations of the Physical Senses

Science has taught us a great deal about the intricate mechanisms of our universe and about the substances of which we are all made, but there is still vast knowledge to be uncovered. We could perceive more and appreciate more if we developed the underlying powers of our sensory organs. Things we should see with our eyes we do not see, things we should hear with our ears we do not hear, because our senses are too habituated, too attached, to experiences of the limited gross physical world. Freedom from that attachment is not negation of sensory enjoyment; it permits a broadening of the God-given sensory powers to their fullest spiritual potential.

On the material plane man has discovered various ways to increase his seeing power. The unaided physical eye receives only limited impressions of color. However, under ultraviolet light, drab-looking pieces of rock in which certain minerals are present will show forth luminescent colors. Remove the ultraviolet light and the rocks assume their original dull hue. Many colors in the physical world, such as the blue of the sky, are really optical illusions caused by the reflection of light on various kinds of particles. Because your eyes register only a limited degree of the creative vibration that makes up everything in creation, you do not see the subtle astral† colors,

---

* "It is quite probable that our entire supply of free oxygen, one-fifth of the atmosphere, has been furnished by photosynthesis."—Encyclopaedia Britannica.

† Within every physical being and object and vibration is its finer astral counterpart, composed of luminous lifetronic energy.

which are hidden in everything around you. Could you but see, you would be amazed at their beauty. Even the most gorgeous shades on earth appear ugly, gross, and wild in comparison to the magnificent hues of the astral world.

So neither your eyes nor your ears register everything possible. You cannot smell astral fragrances, nor perceive with your other physical sense organs the myriad finer forms and impressions passing through the ether. Even if St. Francis were here at this moment in his astral form, you would not be able to see and hear and touch him. Yet it is possible to advance beyond ordinary sensory limitations, for I have seen him.

Often man does not cognize even things that his senses are able to perceive. Those persons who have perceptive eyes enjoy beauty everywhere. Others act as if they had no eyes; even in a beautiful place they fail to "see" anything. When I visited Mexico and saw the "Floating Gardens" of Lake Xochimilco,* their loveliness filled my heart with awareness of the Divine Artist. Another man, standing nearby, seemed equally engrossed. However, something told me he was not seeing what I was seeing, so I asked his reaction to the picturesque scene. "I was thinking of how to drain off the water and make more land," he replied. An engineer, he was seeing the lake in his own way. So we view things according to our different mentalities and moods.

Every soul is encased in a composite vibration of sensations, thoughts, feelings—all the factors that make up a person's being, or consciousness. Each one has a different composition, a different vibration. All the things you have done since childhood are stored in tabloid form as tendencies in your brain. They make you what you are. Because we do not see this tabloid pattern, we wonder why people behave as they do. Some become suddenly elated, or inexplicably angry or moody; even they don't know why. Some are always busy criticizing or gossiping about others, when there is plenty of "housecleaning" to do in their own "home"! The invisible tabloid tendencies in the brain compel each one to behave in certain ways. They bury the soul, preventing the expression of one's

* The gardens are now fixed "islands," the plant roots having long since become anchored to the bottom of the lake, which is extremely shallow.

true Self. How complex is man! each one in himself a full-length novel.

The Infinite Potential of Thought

Man is supposed to get something out of this life besides eating, sleeping, and working. The thinkers begin to wonder about life. They observe and question why things happen, or do not happen, in a certain way. We have a first and then a second set of teeth; why not a third? What causes this regulation? Because of man's unquestioning acceptance of many delusive thoughts of physical limitation, he allows them to control his present sphere of existence. Thinkers do not accept the inevitable; they turn their efforts toward changing it. This is the ingredient that makes progress possible.

I am thrilled when I see the great manufacturing centers, the remarkable inventions, and other exceptional human accomplishments. How much has come from the brain of man! And the brain itself is infinitely more intricate than anything it has produced.

There is a story about a certain king who showed such affectionate regard for his prime minister that others in the court, noticing the monarch's obvious preference, were jealous. Realizing this, the king wanted to show them *why* the minister was his favorite. Some music sounded in the distance, and the king turned to one of his courtiers, saying, "Please find out what is going on." After some time the man returned with the information that it was a marriage procession. "Who is going to be married?" inquired the king. The courtier didn't know, so another courtier was sent out. The man returned with a reply to the king's latest query, but when the sovereign asked another question he could not answer. The result was the same with courtier after courtier. Finally the king called for the prime minister and asked him to go and find out what was taking place. When the minister returned, the king plied him with questions, every one of which the alert and thorough prime minister was able to answer satisfactorily.

A great many persons are dull-minded like the uninformed courtiers. They are not necessarily stupid; just too mentally lazy to make any effort beyond obvious necessity. I can condone physical laziness (there might be a justifiable physiological cause); but there is no excuse for mental laziness! The mentally idle do not like to think, because even that seems too much work for them.

Thought is fascinating. No one will ever be able to tabulate all the tendencies and perceptions of the mind; its capacity is infinite. Yet the mind cannot think an original thought: there is not a single idea that God has not originated already in conceiving His past, present, and future creations. Therefore if you think deeply enough about a subject, the answer to any question about it will come.

You must feel as well as think; if you do not have feeling along with your thoughts, you will not always be successful in reaching the right conclusion. Feeling is an expression of intuition, the repository of all knowledge. Feeling and thought, or reason, must be balanced; only then does the divine image of God within you, the soul, manifest its full nature. Hence Yoga teaches one how to balance his powers of reason and feeling. One who does not have both equally is not a fully developed person.

In God-Consciousness Everything Becomes Beautiful

In my younger days I used to go sight-seeing, but my interest was only in temples. As my consciousness changed with the practice of meditation, I began to look at the world differently; everything seemed transformed and interesting to me. Now I see behind all creation the kingdom of my Father. It is enchanting beyond any dreams of this world! And sometimes I see the beauties of His kingdom showing through the gross physical creation.

As you progress spiritually and draw closer to God, He reveals to you more and more wonders of creation. Even in the dead and ugly-looking stalks of a wheat field after the harvest you will see life. It played its part there, and to the ordinary eye it is gone; but with the divine eye* you will see, even in the outer desolation, the beautiful colors of dancing electrons and protons.

Behind every material object is an astral blueprint of col-

---

* The spiritual or third eye in man; the eye of intuitive perception.

ored light. In the astral world everything is motion, everything is living; there is nothing called "dead." Even in the physical world death is not cessation of life, only a change into a different form. Life is still throbbing in the "lifeless" object. In the bones of dead animals I have beheld rich colors and vibrating light.

You see only the gross material products coming from God's hidden factory behind creation; but if you went into the factory itself, you would behold in what marvelous manner everything in this world has been brought into manifestation.

The factory behind creation is beyond imagination; the whole universe is a single thought in the mind of God! So simple, yet the galaxies are guided by mathematics inconceivable by man. Everything runs in perfect order. What tremendous intelligence is manifested in creation! The Infinite is working in everything. All the different eddies of motion called life are controlled by that Cosmic Intelligence.

Every hundred years a billion and a half persons leave this earth, and more than that many are born. What complexities of supply and demand are created thereby! Even so, the Divine Intelligence has given ample food to take care of human needs. Man alone is responsible for lack and misery on earth. By this time we could have had a millennium—everyone healthy and supplied with all of life's necessities, living in a happy and peaceful way in a wisely governed existence. But man's selfishness, and power in the hands of the inept, destroy such a possibility. Abraham Lincoln expressed the highest ideal of government when he said it should be "of the people, by the people, and for the people." He was a deeply spiritual man. Even so, he had to suffer because of the ignorance of a few.

This World Is a Temporal Place

It is natural to wonder where exceptional men such as Lincoln, and departed dear ones, once so tangible! have gone after death. Such questions arise in the mind, not to discourage you, but to awaken in you a realization of the temporal dream-nature of life. The Bhagavad-Gita* tells us: "That which is night (of slumber) to all creatures is (luminous) wake-

* II:69.

fulness to the man of self-control. The seeming state of wakefulness of the ordinary man is perceived by a sage to be, in reality, a state of delusive sleep."

Thus most people are sleeping soundly throughout this dream-life; only the man of realization is awake. He is not interested in the activities that engross the ordinary man who busies himself seeking wealth and sense pleasures, and wasting time in shallow social engagements. Man makes a nervous wreck of himself pursuing the fleeting attractions of this world, whereas the joy and wonder of God, which is beyond description, would give him so much more: happiness and fulfillment unending!

Only a little while you live as an individualized image in God's dream-world. You are dreaming your mortal existence; it is part of God's cosmic dream. Every day you are living in this dream of physical being. Every night, in deep sleep, it is gone. And one day, when you awaken in God—who is your real Self—the dream will be gone forever.

Seek the Lord Who Is Hiding Behind Creation

Use your time rightly, to discover the factory of the Divine behind this world. Once for an entire day I beheld in vision the infinite wonders of creation, and I prayed:

"O Father, when I was blind I found not a door that led to Thee. Thou hast healed my eyes; now I discover doors everywhere: the hearts of flowers, the voices of friendship, memories of lovely experiences. Each gust of my prayer opens a new entrance to the vast temple of Thy presence." *

Be adamant, strong, and unflinching in your determination to discover the One who is hiding behind this creation. Snatch yourself away from the demands of the world, and do not go to bed at night until you have consciously communed with God. I seldom retire before four o'clock in the morning; only during the night can I find freedom from my responsibilities and be wholly with God.

The ordinary man with his everyday responsibilities can be just as busy as the president of the United States. Busy, busy, busy! that is life's demand. You have to reserve time each

* "Doors Everywhere," in *Whispers from Eternity*.

day to get away from the world and be with God. Control your life, and set aside time to practice meditation for communion with Him. Then everything in this world will be a wonder to you.

As scientists made their discoveries by following certain disciplines and physical laws, so will you find God without fail when you scientifically follow spiritual laws. You are helping yourself in the highest way when you study and apply these laws as set forth in the Self-Realization Fellowship teachings.

Forget not the things I have told you. "A word to the wise—those who are spiritually awakened—is sufficient." Yet Jesus said: "The harvest truly is plenteous, but the laborers are few."* If you receive these teachings and practice them, you will realize every truth I have told you. It is not complicated; I have given only those spiritual techniques that will enable you to perceive and commune with God. No matter how unpleasant your circumstances in this world, when you discover God you will see Him working through you and manifesting in everything, and you will be filled with His love and joy.

India's *rishis* remind us that health and prosperity, material accomplishments and possessions, are not lasting. Why concentrate only on goals that are perishable? What is lasting is the ever-new joyous contact of God and the attainment of Self-realization—finding out who you are, knowing that the image of God is within you. When you have that realization, you will be a satisfied person. The scriptures of India describe one who attains this state as a *siddha*, "successful one." When I was teaching congregations of hundreds and thousands I was often called "successful." That did not impress me. One may be recognized by the whole world and yet be unknown to the only One whose attention matters; and he who attracts the notice of God may be entirely unknown to the world. Which would you prefer? I wanted only the recognition of my Father. The acclaim of the world can be so intoxicating that man forgets to cultivate the all-fulfilling approbation of the Lord.

It is natural for man to yearn for the role of king on this earthly stage, but if all were kings, there could be no play. Your part is just as important as anyone else's. The point is that you

* Matthew 9:37.

must play your role according to the Divine Director's wish; when you live your part to please God, you will be successful. This should be the constant prayer in every human heart:

"My Lord, work Thou through my hands; they were made to serve Thee and to pick flowers for Thy temple. Mine eyes were made to behold Thy presence in the flickering stars, in the eyes of soulful devotees; my feet were made to take me to Thy temples everywhere to sip the nectar of Thy sermons to seeking souls; my voice was made only to speak of Thee. I taste wholesome food that I may be reminded of Thine all-nourishing goodness; I inhale the perfume of flowers that I may breathe Thy fragrant presence there. I dedicate my thoughts, feelings, and love to Thee. All my senses are in harmony with Thy celestial orchestra of fragrance, beauty, and joy playing their refrain in the eternal symphony of the cosmos.

"Lead me from darkness to light. Lead me from hatred to love. Lead me from limitations to Thine inexhaustible power; lead me from ignorance to wisdom. Lead me from suffering and death to everlasting life and enjoyment in Thee. Above all, lead me from the delusion of human attachment into realization of Thy love eternal, which plays hide-and-seek with me in all forms of human love.

"Father, Mother, Friend, Beloved God, reveal Thyself unto me! Leave me in ignorance no longer. All delusion I cast from the sacred shrine of my soul. Be Thou the only King sitting on the throne of my ambitions, the only Queen in the castle of my love, the only Deity in the temple of my soul. Keep me awake in Thy consciousness, that I may pray and demand unceasingly until Thou dost open all doors into Thy home of wisdom, and there receive me, Thy prodigal child, and entertain me with the fatted calf of immortality and eternal joy."

The Invisible Man

*First Self-Realization Fellowship Temple at
Encinitas, California, March 3, 1940*

It seems preposterous to think of man as invisible. We are visible to ourselves every day as a physical body. But there are many ways in which we manifest our essential invisibility. For example, close your eyes. Your form is invisible to you; how do you know you exist? You are aware of the body's weight; you can hear, smell, taste, and touch. Nevertheless you are real to yourself only in terms of ideas. You are an invisible nucleus around which many thoughts are revolving. Now open your eyes. Are you the form that you see, or that inner being you were just now conscious of with eyes closed?

The visible man is of little importance; the invisible self, or soul, is of utmost importance. During sleep you are unaware of the visible man; but you *are* aware of yourself, for when you wake up you know whether you slept well or poorly. Therefore your invisible self is real. Take that away and your outer visibility is meaningless. Without the invisible self the body would be as worthless as a corpse. The invisible man within is the real one. But strange to say, man doesn't try to analyze what that invisible self is. He is so interested·in the form he can see, thinking constantly about his physical appearance and well-being, he doesn't stop to reason out that the inner unseen self is the reality.

Within the physical body, yet invisible to physical eyes, is an identical body of light, the astral encasement of the soul. If one of your fingers has been cut off, you still feel as if that finger were there. Anyone who has lost a limb knows this sensation. There is an invisible astral counterpart for all the bodily parts. Behind your physical heart is an invisible heart. Without it, your visible heart would not beat. You have invisible organs of sight and hearing, an invisible brain, invisible bones and nerves. These parts—tissues of light and energy—constitute the astral body of the invisible man. The astral body looks exactly like the visible one, except that its form, being made of light and energy, is exceedingly subtle.

If you are physically afflicted you should not say, "My sight is gone," or "I have lost a hand." Your invisible eyes and hands are still present. Though your physical arm may be paralyzed, your invisible arm is not disabled. Never believe that the invisible organs are in any way affected by disease of the physical organs, because your negative thought would impede the flow of intelligent life energy into the physical body parts.

Electrical currents are passed through a wire. Which is more important, the wire or the electricity? The wire exists merely for the passage of the electricity; the electricity does not exist for the wire. So the body exists for the use of the invisible man, the soul, not he for the body. However, the physical body must be in a certain condition for the invisible self to remain there.

What a pity that this invisible self is tied to the body! If it were not, we could go walking on the water and fly in the sky and come back into the physical body again. The astral body of the invisible self has sensory perceptions much greater than those of its physical counterpart. Man has invented machines that in some ways are better than the physical body, which has many limitations. But when your consciousness of the invisible astral body is developed, you will realize that it can hear what the physical ears cannot hear, and see what the physical eyes cannot see. It can also smell, taste, and touch objects far beyond the range of the physical senses. And you can make it large or small at will, just as pictures on a movie screen can be made large or small by the man in the projection booth.

Investigate the Electricity That Lights the Body Bulb

You are always looking after the physical body-bulb. Have you never thought how wonderful it would be to investigate the electricity that lights the bulb? Visible man is composed basically of sixteen elements, chemicals that can be purchased in a store. Your body is worth only about ninety cents; in depression times even less! Why not cultivate a better acquaintance with the invisible man? It is he who has power and friends and love. Without him, visible man has nothing but the chemicals of which he is made.

Turn the spotlight of your attention inward, away from the limited visible man. The physical body has backaches and stomachaches; it suffers deterioration in old age; it is the nastiest little animal! always crying and whining for something. The visible man cannot bear a bad fall, and he sometimes shrinks at even a pinprick; the invisible man is unhurt by anything. He is free. He can banish all the troubles of the physical body. The invisible man within you is what you are. "The One who pervades all things is imperishable. Nothing has power to destroy this Unchangeable Spirit."*

You think you are the body, but you are not. A piece of ice can be melted into liquid and then made to disappear by evaporation. The process can be reversed, condensing the vapor into liquid and freezing the liquid into solid form as ice once again. The ordinary man has not yet learned to perform similar transformations with his bodily atoms, but Christ showed that it could be done.

Man's Body Is Composed of 35 Thoughts of God

The human body of 16 material elements is nothing more than a shadow of the invisible man, who has two bodies—an astral form made of electrical currents, and a causal form made of ideas. Your astral form of light consists of 19 elements and your invisible causal form is made of 35 thoughts—the 19 ideas that produced the 19 electrical elements of your astral body;† and the 16 ideas that produced the 16 gross material elements of your physical body. God first created the iron and potassium and other chemical elements in idea; then He materialized them to make your physical body. The real you is invisible, because even your physical body, as well as everything else in creation, was first conceived in thought.

So your body is essentially a causal form of 35 thoughts

* Bhagavad-Gita II:17.
† See *astral body* in glossary.

within an astral body of 19 elements of light and energy, which in turn is encased in a physical body of 16 chemicals. When you die, the visible physical body will vanish, but the astral body of the invisible self within will be real to you; you will be aware of your astral form. By higher spiritual advancement you will see that your subtle astral body can be reduced to 35 thoughts, and that your consciousness behind those 35 thoughts is the Reality; for your consciousness, or soul, is a spark of the cosmic consciousness of God.

When you are viewing a motion picture you see many figures on the screen, but if you look up you see only one beam of light projecting those images. Similarly, from the brain flow five currents of energy, the vibratory creative elements of earth, water, fire, air, and ether, which condense to materialize this physical body on the screen of creation.*

Motion pictures used to be silent; now there is sound, and they are experimenting with odors, so that when you see a garden on the screen you will also smell the fragrance of the flowers. When those light-produced forms can be made true to touch and taste also, you will have produced the fivefold aspects of God's creation. The five senses by which man apprehends creation have their correspondences in the five elemental electricities—ether (sound), air (touch), fire (sight), water (taste), and earth (smell)—from which creation was materialized. Someday the whole world will appear to you as a kind of motion picture—forms of light that are true to the five sensory perceptions. The terrible things that are happening in the world now are distressingly real; but when you are able to behold them as creations of light and shadow, you will understand that they are only a show, a part of God's play.

* The cosmic vibration, or *Aum*, structures all physical creation, including the human body, through the manifestation of five *tattwas* (elements): earth, water, fire, air, and ether. These are intelligent vibratory forces. Without the earth element there would be no state of solid matter; without the water element, no liquid state; without the air element, no gaseous state; without the fire element, no heat; without the ether element, no background on which to produce the cosmic motion picture show. The creative cosmic vibration enters the body of man through the medulla, and is then divided into the five elemental currents by the action of the five lower *chakras*, or centers: the coccygeal (earth), sacral (water), lumbar (fire), dorsal (air), and cervical (ether).

You are only dreaming that you have a body of flesh. Your real self is light and consciousness. You are not the physical body. The visibility of the body deludes our material consciousness. If you cultivate superconsciousness—awareness of your real self, the soul—you will realize that the body is simply a projection of that invisible self within. Then you can do anything with the body. But don't try just yet to walk on water!

In the motion-picture house you are engrossed in the images on the screen. They look so real! You are not conscious of the light overhead by which the images are being projected. But if you look up you can see that the visible is proceeding out of the invisible; the forms on the screen are all proceeding out of that one light from the projection booth. What is the difference between the light and the pictures? If there were no light, could pictures have been materialized? Similarly, if there were no invisible man, there would be no visible man. When the invisible man leaves the physical form, the body disintegrates. Those who understand the subtle relationship between the visible and the invisible man can dematerialize and materialize the physical body at will.* We are coming to that evolutionary period during which we will realize increasingly that we are really invisible beings, or souls.

The Invisible Man Is Free from Suffering and Death

To live only in the consciousness of this visible body of flesh is spiritually retarding, for the body is subject to the sufferings of disease, injury, poverty, hunger, and death. We should not desire to think of ourselves as this visible, vulnerable, destructible body. The invisible man within us cannot be hurt or killed. Should we not strive more to realize our unknown immortal nature? By increasing our knowledge of this

---

* Great masters who have attained God-realization are able to arrange the atoms at will to create any form they wish. Paramahansa Yogananda related in his autobiography that his beloved guru, Swami Sri Yukteswar, appeared before him in the flesh three months after his death. Not only was it a visible form; Paramahansaji mentions embracing his guru "with an octopus grip," and detecting "the same faint, fragrant, natural odor which had been characteristic of his body before." Further, guru and disciple talked with each other at length, as described in *Autobiography of a Yogi*, chapter 43, "The Resurrection of Sri Yukteswar." *(Publisher's Note)*

invisible self we will be able to control the man visible, as great masters do. Even when the visible man is in distress, he who is aware of his divine powers as the invisible man within can remain detached from physical suffering.

How will you gain such control? First you must learn to live more in silence; you must learn to meditate. It may seem uninteresting at first; you have kept so closely in touch with this visible body that you have difficulty in thinking about anything except its ceaseless troubles, desires, and demands. But make the effort. Keeping your eyes closed, repeat again and again, "I am made in the image of God. My life cannot be destroyed by any means. I am the invisible man everlasting."

Everything Is the Result of an Idea

That invisible man is made in the image of God, free as the Spirit is free. In the visible man lie all the troubles and limitations of the world. Whenever we are conscious of our bodies we are tied to the body's limitations. Hence the great masters teach us to close our eyes and remind ourselves, by meditation on the invisible self, that we are not restricted to what our physical bodies can do. I used to affirm with deep conviction: "I am not limited by my physical body. Wherever I want to go, I am instantly there." You may say, "That is only a thought." Well, what is thought? Everything you see is the result of an idea. You could not visualize anything without thought. Invisible thought gives all things their reality. Therefore if you can control your thought processes, you can make anything visible; you can materialize it by the power of your concentration.

Suppose you are sitting in silence and I ask you to concentrate on this temple in which we are gathered. Again and again you try, until your mind has gone very deep; then you will see the temple just as it appears now to your physical eyes. Invisible thoughts can be materialized into visual experiences.

If you close your eyes, you cannot see your body, yet it is real to you. Why think that the invisible self is unreal, just because you cannot see it? In meditation you peer into the darkness behind closed eyes and center your attention on the soul, the invisible self within you. Learning to control your thoughts and interiorize your mind, by scientific guru-given techniques of meditation, you will gradually develop spiritually: your meditations will deepen and your invisible self, the soul-image of God within, will become real to you. In this joyous awakening of Self-realization, the limited body consciousness that was so real becomes unreal; and you know that you have found your true invincible self and its oneness with God.

Realize Your Immortality Now

You will also understand how the invisible man is "tied" to the physical body—by attachments, the mental and emotional cords of desires for certain experiences on the physical plane. When by deeper meditation you can untie those cords, he will be free and you will know that you are a real image of God. Seek out that invisible man who is held captive in the jungle of physical sensations and matter.

If you once understood the invisible man and the miracle of his outer physical body, his secondary body of light, and his inner body of ideas, you would realize what a wonderful creation you are! Concentrate on that invisible you. The visible man is a delusion; the invisible man within is real. When you know this you will know that you are not bones and flesh; you are the indestructible invisible man.

You cannot die! Dwell no more on thoughts of growing older and being ready for the grave. You are only getting ready for your immortal state! Nothing dies. The ideational blueprint of your body is always present in the ether. You feel that your loved ones who pass on are gone forever because you haven't the power of concentration necessary to behold them in their subtle forms in the astral world where they are. Keep your mind on these truths, repeating them to yourself whenever you have a quiet moment, "I am a prototype of God's thought. I am eternal, ever roaming in the kingdom of God." You *are* that deathless invisible man, and ever will be. Why not realize your immortality now?

Your two physical eyes deceive you into thinking that this world of duality is real. Open your spiritual eye and behold your invisible form. If in the inner silence your spiritual eye is open, the invisible becomes visible. Whenever you are thinking, dreaming, or concentrating deeply, you are that invisible man. He is real; the visible man is the shadow. Forget the shadow and remember the real. Be one with the invisible man—the reflection of God.

What Are Ghosts?

Self-Realization Fellowship Temple,
Hollywood, California, July 22, 1945

There are all kinds of tales about ghosts, devils, witches, vampires; and not a few persons have claimed to have had various experiences with such creatures. Of the several cases that have come to my attention, most of the persons involved suffered from overly strong and diseased imaginations. One of them, a woman, had chanced to read a book about vampires, and her imaginings were so vivid that she believed one of them was sucking her blood away each night. Whenever she visited me, she became well; but the idea of the nightly presence of a vampire was so strong in her that after a time she would become ill again. She died prematurely, destroyed by her own thoughts.*

In the sixteenth century, belief in witchcraft was widespread, and hundreds of persons suspected of being witches were falsely accused of being in league with the devil and were put to death. Joan of Arc was burned at the stake as one bewitched. Even Jesus Christ, who was healing the sick and doing only good, was accused of being in touch with Beelzebub. It is true that at various times evil spirits in possessed persons recognized Jesus and spoke to him, saying, "Let us alone; what have we to do with thee, thou Jesus of Nazareth? art thou come to destroy us? I know thee who thou art: the Holy One of God."† Jesus himself spoke of Satan‡ and of evil spirits, which

---

* In the presence of a God-conscious master such as Paramahansa Yogananda, receptive devotees are often healed of mental or physical illness. Permanent cure usually depends on the continued faith and receptivity of the person healed. Persons who revert to wrong thinking, as this woman did, permit the illness to return. *(Publisher's Note)*

† Luke 4:34.   ‡ Luke 4:1–13.

he exorcised from many persons, in one case casting the evil spirits into the bodies of a herd of swine. *

There is another world, the astral, hidden behind this universe. Its inhabitants are garbed in an astral form made of light. Lacking a physical body, they are "ghosts," invisible to us. Ordinarily they are confined to their own sphere, just as we are limited to our own physical world. If it were a simple matter for the ill-intentioned among astral beings to penetrate the earth plane and hurt us, we would be living in terror all the time. There is enough horror already on this earth of ours. Are not millions of deadly germs floating around? Certainly God would not add the interference of spooks to our sufferings!

There are, however, a few astral beings known as "tramp souls." They are earthbound because of strong attachments to the world, and are desirous of entering a physical form for sense enjoyments. Such beings are usually unseen; and they have no power to affect the ordinary person. Tramp souls do occasionally succeed in entering and taking possession of someone's body and mind, but only when such a person is mentally unstable or has weakened his mind by keeping it often blank or unthinking. It is like leaving a car unlocked with the key in the ignition; some vagrant may get in and drive off. Tramp souls want a free ride in someone else's physical-body vehicle—anyone's—having lost their own that they were so attached to. It was in such cases of possession that Jesus exorcised the vagrant spirits. Tramp souls cannot stand the high vibration of spiritual thoughts and consciousness. Sincere seekers after God who practice scientific methods of prayer and meditation need never fear such beings. God is the Spirit of all spirits. No harm from negative spirits can come to one whose thoughts are on God.

The Triune Nature of Man

To understand better what astral beings are, let us first understand what we are. When God created us, we existed first only as consciousness. We were a creation of His mind. Is it not true that whenever you create something new, the initial step is to visualize a model of it in your mind? Then you gather

* Luke 8:26–33.

together the materials, and finally you construct the tangible image of your idea. In the same manner, we and everything in creation are triune: mental (the idea), astral (the building material), and physical (the gross end-product).

The physical body is made of 16 elements. How God combined the chemical materials of physical elements to express intelligence is a marvel! Nevertheless, this body is anything but perfect. We can conceive of a much better one! I would like to create a body that would be like asbestos, able to go through fire and not burn; one in which there could be no broken bones, no unpleasant coughing. The physical body has pains and aches: its "spark plugs" are often "missing"; first one part and then another gives out, and finally the heart fails.

Americans like to get a new car every year, but they have to keep this old body-model sixty or seventy years! Yet even when it is falling apart, still you want to hang onto the model you have, until finally the Lord says, "Come on, get out of it!" Then you spring from the worn-out physical form and see that you are encased in a luminous body, an astral body of light and energy.* You rejoice to find that you can hear, you can see, you can touch; and that your new form possesses no bones to be broken, no flesh to be hurt.

Our astral body is composed of 19 elements, which are mental, emotional, and lifetronic. These are intelligence; ego; feeling; mind (sense consciousness); five instruments of knowledge (the subtle powers behind the physical sense organs of sight, hearing, smell, taste, and touch); five instruments of action (the powers for the executive abilities to procreate, excrete, talk, walk, and exercise manual skill); and five instruments of life force (those empowered to perform the crystallizing, assimilating, eliminating, metabolizing, and circulatory functions of the physical body).

---

* There are many planes or spheres in the astral world, constituting the heaven or hell of life after death. "In my Father's house are many mansions" (John 14:2). A person's good behavior while on earth draws him to one of the higher spheres of light, peace, and joy. Evil deeds attract one to a lower, dark sphere where his experiences may be akin to hellish nightmares. One remains in the astral world for a karmically predetermined time, and then again takes rebirth on earth in physical form.

These are all subtly made. We can hear, smell, taste, touch, and see in the dream world through the *power* that is in the five senses. And in the astral world, even without the physical organs of the ears, eyes, nose, tongue, and skin, we still have with us the power of all five sense perceptions. The astral body is weightless and travels as light travels. You can at will make the astral body very small like an atom or you can make it very large. Why not? God, the divine operator of the cosmic movie of creation, can enlarge or reduce the size of the picture on the screen. He is the projectionist, running the film from the booth of eternity. You are an individualized expression of His infinite light. Your astral body is therefore much freer from the cosmic limitations that so strongly bind the physical form.

But God had first to think of what materials He wanted to put into the physical and astral bodies before He actually created them. We therefore have also a causal or idea body of 35 elements: the 16 ideas that go to make up the elements of the physical body, and the 19 ideas that constitute the elements of the astral body. From the causal thought-forms the astral body's five instruments of life force make visible the astral body of light and the physical body of gross matter. The following experiment illustrates the idea. Close your eyes and visualize a horse on the left. At first your concept is fuzzy, but if I suggest a *white* horse, you can more easily visualize it. Now think of a black horse on the right side. You are creating mental or causal images. Switch them about so that the white horse is on the right side. If you can visualize a little more strongly, you will be able to see these thought-forms as real images. That is what you do in a dream: your mind is more concentrated then, causing your thought-forms to become visible to you. Dreams and visions are astral in essence, being composed of light and energy. Could you actually make the astral images of the black and white horses true to the physical senses, you would have materialized a physical creation.

So essentially we are made of 35 ideas, which make up the ideational or causal body of man. Encased within the 35 thoughts is the spirit of God, which is called the soul. Just as one flame emerges from the tiny openings of a gas burner as many individual flames, so are we all one light, flowing from God into many bodies.

At Death We Are Still Encased in the Astral and Causal Bodies

When you die, your physical body of 16 elements disintegrates, but the 19 elements of your astral body remain intact. Where, then, are all those souls who have left this earth? They are roaming in the ether. "That is impossible," you say. So let us make a comparison. If a primitive tribesman came here and I told him that music is audible in the ether, he would laugh at me, or perhaps become frightened; but if I then brought a radio and tuned in a station where music was playing, he would no longer be able to deny the truth of my statement. I could similarly show you right now that astral beings are roaming in the ether, and you couldn't deny it. The astral world is right here, just behind the gross vibration of the physical cosmos.

If you were to behold the multitude of astral beings in the ether around you at this moment, many of you would be afraid; and some of you would try to seek among them your departed loved ones. If you concentrate deeply at the spiritual eye you can view with inner vision that luminous world in which are living all the souls who have gone on to the astral plane. In human beings the heart acts as a receiving instrument and the spiritual eye as a broadcasting station. Even if you cannot see your lost beloved ones, if you can calmly concentrate your feeling on the heart, you can become aware of the reassuring presence of those dear to you who are now in astral form, enjoying their freedom from flesh thralldom.

I see many astral beings who have left the material plane, but they cannot see me. I don't make myself visible to them, but I can behold them if I so desire.*

Therefore, we are not fully released at death when we depart from the physical form. Our souls are still encased in the

---

* Great masters watch over their disciples on the astral and causal planes as well as on earth. Such masters can and do materialize in physical or astral form in response to the soul call of a true devotee; but at their own wise discretion. We find an example in Lahiri Mahasaya's summoning Mahavatar Babaji to appear before doubting friends, described in *Autobiography of a Yogi*, chapter 34.

subtle astral and ideational bodies. It is only when man dons a physical form that he becomes a visible being in this world. After the death of his physical body, he remains in the astral form as a "ghost": an intelligent, invisible being, with essentially the same mentality and characteristics he had on earth. Inhabitants of the astral realms can of course see one another in their luminous bodies. But astral beings are not ordinarily visible to us on earth unless we know how to perceive the astral world through the spiritual eye. When souls shed the astral body and go into a mental form in the causal world* they are not nonentities, but they do become truly invisible, even as ideas are invisible.

Jesus said, "Destroy this [body] temple and in three days I will raise it up."† He meant that he had to divest himself of the physical, astral, and mental bodies (by casting out all vestiges of attachment to a form) to become one with Spirit. It took three distinct efforts to do this.

If a departed soul has unfinished desires created while on the earth plane, it continues to feel in the astral those desires and the wish to express itself through a material body. And so that soul in its astral vehicle is drawn again into a united sperm and ovum cell and is once more in a physical form.

The Intelligence in Prana Creates the Physical Body

The *prana* that permeates the physical body is intelligent life force ("lifetrons"). The electricity that illuminates the light bulb does not create the bulb; but the electricity or life force in the united human sperm and ovum cells guides the embryonic and subsequent development of the entire human body. Manifesting as the aforementioned five life forces of the astral body, it is an intelligent or consciously directed force.

It is unwise to ascribe to yourself permanently any defect of your body. Suppose you have lost an arm in this life, and the thought of that loss becomes so impinged on your conscious-

---

* When souls are free from physical desires, they need no longer reincarnate on earth. Such souls then migrate between the astral world and the causal "heaven," reincarnating in the astral until spiritual freedom is attained from that state also. When all causal desires are overcome, one becomes a liberated or free soul.
† John 2:19.

ness that you think you can never again have the use of that arm. When you are reborn the next time, you bring with you that consciousness of a missing arm; and if that negative thought is strong enough it may inhibit the creative action of the intelligent life force that grows the arms of your new body. You should therefore never identify yourself with the flaws of your physical form. They do not belong to you, for you are the pure, perfect image of God—the soul.

So you see, before you took on this physical form you were a ghost, and when you die you will become a ghost again. We are also ghosts when we sleep, for in sleep we are not aware of ourselves as a physical body at all. Since you are a ghost when you are asleep, and you will be one after death, why be afraid of ghosts? That is what you were and that is what you are going to be. The only difference is that when you enter the astral world at death you cannot create at will a physical body like the one you now have. Only great masters who have attained oneness with the Divine Creator can do so. Spiritually advanced souls can condense the subtle vibrations of the astral vehicle into a tangible body.

Death Should Not Be Feared

We fear death because of pain, and because of the thought that we may become obliterated. This idea is erroneous. Jesus showed himself in a physical form to his disciples after his death. Lahiri Mahasaya returned in the flesh the next day after he had entered *mahasamadhi*.* They proved that they were not destroyed. Just because instances of those who have mastered the cosmic laws are few, one should not say that their testimony is not true. You should not ignore the divine demonstrations of Jesus and my *param-paramguru*† Babaji; nor can I put aside the evidence of what I have seen—my resurrected guru, Sri Yukteswarji‡—or what I have experienced in myself. "This soul in essence, the reflection of the Spirit, never undergoes the throes of death or the pangs of birth; nor, having once

---

* The last meditation, during which a master consciously casts off his physical body and merges himself in Spirit, is called the *maha*, or great, *samadhi*.

† Guru of one's guru's guru. (See *paramguru* and *Gurus of Self-Realization Fellowship* in glossary.)

‡ See *Autobiography of a Yogi*, chapter 43, "The Resurrection of Sri Yukteswar."

known existence, is it never nonexistent. This soul was never born; it is everlastingly living, untouched by the *maya*-magic of change. The soul is ever constant through all cycles of bodily disintegrations."*

Many times when some disciple living far away has been ill or dying, he has drawn my astral body there through his devotion. One such incident happened here. Seva Devi was a very devoted student. She became extremely ill, but she never complained about it to anyone. She knew her time had come to leave this earth. One day when I visited her in Los Angeles she said to me, "Please don't hold me here."† Later on, I was staying in the Self-Realization Fellowship Hermitage in Encinitas for a time. I had been given a radio and was waking up early in the mornings to listen to broadcasts from India. One morning I suddenly felt intuitively the subtle astral vibration of Seva Devi; she drew my astral body to her through her devotion. My physical body was as dead. I was told later that Seva Devi exclaimed, just before her passing, "Swamiji is here!" She was aware of being consciously ushered by me into the other world.‡ Some time afterward I saw her glowing astral form; she was sitting in one of my classes, just as real as she used to appear in life. If anyone had touched me at that time, he would have seen her too. However, one who is in that state of astral consciousness does not usually allow others to touch him.

We have passed through death and rebirth so many times, why be afraid of death? It comes to free us. You shouldn't wish for death, but be comforted in the realization that it is our escape from so many troubles; it is a pension after the hard work of life. I am making death very charming!

People also fear death because they have been in this cage of flesh so long that they feel timid about leaving its security. But it is foolish to be afraid. Just think, no more repaired tires on the body vehicle, no more patchwork living. Since it is the

---

* Bhagavad-Gita II:20.

† Through intercession with God, great masters are able to prolong the stay of a disciple on earth.

‡ This is one of the promises of the sacred guru-disciple relationship; at the time of the disciple's death the guru is present to usher him into his new life in the astral world.

Lord's desire that we should have this old model until death comes, we have to keep it and take care of it. But I wish the Lord would give everyone the ability to go into *samadhi* and change his bodily vehicle as easily as did *rishi* Narada. He was singing of God in divine ecstatic communion; and when he returned to ordinary consciousness he saw he had shed his old body and had "reincarnated" in a fresh new youthful form. That is the highest form of transmigration.*

There is in India a story of a dying youth who, hearing the sobs of grief around him, cried:

> Insult me not with your cries of sympathy
> When I soar
> To the land of eternal light and love;
> It is I who should feel for you.
> For me, disease, shattering of bones,
> Sorrow, excruciating heartaches no more.
> I dream joy, I glide in joy, I breathe in joy evermore.

You don't know what is going to come to you in this world; you have to go on living and worrying. Those who die are pitying us; they are blessing us. Why should you grieve for them? I told this to a woman who had lost her son. When I finished explaining, she dried her tears immediately and said, "Never before have I felt such peace. I am glad to know that my son is free. I thought something awful had happened to him."

It Is Possible to Enter and Leave the Body Consciously

Many spiritually developed persons can see their own astral body. St. John says in the Bible, "And when I saw him, I fell at his feet as dead."† When your astral body ascends, or leaves the body, at death, you see your physical body as dead. That same experience occurs when advanced yogis transcend the physical body at will. Thus John, though living, saw his

---

* Transmigration, or the passing of the soul at death from one form to reincarnation in another, follows the natural upward evolution of life, without regression to lower life forms. The Hindu scriptures teach that the soul evolves from the mineral kingdom through the plant and then the animal kingdoms before reaching incarnation in a human form. Thereafter, through repeated cycles of human births and deaths, with their intermittent lessons, the soul ultimately finds perfect expression in the superman, the man of God-realization.

† Revelation 1:17.

material form as dead during the *samadhi* he describes. It is fun to get in and out of the body this way. But many persons who think they can do so are only imagining it. Just because you think it is so doesn't make it so. You have to know the technique.

One man in New York came to me and assured me that he could travel astrally. "I don't think you can," I said. "You are only imagining you can do so." Still he insisted that I test him. "All right," I agreed, "go downstairs astrally and tell me what is in the restaurant there." He was quiet for a moment; then he told me, "There is a big piano in the right-hand corner." I knew he was imagining it, for I had observed that his breathing was normal and so was his pulse.* "On the contrary," I said, "I think you will find there two women sitting at a table." He laughed at me. Then we both went down into the restaurant. No piano stood in the corner, but two women were seated at a table there. At last he understood that he had been fooled by his own imagination.

Often I see with the inner astral vision happenings in the war in Europe, but it seems like a picture show. The world was meant to entertain us, not to torture us. God has made His motion picture of creation very complex, full of contrasts of good and evil. When you go to a movie you like to see lots of excitement. Think how many times you have gone to view a murder mystery; and when the movie ended you said to yourself, "That was a good show!" Learn to look upon this movie of life with the same sense of detachment and enjoyment.

There is a lesson to be learned from the fact that we are now encaged in the human body, and that at night and when we die we become ghosts. We must learn to know our ghostly

---

* Conscious "astral travel" is possible only when one enters a deep state of *samadhi* in which the consciousness is expanded into the superconscious perception of the all-seeing spiritual eye. Through the spiritual eye one can behold any point of space in this world or the astral, and project his consciousness there. One who is advanced enough may also materialize anywhere his astral or even his physical form, which is known as bilocation. In this state of astral *samadhi* the breath and heartbeat are still, and the body is in an immobile trancelike condition. Only when a master has attained the highest spirituality, *nirbikalpa samadhi*, can his physical body continue to function in a normal way while he is inwardly engaged in divine ecstasy.

nature, our invisible, powerful nature. But you cannot do so if you are always concentrating on the body: "I have a headache, I want this and that, I dislike spinach." Preoccupation with material concerns is what you must overcome. How can you do this? Make God the first thought in your life. So long as you keep Him in second place He will not come to you. Gold, wine, and sex were created to hold you to this world; the Lord uses them as tests to see whether you prefer them to His love.

The Power of Black Magic Is in Your Thought

In addition to the fear of ghosts, some people have a dread of black magic and other black arts. Many people tell me that somebody they know is using black magic on them. I say to them, "You are sitting in the castle of God. No one can harm you if you truly believe in God." But when you believe in the negative thought that somebody is injuring you, you give him the power to do so. Suppose someone is sending you a wrong thought, and you accept it; it will hurt you. But you do not have to accept evil ideas. Don't be afraid of malicious persons; no one can affect you unless you are fearful. Fear and keeping the mind blank allow evil to enter; but when you say, "God is with me," nothing but good can come to you from the thoughts of others. Wrap yourself in the thought of God. His holy Name is the Power of all powers. Like a shield it deflects all negative vibrations.

The Cosmic War of Good and Evil

Why be concerned about the negligible threat of the powers of tramp-soul ghosts, or practitioners of the black arts? At every moment a far greater danger to our happiness and well-being exists right within us and around us. Two forces are fighting—the one to save us, and the other to hurt us. We are caught in the cosmic war between good and evil.

This world is ruled by invisibilities or ghosts: God the Father, Christ Consciousness, the seven spirits before the throne of God;* and Satan and his legion of evil powers. The seven spirits before the throne of God are the principal intelligent forces of creation: Holy Ghost (the prime creative vibrato-

---

* Revelation 1:4.

ry power of God, *Aum*, or Amen) and its six individualized creative powers that structure and maintain the physical, astral, and causal universes and the physical, astral, and causal bodies of man.

Originally, Satan was an archangel.* He was given the power to create the world according to God's plan. After he had completed his assignment, he was to go back to God, as God intended all creation to return to Him. But if this intelligent power, personified in the scriptures as Satan, were to retire into Spirit, creation would disappear. To prevent this, Satan implanted evil (that is, material) desires in man, fulfillment of which would necessitate man's return to earth again and again, thus keeping the machinery of creation going. In this way the devil tries to see to it that man doesn't get a chance to go back to God.

There is a great tug-of-war between the devil and God. One cannot dismiss the problem by thinking that Satan is a mere delusion. God would be very ignorant if He didn't know about the evil in the world. And why did Jesus say: "Get thee behind me, Satan" and "Deliver us from evil" if there is no Satan? Why is it necessary to pray to God at all if there is no devil? Evil does exist.

When the Lord created man, He created the devil too. Satan, with his power of *maya*, exists in order to test the children of God. Unless fire melts iron, steel cannot be forged. When disease or suffering comes, you should realize that it is a test of God's *maya*. You must pass these tests. You must not be upset by them. Though Jesus was suffering on the cross, he surmounted that divine test. Many great souls have died of terrible diseases and suffering. Saint Theresa of Avila was afflicted with tuberculosis, and yet she said, "I don't want the Lord to shorten my trials. I want to suffer bravely and work as long as I can." And when her body died she was lifted up in Christ.

---

* "And he said unto them, I beheld Satan as lightning fall from heaven" (Luke 10:18).

"Know thou that all manifestations of *sattwa* (good), *rajas* (activity), and *tamas* (evil) emanate from Me. Though they are in Me, I am not in them" (Bhagavad-Gita VII:12).

This creation is the Lord's hobby. But I constantly plead with Him, "Why do You have such a hobby? Why do You give us such troubles?" Our earth is one of the worst places in creation. There are far better dwelling places than this. But though God allows troubles to exist, He also tries to help us out of them. God and His angels and millions of good spirits are trying to establish their order of divine harmony on earth. Every beneficial quality is created by a good spirit. Good spirits are constantly casting the seeds of helpful thoughts into the soil of your mind. At the same time, Satan, the king of darkness, with his evil spirits is creating disorder and trouble in the world. Who but Satan created disease germs? There have been various plagues, then tuberculosis, and now the latest destroyer is cancer—all diabolical methods of torturing human beings. But God is inspiring many researchers to find new ways to banish disease.

The Temptation of Adam and Eve

To hold man to earth life, Satan created sex; that temptation has been with man since the beginning of time. The Lord created man and woman by will power; their bodies were materializations of His divine wisdom and love.* Man and woman originally had the same power as He to create children by mental fiat. Adam and Eve were empowered by Him to propagate the species by immaculate or divine means. As my guru Sri Yukteswarji explained, the evil force, Satan, tempted Eve to taste the fruit (sex) in the midst of the garden (body).† God had said that the original man and woman were to enjoy all the sensations of the tree of life (astral spinal centers of consciousness and energy that enliven the body and the senses) except the experience of sex, which is in the midst, or center, of the body garden. The "serpent" that tempted Eve is the coiled-up spinal energy that feeds and stimulates the sex nerves. When the emotion or Eve-consciousness in any human being is overpowered by the sex impulse, his reason or Adam also succumbs.

---

* Man expresses more the aspect of reason, with feeling hidden; woman expresses more the aspect of feeling, with reason less predominant.

† Genesis 3:3.

Sexual pleasure is a delusive counterpart of God's bliss. Thus when sex is divorced from faithful love, and used only to gratify lustful instincts, it becomes a tool of the devil to keep man's consciousness locked in the senses, unable to experience God-consciousness, or realization of the Self as Spirit: ever-existing, ever-conscious, ever-new Joy. Sex and desire for wine and money—these are the counterfeits created by Satan to displace the ecstasy of the soul. When Adam and Eve tasted of the sex sensation, they fell from Paradise; they lost that divine consciousness by which they could feel their oneness with God in soul ecstasy, and they were forced out of the garden of Eden. Ever since, human beings have had to reproduce their kind the sexual way, like the animals. Women give birth in a troublesome and painful manner. Then, too, husband and wife have to accept what they get; if a bad child comes, they must rear it. Originally they were able to create what they wanted, through the power of mind, just as God does. What happy days of pristine innocence!

Listen Only to the Voice of God

In the ultimate sense even Satan is really a tool of God. Satan fails to keep his promises to man, and then the disillusioned person seeks the faithful Lord. Why wait for disillusionment? I urge you not to put all your eggs of happiness in one basket. When you are physically strong and well and reasonably contented, suddenly pain comes and you think, "My goodness, what is this?" Self-Realization Fellowship teaches you not to put all your hopes for happiness in the frail basket of your body and the pleasures of this world. How? By teaching you to master the body; and, above all, by teaching you to meditate.

Listen to the voice of God through your good thoughts. God and His angelic spirits are creating these good thoughts; the devil is creating his own kind of thoughts. Every time a bad thought comes, cast it out. Then Satan can't do anything to you. But as soon as you think wrongly, you go toward Satan. You are constantly moving back and forth between good and evil; to escape, you must go where Satan will be unable to reach you: deep in the heart of God.

Jesus: a Christ of East and West

First Self-Realization Fellowship Temple,
Encinitas, California, September 18, 1938
Self-Realization Fellowship Temple,
San Diego, California, February 4, 1945
(Compilation)

Jesus Christ is a liaison between East and West. That great master stands before my eyes, telling Orient and Occident: "Come together! My body was born in the East; my spirit and message traveled to the West." In Christ's birth as an Asiatic, and his acceptance by Western peoples as their guru, is a divine implication that East and West should unite by exchanging their finest distinctive features. It is part of the drama of God that the West was meant to have material power, and the East, spiritual power, so that amity might come through an interchange of their characteristic qualities. The spiritual freedom of the East overrides material suffering. The West needs that kind of spiritual freedom; God's Western children, being more fortunate physically and materially, need to develop spiritually and to receive the spiritual illumination of the East. And the East needs Western material development; God's Eastern children should welcome the help of the West, that they may industrialize Asia, and thus enable her to develop and use her resources to fullest advantage.

The American way of living progressively, plus the spirituality of India—you cannot beat that combination. India is the melting pot of religions; America, the melting pot of nations. America became great because of her love of liberty and because she welcomed all races to her shores—she absorbed the best of all nations. No other country was founded on and has grown on such wonderful ideals; the freedom and exceptional way of life that have been created in America by these ideals must never be lost.

Many in the West believe that Easterners are materially poor because they are spiritually wealthy. This is not true. And many Easterners believe that Westerners are spiritually poor because they are materially rich. This is not the case either. The truth is that we human beings become too one-sided; we need to seek a balance by drawing the best from one another.

Jesus is a divine colossus standing between Orient and Occident, telling East and West to exchange their better qualities. Can you see him there? I see him. He urges the West to spiritualize itself and the East to industrialize itself—the East to accept the Western missionaries of science and industry, and the West to accept the Eastern missionaries of the Spirit. To the West he says: "Love your Eastern brothers. I came from the Orient." To the East he pleads: "Love your Western brothers; they have received and loved me, an Oriental." Isn't that a beautiful thought? It would make a magnificent picture.

Christ is not the property of either East or West—an East-West bond is manifested in his life. He belongs to both, and to all the world. His universality is what makes him so wonderful. Jesus took the body of an Oriental so that in being accepted as guru by the Occidental he would thereby symbolically draw East and West together. Those in the West who have adopted Christ as their own should remember that he was an Oriental. Love and sympathy for Jesus should be expanded into love and sympathy for all Orientals, and for all the world.

God does not prefer Orientals or Occidentals. He loves those who manifest His spiritual qualities. Why, then, was it ordained by God that Christ, a great savior of mankind, came out of the East? God wanted to come with the downtrodden, to show the transcendence of Spirit over matter. We should not conclude that it is necessary to be poor to be Christlike; if Jesus had come in a prosperous country, it would be equally foolish to reason that Christ Consciousness can be attained through material things, or that God favors the materially rich. A balance between spirituality and material development is necessary.

The ideals of Christ are the ideals of the scriptures of India. The precepts of Jesus are analogous to the highest Vedic teachings, which were in existence long before the advent of Jesus.

This does not take away from the greatness of Christ; it shows the eternal nature of truth, and that Jesus incarnated on earth to give to the world a new expression of *Sanatan Dharma* (eternal religion, the eternal principles of righteousness).*
In the Book of Genesis we find an exact parallel of the older Hindu concept of the genesis of our universe. The Ten Commandments of Moses, many of the Biblical legends and figures and rituals, the miracles performed by Christ, the very basics of Christian doctrine, all have concomitance with the earlier Vedic literature of India. The teachings of Christ in the New Testament and of Krishna in the Bhagavad-Gita have an exact correspondence.†

The True Nature of the Star of the East

The parallelisms of Christ's teachings with Yoga-Vedanta doctrines strongly support the records known to exist in India, which state that Jesus lived and studied there during fifteen of the unaccounted-for years of his life—no mention is made of him in the New Testament from his twelfth to thirtieth year. Jesus journeyed to India to return the visit of the three "wise men from the east" who came to pay homage to him at his birth.‡ They were guided to the Christ Child by the divine light of a star—not a physical luminary, but the star of the omniscient spiritual eye. This "third eye" can be seen within the forehead, between the eyebrows, by the deeply meditating devotee. The spiritual eye is a metaphysical telescope through which one can see to infinity in all directions simultaneously, beholding with omnipresent spherical vision whatever is happening in any point of creation. The spiritual eye has been mentioned in the teachings of India, and Jesus referred to it, too: "The light of the body is the eye: if therefore thine eye be single, thy whole body shall be full of light."§ Brought thus to

* The *Sankhya* philosophy defines true religion as "those immutable principles that protect man permanently from the threefold suffering of disease, unhappiness, and ignorance."

† Many parallel references are noted and analyzed in *Autobiography of a Yogi*.

‡ "Now when Jesus was born in Bethlehem of Judea in the days of Herod the king, behold there came wise men from the east to Jerusalem, saying, Where is he that is born King of the Jews? for we have seen his star in the east, and are come to worship him" (Matthew 2:1-2).

§ Matthew 6:22.

the stable in Bethlehem by the guiding light of the spiritual eye, the Wise Men recognized and honored the infant Christ for the great soul and divine incarnation that he was. During the unknown period of his life Jesus repaid their visit.

Even in the name and title of Jesus we find Sanskrit words with a corresponding sound and meaning. The words *Jesus* and *Isa* (pronounced "Isha") are substantially the same. *Is, Isa,* and *Iswara* all refer to the Lord, or Supreme Being. "Jesus" derives from the Greek form of the name Joshua or Jeshua, a contraction of Jehoshua, "help of Jehovah" or "Savior."*

The title "Christ" is also found in India—it was perhaps given to Jesus there—in the word "Krishna," which sometimes I purposely spell "Christna" to show the correlation. "Christ" and "Krishna" are titles signifying divinity, meaning that these two *avatars* were one with God. While residing in physical form their consciousness expressed oneness with the Christ Consciousness (Sanskrit *Kutastha Chaitanya*), the Intelligence of God omnipresent in creation.† This consciousness is also called the "only begotten son of God" because it is the sole perfect reflection in creation of the Uncreated Infinite.

To understand what Christ Consciousness means, consider the contrast between your consciousness and that of a little ant. The ant's awareness is limited by the minuscule size of his body; your consciousness resides throughout your relatively capacious form. If anyone touches any part of your body you are aware of it. Creation is the body of God, and His con-

---

* Ref. Smith's Dictionary of the Bible; De Wolfe, Fiske and Co.; Boston, Mass.
† There are many derivations given to the word "Krishna," the most common of which is "dark," referring to the hue of Krishna's complexion. (He is often shown as dark blue to connote divinity. Blue is also the color of the Christ Consciousness when epitomized in the spiritual eye as a circle of dark blue light surrounding the star mentioned earlier in this talk.) According to M. V. Sridatta Sarma ("On the Advent of Sri Krishna"), of the various other meanings given to the word "Krishna," several are found in the *Brahmavaivarta Purana.* He states that according to one of these derivations, "*Krsna* means the Universal Spirit. *Krsi* denotes a generic term, while *na* conveys the idea of the self, thus bringing forth the meaning 'Omniscient Spirit.'" In this we find a parallel to the Christ Consciousness as the Intelligence of God omnipresent in creation. It is of interest that a colloquial Bengali rendering of "Krishna" is *Krista* (cf. Greek *Christos* and Spanish *Cristo*). *(Publisher's Note)*

sciousness omnipresent therein is called the Christ Consciousness. He is aware of whatever we do within His universal form, just as we are conscious of our little selves. Through oneness with that Christ Consciousness Jesus was able to know, without being told, that Lazarus was dead.

The wonders of God's creation cannot be discovered by a cow; it is the unique potential of human beings to attain the omniscience of oneness with Christ Consciousness. I ask those who do not believe in God: "Whence came the intelligence in man and in the universe, if it is not produced in some divine 'Factory' hidden behind the ether?" Such mysteries prompted Einstein to say that space looks very suspicious. Space is concealing God; His Intelligence is hidden there, for out of the "nothingness" of space comes everything.

Being one with this Intelligence, which guides every atom in creation, Jesus could materialize his form anywhere he wished. And he can still do so, just as he used to appear every night to St. Francis in Assisi. Jesus was conscious not only of his microcosmic physical form, but also of all creation as his macrocosmic body; he could truthfully say: "I and my Father are one."* He experienced his presence in all atoms, even as does his Father. Jesus alluded to the omnipresent Christ Consciousness when he said, "Are not two sparrows sold for a farthing? and one of them shall not fall on the ground without [the sight of] your Father."†

Christ came at a critical time in history, when the world was sorely in need of spiritual hope and regeneration.‡ His message was not intended to foster multifarious sects, each claiming him as their own. His was a universal message of unity, one of the grandest ever given. He reminded mankind that it is written in the scriptures, "Ye are gods";§ and St. John voiced the inspiration and spirit of Christ's teaching when he said, "But as many as received him [the Christ Consciousness

* John 10:30.

† Matthew 10:29.

‡ In the Bhagavad-Gita the Lord says: "O Bharata, whenever virtue (dharma) declines and vice (adharma) predominates, I incarnate as an avatar. In visible form I appear to destroy evil and reestablish virtue" (IV:7–8).

§ John 10:34.

manifested in Jesus and in all creation], to them gave he power to become the sons of God."* Was there ever a greater message? Jesus assured the downtrodden, the white and the dark man, the Oriental and the Occidental, that they are all children of God; whoever is pure in heart, no matter what his race or color, can receive the Lord.

The charcoal and the diamond receive the same rays of the sun, but the diamond reflects their radiance. So, both in the Orient and the Occident, those who have diamond mentalities shall reflect God and be called the sons of God, and those who keep themselves dark with evil qualities shall not be able to reflect His light.

Train Your Heart to Feel the Brotherhood of Man

All mankind should open its heart to Jesus' great message: "[God] hath made of one blood all nations of men."† That is the Christ inspiration I love so much. I want to make that message a living reality, to give it a practical application. Color prejudice is the most foolish of all man's displays of ignorance. Color is only skin deep. God gave darker skin pigment to races that originally lived under climatic conditions requiring greater protection from the sun, a purely practical measure; therefore white, olive, yellow, red, or black skin is nothing to be particularly proud of. After all, the soul wears a bodily overcoat of one color in one lifetime and other hues in other incarnations. So the color of one's complexion is a very superficial thing. To have any color prejudice is to discriminate against God, who is sitting in the hearts of all the red, white, yellow, olive, and black peoples of the world. Besides, it is well to remember that whoever hates any race will surely reincarnate in that bodily form; thus does the karmic law force man to overcome his soul-stifling prejudices. Train your heart to feel the brotherhood of man—that is most important.

Although Jesus' teachings were preordained to establish their strongest foundation in the West, he chose an incarnation in an Oriental body, and in the Jewish race, which has had a long history of persecution, because he wanted to demonstrate

* John 1:12.
† Acts 17:26.

the folly of judging others according to distinctions of race and color. True Christianity must be lived; racial divisions must be banished. Prejudices and lack of real brotherhood are causes of war and disunion among God's children. We must work at eradicating all incitements to war; in hate and prejudice lie bombs and misery. Jesus warned: "...for all they that take the sword shall perish with the sword."* It is not the sword, but the practice of Christ principles that shall ultimately free the world. In the highest sense, God alone protects you. You can best help this world by ideal living, as taught by Christ and all spiritually enlightened ones. Above all else, love God; don't you see that the whole answer is in His hands? When He will push aside the screen of mystery, you will see the answer to all that was theretofore obscure and unfathomable.

Some Westerners consider the Hindus heathens; they don't know that many Hindus consider Westerners heathens also—ignorance is fifty-fifty everywhere. I am sometimes asked if I believe in Jesus. I reply: "Why such a question? We in India reverence Jesus and his teachings, perhaps more than you do."

In order to love Christ you must live what he taught, you must follow the example of his life. Jesus said: "...whosoever shall smite thee on thy right cheek, turn to him the other also."† India has practiced this teaching more than any other nation. Many who call themselves Christian do not even apply it; they say that it is a beautiful philosophy, but if you were to slap them they would return twelve slaps, a kick, and maybe a bullet! Anyone who so retaliates is not a true Christian, or lover of Christ, for that is not the spirit of the all-forgiving Jesus.

Every time you see the symbol of the Cross it should remind you of what it stands for—that you must bear your crosses with right attitude, even as Jesus did. When you mean well and still you are misunderstood or mistreated, instead of being angry you should say, as did Christ: "Father, forgive them for they know not what they do." Why forgive one who wrongs you? Because if you angrily strike back you misrepre-

* Matthew 26:52.
† Matthew 5:39.

sent your own divine soul nature—you are no better than your offender. But if you manifest spiritual strength you are blessed, and the power of your righteous behavior will also help the other person to overcome his misunderstanding.

Those eternal principles of truth and righteousness taught by Jesus we take very seriously in India—we take them literally, without rationalizing them to suit our purposes. Jesus said: "And everyone that hath forsaken houses, or brethren, or sisters, or father, or mother, or wife, or children, or lands, for my name's sake, shall receive an hundredfold, and shall inherit everlasting life."* That spirit of renunciation for God is all-pervasive in India. Especially in olden days it was the ideal of every man to give at least one part of his lifetime to God alone.

God Does Not Like to Be Forgotten

Complete renunciation is not necessary for everyone, but if you forget God while fulfilling your material duties, God will not like it. Give time to Him alone, without work. I always save time in the morning and night for God, and the rest of the day I serve Him wholeheartedly. The Lord says in the Gita: "Whatever actions thou dost perform...dedicate them all as offerings to Me. Thus no action of thine can enchain thee with good or evil *karma*."† You came on this earth for God. It is His world, not yours. You are here to work for Him. Life will very much disappoint and disillusion you if you labor only for yourself, because eventually you will have to leave everything; you will be forced to practice renunciation then!

The message of Christ is one of compassion and forgiveness, renunciation (in spirit if one cannot do it in actuality), morality, brotherly love and unity and equality, and supreme love for God. Remember Jesus' admonition: "And why call ye me, Lord, Lord, and do not the things which I say?"‡

The authenticity of the life of Christ has been questioned by many agnostics. Some have propounded the theory that Jesus was legendary, his life a mere fictitious drama. I know that Christ is real, for I have seen him many times.

Jesus was not as fair complexioned as most of you in the

* Matthew 19:29.   † IX:27-28.   ‡ Luke 6:46.

West. He had dark skin. And his eyes were not pale blue, as many artists paint them; they were dark. Nor was his hair blond; it also was dark.

A Vision of Christ at the Yogoda School in India

One day at my school in Ranchi, I was sitting with the young boys when I saw someone coming toward us, from behind the boys, and wondered who it was. Then I saw it was Jesus; his feet were not touching the ground as he approached. He came very close to us and then vanished.

A few years later, in Boston, I again saw Jesus. I was meditating and deeply praying to God because I felt that for three days I had forgotten Him—I had been so engrossed in fulfilling the responsibilities He had given to me. I told the Lord: "I am going to walk out of this work!" The right attitude is to love God and love His work because of Him. Those who do missionary service, but never make the effort to meditate or commune with God, never find Him. Because I felt that the activities of my ministry had taken me away from God, I prayed, "Lord, I will go away. I will not remain in America and do Your work unless I know You are with me." Then a Voice came through the ether like a beam of light: "What do you want? You cannot go." Many times in my life God has thus prevented me from carrying out my desire to run away from my duties to this cause, to be only with Him. I replied to the Divine Voice: "Let me see, on a sea of gold, Krishna and Jesus and their disciples." Even as I made this inward request, I saw those divine ones coming toward me! "It is a hallucination," I thought. "If the person meditating with me sees this also, then I shall believe." Instantly my companion exclaimed aloud: "Oh, I see Christ and Krishna!" Then I rationalized, "This is thought transference." I was doubting and praying to God to help my unbelief when the Voice said: "When I leave, the room will become filled with the fragrance of the lotus, and whoever comes shall notice it." As the vision vanished, the whole room became permeated with a marvelous lotus essence. Others entering the room even hours later noted the aroma. I could doubt no longer.

Mahavatar Babaji ordained that I come to America to interpret the teachings of Christ for the purpose of showing their parallelism with the yoga teachings of India's Lord Krishna. In the immortal truths expressed by these two *avatars* lies the answer of the ages. That is why Babaji, who is in divine communion with Christ, gave me the special dispensation of carrying this message to the West.

So long as breath will be in the body, I will try to bring East and West together to fulfill the purpose for which Christ came on earth in an Oriental body. His soul in the West, his body in the East; bringing soul and body together unites East and West.

Truth Is a Universal Experience

Help to spread the message of Self-Realization Fellowship. There is nothing vague or mysterious about Self-Realization teachings. You can realize these truths for yourself. Truth is truth, and it is a universal experience. After I heard my guru, Sri Yukteswarji, teach, I could see the blemishes in the talks of those who tried to make me understand something they did not understand themselves. A salesman should never try to sell something he does not believe in. One should teach only those things he has practiced and experienced.

Devotees of this path should sincerely study the *Self-Realization Lessons* and meditate deeply each night before going to bed. Jesus promised to send the Holy Ghost, the Great Comforter.* Through the practice of the Self-Realization techniques of meditation, the faithful student is enabled to realize the fulfillment of that promise. Worshiping Jesus is not truly meaningful until one can expand his consciousness to receive within himself the Christ Consciousness. That is the second coming of Christ. Unless you do your part, a thousand Christs come on earth would not be able to save you. You have to work for your own salvation. Then Christ can help you.

The first two lines of Rudyard Kipling's poem became famous: "East is East and West is West, and never the twain shall meet...." But just because I eat curry and you eat apple pie, why should there be division between us? Division is imaginary lines drawn by small minds. It is the result of superiority complexes, and is the cause of wars and pernicious

* John 14:16,26; 15:26. (See page 136.)

troubles. We must destroy division. Look to the example of the great Christ who came in the East and stands as a lofty ideal before both East and West, telling them, "Here am I in the midst of you; learn from one another, balance your spirituality and material development." There he stands—a Christ of East and West—linking the two hemispheres with this message of unity. Can you not see him?

Christ and Krishna
Avatars of the One Truth

Self-Realization Fellowship International Headquarters,
Los Angeles, California, January 15, 1933, and April 14, 1935
(Compilation)

He is a master whose consciousness has been refined to receive and reflect perfectly the light of God. The sun shines equally on a piece of charcoal and a diamond, but only the diamond reflects the sun's light. God's light also shines equally on all stages of life, but the reflection is greater from some than from others. The divine light is fully reflected by the man of realization.

Every human being is essentially a soul, covered with a veil of *maya*. Through evolution and self-effort, man makes a little hole in the veil; in time, he makes the hole bigger and bigger. As the opening enlarges, his consciousness expands; the soul becomes more manifest. When the veil is completely torn away, the soul is fully manifest in him. That man has become a master—master of himself and of *maya*.

The great ones are not specially manufactured by God. They became masters through their own efforts. They had to work and fight for liberation, just as all the rest of mankind is struggling toward the light of soul freedom.

Divine incarnations such as Jesus Christ and Jadava* Krishna had somewhere, sometime, developed that spiritual stature which foredestined their birth as *avatars.*† Such beings are free from the karmic compulsions of rebirth; they return to earth only to help liberate mankind.

---

* One of the several names of Krishna. (See glossary.)

† This Sanskrit word means "descent"; its roots are *ava*, "down," and *tri*, "to pass." In the Hindu scriptures, *avatara* signifies the descent of Divinity into flesh.

Even though liberated, the divine ones play, at God's behest, their human roles in the seeming reality of the earth-life drama. They have their weaknesses, their struggles and temptations, and then, through righteous battle and right behavior, they attain victory. In this way they show that all men can be and are meant to be spiritually victorious over the forces that would keep them from realizing their inherent oneness with God.

A Christ and a Krishna created perfect by God, without any effort of self-evolution on their part, and merely pretending to struggle and overcome their trials on earth, could not be examples for suffering humans to follow. The fact that the great ones too were once such mortals, but overcame, makes them pillars of strength and inspiration for stumbling mankind. When we know that divine *avatars*, in order to make themselves perfect, once had to go through the same kinds of human trials and experiences that we do, it gives us hope in our own struggle.

A God-realized master is known by his spiritual deeds. Miracles are not the most important of these. Some of the miracles that Christ performed can be duplicated in other ways by scientists today. On the spiritual side, Christ himself said: "He that believeth on me, the works that I do shall he do also; and greater works than these shall he do."* Miracles such as you have heard about I have seen demonstrated many times by the masters; but these are not the criterion of their greatness. The power to perform miracles comes naturally to those who know God, because they are in tune with His cosmic laws; but those who become attached to miracles will lose Him. God alone must be the goal of our hearts. A master's most important spiritual accomplishment is the conquering of *maya*, delusion: the attainment of that realization which makes God supreme in one's life—more important than life itself.

Christ performed his greatest miracle when he allowed himself to suffer on the cross, saying, "Father, forgive them, for they know not what they do."† He could have retaliated with

* John 14:12.
† Luke 23:34.

spiritual power and saved himself. His victory has immortalized him as an example for the ages. If he was able to overcome his mortal consciousness to express divinity, other men can do the same.

The manifestation of God in the life of divine beings is sometimes measured in terms of the quantitative and qualitative good they do. But great ones who fully manifest God are equally one with Him. So it is impossible to make comparisons between the masters (or *avatars*), and foolish to try, because being one with God they are all the same; they are all equal before Him.

But to me Krishna and Christ stand supreme. By the greatness of his loving sacrifice, Christ has influenced the whole world. Krishna manifested a different aspect of the Infinite Father. In contradistinction to Christ, who was a renunciant, Krishna was a king; and I bow to one who can be a king and remain a divine one at the same time. To be in the world but not of the world is very difficult, for you live in the midst of temptations and desires and yet must remain untouched by them.

Krishna came on earth much earlier than Christ, about three thousand years before, some scholars say. The lives of Christ and Krishna have not only a great spiritual concomitance; there are also parallels in the personal stories that come down to us. Both Jesus and Krishna were born of devout, God-loving parents. Krishna's parents were persecuted by his wicked uncle, King Kansa; King Herod's threats tormented the mother and father of Jesus. Jesus has been likened to a good shepherd; Krishna, during his early years in hiding from Kansa, was a cowherd. Jesus conquered Satan; Krishna conquered the demon Kaliya.* Jesus stopped a storm on the sea to save a ship carrying his disciples; Krishna, to prevent his devotees and their cattle from being drowned in a deluge of rain, lifted Mt. Gowardhan over them like an umbrella.

Jesus was called "King of the Jews," though his kingdom was not of this world; Krishna was an earthly king as well as a divine one. Jesus had women disciples, Mary, Martha, and

---

* Satan and Kaliya represent evil, or ignorance of God.

Mary Magdalene, who helped him and played a vital role in his mission; Krishna's women disciples, Radha and the *gopis* (milkmaids), similarly played divine roles. Jesus was crucified by being nailed to a cross; Krishna was mortally wounded by a hunter's arrow. The destinies of both were prophesied in the scriptures. These two *avatars*, both Orientals, are generally recognized in the West and East respectively as the supreme incarnations of God.

Jesus Christ and Bhagavan Krishna gave to the world two of the greatest books of all times. The words of Lord Krishna in the Bhagavad-Gita and of Lord Jesus in the New Testament of the Bible are sublime manifestations of truth, great models of spiritual scripture. These two bibles give essentially the same teaching. The deeper Christianity that was preached by Jesus has been lost sight of today. Christ taught devotion and yoga, as did Krishna; and it was my *param-paramguru*, Mahavatar Babaji, who first spoke of showing the unity of Christ's teaching and Krishna's Yoga philosophy. * To fulfill this mission is the special dispensation given to me by Babaji.

The Universal Consciousness

I am glad that Christianity was not called "Jesusism," because Christianity is a much broader word. There is a difference of meaning between *Jesus* and *Christ*.† Jesus is the name of a little human body in which the vast Christ Consciousness was born. Although the Christ Consciousness manifested in the body of Jesus, it cannot be limited to one human form. It would be a metaphysical error to say that the omnipresent Christ Consciousness is circumscribed by the body of any one human being.

Jadava Krishna is the Christ of the Hindus. These two great *avatars*, Jadava and Jesus, fully manifested the Christ Consciousness, the *Kutastha Chaitanya* or divine guiding Intelligence that is in every atom of creation. "But as many as

---

* Mahavatar Babaji had requested my guru, Swami Sri Yukteswar, to write a book showing that there is no real discrepancy between the scriptures of East and West. That book is *The Holy Science*.

† See *Jesus: a Christ of East and West*, p. 283.

received him (the universal Christ Consciousness), to them gave he power to become the sons of God."*

Jesus said: "Are not two sparrows sold for a farthing? and one of them shall not fall on the ground without [the sight of] your Father."† God's consciousness is everywhere. He knows simultaneously everything that is going on in the world. You are aware of whatever is happening in any part of your body, and in the same way God feels everything that is going on in His body—the cosmos. When you can feel His omnipresent consciousness in your fingertips, in your heart and head and wherever there is any vibration of creation; when you can feel yourself in every speck of space; when your sympathy and love have spread everywhere and you feel oneness with everything, you are in Christ Consciousness. Both Jesus and Jadava were one with the omnipresence of Christ Consciousness.

If you put some salt water in a bottle and cork it, and then place the bottle in the ocean, the water in the bottle cannot mix with the water of the ocean. Remove the cork and they become one, being composed of the same ingredients. So when we remove the cork of ignorance from the bottle of our consciousness, as did Jadava Krishna and Jesus Christ, we become one with the vast Universal Consciousness.

From Christ and Krishna we learn that the purpose of religion is to expand human consciousness and unite it with the omnipresent Christ Consciousness. How? The social way is by cultivating divine love for everything that is. To love all impartially is to know Christ Consciousness. The transcendental way is by direct communion with the Christ Consciousness through yoga meditation.

The body continuously reminds you that you are flesh. Yet every night in sleep God banishes your consciousness of the flesh to show you that you are not the body. You are not the wave, but the Ocean behind the wave. You are not this mortal consciousness, but the Immortal Consciousness behind it.

Jesus declared: "I and my Father are one."‡ He who knows God becomes one with God. The consciousness of such a devotee is not only in the body; he feels oneness with the Spirit

---

* John 1:12.   † Matthew 10:29.   ‡ John 10:30.

behind his body and mind. When the wave dances on the sea it thinks it exists as a separate entity. But once it realizes, "I cannot exist without the ocean," the wave sees that it *is* the ocean, that the ocean has created a little wave out of itself. Similarly, God can manifest Himself as a soul within the form of man, but He cannot be limited by that form. The Bhagavad-Gita says: "The Supreme Spirit existing in the body is the detached Beholder, the Consenter, the Sustainer, the Experiencer, the Great Lord, and the Highest Self."* Jesus understood that "The Father has become myself." This truth is also brought out in the Hindu scriptures: *"Tat twam asi,"* "That thou art."

Concepts of God and Trinity Agree

Hinduism as well as Christianity believes in one God. A few misunderstanding Westerners who have visited India have brought back stories that prejudice others against Hindu religious practices. I could similarly go back to India and say that I found America to be a place of murderers, racketeers, and drunkards; but I realize that such persons do not constitute the whole of America. There are defects in India as there are defects in America and everywhere else. Some Indian teachers instruct their followers to concentrate on an image representing a particular aspect of the Infinite Spirit. The visible image helps devotees to increase their concentration and devotion in prayer to the unseen Spirit. Uninformed Westerners conclude that Indians as a whole worship idols. But we worship only Brahman, Spirit. The concept of one God is the same in Hinduism as in Christianity.

The concept of the Trinity is also exactly the same in the Hindu and Christian scriptures. The Trinity is not a negation of the one God; it illustrates a metaphysical truth, that the One became Three when God made this creation.

In the beginning—when there was no creation—there was Spirit. But Spirit wanted to create, and by His wishful thought He projected a great sphere of light, or cosmic energy, which became the universe. That cosmic energy is the Holy Ghost. "Ghost" means something invisible and intelligent. "Holy

* XIII:23.

Ghost" refers to the spiritual vibration or energy of creation in which the intelligence of God is immanent as Christ Consciousness, "the only begotten Son,"* God's pure reflection in creation. This Christ Intelligence holds the universe in balance. God the Father is the Intelligence beyond creation; the Son or Christ Consciousness is His Intelligence in creation; and the Holy Ghost is the intelligent vibration of creation itself. Long before Christ spoke of it, the Trinity was described in the Hindu scriptures: "Aum, Tat, Sat"—Cosmic Vibration, Christ Intelligence, and God the Father.

The Bible tells us of Jesus Christ's promise that when he was gone from this world he would send the Comforter,† the Holy Ghost. Every vibration emanates a sound. The Holy Ghost is the Cosmic Intelligent Vibration, whose sound is the Aum or Amen heard in deep yoga meditation. Saint John spoke of it when he said: "I was in the Spirit on the Lord's day, and heard behind me a great voice, as of a trumpet."‡ That sound is the Holy Ghost. In its vibration is our comfort.

We are living in a new age in which God's voice of cosmic vibration, of Aum and Amen, can be heard from the two ends of the two hemispheres in the scriptures of Krishna and Christ. It was in the land of India that Krishna spoke of the Aum sound§ and it was another Oriental Christ who spoke of this same vibration, calling it Amen or Holy Ghost, as the means of communing with God.

By attuning your consciousness within in meditation, you can hear and commune with the Aum or Amen vibration in which you meet the great Comforter. In communion with the holy Comforter you realize the immanent Christ Consciousness. In deeper communion with the Christ Consciousness

---

* John 1:18.   † John 14:26.   ‡ Revelation 1:10.

§ The author here refers to a verse in the Bhagavad-Gita wherein the Lord in the form of Krishna says: "I am the Aum (Pranava) in all the Vedas; the sound in the ether..."(VII:8). In his Autobiography, Paramahansaji has explained that the wisdom of the Vedas, India's most ancient scriptures, was divinely revealed from age to age to the rishis, "seers"; and that it was a revelation by sound, "directly heard" (shruti). Having by deepest meditation attuned their consciousness to the cosmic vibration of Aum, the rishis heard within the timeless truths about Spirit and creation. (Publisher's Note)

you realize you are one with God. As soon as you know the Holy Ghost you know Christ Consciousness, and when you know Christ Consciousness you know that you and your Father, Cosmic Consciousness, are one. The divine Christ Consciousness hidden in every atom of creation is the same as the Cosmic Consciousness of the Father beyond creation. First you must know how to commune with the Trinity. Through such communion, you become one with Spirit; then there is no longer a Trinity: Father, Son, and Holy Ghost are seen to be the one Spirit.

The Pitfalls of Body Consciousness

Consider the limitations of this physical body. Looking outward you see disease, suffering, pain, and heartaches; but on the other, inner side of this body, in the subtle centers of spiritual consciousness, is the Comforter. When your mind follows the stream of ordinary outward consciousness you will know Hades; but when by meditating on *Aum* your mind follows the stream of the inner consciousness, you will find the great Heaven that exists behind this body. That is why Jesus said, "Take no thought for your life, what ye shall eat, or what ye shall drink; nor yet for your body, what ye shall put on. Is not the life more than meat, and the body more than raiment?"* As soon as you become concentrated on the limited physical body you will fall into the pit of misery. It is popular in these times to seek prosperity, but you may become ill and unable to enjoy your abundance. Therefore Jesus warned that we should seek the kingdom of God first. Your consciousness must be with God. This is man's highest duty. "For all these things do the nations of the world seek after; and your Father knoweth that ye have need of these things. But rather seek ye the kingdom of God; and all these things shall be added unto you."† Health or no health, power or no power, seek God first. When you seek with that determination, "all things shall be added unto you"—not before.

Christ went even further: "There is no man that hath left house, or brethren, or sisters, or father, or mother, or wife, or

* Matthew 6:25.
† Luke 12:30-31.

children, or lands, for my sake, and the gospel's, but he shall receive an hundredfold now in this time, houses, and brethren, and sisters, and mothers, and children, and lands, with persecutions; and in the world to come eternal life."* In these words Christ teaches physical renunciation as the highest way of attaining God. Isn't it foolish not to renounce a few material things in order to realize the kingdom of heaven? But seldom do even devout Christians follow what Christ said here; not many are able to follow this path. Yet renunciation is not self-punishment; it is the investment of a few temporal trinkets in order to gain the eternal treasure—God. Worldly persons have left God for perishable acquisitions, but I have left perishable things for God.

The Gita also advises renunciation. Krishna says: "Forsaking all other *dharmas* (duties), remember Me alone; I will free thee from all sins (accruing from nonperformance of those lesser duties)." † The shame and trouble and misery that will arise from forsaking worldly duties God will forgive you. But the Gita says more: "The sages call that man wise whose pursuits are all without selfish plan or longings for results, and whose activities are purified by the fire of wisdom. Relinquishing attachment to the fruits of work, always contented, independent (of material rewards), the wise do not perform any (binding) action even in the midst of activities."‡ Therein Krishna declares that it is not necessary to forsake all things outwardly to find God, if everything you do is without selfish motive, and done only to please Him. To forget God for worldly duties is to show colossal ingratitude, for we cannot do our duty to our family and others without the power borrowed from Him.

In India hundreds go away into the forest just to think of God alone. That is the way that Christ taught when he called to his disciples, "Follow me."§ They left their work and their homes and forsook all, even their lives, for God.

Significance of Krishna's Life for Modern Man

Lord Krishna says in the Gita that what man really needs to do to find the kingdom of heaven is to renounce the *fruits* of

* Mark 10:29–30.   † XVIII:66.   ‡ IV:19.   §Matthew 4:19.

action. God has sent man into this life so circumstanced with hunger and desires that he *must* work. Without work human civilization would be a jungle of disease, famine, and confusion. If all the people in the world were to leave their material civilizations and live in the forests, the forests would then have to be transformed into cities, else the inhabitants would die because of lack of sanitation. On the other hand, material civilization is full of imperfections and misery. What possible remedy can be advocated?

Krishna's life demonstrates his philosophy that it is not necessary to flee the responsibilities of material life. The problem can be solved by bringing God here where He has placed us. No matter what our environment may be, in the mind wherein God-communion reigns, Heaven must come.

"A heaven without Thee, O God, I want not! I love to work in the factory if I can but hear Thy voice in the noisy wheels of the machinery. A material life without Thee, my Lord, is a source of physical misery, disease, crime, ignorance, and unhappiness." *

To avoid the pitfalls of the two extremes, renunciation of the world, or drowning in material life, man should so train his mind by constant meditation that he can perform the necessary dutiful actions of his daily life and still maintain the consciousness of God within. All men and women should remember that their worldly life can be freed from endless physical and mental ills if they add deep meditation to their daily routine of living. A balanced life of meditation and activity, without attachment to the fruits of action, is the example set by Krishna's life.

The message of Krishna in the Bhagavad-Gita stands as the doctrine best suited to our modern busy life of many worries. To work without the peace of God is hades. To work with God's happiness ever bubbling in the soul is to carry a portable paradise within you wherever you go. To be constantly worried even in pleasant surroundings is to live in hades; to live in the inner, boundless soul-peace, even though housed in a rickety shack, is real paradise. Whether in a palace or under a tree, we must carry with us always this inner heaven.

* *Whispers from Eternity.*

The yogi enjoys everything with the consciousness of God. But at the same time he can say: "If I don't see the face of food, I shall never miss it." The conditions of the world should not bother you. Be not attached to anything. Jesus fasted for forty days and kept his mind always on God.

If you are in the world and have no attachment to it, you are a real yogi. To remain in the candy store and not touch the candy is true renunciation. However, milk will not float on water unless you make butter of it. The only way to find happiness and emancipation is to seek God and live by His laws. Jesus said: "If thy hand offend thee, cut it off."* That kind of determination is needed. You must realize in your heart and soul this truth: "Lord, You alone are mine. I am here just to please You."

Renounce not only outwardly but mentally too. Jesus did not mean that man should not eat or put on clothes; he himself ate food and wore clothing. He did mean that one should be mentally nonattached to dress and food. He was teaching that renunciation must be accomplished mentally as well as externally. "Take no thought...for your body"† means "Don't worry too much about food and clothing and the demands of the body." It is more important to be clean inside than outside. If you can be pure within and also clean without, that is even better.

Moral Doctrines Universal in the Scriptures

We find the main moral doctrines of religion in both the Bible and the Hindu scriptures. The message of the Gita includes the precepts of the Ten Commandments of Christianity, and also the reason why it is wrong to break them. The Gita wisely warns: "He who ignores the scriptural commands and who follows his own foolish desires does not find happiness or perfection or the Infinite Goal."‡ You can be moral without being religious, but the principles of morality are a necessary beginning in the practice of religion; for true religion is deeper than morality—it is contact with God. You should not concentrate on your faults, nor think of yourself as a sinner.

* Mark 9:43.   † Matthew 6:25.   ‡ XVI:23.

Affirm that you are a child of God, and dwell on what Jesus said: "I and my Father are one."

Reincarnation in the Gita and the Bible

Reincarnation, so beautifully expounded by Krishna in the Bhagavad-Gita, is one of the most helpful and inspiring spiritual doctrines; without it we cannot understand the justice of God. Why would a baby be born crippled? Why would God send to a family two babies who are strong and whole, and one who is lame? If we are all made in God's image, where is the justice of this? Only reincarnation can explain it. The crippled baby is a soul that in some past life transgressed God's laws and, as a result, lost the use of his legs. As it is the mind that molds the body, and this soul had lost the consciousness of having healthy legs, it was unable to create a perfect pair of limbs when it came back again in this life. And so we must come, and come again, until we regain our lost perfection. He who becomes perfect shall not have to return to earth anymore.

Those who have overcome desire shall be one with God. Jesus spoke of this when he said: "Him that overcometh will I make a pillar in the temple of my God, and he shall go no more out."* The Gita similarly promises: "O Arjuna! this is spoken of as the 'established in Brahma (Spirit)' state. Anyone entering this state is never deluded. Even at the very moment of transition (from the physical to the astral), if one becomes anchored therein, he attains the final state of Spirit-communion."† When you overcome physical desires, you shall go no more out of God. Desire brings you back to this earth. We have been prodigal children, and unless we forsake desires we cannot go back to God. If suddenly we have to leave this earth with desires still in our hearts, we must come here again until we work them out. It is necessary to regain self-perfection before we can return to God. When the storm is on, the wave rises out of the ocean, but as soon as the ocean is calm again, the wave can sink back into the sea. So it is with us. As soon as this storm of material desires is over we can melt again into the ocean of God.

* Revelation 3:12.
† II:72.

Early Christianity taught reincarnation. Jesus had revealed his knowledge of this truth when he said: "Elias is come already, and they knew him not.... Then the disciples understood that he spake unto them of John the Baptist."* When he said, "Elias is come already," he meant that the soul of Elias had reincarnated in the body of John the Baptist.

Christ Born an Oriental to Unite East and West

God made Jesus Christ an Oriental in order to bring East and West together. Christ came to awaken the divine consciousness of brotherhood in the East and West. It is true that Christ lived in India during most of the eighteen unaccounted-for years of his life, studying with India's great masters. That doesn't take away from his divinity and uniqueness; it shows the unity and brotherhood of all great saints and *avatars*.

The great ones come on earth to show that the Christ Consciousness they have attained is what all who live here must seek. You must expand your consciousness and banish your suffering. Eating food doesn't make physical pain go away. Acquiring possessions doesn't stop mental suffering. Reading spiritual books doesn't satisfy the soul. The masters of India say that the purpose of religion is not to create certain doctrines to be followed blindly, but to show mankind the perennial method of finding everlasting happiness. As the businessman tries to alleviate the suffering of others by supplying some need; as every man is an agent of God for doing some good on earth, so Christ, Krishna, Buddha—all the great ones—came on earth to bestow on mankind the highest good: knowledge of the path to Eternal Bliss, and the example of their sublime lives to inspire us to follow it.

Someday you will have to leave the body. No matter how powerful you are, the body will eventually have to be buried beneath the sod. There is no time to be wasted. The Yoga methods taught by my beloved Christ and my beloved Krishna do destroy ignorance and suffering, by enabling man to attain his own Self-realization and union with God. In the name of the Originator of Christians and Hindus, let us break down the walls of suffering and ignorance, and worship God truly. Too

* Matthew 17:12-13.

often in His name the demons of avarice and prejudice have danced in God's temples. We must restore to His altars the Lord of peace and joy. Let us behave on earth not as Americans or Indians with conflicting customs and beliefs, but as children of one Father. "Christian" and "Hindu" are only names. Let us live as a great divine family in a United World of Oneness, knowing within and without the harmony and bliss of Spirit.

* * *

A Vision of Christ and Krishna

An experience recounted by
Paramahansa Yogananda in "Whispers from Eternity"

I beheld a great blue valley encircled by mountains that shimmered jewel-like. Around opalescent peaks vagrant mists sparkled. A river of silence flowed by, diamond-bright. And there I saw, coming out of the depths of the mountains, Jesus and Krishna walking hand in hand: the Christ who prayed by the river Jordan and the Christna who played a flute by the river Jamuna.

They baptized me in the radiant waters; my soul melted in fathomless depths. Everything began to emit astral flames. My body and the forms of Christ and Krishna, the iridescent hills, the glowing stream, and the far empyrean became dancing lights, while atoms of fire flew. Finally nothing remained but mellow luminosity, in which all creation trembled.

O Spirit! in my heart I bow again and again to Thee: Eternal Light in Whom all forms commingle.

The Ten Commandments

Eternal Rules of Happiness

First Self-Realization Fellowship Temple at
Encinitas, California, March 6, 1938

The sudden cataclysms that occur in nature, creating havoc and mass injury, are not "acts of God." Such disasters result from the thoughts and actions of man. Wherever the world's vibratory balance of good and evil is disturbed by an accumulation of harmful vibrations, the result of man's wrong thinking and wrong doing, you will see devastation such as we have recently experienced.*

The world will continue to have warfare and natural calamities until all people correct their wrong thoughts and behavior. Wars are brought about not by fateful divine action but by widespread material selfishness. Banish selfishness—individual, industrial, political, national—and you will have no more wars.

When materiality predominates in man's consciousness, there is an emission of subtle negative rays; their cumulative power disturbs the electrical balance of nature, and that is when earthquakes, floods, and other disasters happen. God is not responsible for them! Man's thoughts have to be controlled before nature can be controlled.†

Rama, an *avatar* who was one of India's great Hindu emperors, reigned over the kingdom of Ayodhya, whose inhabi-

---

* A reference to local floods after unusually heavy rains.

† "Man's vaunted 'conquest of nature' is the expression of a power complex—vain humbug. Nature is that which we *obey*. The scientist is deciphering the rules we have to obey. Every rule disclosed has had within it its own power to ensure obedience."—G. Scott Williamson and Innes H. Pearse, *Biologists in Search of Material* (Faber & Faber, London, 1950).

tants all lived righteously. It is said that during the golden era of Rama's rule no accidents or premature deaths or natural disasters disturbed Ayodhya's perfect harmony. There will be more harmony and health in every home as the individual members of the family live more rightly. When family members selfishly take away from one another, the house naturally will be filled with disharmony. So also with the nations; only when mankind lives rightly will the kingdom of God come on earth. But time is short. You are here today, and tomorrow you are gone. As a human being, it is your highest privilege to seek God. You should use the freedom He has given you in this life to prove by experiment the eternal spiritual truths.

Sin is that which causes you suffering. Virtue is that which makes you lastingly happy. If there is no spiritual harmony in your mind, even a new house and a new car cannot make you happy; you will have your hades with you just the same.

Real happiness can stand the challenge of all outer experiences. When you can bear the crucifixions of others' wrongs against you and still return love and forgiveness; and when you can keep that divine inner peace intact despite all painful thrusts of outer circumstance, then you shall know happiness.

"He who ignores the scriptural commands and who follows his own foolish desires does not find happiness or perfection or the Infinite Goal. Take the scriptures as your guide in determining what should be done and what should be avoided. Act in accordance with the wisdom given in the holy books."* Those who are inwardly content are living rightly. Happiness comes only by doing right. Be happy here and you will also be happy in the beyond. Death is not an escape. You must be good now if you want heaven in the future. According to the law of cause and effect, you are after death exactly what you were before. So "make hay" by gathering wisdom while the sun of opportunity shines.

The Ten Eternal Rules of Happiness

The Ten Commandments† might have been more aptly named the Ten Eternal Rules of Happiness. The word "com-

* Bhagavad-Gita XVI:23–24.   † Exodus 20:3–17.

mandment" is an unfortunate choice, because few persons like to be commanded. As soon as you tell a child not to do a thing, he at once wants to do it.

These Ten Commandments are being broken every day, everywhere. Unless their spiritual meaning is understood, people will always rebel against them. The Ten Commandments are eternal rules of conduct that have been set forth in all the great world religions. However, the scriptures for the most part do not explain the psychology and utility of these commandments. People accept them in church but do not act upon them outside of church, rationalizing that these precepts are impractical. Yet the breaking of the Ten Commandments is the primary source of all the misery in the world.

What is the utility of the commandments? In the Bhagavad-Gita we are told to forsake all else and remember God alone. "Absorb thy mind in Me, become My devotee; resign all things to Me; bow down to Me. Thou art dear to Me, so in truth do I promise thee: thou shalt attain Me."* This corresponds to the first of the Ten Commandments given to Moses:

"Thou shalt have no other gods before me." God-realization should be the goal of living. Material duties cannot be performed without power borrowed from God. To perform one's ordinary duties, and forget Him, is the highest sin. Sin means ignorance, acting against one's highest good. How many times have you felt a burning sorrow in your heart? Why? Because you didn't act rightly; because God was not first in your heart. The Gita says: "Forsaking all other *dharmas* (duties), remember Me alone; I will free thee from all sins (accruing from nonperformance of those lesser duties)."† There should be no other god in your life who means more to you than God. Even though Jesus was one with the Father, he said: "I do not know all the things that my Father knows."‡

As soon as man begins to worship possessions, name, fame—anything less than God—he finds unhappiness. "Those who worship lesser gods, O Arjuna, they go unto them; My

---

* XVIII:65.   † XVIII:66.

‡ "But of that day and hour knoweth no man, no not the angels which are in heaven, neither the Son, but the Father" (Mark 13:32).

devotee comes unto Me." * Only God can fulfill man's dreams of lasting happiness. No diversion should be allowed to replace worship of the Supreme Lord. If you study the Hindu scriptures you will see how they correspond with the Ten Commandments of the Bible.

"Thou shalt not make unto thee any graven image." Symbol worship is all right for a few, but it has more bad than good results. To worship the cross of Christ and forget what the cross stands for is to worship a "graven image," because you have lost sight of its significance. When a great spiritual teacher passes on, his image, or some symbol of his life, is usually kept and venerated, and this is all right provided you remember and emulate his qualities. But if you worship an image without conscious regard for what it represents, then you have forgotten the Infinite. To have a picture or a statue of Jesus is acceptable if it helps you to dwell on his divine qualities. Then you are not worshiping a graven image, but the ideal the image represents to you. Whatever worship ritual you perform with the consciousness of Spirit is pleasing to the Lord. But in Moses' time many worshipers had forgotten God; they were venerating mere objects, even sacrificing goats to them.

In India it is customary to make a picture or statue of a saint, or perhaps to fashion an image symbolic of a specific manifestation or quality of the Divine, and place it in a temple. The people offer flowers to God or to the spirit of the saint represented by the picture or statue, and meditate on the divine qualities it symbolizes. Such worship is acceptable in God's eyes. † True devotees do not allow their consciousness to dwell on the object, but concentrate with deepest love and attention on the Spirit behind it. A great saint of India used to go into *samadhi* (ecstatic communion with God) whenever he offered his devotion before the image of the Divine Mother in the temple where he worshiped. "I was placing flowers at the feet

---

* VII:23.

† "Whatever embodiment (an *avatar*, a saint, or a deity) a man faithfully worships, it is I who make his devotion unflinching. Absorbed in worshiping that embodiment with deep faith, the devotee thus gains the fruits of his longings. Yet those fulfillments are verily granted by Me alone" (Bhagavad-Gita VII:21–22).

of a stone symbol," he said, "when suddenly I beheld that, untouched by my body, I was one with the Sustainer of the universe. I began placing flowers on my own head."

If you can do so, it is much better to concentrate inwardly on God than to focus your attention first on an external intermediary symbol, and then transfer that concentration to the Spirit. God is infinite. How could an image encase Him? This is the reason behind the second commandment. We should not worship an image as God, because He is infinite.

Being infinite, God cannot be limited to any form, human or stone; yet He is manifest in all forms. One can rightly say that God manifests in every man as well as in great saints, for He is present in all. The sun shines equally, also, on a piece of charcoal and a diamond. But the diamond receives and reflects the sun's light, whereas the charcoal does not. Similarly, all people are exposed to the light of God, but not all receive and reflect that light. To do so they must purify themselves by meditation and by following the Ten Commandments.

"*Thou shalt not take the name of the Lord thy God in vain.*" When you say the name of God, you must be inwardly aware of what you are saying. Were it possible to look into others' minds when they are praying, you would see that a great many are thinking about almost anything but the Lord. They are taking the name of God in vain. When we pray we should try our utmost to concentrate our whole attention on God, instead of saying "God, God, God" and letting our minds dwell on something else. An aunt of mine had the habit of saying her prayers on beads. She could almost always be seen busily fingering her beads. But she approached me one day and confessed that although she had been doing this for forty years, God had never answered her prayers. No wonder! Her "prayers" were hardly more than a nervous physical habit.

Don't think of anything but the Spirit when you are praying. Try your utmost to be sincere. The use of beads in prayer, and *japa*, repetition of the name of God, are good when practiced with devotion and concentration. But these all too often become mechanical; they are lower forms of worship. But to whisper "God" in your heart on beads of love—that is true worship. It is insulting to God also if you sing hymns or chant to Him with an absent mind. The Bhagavad-Gita similarly stresses the importance of a concentrated mind while worshiping God. When you pray, your heart and your mind should be filled with the love of God. "He attains the Supreme Effulgent Lord, O Arjuna! whose mind, stabilized by Yoga, is immovably fixed on the thought of Him."*

"Remember the sabbath day, to keep it holy." Out of a week of seven days, how few people devote even one to God! To keep apart one day for Him is in the best interests of your own welfare. Sunday is the sun's day—the bright day of wisdom. Many never use it to think of God, though to do so is the highest wisdom. If on that day, you could just be alone and quiet for a little time, enjoying that stillness, you would see how much better you feel. Observe the sabbath in this way; it will be a salve to the lacerations of the preceding six days. Everyone needs one day a week in the spiritual hospital to heal his mental wounds.

Don't observe the sabbath as a forced duty; enjoy it. When it becomes for you a day of peace and joy and contentment, you will look forward to it. Seclusion is the price of greatness. You may be surprised at what seclusion with God will do for your mind, body, and soul. In the early morning, and before retiring, you should immerse yourself in His peace.

India's sages counsel not only a regular day for seclusion, but stress the need for quiet meditation during four specific periods every day. In the early morning, before you get up or see anyone, remain calm, feeling peace. At noon, be quiet for a while before taking lunch; and before your evening meal, have another time for peace. Before going to bed, go into that silence again. Those who faithfully observe silence in seclusion during these four times of the day cannot but feel in tune with God. Whoever cannot manage four times a day should observe each morning and evening a period devoted to God. By doing this you will have a different, happier life.

If you continually write out checks without depositing anything in your bank account, you will run out of money. So

* VIII:8.

it is with your life. Without regular deposits of peace in your life account, you will run out of strength, calmness, and happiness. You will finally become bankrupt—emotionally, mentally, physically, and spiritually. But daily communion with God will continually replenish your inner bankroll.

Four times a day sit quietly in meditation and think with all the love and longing of your heart: "I am with the Infinite now. 'Father, reveal Thyself, reveal Thyself.'" Strive to feel the peace of His presence. Bathe your mind and body in that peace, and you will be much more successful in life. The calm man doesn't make mistakes. When thousands of others are failing, he succeeds. You must be calm to be successful. Those who do not observe the sabbath by feeling this divine peace develop great moodiness. They become nervous automatons. Through the portals of silence the healing sun of wisdom and peace will shine upon you.

The sabbath should be a day of rest and cultivation of divine peace. However, activity that expresses wisdom and peace is also appropriate on the sabbath.

"Honor thy father and thy mother." The human father and mother should be honored as the representatives of God, the supreme Parent, who has empowered them with His gift to create man. The mother is God's unconditional love incarnate, because a true mother forgives when no one else does. The father is a manifestation of the Heavenly Father's wisdom and protection of His children. One should not love father and mother apart from God, but as representations of His protecting love and wisdom. The Supreme Spirit becomes the father and mother to help each child. Therefore honor Him in your parents.

"Thou shalt not kill." The meaning is that one should not kill for killing's sake; for then you become a murderer. One should not take another's life in a moment of violent emotion. But if your country is attacked and goes to war, you should fight to protect those whom God has given to you. You have a righteous obligation to defend your family and your country.

"Thou shalt not commit adultery." The ideal of sexual union should be the creation of children made in the image of God, and the expression of the pure love of the soul that is felt

between marriage partners who behold only God in each other. Those who live solely on the physical plane, never thinking of love or the high purpose for which the sex sense was intended, are, in the spirit of this commandment, committing adultery. One is then no better than the animal, who has his sex and goes his way.

Except for the purpose of procreation, and the expression of mutual true love in the holy state of matrimony, the creative urge is intended by God to be transmuted into energy and divine realization. Insofar as you can absorb the sexual power, you can develop great mental powers to write, paint, or express yourself creatively in a thousand other ways. As you ultimately control and spiritualize the creative energy, you will feel great peace and love and bliss in God. Saints who have thus spiritualized the sexual energy are very powerful, able to demonstrate wonderful achievements in the world and in the interior search for Truth.

Thus the highest use of sex is the sublimation of its power in order to manifest spiritual thoughts and ideals and wisdom. It is detrimental to your mental and physical well-being if you concentrate on sex apart from the expression of marital love or the procreative purpose of married life. One should not dwell on sex thoughts or act promiscuously on sex thoughts. When you can exercise this restraint you can develop the right attitude toward sex and its wholesome divine purpose.

The universe and man were immaculately created by God's will. In the beginning, man also was empowered to create immaculately by will, as God did. Man lost this power when he was tempted to concentrate on sexual rather than spiritual expression of the divine creative power. To be enslaved by sex is to lose health, self-control, and peace of mind—everything that man needs to be happy.

"Thou shalt not steal." If all the people in a community of 1,000 steal from one another, each will have 999 enemies. Therefore one should not unfairly take from others their property or love or peace or any other possession. If you feel no desire to take what does not belong to you, that which you need or wish for will come to you. Stealing begins in the mind, when you begin to covet what others have. The seeds of desire

must be removed from the mind. Spiritual unselfishness is the way; then one automatically attracts abundance.

Unless material selfishness is abandoned, there can be no happiness in the world. Happiness will come only by spiritual cooperation, when all men begin to feel for others' necessities as for their own, and to work for others as earnestly as for self.

"Thou shalt not bear false witness against thy neighbor." To harm anyone through distortion of truth is another way of disrupting social happiness. If you want to be treated well, you should treat others well. It is important to speak the truth at all times.

To be always truthful one must understand the difference between fact and truth. Your truthfully pointing out that a man is lame only hurts; it does no good. Therefore one should not speak unpleasant facts unnecessarily. To tell a truth that would betray another person, and to no worthy purpose, is also wrong. One should not speak untruth to avoid speaking truth, but rather remain silent. Never carelessly or maliciously reveal information that could embarrass and hurt others.

"Thou shalt not covet thy neighbor's house, thou shalt not covet thy neighbor's wife, nor his manservant, nor his maidservant, nor his ox, nor his ass, nor any thing that is thy neighbor's." Covetousness is the source of discontent. Learn to differentiate between "necessary necessities" and "unnecessary necessities." The more you covet what others have, the more unhappy you will be. You will spend your life in misery and never find contentment. Seek spiritual riches within.

What you are is much greater than anything or anyone else you have ever yearned for. God is manifest in you in a way that He is not manifest in any other human being. Your face is unlike anyone else's, your soul is unlike anyone else's, you are sufficient unto yourself; for within your soul lies the greatest treasure of all—God.

How to Read Character

Self-Realization Fellowship international headquarters,
Los Angeles, California, January 11, 1942

By studying the character of others, one can become alert to ways in which he can improve his own nature. To study character in a negative way, however, is not right, and has a devastating effect. Everyone shuns a "character detective," who exposes others' faults. Many people who enjoy criticizing cannot themselves stand criticism, and may even have the same flaws they so righteously deplore in another.

Character study is important primarily in this respect: one needs constantly to take note of virtues in others and to implant those good traits in himself. I study character when I choose people with whom to work. But I have an entirely different standpoint for choosing. Sometimes I let a person that I know is "bad" be with me, in the hope that he will change. If he responds to my spiritual thought for his welfare he becomes better; and if he doesn't, well, I take that chance. I am like a medical doctor who risks exposure to a disease in order to help a patient. All doctors have to take that chance because their desire is to serve. So it is with a spiritual doctor; he undertakes to judge others and show them their defects in order to help them improve.

Jesus said: "Judge not, that ye be not judged."* He condemned that criticism of others which is done solely out of desire to hurt. Such behavior is unkind and spoils friendship. Criticism has no use whatsoever unless it is given with sincere love, and only when wanted. It should be offered with a loving desire to help the other person. Those who have learned self-control have the right to help others. From that point of view character study is worthwhile.

* Matthew 7:1.

317

Physical Appearance an Index of Character

One type of character study is based on physiognomy. It is said that the salient characteristics of man are revealed in his body—a very sweeping statement. Not all one's physiological characteristics do tell the real tale of the inner life.

Aristotle studied physiognomy as a guide to character. Hindu teachers go deeper. They say that the main thoughts of all one's incarnations are reflected in the eyes. Though the eyes reveal the whole story of the soul, not only of this life but of past lives, still it requires a master's mind to analyze the revelation of your past lives reflected in this life.

Once in a while you are walking along and suddenly notice something in the eyes of a passer-by, and you think, "I don't like him," or as the case may be, "I like him." Eyes tell the whole story. Fear, anger, jealousy, greed, generosity, love, courage, spirituality—all these qualities, good and bad, cause corresponding reflections in the eyes. Detectives can control their facial muscles so as not to betray by their expressions what they are thinking, but they cannot hide the suspicion in their eyes. A yogi has calm eyes because he is thinking of the tranquil Spirit.

Facial and bodily features have been studied, even the bumps on the head have been analyzed; but physical appearance does not always tell the story, and different cultures draw different conclusions from their observations. Some say that fat people are luxury-loving and don't like to work, and that thin people are more spiritual. Yet in India, fatness in a spiritual person is viewed favorably. Caesar was wary of Cassius' "lean and hungry" appearance, in which he saw a threat to his power. Some writers have theorized that those who are thin think too much, hence flesh doesn't build up on them. A study of history shows that both lean and stout people have been good rulers.

If you are persistently fat now, you were fat many times before; or if in this life you are chronically thin, you have been thin for several incarnations. You have inherited the tendency from the past; and no matter what you eat, that thought-pattern tends to manifest itself.

Physiognomy as a revealer of character is true if one takes into account the fact that all the thoughts that have passed through a particular mind during many incarnations show in the body. But it takes the intuitive power of a master to "read" one's physiognomy completely and correctly.

For example, Socrates was very ugly. He met a great astrologer who said, "Socrates, you are the most evil and wicked person I know." Socrates' students were very angry at the astrologer, but their teacher replied: "You are right. I have been all that in the past. But though I have overcome it by wisdom now, still the things I did then are registered in this body, making it appear ugly."

No two faces are the same. Each is different because of characteristics that have manifested themselves in this life and in past lives. So it is not a matter of simply judging people as bad or good because their present looks are repellent or pleasing. St. Francis was not physically attractive, whereas his disciple Brother Masseus was a handsome man. But Masseus did not possess as great a spiritual beauty as St. Francis.

Emotions as a Clue to Character

There is another branch of investigation related to physiognomy; that of pathognomy, the study of man's feelings and emotions through the outward signs of his facial expressions and bodily movements, and through study of his emotional reactions to various incidents in his life. Feelings and habits indicate one's characteristics; but some people have cultivated the ability to hide their true feelings because they don't want to expose themselves to others. Two husbands heard the news that their wives had drowned. One was showing great grief and the other was not saying anything; but the one who showed sorrow outwardly felt less love for his wife than did the husband who didn't reveal by his facial expression any pain at all. So pathognomy, finding out the true feelings and reactions of people, is a very deep study.

You can analyze people more surely according to their feelings than according to their physical appearance. I combine the two methods for the most accurate analysis. All those who come to me for training I place in certain situations to see how their minds and feelings will react. If they respond adversely I try to correct them; but I don't do this unless the person has asked to be corrected, and has given me the authority and permission to guide him.

Some people are emotionally stirred at the slightest thing. Musicians in this country are as a rule very emotional, and most of your music is emotional, because it is written around the theme of human love. In India music centers around the thought of God. That is why it tends to quiet the storms of emotion and to bring out deep spiritual calmness. Not all Western musicians are emotional, of course; nor are all Indian musicians spiritual, though for the most part they are. The Sanskrit word for musician is *bhagavathar*, "he who sings the praises of God."

In dealing with emotional people you can seldom bank on their stability. Today they are enthusiastic about you and tomorrow they leave you. I have seen such persons come to the *ashram*, and within a few days they would make me feel they were going to be as firmly loyal as the disciple John. Next month I would find they had gone. If anything hurts me, it is when an avowal of friendship is withdrawn by a breach of that trust. When I give my friendship to anyone, I never take it back.

Even-Mindedness, a Key to Development

One can easily tell the difference between the motor type and the thoughtful type of man: the former always wants to work and the latter wants to think things through. Both types are needed. Motor types like to act at once. They should be taught to direct their energies into spiritually rewarding activities. In order to help each type to create a harmonious balance, I advise motor types to meditate and think more, and thoughtful types to meditate and work more.

People addicted to bad habits—overeating, smoking, drinking—have to be carefully handled. Any obstruction of desire causes anger. If you take food away from a greedy man he will be wrathful. It is useless to try to help such sense slaves until they themselves indicate a real desire to improve.

Swami Shankara said that even-minded people will know God. The Master of the universe sits on the altar of even-mindedness. By even-mindedness man enjoys the perfect equilibrium of peace.

One of the three basic qualities predominates in every man, according to Hindu philosophy.* *Sattwa* is the quality of those who have spiritual tendencies. They eat properly, cultivate good habits, and are devoted to the Lord. The *rajas* quality is manifested in those who are active; such persons keep busy with work until they die. Those in whom the *tamas* quality is uppermost fill their lives with quarreling, anger, jealousy, sensuality, and laziness.

Any habit that holds you from spiritual attainment should be overcome. You must be the master of your thoughts and actions. It is better to be the active rajasic type and to have your habits under control than to be the tamasic type; but the sattwic type in whom goodness manifests itself is ideal. Those who want to improve themselves should mix more with sattwic types.

Very few people know in what lies their own good. By this one criterion you can judge anyone. Ninety-nine percent of all people fail under this test. Tell a person, for his own good, to do a particular thing, and he will do exactly the opposite. Why? Because he can't help himself; his materialistic habits are too strong. Very often people won't do what you suggest, even though they know it is good for them, just to prove that you can't influence them. Those who really want to improve should mix more with those who are calm and self-controlled. Try to mix with people who are normal, and better still, with people who are supernormal. The weak should seek out the strong and the strong should seek out those who are even stronger. A wrestler will never increase his strength unless he works out with a stronger man.

Animal Characteristics in Man

After judging the mental qualities of *sattwa, rajas,* and *tamas* in others, you can analyze their physical behavior. Some

---

* All creation is subject to the influence of three inherent *gunas* or qualities: *sattwa, rajas,* and *tamas*—spiritual or elevating, activating, and obstructing.

say that women are "catty." But men can be just as catty. The cat eats the tame canary and then sits as calmly as any yogi in order to feign innocence of his unwelcome act. Some people enjoy being destructive to others' peace and happiness. Their whole purpose is to disturb and upset; like predatory wolves, they go about in society and seek out fights.

Certain types of people have been compared to the jay—chattering all the time. It is said that man was created first, and that the god Twashtri then took the gentleness of the moon, the softness of the down from the swan's breast, the beauty of the flowers, and the chatter of the jay, and, combining these things, made woman. And man was so happy. But after a while he went to Twashtri and said, "She is a beautiful creature. I really appreciate her. But she talks without rest and she has become the bane of my life. Take her back." Then after two months the man again visited Twashtri. "I am very sad," he said. "Please return the woman to me." But after a while he came again and said, "Please take her back." This time Twashtri said, "No, you have to keep her!" Poor man! he couldn't live with her, but neither could he live without her.

Women can complain, for their part, about men. Unless man and woman understand each other's nature, they ignorantly torture one another. Both were created equal in God's eyes; no man can come without woman, and no woman can come without man. It is the duty of man and woman to attain within themselves a balance between their respective predominating and hidden qualities. Man is guided more by reason and woman more by feeling. Each should strive for an inner balance of both reason and feeling, and so become a "whole" personality, a perfected human being.

Some people behave like donkeys. No matter how much they have suffered from the consequences of sense slavery, they stubbornly go on nourishing their bad habits. They seem to have no memory whatsoever, quickly forgetting the painful results of sense indulgence and so never learning from their experiences.

In nature all the different animals represent different emotions and characteristics; but man has them all in himself. He can act like the snake or the wolf or the fox or the lion. Within us is the essence of hades and heaven. We should learn to express more of the heavenly qualities.

Intuition Is the Surest Judge of Character

Though an interesting study of character is possible through analysis of the eyes, the emotions, and the physical features, as has been pointed out, the greatest and highest way to learn about character is through soul intuition. If your mind and feeling remain perfectly calm, you will be able to feel intuitively and exactly the nature of each person you meet.

My task is to take all kinds of people for training and help. It is not good to set a limitation on any human being, confining his possibilities to a certain analysis; but whether he changes or remains the same, intuition will be able to tell you, more than your diagnosis of the eyes, feelings, or physical features, whatever the nature of that person is. Intuition is the greatest analytical power. As a mirror reflects all things held before it, so when your mind-mirror is calm, you will be able to see reflected in it the true quality of others. If you are busy doing good to all, remaining calm and meditative, the true character of whoever comes to you will be revealed to you.

How to Be Happy at Will

Date and place unknown

As you watch the faces of human beings, you can usually classify their expressions into four basic types, with corresponding mental states: smiling faces, bespeaking inner and outer happiness; grim faces, denoting sadness; dull, unsmiling faces, revealing inner boredom; and calm faces, reflecting an inner peace.

A desire satisfied produces pleasure. A longing unfulfilled creates sadness. Between the mental crests of happiness and sadness are troughs of boredom. When the high waves of pleasure and pain and the depressions of boredom become neutralized, the state of peace manifests.

Beyond the state of peace there is an ever-new state of bliss, which the individual can find within himself and recognize as the true native state of his soul. This bliss is buried beneath the exciting mental waves of exuberant pleasure and deep depression and the hollows of indifference. When these waves disappear from the mental waters, the placid state of peace is felt. Reflected in the calm waters of peace is the ever-new bliss.

Basis of Reactions

Most people in the world are tossing on the waves of exciting pleasure or pain, and when these are wanting, they are bored. As you watch the faces of others during the day—at home, in the office, on the streets, or at gatherings—you can see that there are only a few who manifest peace.

When you see a merry countenance and ask that person, "What makes you happy?" he is likely to answer in this way: "I had a raise in salary," or, "I met an interesting person." Behind happiness lies the fulfillment of a desire.

When you see a doleful face and make sympathetic inquiry, its owner may reply, "I'm a sick man," or, "I lost my wallet." His desire to regain health (or his lost money) has been contradicted.

When you see a face registering a sort of blank neutrality, and you ask, "What's the matter? Are you unhappy about something?" he promptly answers in the negative. But if you press him, "Are you happy?" he will say, "Oh, no, I'm just bored."

Negative and Positive Peace

You may meet a refined, well-to-do man living on an estate, looking healthy and plump, and neither unduly happy nor sad or bored. In such case you might say he is peaceful. But when that comfortably fixed person has too much of this kind of peace—which few people have the good fortune to experience—he thinks within, "I've had enough peace—I need some excitement and diversion." Or he may remark to a friend, "Please give me a knock on the head to make me feel that I'm alive!"

The negative state of peace is derived from the absence of the three mental states of happiness, sadness, and boredom. Without change or excitement, protracted negative peace becomes stale and unenjoyable. But after long-continued indulgence in the happy, sad, and bored states, negative peace is enjoyable. For this reason, the yogis advocate the neutralization of the waves of thoughts by concentration to achieve mental peace. Once the yogi has stilled the waves of thought, he begins to look beneath the lake of calmness, and finds there a positive state of peace—the ever-new joy of the soul.

I met a very wealthy man in New York. In the course of telling me something about his life, he drawled, "I am disgustingly rich, and disgustingly healthy—" and before he could finish I exclaimed, "But you are not disgustingly happy! I can teach you how to be perpetually interested in being ever newly happy." He became my student. By practicing *Kriya Yoga,* and by leading a balanced life, ever inwardly devoted to God, he lived to a ripe old age, always bubbling with ever-new happiness. On his deathbed he told his wife, "I am sorry for you—that you have to see me go—but I am very happy to join my Beloved of the Universe. Rejoice at my joy, and don't be selfish by sorrowing. If you knew how happy I am to go to meet my beloved God, you wouldn't be sad; rejoice to know that you will someday join me in the festivity of eternal bliss."

Drink Deep of Bliss

Now, after observing faces that register pleasure, sorrow, boredom, or temporary peace, wouldn't you rather that your face reflect the contagious ever-new joy of Spirit? To be able to do this you must drink and drink of His bliss from the cask of deep meditation until you become a bliss alcoholic, manifesting bliss in sleep, dreams, wakefulness, and all circumstances of life that might otherwise tend to make you boisterously happy, or abysmally sad, or saturated with boredom or temporary negative peace. Your laughter must echo from the caverns of sincerity. Your joy must flow from the fountain of your realized soul. Your smile must spread over all the souls you meet and over the whole universe. Your every look must reflect your joyous soul and spread its contagion to gloom-drunk minds.

Stop dreaming that you are just an ordinary mortal, constantly going through mental ups and downs. No matter what happens, remember always that you are made in the true image of Spirit. The living joy in all things—the Fountain of Cosmic Bliss—must shower you with Its spray, and send joy trickling through your thoughts, through every cell and tissue of your whole being.

Remember, for many hours in the state of deep dreamless sleep, which is unconscious soul-perception, you are happy all the while. So during the day, regardless of how much you are disturbed by nightmarish mental trials and upheavals, you must keep trying all the time to be inwardly ever newly joyous, like the ever-fresh laughing waters of a gurgling brook.

As a man can be drunk with liquor all the time by continuously imbibing it, so also can you be drunk with true happiness by continuously perceiving the joyousness of your soul after meditation. When you can constantly feel the blissful after-state of meditation, you will live in ecstasy; you will be one with the ever-new Joy of your soul, and whosoever will be around you will be like you—even as the constant touch of sandalwood makes the hand fragrant. "Their thoughts fully on Me, their beings surrendered to Me, enlightening one another, proclaiming Me always, My devotees are contented and joyful."*

* Bhagavad-Gita X:9.

Steps Toward the Universal Christ Consciousness

February 17, 1935

In this world we are limited by our thoughts. It is natural for us to be partial to our own ideas, but because of this partiality we often fail to recognize that the ideas of others may be bigger and better ones. When we learn to be open-minded and not opinionated about anything, we grow in understanding and wisdom.

A person is mentally free when his judgment is no longer influenced by the prejudices, customs, and conventions that are imposed on him by racial, national, and familial background. In the West you sit on chairs; in the East we sit on the floor, because the climate is extremely warm and the air is cooler near the floor. But one cannot say that everyone should sit on the floor just because the East finds it more comfortable to do so. National customs and conventions limit our outlook considerably; but as soon as we become free from blind slavery to our provincial prejudices and habits, we can see truly what is right or wrong in any other nationality.

As individuals we are to some extent limited by our desire to do whatever contributes to our own personal good. Thus each human being is more or less fenced in by his egoistic desires and experiences. As he increases the range of his experience, his consciousness begins to stretch; it is like a rubber band that can be expanded infinitely without breaking. Indeed, the more you stretch your consciousness, the greater it will be.

Learning to love our relatives is simply a training in stretching our consciousness. It is a preliminary practice in loving all others as we do our relations, whom we think of as our own. We have to learn to look on family and strangers alike,

328

because all are children of God. He has given you certain family members with whom you are practicing stretching your consciousness. When the husband serves the wife, and she serves him, each with the desire to see the other happy, Christ Consciousness—God's loving Cosmic Intelligence that permeates every atom of creation—has begun to express itself through their consciousness. Whenever you do something for someone else, without any selfish motive, you have stepped into the sphere of Christ Consciousness.

If you limit your love to your family, however, you have only that much capacity to express Christ Consciousness. When you love your neighbors as your family, your consciousness expands and you express a greater degree of Christ Consciousness. When you feel for all people with the love that you feel for your own loved ones, when you have that soul preparedness to do for anyone else as you would do for your own, then you are exactly expressing Christ Consciousness.

Selfishness is destructive to one's own interests; hence it is an unwise policy in any relationship or endeavor. Many of the customs in India give wonderful practice in expanding the consciousness through unselfishness. The mother never eats until the children and the father have had their food. As a result they feel for her and have a sympathetic desire to share choice tidbits with her. However, to feel concern only for yourself and your own few loved ones is still selfish. When you do something for others as feelingly as you do for self and family, you leave the little territory of selfishness and enter into the vast realm of Christ Consciousness.

So the first step toward Christlike unselfishness is to expand your consciousness to include your neighbors' interests and well-being. It is not necessary to give everything away; but you should have an intense desire to help others, and be prepared, mentally and physically, so that when the occasion arises you can do the same for your neighbors as you would do for yourself. You can do it, but you don't. Whenever you find a lonely heart, or a brother weeping by the wayside, and your heart goes out to that soul, your consciousness impinges on the Christ Consciousness.

Human love has its limitations. Family feeling is hemmed in by clannishness. Patriotic love is greater, for when you are ready to give up your happiness for the welfare of your country, you have expanded your consciousness on a much wider scale. And when you can feel for all nations as for your own country, your love manifests in an even greater way—you become a wider channel for the expression of that universal Christ Consciousness which Jesus had. He could say, "Who is my mother? and who are my brethren?"* because he was aware that there is only the one love of God manifesting through all individual human relationships.

In my consciousness I see no difference in an American, an Indian, an African, a German, a Frenchman, or an Englishman —that comes from the training I received from my guru, Swami Sri Yukteswar. Most parental, social, and educational training tends to foster prejudices. I love all races and nationalities alike. I do not want to be limited by attachment to any one country. After all, we are only Americans or Indians for a little while; when we die we are all the same. If we are conscious of being world citizens, we have an expanded consciousness.

Psychological Expansion of Consciousness

You can stretch your consciousness psychologically so that you no longer feel for your little self, but rather for the good of the whole world as your expanded self. That is one way of expressing Christ Consciousness.

Every day you think thousands of thoughts—about a thousand an hour. When you are writing you are thinking, in about an hour and a half, twenty-five hundred thoughts. The ordinary human being thinks about twelve thousand thoughts a day. A deep thinker puts forth about fifty thousand. I have found that by concentrating it is possible to produce as many as five hundred thousand thoughts in a day.

I used to know a man in India who knew eighteen languages and was a Master of Arts in twelve of them. Think how many thousands of thoughts were passing through his brain! Yet he was never mixed up.

---

* Matthew 12:48.

You are to some extent conscious of every thought that you think during wakefulness. If you receive a pinprick anywhere on your body you are instantly aware of it. That means your consciousness is present in each of the trillions of cells in the body. At the end of sixty years can you remember all the thoughts that you have had? It seems impossible. Yet all events of your life have been recorded in your subconscious mind, and that mind does recall most of those thoughts that were outstanding. The more you develop concentration and memory, the more you can recall.

Conscious, Subconscious, and Superconscious Memory

The scope of the mind is very grand. God has given you waking consciousness, subconsciousness, and superconsciousness. Your conscious mind has certain limitations; after a few years it begins to forget various things. But your subconscious mind has a greater memory capacity; every thought and experience is stored in the repository of subconsciousness. Your conscious mind may forget every word that I am saying, but your subconscious mind is registering them all.

Behind the subconscious is your superconscious mind, which never forgets anything. The superconscious mind has kept a record of everything you have done, every thought you have thought. When death comes, all these thoughts and experiences flash through your mind before you leave the body. Those impressions that are strongest determine the environment and habits of your next life.*

As an ego your consciousness is present everywhere within yourself, and is therefore present in each thought that you think. If you can expand your consciousness beyond ego into the realm of superconsciousness, you can watch from that point all the thousands of thoughts passing through your conscious mind. Those who have developed the superconscious mind can remember all the thoughts of a lifetime, and of previous lives as well. In divine memory nothing is forgotten. Our thoughts are real and they are eternal, ever present in the ether.

* "That thought with which a dying man leaves the body determines—through his long persistence in it—his next state of being" (Bhagavad-Gita VIII:6).

All the sounds of the earth are recorded, also, in your super-conscious mind. Thus Jesus could say: "Are not two sparrows sold for a farthing? and one of them shall not fall on the ground without [the knowledge of] your Father." *

Think of fifteen hundred million people and the twelve thousand thoughts that each one thinks every day. If your consciousness is aware of all those thoughts, several trillions of them, then you have Christ Consciousness: omniscience, conscious awareness of everything in creation.

God gives man a mental barrier so that no one else can know his thoughts. You are alone with your thoughts even though you may be with many people. Even those who have Christ Consciousness do not intrude on the thoughts of others unless they have been ordained by God to guide others, or have been requested by their disciples to take that liberty in order to help them perfect their *sadhana.*

Sympathy a Key to Christ Consciousness

If you would develop Christ Consciousness, learn to be sympathetic. When genuine feeling for others comes into your heart, you are beginning to manifest that great consciousness. When you talk unkindly about others, you are far from the universal sympathy of Christ Consciousness. Jesus said: "Bless them that curse you."† He practiced divine sympathy. Jesus fought against those who were doing wrong; but he hated no one, because he saw God in everyone. Lord Krishna said: "He is a supreme yogi who regards with equal-mindedness all men...."‡ Do not sully your own thoughts and tongue by criticizing others. Be sincere with everyone, and above all, be sincere with yourself. God watches you. You cannot deceive Him.

God is the whisper in the temple of your conscience, and He is the light of intuition. You know when you are doing wrong; your whole being tells you, and that feeling is God's voice. If you don't listen to Him, He becomes quiet. But when you wake up from your delusion, and want to do right, He will guide you. He is always waiting for the time when you will return Home. He sees your good and evil thoughts and actions, but they do not matter to Him. You are His child just the same.

---

* Matthew 10:29.   † Matthew 5:44.   ‡ Bhagavad-Gita VI:9.

In your heart must well that sympathy which soothes away all pains from the hearts of others, that sympathy which enabled Jesus to say: "Father, forgive them; for they know not what they do." His great love encompassed all. He could have destroyed his enemies with a look, yet just as God is constantly forgiving us even though He knows all our wicked thoughts, so those great souls who are in tune with Him give us that same love.

The transcendental way to develop universal sympathy is meditation. The man whose mind dwells in the superconscious state is always happy, always wise and loving, and always retains the after-effects of meditation. If you can retain effortlessly that consciousness you feel just after meditation, you have attained superconsciousness. When someone unknown comes before you, you will instantly know all about that person's life. But Christ Consciousness is still farther beyond: you feel everything in the universe in your consciousness at the same time.

By developing sympathy for all, you can expand your consciousness and learn everything there is to be known. Just as you are aware of your body and limbs and thoughts and brain simultaneously, so when you have Christ Consciousness you will feel the bodily sensations of every human being you meet, and know all the thoughts they have ever had. When the scribes and the Pharisees brought an adulteress before Jesus for judgment he said, "He that is without sin among you, let him first cast a stone at her."* How did Jesus know about their private lives? He lived in the all-permeating divine Christ Consciousness. In that consciousness you are able to feel what others are doing and thinking. Sometimes you even forget momentarily in which body you are living.

Metaphysical Way to Christ Consciousness

The metaphysical way to Christ Consciousness is through meditation and holding on to the after-effects of meditation. There are persons who read a few books on truth and then say that they have attained Christ Consciousness, but you can have that consciousness only through deep meditation and

* John 8:7.

unceasing spiritual effort. So don't say you have Christ Consciousness until you have attained what I have described. Your present consciousness is limited by the body, but when you expand it by deep meditation, you will become aware of the feelings of all peoples. You will be able to know all things. Marvelous realizations will come to you. Sometimes, when that state comes, you feel yourself simultaneously in the stars, in the moon, and in every blade of grass.

We are a part of the divine Christ Consciousness present in all creation. Each individual intelligence is a part of that vast Christ Intelligence. We are like the jets in the burner of a gas stove. There are many little holes through which the flames are pouring, but under the burner there is only one flame. We are little flames coming from the big flame of Life. Beneath all the tiny jets of human life is One Life; behind the flowers, behind all nature, is One Life.

When you feel your consciousness in every pore of creation, you have Christ Consciousness. Beyond creation is Cosmic Consciousness. When you lift your consciousness from creation and see the vast eternal joy of God alone, you will be in Cosmic Consciousness. When you are in tune with that Cosmic Consciousness which is beyond this creation, you will understand that God begot His Intelligence in the womb of creation, the "Virgin Mary"; and that this Intelligence of God the Father, which is reflected or "born" in every atom of creation, is the Christ Consciousness or "only begotten Son."

The "Sons of God"

The Indian name for this universal Christ Consciousness is *Kutastha Chaitanya*. In India we might also call it Krishna Consciousness, because the consciousness of our great *avatar* Jadava Krishna, like that of Jesus Christ, was in tune with the Christ Consciousness in everything. These two great ones had discovered the One Life behind all life. By divine concentration and will in meditation, they had withdrawn their consciousness from the material world and seen that behind everything in creation is the one reflection of God, the only son of God— the Christ or Krishna Consciousness.

Jesus, Krishna, Buddha, Babaji—all are Christs. They had

expanded their consciousness to receive Christ Consciousness. St. John declared: "As many as received him [the Christ Consciousness that was manifest in Jesus], to them gave he power to become the sons of God."*

My guru, Swami Sri Yukteswar, manifested the Christ Consciousness. He was always calm, and all my thoughts and feelings were reflected in the mirror of his calmness. Sri Yukteswarji wasn't interested in what others were saying; he was interested in what they were thinking. It was impossible to dissemble with a true teacher such as my guru! His consciousness was aware of all that was going on.

The Christ Consciousness dwelt also in Lahiri Mahasaya. One day when he was discoursing to his disciples on Christ Consciousness as explained in the Bhagavad-Gita, Lahiri Mahasaya suddenly cried out, "I am drowning in the bodies of many souls off the coast of Japan!" The next day his disciples learned from a newspaper account of the deaths of a number of persons whose ship had foundered the preceding day near Japan.

Life and death are but a passing from dream to dream. They are only thoughts: you are dreaming you are alive, and you are dreaming you are dead. When you get into the great Christ Consciousness, you see that life and death are dreams of God. Because Jesus lived in that consciousness he could say: "Destroy this [bodily] temple, and in three days I will raise it up."† He knew he could transform that dream of death into a dream of life, even as God can.

Develop sympathy and unselfishness if you would expand your consciousness. I have no consciousness of possession. I can leave everything in a moment if God calls, for I am not bound to anything. And yet all things are mine. In Christ Consciousness the whole world—everyone and everything in it— is your own. The whole of space and everything in it belongs to you.

When you begin to feel the sensations of others as though they were happening in your own body, you are developing that Christ Consciousness. When you cultivate this consciousness and therein understand that everything is yours,

* John 1:12. † John 2:19.

you will have no prejudices about race or color. In that consciousness you feel the love of a million mothers in your heart, not just for a few but for everyone. You do not imagine it, you feel it—this love that Jesus, Krishna, all of the great ones manifested—this universal intelligence and love which is called Christ Consciousness.

Even-Mindedness
in a World of Change

*First Self-Realization Fellowship Temple at
Encinitas, California, August 3, 1939*

In the West we find emphasis on physical comfort. When
the weather is too warm the Westerner suffers without something to cool him, and when it is too cold he is miserable without warmth from artificial heat. But the masters of India teach
a different philosophy. They say that sensitivity to heat and
cold, pleasure and pain, accrues from the delusive suggestions
of the senses and man's habit of catering to sensations; and
that he who is wise rises above all dualities. The great ones do
not suggest that man discipline himself to the point of doing
injury to his system; rather, they advise that when cold or heat
is intolerable, one should free himself mentally from the sensation, at the same time seeking a commonsense remedy for the
condition.

The Gita teaches: "Those who are attached to sense pleasures cannot gain the mental equilibrium of meditation; they
fail to receive union with God through ecstasy (*samadhi*)."*
Learning to disconnect oneself mentally from the disturbance
of sensations brings peace of mind. That man who remains untouched by the sensations that come and go, being neutral to
their ever changing stimuli, manifests the soul's essential
changelessness; in that unchanging consciousness he becomes
one with the Changeless Infinite.

Slavish response to the various sensations of the body disturbs both mind and soul. With the disturbance of the soul
man loses his true nature, which is calmness. God is present
in the coldest and the hottest regions of the earth; He is at the
North Pole and in the African desert. He is not affected by any

* Bhagavad-Gita II:44.

extremes of His earth-creation, and we, being made in His image, should behave like Him. He put us in this body that is subject to conditions of heat and cold, pain and pleasure; but He wants us to look on these dualities with even-mindedness. He wants us to rise above them. We should develop endurance, without being rash. When we cannot avoid excessive heat or cold, we should simply disconnect the mind from it. The more we strive to practice this, the more the mind will free itself so that no unwanted sensations can touch the consciousness.

Pain Is Perceived Only in the Mind

The skin's surface does not feel touch sensations; they are experienced in the brain. One cannot taste, touch, smell, hear, or see except through the mind. We seem to experience taste on the tongue, but it is actually the brain that registers flavor. Similarly, when some part of the body hurts, the pain is really in the mind, not in the body-part. We have two instruments for perceiving pain: the nerves and the gray matter of the brain. But we perceive only if the mind allows a connection between them. Unless the mind says there is pain, there is no pain. This is the marvelous discovery of India's great masters. Under chloroform you do not feel pain, because sensations do not reach the mind. At the nerve endings there are fine fibers through which the pain sensations are relayed to the brain. Chloroform prevents the relaying of these pain signals.

The brain is the sensitive instrument of the mind, and all the sensations of the body are reported to the mind through the nerves and the brain. The mind, being identified with the brain, receives and interprets these sensations. A mind made strong by the practice of powerful and positive thinking is less affected by sensations of pleasure and pain. It recognizes sensations in the way God intended—as a form of academic experience.

Sensitivity was given to man only to protect the body; without sensation, one could cut himself badly and not know it. Sensitivity was never intended to cause pain. Animals have not developed this faculty to the degree that man has, hence they experience less pain. Otherwise, the cruelty practiced on animals in some methods of killing would be intolerable. The lobster is put in boiling water while it is still alive!

Because pain and pleasure are created by the mind, pain in the body can be lessened by practicing control of the mind. Then one can experience a sensation without its producing pain, receiving only its guiding or warning message. The Bhagavad-Gita goes very deeply into it, and that is what the Gita tells us. Oversensitivity to pleasure and pain strengthens their effects; reduced sensitivity makes one less subject to pain and less enslaved to sense pleasures. I have trained my body and mind to be less sensitive and have found myself free from sense disturbances. That training is the way to gain freedom.

There was a doctor who had such mind power that he was able to perform a major operation on himself. The very thought makes the mind protest that one could not do it, because the mind has been enslaved by bodily attachments. But mind can be made powerful by training. The more you discipline your mind, the more it will be under your control. A pampered child suffers greatly over even a little hurt; a Spartan-trained child may hardly wince at serious injury.

You Can Free Yourself from the Sensory Dictators

In this respect the system of training given in India under great masters is entirely different from that given in Western schools. Indian masters train their students to free themselves completely from slavery to the body and its sensations. The comforts and conveniences developed in the West encourage pampering the body; as a result, little or no effort is made to cultivate mental strength. In India we are trained from childhood to nip in the bud the dictates of sensations. In my school at Ranchi we had the children sleep on little mats on the hard floor, and they grew healthier. Westerners are conditioned to too many external necessities in order to sleep well or be at peace. In India we were taught to sit on the hot sand in meditation. Gradually we could sit in the heat all day long; and in the cold, likewise. As a result of this training I found such mental strength that nothing can affect or disturb my consciousness. When I disconnect my mind from the sense telephones, I am not bothered by anything.

Some years ago the weather was terribly hot—extremely so. Everyone else was panting. I was getting by mental association the discomfort they were feeling. I had intended to do some writing, but I was so uncomfortable I could not concentrate. Then I chided myself, "What is the matter with you?" And I prayed: "Lord, the same electricity makes the heat in the oven and ice in the refrigerator. It is cool here." All around me the atmosphere became cool, as though a sheet of ice surrounded me. I began to feel great inspiration and wrote without any difficulty.

Another time, many years ago, I was traveling across country in an open touring car. Accompanying me were several young men, all Self-Realization students, one of whom served as my secretary. He and I slept in the car, sharing one small blanket. The night was freezing cold. When I went soundly to sleep he pulled the blanket completely off me; and when I half wakened from the cold I subconsciously pulled the blanket off him! This went on for some time. Then my mind said: "Why are you behaving this way? It is all right. You are warm!" I threw off the blanket and began to meditate. My body became as warm as toast. The students were shuddering with cold when they awoke two hours later and discovered me sitting there, immobile. I was in divine ecstasy. They thought I had left my body! Roused from *samadhi* by their exclamations, I smiled and said, "What is all this commotion about? Let us resume our journey." "But you were sitting in this bitter cold with no coat or blanket!" they protested. Nevertheless, I did not catch cold. I was the only one who was warm!

What you must do is discipline your mind to be more positive. If you make up your mind you are not going to catch cold, you will be less likely to catch one. The mind must be trained to overcome pain as well. Mental sensitivity magnifies pain. To magnify pain is to forget the indomitable image of God within you.

Habits Begin to Form at Age Three

The ancient sages of India taught that all habits begin to form in man at the age of three. It is very difficult to change them after they are set. If your family and environment create early prejudices in your mind, you may carry them throughout life. One of the first things I learned from my guru, Swami Sri

Yukteswarji, was to overcome mental prejudices toward sensations. At the time I first came to him for training, I invariably caught cold if I didn't use a blanket when the weather was chilly. But Master taught me differently. As a result I became free of the cold-catching tendency I was virtually born with. Until Master's training, I had caught colds one right after the other.

Some people say we should depend only on mind, and others believe we should cater to bodily sensations. Both positions are extreme. According to one theory, it is good to have a physical examination regularly to see how the body is getting along, just as one has his car checked over periodically. This is sensible enough, but remember, you are not a machine. If your mental well-being is too dependent on the condition of the body, a time will come when the mind is so enslaved by the body's demands that no amount of any kind of physical aid helps. This explains why we have chronic diseases. The physical debility became chronic because the mind simply refused to be master of the body.

In the beginning it is better to follow the moderate path. If you have a cut, put a little iodine on it, but don't depend wholly on medicines. Take adequate, sensible precautions until gradually you can depend more on the mind. Even great masters have used medicines, which are, after all, God-created herbs and chemicals. Medicine is not necessary to a master, but to show that God's power works in countless ways he may sometimes choose to use pharmaceutical remedies. In any event, victory lies in the power of the mind. When you know with absolute conviction that you can do without all medication with no ill effect, you are victor.

A certain master who had broken his arm had it treated and bandaged. When a rich man came to visit him shortly after, his worried disciples thought that the visitor, seeing their master with his arm in a sling, might become disillusioned. "Don't pay any attention to these devotees," the saint remarked. "They imagine that because you see my broken arm you will think God doesn't look after me anymore. And it is paining, too!" Another time this same master was in ecstasy, singing about God, when he fell on a small pile of hot charcoal nearby. Still he went on singing to God. When the disciples picked him up, they discovered some of the hot coals clinging to his back, burning the flesh. The devotees were alarmed, but the master laughed and said calmly, "Well, why don't you remove them?" He never complained of any pain. Such is the mental aboveness masters show. On this occasion the saint demonstrated that he was above pain, and on the other he showed that he was capable of human suffering and of bearing it humbly.

Develop an adamant attitude toward the body. "The ideas of heat and cold, of pleasure and pain, are produced by the contacts of the senses with their objects. Such ideas are limited by a beginning and an end. They are transitory in their behavior. Bear them with patience."* Why be so sensitive about a little cold or a little pain? Think of the agony of those who suffer in war. But even stronger than the patriot is the spiritual man; he develops a greater mental courage through disciplining his mind to endure, and ultimately rise above, every kind of pain and trouble.

Man's Life Is Totally Independent of the Body

The body is only a flesh-covered cage of bones in which the bird of life stays for a time. The life itself is totally independent of the body. But the life has become identified with the limiting conditions of the body; hence it suffers. If you analyze body and mind you will find there is no connection between them, except what you give. Only in the daytime do you accept the sensations of the body. At night in sleep, when your mind is detached from the body, you are not aware of its sensations; you feel a deep peace.

Being made in the image of God, man can live in the body completely separate from physical sensations. But instead he adopts the conditions of the body as though they were his own. To be free of sensations, one has to separate himself mentally from the body. Therefore the saints teach mental detachment from both pleasure and pain. To understand and experience mental aboveness, one must practice it. I have proved this truth

* Bhagavad-Gita II:14.

to myself, and I know how wrong it is to be sensitive. Catering to sensations is the cause of all suffering and misery. God didn't intend for us to suffer; He created sensory perceptions to guide and entertain us in the form of mental pictures. He meant for us to use the body-instrument wisely, not to become so identified with it that it makes us miserable. St. Francis called the body "Brother Donkey." If one loves a pet dog with a deep attachment, he will be sensitive to his pet's sensations, even though he is not physically connected with the dog's nervous system. In the same way, our body-suffering is due to too much mental attachment to "Brother Donkey."

The mind must acquire greater control over the body. To be able to live by the power of mind is wonderful, because the mind can do whatever you want it to. How to start depending more on mind? Little by little habituate yourself to heat and cold, to sleeping on a hard bed, to being less dependent on accustomed comforts.

While I have been speaking to you I have been utterly unconscious of the high temperature today; but just now as I mentioned the heat, I began to feel it. Once I was lecturing in Milwaukee when the weather was extremely hot. In addition, the heat inside my body had increased greatly, as it does when I am speaking of spiritual things. My mind said, "You cannot continue the lecture without wiping your face; it is wet with perspiration." I reached into my pocket for a handkerchief, but found none. Then I looked in the spiritual eye and suggested to my mind, "There is no heat at all." Immediately the feeling of oppressive heat vanished; I was calm and cool.

The Right Way to Look at Death

Practice these things and see if what I am saying is not true. You can increase pain by sensitiveness and lessen it by mental detachment. When a dear one dies, instead of grieving unreasonably, realize that he has gone on to a higher plane at the will of God, and that God knows what is best for him. Rejoice that he is free. Pray that your love and goodwill be messengers of encouragement to him on his forward path. This attitude is much more helpful. Of course, we would not be human if we did not miss loved ones; but in feeling lonesome for them we don't want selfish attachment to be the cause of keeping them earthbound. Extreme sorrow prevents a departed soul from going ahead toward greater peace and freedom.

Most of the people living on earth today were not here a hundred years ago. Others were here before us. And we who are now walking the streets of the world will not be here a hundred years hence. It will be all over for us, and the new generation will not give us a thought. They will feel, as we do now, that this world belongs to them; but one by one they too will all be taken away. Death must be good, otherwise God would not have ordained that it happen to everyone. Why live in fear of it?

Those who are afraid of death cannot know their true soul nature. "Cowards die many times before their death; the valiant never taste of death but once."* The coward lives over and over again a mental picture of pain and death. The valiant experience only the final death, quickly and without pain. If one dies of natural causes or is spiritually advanced, the body of sensations simply drops off, and when the consciousness reawakens on another plane it has all the sensations of the body without any physical form. Awareness is all mind, just as it is in dreams. This is not difficult to picture. In death one merely sloughs off his gross physical body, which is only a lower form of mind and the cause of all manner of troubles for the soul.

Exude Peace and Goodness

There are roughly two kinds of people: those who continually lament what is wrong with the world, and those who smile away life's difficulties and remain always positive in their thinking. Why take everything so seriously? How wonderful this world would be if everyone were more positive, more harmonious!

In the jungle of civilization, in the stress of modern living, lies the test. Whatever you give out will come back to you. Hate, and you will receive hate in return. When you fill yourself with inharmonious thoughts and emotions, you are destroying yourself. Why hate or be angry with anyone? Love your enemies. Why stew in the heat of anger? If you become riled, get over it at once. Take a walk, count to ten or fifteen, or

* Shakespeare; *Julius Caesar*, Act II, Scene 2, line 32.

divert your mind to something pleasant. Let go of the desire to retaliate. When you are angry your brain is overheating, your heart is having valve trouble, your whole body is being devitalized. Exude peace and goodness; because that is the nature of the image of God within you—your true nature. Then no one can disturb you.

Good and Evil Are Created in the Mind

In the ultimate sense, everything starts in the mind. Sin is created in the mind. Little children go naked without any consciousness of sin. To the pure-minded everything is pure. To the immoral everything is evil. An undisciplined mind causes great havoc in our lives. Sense-enslaved minds are the perpetrators of all wars, cruelties, and injustices.

God put you in this sensate physical form with the intention that you live in the world as an introspecting soul, enjoying the movies of creation without becoming identified with them. That is how God wants you to live: to demonstrate mind-control not only when everything is rosy, but in the midst of your troubles also. Far from just talking about it, Self-Realization teaches you that self-mastery. The dance of life and death goes on all the time; but man has the mental power to rise above all sensory experiences of change, to be unaffected by life's inconstancy. The Bhagavad-Gita offers us sublime assurance of this freedom: "The relativities of existence (birth and death, pleasure and pain) are overcome by those who view this world with equal-mindedness. Verily they are enthroned in the taintless, the perfectly balanced Spirit."*

When you manifest changelessness you become a king among souls. Changeless within, even though body and mind are constantly changing, you become one with the Changeless Infinite.

The teaching of the Gita is inimitable. It deals in minute detail with life as it is, and shows how man should behave under all circumstances. It is correct to say, "I am made in the image of God"; but having lost touch with that image you must learn how to become one with it again. The message of the Gita shows the way. Gold that has been covered with

* Bhagavad-Gita V:19.

several layers of clay will still be there, though hidden. To discover it you must break through the clay. Similarly, many claylike strata of habits and sensations cover the golden soul. This "mud" is the cause of man's nervousness and fear—of all ungodlike qualities. To remove the "mud" one must develop an impervious mental attitude toward the body and the senses. What fears we have about the body! I have pictured and experienced in my mind all kinds of suffering, and have overcome them.

When the Soul Commands, the Mind Obeys

In order to realize you are made in the image of God you must rise above fear and anger and destroy oversensitivity. Don't be finicky. Say to yourself: "Today I sleep in a bed; tomorrow I lie on the ground, it doesn't matter. All is the same to me." Practice this mental neutrality, and the mind will do exactly what you tell it. The mind is extremely tricky, but if you train it, it will behave. When you say, "I can't live without beefsteak," the mind echoes, "I can't live without beefsteak." But if you, the soul, give the command, "Slavery, begone!" the mind will obey. So be not the servant of the body or the mind. Freedom from sense slavery is the only way to peace and happiness. No matter what the circumstances, rise above all mental sensitivity and make yourself truly and everlastingly happy.

> The state of complete mental tranquility, attained by yoga meditation, in which the self (ego) is satisfied by the vision of the Self (soul);
>
> The state in which the sense-transcendent bliss becomes known to the (awakened intuitive) intelligence, and in which the yogi remains enthroned, never again to be removed;
>
> The state that, once found, the yogi considers as the treasure beyond all other treasures—the state in which he is immune to every grief;
>
> That state is known as Yoga—the pain-free state. The practice of Yoga is therefore to be observed resolutely and with a stout heart.*

* Bhagavad-Gita VI:20–23.

The Balanced Life
Curing Mental Abnormalities
1925

Try to visualize a group of misproportioned human figures—one with a peanut-sized head and a body as fat as a balloon, another with one arm developed like that of a Sandow, but with the physique of a dwarf, and another with a top-heavy head fitted to a frail Lilliputian body. Would it not be (according to your mood) a very amusing or pathetic spectacle if you suddenly beheld a crowd of such people?

Now visualize another group of people who are normal so far as their physical form and appearance are concerned, but who are mentally unsound and deformed. As clothing hides scars, sores, and some deformities, so also the neat-looking garb of human flesh often covers serious mental maladies.

If you were confronted with a vast crowd of average people, well-dressed and physically healthy, and if you were gifted with the power to see their mental bodies, what a surprise and heartache you would have. You would observe their mental bodies—with reason as the head, feeling and senses as the trunk, and will as the hands and feet—to be abnormal, diseased, and deformed. You would see that some have a tiny head of undeveloped wisdom attached to a bulging trunk of sense appetite. Some would possess a withered body of pep and feeling, with the arm of business faculty very much overdeveloped in proportion. Others perhaps have a large, creative brain, but the trunk of sympathy and feeling is shrunken and dried up. Still others, normal in head and body, would be seen to possess impotent paralytic legs of will and self-control. You could go on and on.

Such multitudinous psychological deformities in pathological mental bodies, underdeveloped in some directions and overdeveloped in others, lie concealed within man, causing

347

suffering to his soul and hampering its expression on the material plane.

It would not be out of place here to name a few of such psychological diseases, so that these invisible but prime causes of all havoc in human life may be detected and their presence made known to the unconscious sufferers. Such persons may thus learn the nature, silent growth, and symptoms of these defects and guard against the secret onslaughts of their happiness-destroying powers.

Spiritual Melancholia

This disease is prevalent among those who are mentally and physically idle under the pretext of being too busy with spiritual things. These sufferers neglect the great and small duties of material life in the name of serving God, and thus invite the devil to work his mischief in them. They suffer from pessimism and lack of appreciation for all things good and beautiful in the material life. This is a contagious disease, and all spiritual aspirants must guard themselves against it by keeping their blood of energy warm and immune with constant healthful worthwhile activity.

Spiritual Indigestion

This results from indiscriminately swallowing a lot of mental patent medicines in the form of pseudo-spiritual books and lessons by quack spiritual doctors. This disease kills not only the real hunger for Truth, but also destroys the power to discriminate between good and bad teachings. He who eats theological ideas all the time, and eats anything that he can get, will not only overeat but will consume poisonous ideas along with the good, inviting first, spiritual indigestion, and finally, spiritual death. Long-continued overstudy of all sorts of philosophical principles and treatises, without any effort to assimilate them and test them out in one's own practical experience, results in doubt, indifference, and disbelief in all spiritual laws.

Sowing Mental "Wild Oats"

Those afflicted with this disease lead a purposeless life, through having too much time or money on their hands and lacking a true aim in or understanding of life. They are whimled, doing anything that comes into their heads, filling life with cheap novels, exciting movies, or other unproductive pastimes. They do not realize their malady until some terrible shock or nervous breakdown overtakes them.

Mental Cold

This disease is called despair. You don't know when you are going to catch it and suffer from its unpleasant symptoms: congestive pains of despondency, intolerance, and impatience. Worst of all, it hangs on for a long time, and the victim easily becomes reinfected even after seeming recovery.

Mental Catarrh

This disease consists in harboring chronic worldly worries. Sufferers usually neglect to use their powerful weapon of will and therefore passively yield to their constant fears instead of fighting and routing them.

Psychological Fixation

Its victims become one-sided in the pursuit of happiness. They begin to think that money is happiness, or that fame is happiness, or health, or power. They sacrifice everything else —youth, reputation, peace of mind—on the altar of their all-consuming ambition. They learn too late that the balanced life —observing all the laws of nature and of God, and combining activity with calmness—alone can bring happiness and fulfill man's natural destiny.

Sufferers from psychological fixation become wholly obsessed with some one ambition until their perspective on life is warped and distorted. One man, for instance, was very successful in his business and amassed a million dollars; but before he could use it he died of excessive worry and a nervous breakdown. Others, to gain fame, sacrifice their self-respect and sincerity. Sufferers from this disease of one-sidedness miss their true goal and can never derive real satisfaction from the possession of the longed-for objective, since man's nature is many-sided and demands all-round development.

Religious Fixation

This ism-fanaticism among so-called spiritual people results from clinging to some dogma or opinion without putting it to the test of experience, and causes paroxysms of anger and hatred against the tested laws of Truth and liberal rational thought. This religious madness leads to disobedience of God's simple laws of mental efficiency, material prosperity, and physical health.

Spiritual Principles Should Be Taught

Physical diseases, being tangible, painful, and repugnant, arouse our active resistance, and we seek to remedy them by exercise, diet, medicine, or some other definite method of cure. But psychological diseases, though the root cause of all human woes, are not prevented or attended to promptly and are allowed to wreck and devastate our lives.

Educators, physical culturists, preachers, reformers, doctors, and lawmakers will hasten the true progress of civilization only when they themselves first learn, and then teach others, how to develop harmoniously all the factors of life and of man's nature. This is the true education and all-round human culture that all the world is seeking.

Educational authorities deem it impossible to teach spiritual principles in public schools because they confuse them with the varied conflicting religious dogmas. But if they would concentrate on the universal principles of peace, love, service, tolerance, and faith that govern the spiritual life, and devise practical methods of growing such seeds in the fertile soil of the child's mind, then the imaginary difficulty would be dissolved. It is a great mistake to ignore this problem just because it is seemingly difficult.

Many college graduates leave their universities with a top-heavy, book-inflated head, and are unable to walk straight on the path of life because their legs of will and self-control have been almost paralyzed through disuse. They tumble headlong into the pit of wrong marriage, sex misuse, inordinate dollar-craving, and business failure because they have not been taught any use of their college-sharpened mental blades of smartness except to hurt themselves. Many young men seem to take pleasure in doing those things that react to their own disadvantage and suffering in the end. Last year in America young men ranging in years from fifteen to thirty stole a billion dollars by the "hold-up" method. Who was responsible? We are—all of us. They also are vicious who do not prevent the spread of vice, and who do not teach others to be virtuous through their example. Schools, colleges, and society have not tried scientifically to prevent crime by eliminating its true mental cause.

"How to Live" Schools Are Needed

Why not take the proper educational steps to avoid this annual theft of a billion dollars, and use some of those millions for creating "how to live" schools, where the art of living and a balanced development of all human faculties would be taught?

I consider properly organized schools as gardens where infant souls are grown and nurtured. The gardeners should be well selected and given cooperation by parents and the public. We should never neglect teachers, for they are soul molders. The care and spiritual nourishment of the early life of a human plant usually determines its later development.

I sincerely praise the modern school system of America and its constantly improving methods of intellectual and, to a certain extent, physical training. But I cannot fail to point out its main shortcoming: a lack of spiritual background. The system badly needs to be supplemented with moral and spiritual training. The boy who belongs intellectually to Class A, or who is a great baseball or football player, often attracts notice and is encouraged by the teacher, but very few observe or warn him rightly if he is leading a dark Class D moral or spiritual life.

Where is there such a school, one that adopts definite measures for developing the whole nature of man, teaching him the true art of life and fitting him to go through the various minor tests and ultimately the final examination of life? Such schools are urgently needed to teach the arts and sciences of all-round growth.

In such a "how to live" school, the science of physical, mental, and spiritual development should be taught to children whose minds are still plastic and whose energies are as yet unguided into any definite channel. Adults too may master the subjects in night school, if they will exercise willingness and patience while the good habits are displacing the undesirable ones.

After a thorough training, the students of such a school should undergo ceaseless introspective examination throughout life; and the various diplomas won will be health, fame, efficiency, wealth, and happiness.

The results of the final examination at the end of this earthly sojourn will be determined by the sum total of achievements and mental and spiritual diplomas won at the various examinations throughout life. Those totally successful in this last great examination will receive a diploma of divine self-sufficiency, a free and joyous conscience, and blessings, engraved eternally on the parchment of the soul. This rare reward is incorruptible by moths, beyond the reach of thieves and the eraser of time, and is awarded for honorable entry into the Fellowship of Truth.

Increasing the Power of Initiative

Circa 1930

Looking at the vast panorama of this world, at the crowds of humanity rushing hot-haste through their span of life, one cannot but wonder what it is all about. Where are we going? What is the motive? What is the best and surest way to reach our destination?

Most of us rush aimlessly, like runaway automobiles, without any plan. Dashing heedlessly along the road of life, we fail to realize the purpose of our travel; we seldom notice if we are on winding devious ways that lead nowhere, or on straight paths that lead directly to our goal. How can we find our goal, if we never think of it?

Many people, though unaware of life's destination, nevertheless have enough initiative to determine what they want and to seek it. In connection with their personal desires and with changing their environment, they try to use the initiative within them to create what they want. What is that initiative? It is a creative faculty, a spark of the Infinite Creator within each one of us.

Think of a dozen people you know; aren't the minds of most of them like one-horsepower engines? Many people make similarly limited use of their creative energies. The whole process, the main activity of their lives, consists chiefly in eating, working, amusements, and sleeping. When life is so lived, what is the difference between man and the animals? One difference, psychologists say, is that man is the only creature that laughs. It is good to laugh; if you don't employ that power, you lose one aspect of strictly human development. Don't be like those who, day in and day out, take life so seriously they are afraid even to smile. They don't enjoy life at all.

Besides the unique ability to laugh, man has another supe-

rior quality, one of the greatest of all qualities—initiative.
What is this mysterious faculty? America is a land of initiative
in business, in applied mechanics; India is a land of initiative
in spirituality. Initiative is the power to create; to create
means to do something that nobody else has done; it is trying
to do things in new ways, and trying to create new things. Initiative is that creative ability which is derived directly from
your Creator. What have you done in your life with this divine
gift? How many people really try to use their creative ability?
Weeks, months, years pass, and they are always the same; they
have not changed, except in age. The man of initiative is as
glorious as a shooting star—creating something from nothing,
making the impossible possible by the great inventive power
of the Spirit.

Don't Be a One-Horsepower Person

There are three kinds of people with initiative—the extraordinary class, the medium class, and the common class;
and there are hundreds of others huddled together in a "no
man's land" of nonentity. Ask yourself this question: "Have I
ever tried to do anything that nobody else has done?" That is
the starting point in the application of initiative. If you
haven't thought that far, you are like hundreds of others who
erroneously think they have no power to act differently than
they do. They are like sleepwalkers; the suggestions coming
from their subconscious mind have given them the consciousness of one-horsepower people. If you have been going through
life in this somnambulistic state, you must wake yourself by
affirming: "I have man's greatest quality—initiative. Every
human being has some spark of power by which he can create
something that has not been created before. Yet I see how
easily I could be deluded with the mortal consciousness of
limitation that pervades the world, if I allowed myself to be
hypnotized by environment!" But if you say, "Every avenue of
activity is already overcrowded; why try at all?" you are allowing yourself to be hypnotized by a frustrating worldly consciousness. That is why in every walk of life so many men,
lacking initiative, remain unsuccessful.

On the spiritual side, also, many people passively follow

the same path throughout life. Even though unsatisfied, they unthinkingly remain in the denomination to which their families belong. Or perhaps they were born Baptists, but a change of residence places them near a Congregational Church, so they become Congregationalists. Man ought to adapt himself conscientiously, according to his inner dictates, to all life's experiences. He should not act blindly.

My guru, Sri Yukteswarji, used to say, "Remember this: if you have within you that faith which is truly divine, and if there is something you desire that is not in the universe, it shall be created for you." I had that indomitable belief in an inner strength, in the spiritual strength of my will, and I always found that some new opportunities were created to give me the things I wanted.

The power of initiative within you remains undeveloped, unformed, unexploited, unused. That power is native to the soul; it has actually been given to all of you, but you have not used it. How can you acquire initiative? If you have not developed the power to think creatively for yourself, or the initiative to make your own way, your first attempt should be to try to improve on what someone else has done. The effort to make improvements on the inventions of others is the most common form of initiative.

The second or medium quality of initiative is shown by people who write or invent something new, but of no particular significance.

The best or most extraordinary quality of initiative is that which makes you stand out before the world in a blazing flame, like a Burbank or an Edison. Those were men of invincible initiative, spiritual initiative. Was God partial to these great men, that they possessed this particular greatness? Were they chosen by Divine Will to take so much glory? No. They simply used their initiative to bring forth the greatness and the glory that is every man's birthright as an immortal child of God. Those who look for personal glory are never great; inflated with pride, they lack any real support from God. Those who enjoy giving—whether it be strength, courage, music, art— are great men.

Most people who have become great have been subconsciously guided: they had a tinge of greatness in their heredity that gave them an initial advantage. They used that hereditary advantage in their life to become extraordinary, to become outstanding. If you have a quality of greatness, you have been unconsciously led by forces of mind whose power enabled you to change your environment by reincarnating, and in that new environment to bring forth the greatest flowering of your initiative. In this sense, great men are "born."

You Must Discover the Power You Have

But I know that great men can also be made, or developed from seemingly nothing. There is a way to become great, to acquire this extraordinary power of initiative. By wisdom, by right training, and by practice of the Self-Realization teachings you can develop that power of initiative and bring it into full play. The ones who made the struggle long ago are the ones who now see the fruition of their activities. You must discover the power you have; you must strive to overcome apparent impossibilities.

You must be prepared to withstand the critical opinion of the world in order to succeed in a great way in any vocation. You must stay away from one-horsepower people in order to be original—to think differently, to speak a little differently. And be untiring in your zeal. The man of extraordinary initiative swallows up all difficulties, believing in his heart that he is right. With unflinching steadiness march on your path, realizing that behind you is the infinite Creative Power.

You must first get yourself into conscious contact with that Infinite Power. It is the Source of all initiative, and when you contact that superconscious Power, your conscious and subconscious minds also become filled with power. Long ago I was apprehensive lest the little initiative I had developed would disappear quickly under difficult tests. I know now that within myself is that great infinite Principle, which is the Source of all art, all music, all knowledge. If That is behind me, I cannot fail.

Whenever you want to create something wonderful, sit quietly and go deep in meditation until you have contacted that infinite, inventive, creative Power that is within you. Try something new, but always be sure that that great creative Principle is behind anything you do; and that creative Principle will see you through. Every human being is meant to be guided by the boundless creative power of Spirit. You have choked with doubt and laziness the fountain of creative power within you. Clear it out! Show dauntless determination in everything you do.

Most people are content to feed themselves on dead quotations, to go on collecting the ideas of others, without ever showing the individuality that is within themselves. What is distinctive about you? Where is the great uniqueness of God's power in you? You have not been using it.

The Lord's Infinite Power Sustains You

I was reluctant, at first, to become a teacher—the implications frightened me. A teacher has to be a shock-absorber; the minute he becomes disturbed, he cannot help those who seek his aid. A true teacher has to love everybody; he has to understand humanity, and to know God. But when Sri Yukteswarji told me that my role in this life was to be that of a teacher, I called on the Lord's infinite power to sustain me. When I started to give lectures, I made up my mind that I would speak not by book learning but by inner inspiration, holding the thought that behind my speech was the inexhaustible Creative Power. I have also utilized that Power in other directions, to help people in business and in many different ways. I have used mortal mind to reflect Immortality. I did not say: "Father, do it," but, "I want to do it, Father. You must guide me; You must inspire me; You must lead me."

Do little things in an extraordinary way; be the best one in your line. You must not let your life run in the ordinary way; do something that nobody else has done, something that will dazzle the world. Show that God's creative principle works in you. Never mind the past. Though your errors be as deep as the ocean, the soul itself cannot be swallowed up by them. Have unflinching determination to move on your path unhampered by limiting thoughts of past errors.

Life may be dark, difficulties may come, opportunities may slip by unutilized, but never within yourself say, "I am

done for. God has forsaken me." Who could do anything for
that kind of person? Your family may forsake you; good fortune
may seemingly desert you; all the forces of man and nature
may be arrayed against you; but by the quality of divine initiative within you, you can defeat every invasion of fate created
by your own past wrong actions, and march victorious into
paradise.

Though you be defeated a hundred times, be determined
that you are nonetheless going to conquer. Defeat is not meant
to last for an eternity. Defeat is a temporary test for you. Naturally God wants to make you invincible, to have you bring into
play the almighty power that is within you, so that on the stage
of life you can fulfill your high destined role.

God Meant the World for Our Entertainment

How are you going to find out what role suits you? If we all
want to be kings, who will be the servants? On the stage the
parts of a king and of a servant are equally important if the
roles are played well. You must remember that this is why we
are sent into this world with differences, with desires for various vocations. God meant the world to be a play, a huge spectacle for our entertainment. But we forget the Stage Manager's
plan and want to play our part as we see fit, and not as He
desires.

You fail on the stage of life because you are trying to act a
part different from the one divinely designed for you. Sometimes the buffoon attracts more attention than the king; so no
matter how obscure your role, play it conscientiously. Tune
yourself with Spirit, and in this earth-drama you will play your
part well.

You are not meant to suffer. Those who play tragic parts
must realize that they are but enacting a role. Never mind
which part you have to play; always strive to act it well, in
harmony with the direction of the Stage Manager, so that your
little role will enlighten others. Realize that an aspect of the
infinite power of Spirit is performing through you on the stage
of the world.

Infinite Spirit creates new success. Infinite Spirit does not
want you to be an automaton. Attune yourself to Cosmic
Power, and whether you are working in a factory, or mixing
with people in the business world, always affirm: "Within me

is the Infinite Creative Power. I shall not go to the grave without some accomplishments. I am a God-man, a rational creature. I am the power of Spirit, the dynamic Source of my soul. I shall create revelations in the world of business, in the world of thought, in the world of wisdom. I and my Father are One. I can create anything I desire, even as my creative Father."

Who Made God?

Circa 1949

The enigmas of God's creation, and of how He Himself came into being, almighty and powerful, have been pondered in every heart that yearns to know about God. No scripture has fully elucidated these seemingly unanswerable questions. But if you contemplate and try to feel the entire perception of the subject as I shall describe it, you will find the answers to these questions—answers that I received from the very depths of my soul and from God.

The Infinite, God, is the ultimate cause of all finite creation. He projects the power of *maya,* the storm of delusive relativity—the illusion that the One has become the many—which, blowing over the ocean of His Being and His vibratory wish to create, stirs into manifestation the waves of finite creation. "Unborn though I am! changeless, Lord of Creation and Controller of Cosmic Nature (Prakriti)! yet, entering Nature I wear the cosmic garment of My own *maya*-delusion (which does not change Me)."*

Manifesting Himself as the creative Cosmic Intelligent Vibration, and using the help of the storm of delusive relativity, God forms out of Himself all finite vibratory waves of mind, energy, and matter: electrons, protons, atoms, molecules, cells, and blocks of solid matter—clusters of island universes floating in the sphere of space, surrounded by wandering radiations.

Thus Intelligent Cosmic Vibration is the first manifested cause of all created things, though the different finite forms of matter are created or caused secondarily by arrangement and combinations of certain basic forms: cells derive from molecules, molecules from atoms, atoms from electrons and

* Bhagavad-Gita IV:6.

protons, electrons and protons from lifetrons, and lifetrons from thoughttrons* of the Infinite.

Creation exists, and is caused by God; therefore God exists. We can say that intelligent creation exists because of an intelligent God. But who created God, out of whom all things else have come? The Infinite Himself.† The law of causation applies only to finite objects; it does not apply to the Infinite. As all waves on the ocean become dissolved in the ocean, so all finite objects manifesting from the aforesaid finite causes lose themselves in their Eternal Source. Similarly, the law of causation operates outwardly in creation, but is lost in the Infinite.

Through the law of causation, our original parents—the finite creations known as Adam and Eve, who themselves were special creations of the Infinite—helped to create all humanity. Because we are created by our parents—and our parents by our grandparents, and all mankind has come from Adam and Eve—we ask who created God. We apply to the Infinite the law of causation that created us. This is erroneous reasoning.

Varying Perspectives

When you are dancing with the waves of the ocean, you can't get a perspective of the ocean as a whole; but from the air you have a bird's-eye view of its vast expanse. Similarly, when you concentrate on creation and are immersed in it, you cannot see anything but creation and the law of causation working therein. But when with closed eyes you learn how to look within, you see neither finite forms nor the law that created them, but glimpse the formless, causeless Infinite.

---

* The name given by Paramahansa Yogananda to the first and most subtle manifestation of the creative vibration emanating from Spirit; the primal ideas behind all matter. Thoughttrons compose the ideational or causal universe, from which emanates the astral universe of lifetrons, intelligent life energy; from which in turn emanates the physical universe of gross atomic energy. (See *causal world* in glossary.) *(Publisher's Note)*

† "Not-Being was not, Being was not then....
The One breathed windless, of its own power.
Beyond this there was naught whatsoever....
The root of Being in Not-Being was found
By sages tracing it with understanding in their hearts."
—Rig Veda X:129

In the wintry land near the North Pole, an Eskimo who was hunting seal looked up and saw a Hindu traveler approaching him.

"Where did you come from, my friend?" he asked.

"My home is India," the stranger replied.

"Well, well!" said the Eskimo. "Do Hindus find plenty of good seal meat in India?"

"Oh, no, we don't have any at all," replied the amused visitor. "Hindus live mostly on vegetables."

"What a foolish statement," thought the Eskimo. "No one can live without seal meat!"

Just as the Eskimo, knowing no other diet, thought all people ate seal meat, so finite creatures, being themselves created by the law of causation, naturally think that the Infinite God also came into being through the law of causation.

Spirit Is Free from Causation

So it is foolish error for finite, causation-born human beings even to question, "Who made God?" The Infinite made the law of causation that created all finite things, though the Infinite Itself exists without having been caused. As an absolute monarch may make all the laws in his kingdom without being bound by them, so the King of the Universe makes all the laws in His kingdom, including the law of causation that governs His finite creation; but He is not subject to His laws. "I, the Unmanifested, pervade the whole universe. All creatures abide in Me, but I do not abide in them."* Though present in all things, God is in no way bound by finitude.

Therefore the Infinite *is*. We deduce His existence and omnipotence from His powerful manifestations in creation. His power is fully active in the manifested state. And during cosmic dissolution, all power, cosmic intelligence, and the law of causation become inactive and dissolve into the Absolute, there to await the next cycle of God's creative manifestation. The forces of the storm that create waves in the ocean are manifest in the waves. But no power is manifested when the ocean is still. Similarly, in the creative state, the Infinite manifests

* Bhagavad-Gita IX:4.

intelligence, mind, vibration, forces, and matter. And in the unmanifested state, the Infinite exists solely as Spirit, in which all forces lie dissolved. Out of space come light, nebulae, and weather, and into space they dissolve and hide again. That sphere beyond manifestation is the hiding place of Spirit.

The Infinite, beyond the categories of vibratory intelligence, energy, space, and time, is thus a thing in Itself. It can be felt and known as the eternal Power that exists without a beginning or end. Creation is caused by God, but God simply *is*. No one, nothing made God—He has been and will be what He is forever and forever. "O Arjuna! there is nothing higher than Me, or beyond Me. All things (creatures and objects) are bound to Me like a row of gems on a thread."* This cannot be understood so long as you consider yourself a created being, subject to laws of cause and effect. But as soon as you become one with God in ecstasy, you will know exactly how and what God is—Beginningless, Endless, Causeless. Then, being one with Him, you will know that you too are the Causeless Eternal. As a mortal man you are a creation made by God; as an immortal man of realization, you will know yourself as a wave in the ocean of God, the one and only, self-sustaining, ever-existing Cosmic Consciousness.

* Bhagavad-Gita VII:7.

The Missing Link Between Consciousness and Matter

Self-Realization Fellowship international headquarters,
Los Angeles, California, 1932

The difference between a stone and the thought of a stone is very great: a stone has weight and dimension, and is visible and tangible; the thought of a stone is invisible and intangible, without weight or dimension. Likewise the physical body of, let us say, Henry Jones, manifests weight, form, dimension, and visibility; the thought of Henry Jones has none of these qualities of matter. Yet a powerful mind, versed in the art of visualization, can in a hallucination or a consciously produced dream see Henry Jones, shake hands with him, weigh him on a scale, and see that he is tall and slight. A visualization, hallucination, or even a dream representation of the body of Henry Jones is more real than the mere thought concept of his body, because dream objects are apperceived by the senses of touch, taste, smell, sight, and hearing.* What then is the difference between a thought of Henry Jones; a visualization, hallucination, or dream perception of Henry Jones's body; and his living physical body?

Difference Between Illusion and Delusion

One could take the view that the physical form of Henry Jones is real because visible to all, and that the dream conception of him is unreal because visible to only one person. Is it not possible, however, that the reality of the physical body of Henry Jones—and of all other human beings—is a delusion?

---

* The instruments of sensory perception (eyes, ears, etc.) belong to the physical body, but sensory perception itself is a function of man's astral body of subtle electricities. Thus, in dreams and hallucinations the senses function through the subconscious mind, independent of their physical instruments. (See *astral body* in glossary.)

From India has come the philosophical concept of *maya*, delusion or mental error common to all individuals; and of *avidya*,*
illusion or mental error as experienced by each individual.

On the other hand, one individual may understand certain
truths that are not similarly realized by all. Thus men of divine
understanding, who have experienced the truth about the nature of God and man, are sometimes wrongly accused of illusions and hallucinations by those who are yet in thrall to cosmic delusion. It is not right for those under *maya* to decry the
testimony of one who is not. Only he who has transcended
cosmic delusion through his own inner realization may correctly judge the truth.

The average person thinks of the physical body perceived
by the senses as real, and regards a mental, imaginary, or dream
concept of the body as unreal. Let us suppose that by television
a picture of Henry Jones's form is transmitted from Detroit to
the *Los Angeles Times* headquarters. Are the viewers in Los
Angeles seeing the real Henry Jones? The ordinary person
would say *yes*.

The Cosmic Magician's Grand Illusion

A metaphysical master sees delusion within delusion as
illusion. He can see the physical body of Henry Jones as a delusive form—like a mirage of a city—not nothing, but something, yet not what it appears to be. The man of realization
would ask what makes us so sure that the physical body is not
a delusion shared by everyone? Can we be certain that all
human beings are not merely dreaming about the body of
Henry Jones and other material forms? If man really is circumstanced by God to dream within a cosmic dream, then we all
may be dreaming the existence of the body of Henry Jones. In
which case we cannot distinguish whether the body of Henry
Jones actually exists or not.

By certain stereoscopic and vitaphonic effects, the great
magician Thurston might show to his audience the form of
Henry Jones floating in the air and talking, and suddenly spirit
it away. Is it not possible, then, that the great Cosmic Magician
might be showing us true-to-sound, true-to-sight, true-to-

* See *avidya* and *maya* in glossary.

touch superpictures of the body of Henry Jones and of everyone and everything else in creation? If so, then anyone under the influence of this stereoscopic vitaphonic superdrama might create the form of Henry Jones by mental motion pictures of his own—"home movies," you might say. In this case, the people who are under the cosmic delusive influence created by God would think, "That person is suffering from illusion," even though they themselves are victims of the cosmic delusion by which they see the metaphysically untrue, but mundanely true body of Henry Jones. So, if everything in creation consists of dream pictures in the consciousness of man, then all is delusion, and the mental picture or hallucination of one person, based on the reality of the physical body of Henry Jones in this cosmic dream-world, is delusion within delusion, or illusion.

The wise man who awakens from the influence of the cosmic dream perceives the physical body of Henry Jones and all matter as a delusive cosmic dream, and the mental concept of matter or Henry Jones as a delusive dream within God's cosmic dream. A mental error or illusion in one person can be corrected by others who do not participate in the error; but an error shared by all cannot be corrected by any except those who have attained Self-realization, and who thereby know the truth that "things are not always what they seem"* to the senses.

How Consciousness Became Matter

The only difference between consciousness and matter, mind and body, is rate of vibration. Vibration is the motion of energy. How did this motion originate from the Cosmic Intelligence? All the vibrations in the ether are manifestations of the Intelligence-guided cosmic energy. Spirit as the unmanifested Absolute is without vibration or motion. Spirit manifested as the Creator is God the Father. The Creator first stirred His still Spirit with the motion of thoughts; thus God the Father's first projection of creation was cosmic intelligent motion, or vibration of thought.† This motion became stronger

---

* *Phaedrus,* Book IV, Fable 2, 5.

† The great Albert Einstein was very close to the truth when he wrote: "I want to know how God created this world. I am not interested in this or that

and grosser until it changed outwardly and manifested as cosmic light and cosmic sound (registered in the human body as the visible spiritual eye and the audible cosmic sound of *Aum* or Amen). The vibration of the conscious cosmic energy became progressively more gross, until it began to manifest as divine, semi-intelligent, instinctively guided electronic energy, and finally as the still grosser forms of gaseous, liquid, and solid energy.

Likewise the microcosm, or body of man, came into being first as a vibratory thought-form, the causal body. This in turn produced the grosser vibrations that make up the astral or energy body of man, which produces the still grosser vibrations that structure the solid physical body. Just as man uses electrically projected light and shadows and sounds to create a stereoscopic vitaphonic picture of a human being on a movie screen, so the Cosmic Operator combines various thought-frozen vibrations of cosmic light and energy to produce in man's consciousness the "picture" of a solid physical body.

Wrong Thoughts Obstruct God's Perfect Thought-Pictures

By partially obstructing light from the projector, the projectionist of a slide film may produce on the screen a picture of a man without a hand; he can easily restore the hand by letting the light flow freely through the film. Similarly, the consciousness or manifestation of disease is nothing more than an obstruction, created by wrong human thought, in the perfect thought-feeling of man that God created. Man is heir to the failings of his forefathers. Hereditarily he has become habituated to imperfection. His wrong thoughts not only obstruct the perfect thought-pictures of life and body, they also impede the free flowing of the cosmic life force, which is responsible for manifesting and perpetuating the delusive picture of the human body.

The amputation of a hand in an auto accident is no more real than is the amputation of the hand of the man on the film screen in the foregoing illustration. However, unless one is an accomplished "projectionist," he may not be able to correct, in

---

phenomenon, in the spectrum of this or that element. I want to know His thoughts; the rest are details."

the superpicture created by God, a distortion of seeming hurt
or disease in his body. The delusive nature of bodily accidents
cannot be known until one can transfer his consciousness into
the operating chamber of Cosmic Consciousness and get ac-
quainted with the secret methods of the Cosmic Projectionist.
By His self-evolved cosmic thought-films and self-frozen cosmic energy, He is trying to show perfect pictures of man (made
"in His own image"), and of all life, all worlds, and the cosmos.
Through ignorance, man has fallen out of tune with the divine
will, and thus obstructs the perfect presentation of God's
stereoscopic vitaphonic superpictures of life.

A block of ice is solid, heavy, cold, and visible. If allowed
to melt, it becomes liquid, yet has the same weight, remains
cold, and is still visible, but in a different form. If electricity is
passed through the melted ice, it becomes invisible hydrogen
and oxygen. So the one block of ice can be changed from a visible, cold, solid mass to invisible, intangible gases with the
same weight. The process may be reversed, and the gases re-
condensed into liquid and frozen into the vanished block of ice.
Similarly, the solid human body can be reduced to liquids and
evaporated into invisible gases; but man has not yet learned
how to bring it back in its original form. Not yet does he know
the link between mind and body, Spirit and matter. That missing link is cosmic energy.

Finely vibrating conscious energy becomes pure consciousness, and, vibrating at increasingly grosser rates, manifests as the body. When by use of his will man attains supreme
control of the energy in his body, he will be able to melt the
vibrations of his solid physical body into astral energy, and the
astral energy into mental energy. And by the same method he
will be able to materialize his consciousness into the astral
body and condense it into the physical body. The Gita refers to
this power. "He who realizes the truth of My prolific manifestations and the (creative and dissolving) power of My divine
Yoga is unshakably united (to Me). This is beyond doubt."*

Scientists today can control chemical changes of the body,
but they do not yet understand the biochemical control of matter. With understanding of the relation of will and body comes

* Bhagavad-Gita X:7.

the realization that the body is not dependent on food chemicals alone, but on energy supplied by the will from the invisible cosmic source. The will is the chief bringer of life force into the body. Like a human dry battery, a human body in a state of suspended animation can live without oxygen, sunshine, solids, liquids, breath, or heart action; but deterioration inevitably follows when consciousness, and therefore will, has completely left the spinal column and the brain regions.

Will, the Cosmic Energizer

Every movement of the body parts presupposes movement of will, and with every action of this invisible radio of will, energy is radiographed into the body from the storage battery in the brain and the conscious cosmic energy surrounding the body. When you are tired you can put energy into the body by eating food, or by inhaling oxygen, or by absorbing ultraviolet rays of sunshine, or by drinking water or other liquids; but as you tense your arm and body in *willing* to lift a heavy weight, you are bringing energy into the body by the invisible mental force of will. In the tensing of body parts with concentrated will,* we find the only instance whereby we can create energy in the body; not from physical sources outside the body, but from the invisible source existing both within and without the body—the intelligent cosmic energy of God.

To attain mastery over cosmic energy, the missing link between consciousness and matter, body and Spirit, is to realize the true nature of the Self—of everything in creation—and the oneness of all with the Creator.

---

* Reference is made to the Energization Exercises taught to students of the Self-Realization teachings. (See glossary.)

Is God a Father or a Mother?

*First Self-Realization Fellowship Temple at
Encinitas, California, May 14, 1939*

I feel pity for those who have never known the love of a mother, for they have missed a great experience. Every mother is a manifestation of God's unconditional love, though human mothers are imperfect, and the Divine Mother is perfect. I pray that all mothers live such a godly and impartial life that their limited human love becomes transmuted into the pure all-embracing love of the Divine Mother.

My mother was everything to me. My joys rose and set in the firmament of her presence. I was still but a boy when Father and I, in Bareilly, received word that Mother was seriously ill. We entrained at once for Calcutta: Mother had gone there to supervise preparations for the wedding of my elder brother Ananta. At a transfer point we were met at the station by my uncle. I felt a terrible conviction that Mother was already dead. I asked anxiously if she was still alive. A train was thundering toward us, and I had inwardly determined to throw myself beneath its wheels if Mother were dead. Correctly interpreting the desperation in my face, Uncle replied, "Of course she is alive!" But when we reached our Calcutta home, Mother was gone. I was inconsolable. I loved Mother as my dearest friend; her solacing black eyes had been my surest refuge. I have described in a poem an actual experience of mine at that time:

> Merely affection-saturated, many black eyes called—
> Offering to nurse
> My motherless sorrow—this orphan life of mine.
> But none matched the love-call glance
> Of those lost two dark eyes.

The love of those two black eyes
Had forever set
From the region of all black eyes that I beheld.
Seeking those two eyes
In birth and death, in life and dreams,
And in all the lands of the unknown,
At last I found
The all-pervading Divine Mother's
Countless black eyes
In space and heart,
In earth-cores, stars, within, without,
Hungrily staring at me
From everywhere.
Seeking and seeking my dead mother,
I found the Deathless Mother.
The lost love of the earthly mother
I found in my Cosmic Mother. Seeking and searching,
In Her countless black eyes
I found those two black eyes.

If only you could share with me the thrill that I felt when I suddenly became aware of those black eyes of my Mother watching me from everywhere, from every speck of space! What an experience it was! All my sorrow became changed into joy.

Human relationships are given to you, not to be idolized, but idealized. If you always think of your mother as the unconditional love of the Divine Mother manifested in human form, you will be comforted when she is gone. The mother who has passed on is not lost to you; she is a representative of the Divine Mother, who came to mother you for a short time and then was taken away, to remain concealed behind the omnipresent love of the Divine Mother. Those who have lost their mother must find the Divine Mother hidden beyond the skies. You don't pray deeply enough. Implore Her with continuous demand, with the resolve not to cease until Her reply comes. If you will pray in this way as earnestly as I did, you will receive an answer from the Divine Mother; and you will see your earthly mother.

Now I behold every woman as a mother. Even when only a little goodness is reflected there, I see the Divine Mother. Men

should look upon all women as mothers; they do not know
what they miss when they look upon woman merely as an object for the satisfaction of passion; they see then only the evil
that is within themselves. In the mother aspect of womanhood
there is purity. Woman was given the motherly instinct to save
man from the pitfall of evil. That is her primary purpose; she
was not created as an object of lust. Nothing is more sacred
than the unconditional sympathy of woman toward man. A
stern, dignified court judge is but a child to the wife in his
home. Every woman should feel love for all the world if she
would manifest the Divine Mother's love. To inspire mankind
with mother love is to bestow the greatest blessing a woman
possesses.

God Is Both Father and Mother

In creating this universe God revealed two aspects: the
masculine or fatherly, and the feminine or motherly. If you
close your eyes and visualize vast, illimitable space, you become overwhelmed and enthralled—you feel naught but pure
wisdom. That hidden, infinite sphere wherein there is no creation, no stars or planets—only pure wisdom—is the Father.
And Nature with her diamond-dazzling stars, the Milky Way,
the flowers, birds, clouds, mountains, sky—the countless
beauties of creation—is the Divine Mother. In Nature you behold the mother aspect of God, full of beauty, gentleness, tenderness, and kindness.* The beauty in the world bespeaks the
creative motherly instinct of God, and when we look upon all

---

* In this context, Paramahansa Yogananda is emphasizing what we have come
to regard as true "motherly" qualities, the gentle and loving responses we find
in a mother's nature. On other occasions, Paramahansaji has also pointed out
that form and qualities presuppose manifestation, and manifestation presupposes relativity. Mother Nature must also enforce the inherent and inexorable
cosmic laws of the universe. Break those laws, and Divine Justice dispenses its
corrective punishment; hence the fierce demonstrations we sometimes behold
in nature. These are results of man's own wrongdoing, which throws the cosmic harmony out of order. (See *karma* in glossary.) But the consistent beauty of
Divine Mother is that if the devotee appeals to Her unconditional love, She
may be persuaded to assuage the retaliatory power of those laws. Thus in Hinduism, Divine Mother is sometimes depicted as Kali; her four arms symbolize
cardinal attributes, two beneficent and two destructive—the essential duality
of Mother Nature. *(Publisher's Note)*

the good in Nature, we experience a feeling of tenderness within us—we can see and feel God as Mother in Nature.

So God is both Father and Mother. The Christian and Hindu scriptures describe God as triune: Father, Son, Holy Ghost—*Sat, Tat, Aum*. The Father is the wisdom aspect of God; Holy Ghost, the mother aspect; the Son is cosmic creation—the emblem or principle through which the father and mother aspects of God express their divine love. We are the children of that love. "As above, so below"—in the human family we see in miniature the greater family of the Holy Trinity: God the Father represented in the human father; Holy Ghost or Nature manifested in the mother; the Son symbolized in the child, expression of the love of both father and mother.

Jesus spoke of God as Father. Some saints speak of Him as Mother. In His transcendental aspect, God is neither Father nor Mother; but when we think of Him in terms of human relationship, He may become for us either Father or Mother. God is both infinite wisdom and infinite feeling. When He manifested Himself in creation, God gave His wisdom a form in the father; and He gave His feeling a form in the mother. Each, alone, is imperfect, only half of God's nature, because the father moves and is moved by reason, whereas the mother moves and is moved by feeling. The father wants to govern the child by reason; the mother, by feeling.

The mother says, "Teach him by love." Sometimes a great deal of love is good; but if you give too much sweetness, and that only, you may spoil the child. Sometimes a little strictness is good, but severe punishment for errors only drives a child to greater error. This is why the two aspects of God must be manifested through the parents in the upbringing of the child; both are necessary for its ultimate welfare. Every father should strive to temper his reason with love, and every mother to temper her love with reason.

When I think of my guru, Sri Yukteswarji, I see in him the sternness of a father and the kindness of a mother, without the weaknesses or blindness of either. Every father and every mother is potentially endowed with both the fatherly wisdom and the motherly tenderness of God. They have to perfect these endowments. Parents so easily become blind to the faults in their offspring! If you can't see your child's faults, there is something wrong with your love. Parents should learn to love their children unconditionally, without allowing love to blind them to errors in a child's action or thinking. They should love their child in spite of any misdeed, but should not support him in his error. Help your children to extricate themselves from the pitfalls of evil, rather than drive them farther down by supporting them in their wrongdoing. They won't return any love to you for that misguided indulgent love.

Pure Reason and Pure Feeling Are Intuitive

Pure reason and pure feeling both have intuitive qualities. Pure feeling sees as clearly as pure reason. Most women have a keenly developed intuition. Only when they become unduly excited do they lose their intuitive powers. Pure reason is also intuitive, if this power is sufficiently developed. Otherwise, should the premise be wrong, the conclusion will be wrong also. Sooner or later, every man who reasons clearly will develop true intuition, which never errs.

A jealous, hateful, angry woman will see these qualities reflected in others. If she continually harbors such destructive emotions, she will lose, alas, her intuitive gifts. For this reason every woman should strive to be less emotional and to keep herself free from wrong emotions. She will then develop that intuitive mother-aspect of God. My mother had great intuition because she was entirely free from jealousy, hate, and anger.

God never forsakes anyone. When, having sinned, you believe your guilt to be measureless, beyond redemption; and when the world declares you of no account and says you will never amount to anything, stop a moment to think of the Divine Mother. Say to Her, "Divine Mother, I am your child, your naughty child. Please forgive me." When you appeal to the mother aspect of God there is no retort—you simply melt the Divine Heart. But God will not support you if you continue to do wrong. You must forsake your evil actions as you pray.

Confession embodies a sound principle. The act of confessing may be likened to calling a doctor when you are ill from transgressing health laws. You are obliged to tell the doctor your symptoms, and he forthwith prescribes for you, and you receive healing. But if you violate nature with wrong practices time after time, you will never remain healed. I know a boy who always boasts, "I can do anything I please, for I will be forgiven next week when I confess." This is the wrong view. If you don't forsake the evil as well as confess it, you will not be forgiven.

The divine man develops both the fatherly and motherly qualities in himself. He can feel toward anyone the same love a mother has for her children. These were the feelings of Jesus when on the cross he said: "Father, forgive them, for they know not what they do." How could he know such love for those who were crucifying him? He had developed both the fatherly and the motherly aspects of God. To Jesus the men nailing him on the cross were not enemies with javelins and spears; they were his children who didn't understand him. Who but a mother could think of them as Jesus did? A mother whose son is torturing her is afraid only of what may happen to him. This is what Jesus understood; this is how he could say, "Father, forgive them."

If you develop the motherly aspect of God, you will feel love for all the people of the world. And if you appeal to God as the Divine Mother, She quickly gives in, for you have appealed to Her tenderness and unconditional love. When you worship God as the Mother, you can stand and face Her and say, "Divine Mother, naughty or good, I am Thy child. I may have been in the clutches of evil for many incarnations, but do I have to make full recompense according to Thy law? I cannot wait so long a time to enter Your presence! Mother, please, forgive me! Why must You exact punishment of me? What is done is done. It is all past. I am not going to sin again." The Divine Mother may reply: "You are naughty; go away from Me." But you must say, "You are my Divine Mother. You have to forgive me." Then She says: "Ask of Me salvation; I will give you salvation. Ask of Me wisdom, and I will give you wisdom. But do not ask of Me My love, for when you take that away I have nothing."* If you continue to cry, "I want Your love!" the Divine Mother

* From an old Bengali song. It has been translated for the West by Paramahansa Yogananda in *Cosmic Chants*. (Publisher's Note)

finally melts: "Since you are My child, and I am your Mother, how can I but forgive you?" And She gives you Her last possession—Her divine love.

A Vision of Divine Mother

In India I used to visit the great saint Master Mahasaya. *
On my first call at his home I happened to disturb him at his devotions. He invited me to sit down, adding: "I am talking to my Divine Mother." His whole countenance shone with the reflection of Her love, and I could feel the intense vibrations of that great love. Whenever I was in his presence while he was communing with the Cosmic Mother, the love I experienced in my heart was a thousand million times more than that I felt for my earthly mother, whom I so dearly loved; at such times I thought I could not exist another moment without my Divine Mother.

"How is it that you can commune with the Beloved Mother and I cannot?" I said to him one day. "Please ask Her if She loves me. I *must* know!" Insistently I pleaded until finally the saint agreed.

"I will make your plea to the Beloved."

That same night in meditation I had a great divine experience: Seeking the seclusion of my small attic room as soon as I arrived home, I meditated until ten o'clock. Suddenly the darkness was lit with a beauteous vision. The Divine Mother stood before me, tenderly smiling.

"Always have I loved thee! Ever shall I love thee!" With these words She disappeared.

It was barely sunup the next morning when I hurried to the saint's home. I saw by his eyes that he was wandering in the gardens of the Infinite; such love of God is rarely seen.

"Did the Beloved Mother say anything about me?" I asked.

"Mischievous little sir!"

"What did Divine Mother say? You promised to tell me," I chided.

Again he answered, "Mischievous little sir!" I knew in my heart that he could see through my subterfuge, yet I had been

* See chapter 9 in *Autobiography of a Yogi.*

deliberately hiding my thoughts in order to learn if my experience the previous night was real.

"Why so mysterious?" I said. "Do saints never speak plainly?"

"Must you test me?" he replied. "Could I add a single word this morning to the assurance you received last night from the Beautiful Mother Herself?"

Bliss flooded my being. I prostrated myself at the saint's feet; I knew the Divine Mother was walking in them. He it was who gave me the revelation and the understanding of the mother aspect of God. He told me that later my guru would come to me, one who would be endowed with the wisdom aspect of God: "Through his guidance, your experience of the Divine in terms of love and devotion shall be translated into his terms of fathomless wisdom."

A Test of Faith

I will tell you a little story about Divine Mother and an experience I had with Her. On the grounds of Self-Realization Fellowship headquarters there is a small wishing well of cast concrete. Shortly after its purchase I was helping the boys to move it into place. The well accidentally slipped and fell with all its terrific weight on my foot. There was terrible pain and much swelling in the foot, which seemed completely mashed. I was carried to my room. My friends wanted to call a doctor.

"If Divine Mother tells me to see a doctor," I said, "I will go to one. If She does not, I won't go."

I waited, hoping to feel inwardly what Her wish might be. Day by day the pain in my leg became almost unbearable; there was no sign from Divine Mother.

The following Sunday I had a large class to teach. It seemed that I would have to be carried to the platform. I could not get my foot into a shoe. Satan tempted me that Sunday, saying, "Why don't you pray to be healed?" But to pray would have been to doubt. Divine Mother knew my plight, and I was willing to abide by Her wish.

"I am not going to pray," I said. "The Mother knows what is wrong with me." Inwardly I vowed my unconditional surrender to Her: "Whether sunk beneath the wave of death or moving on the oceanic waves of life, I am with Thee evermore."

"Look at these people," Satan spoke again. "They will all laugh at you. They have never seen you sick before, and now they will see you with an injured foot."

"I don't care." Once you have Divine Mother's love, neither praise nor blame can touch you.

I was limping along toward the platform where I was to speak, when inadvertently I slipped on the threshold; my injured foot was badly twisted. So great was the pain, I felt as if every bone in it had splintered. But the moment I stepped forward again the terrible swelling collapsed suddenly, all pain gone; I was able to slip my foot into a shoe.

That was one of the greatest demonstrations of the power of love that I have ever experienced. I walked as if nothing had ever been wrong with my foot. Needless to say, I was thrilled— not because of the healing, but because of the Divine Presence. She wanted to see if I would pray for a healing. Had I prayed, perhaps in due course of time the injured foot would have had a natural recovery; but I would not have had that all-assuring divine experience.

Another time, in Palm Springs, I was singing to the Divine Mother: "Mother, I give You my soul call. You can't remain hidden anymore! Come out of the silent sky, come out of my cave of silence."* Suddenly She appeared! I saw Her in the stones, the palms, everywhere! God has no form, but to please a devotee He can take any form that devotee desires. You have no idea how wonderful the Divine Mother is; how great She is; how loving She is!

There is no greater experience than to feel and know that the Cosmic Mother is with you. Watch for the presence of the Mother, because She will look after you in every way, whether your trouble is sorrow, pain, or sickness. Pray to God as the Divine Mother when you crave solace, and when you seek wisdom pray to God as the Divine Father.

Mothers, do not limit to your child alone the all-forgiving love you bestow on him. Give to everyone the love and under-

* "I Give Thee My Soul Call," from *Cosmic Chants*.

standing of the Divine Mother, and you will be bound no longer by the limitations of an earthly mother's love; you too will be a divine mother. When you can truly say, "I feel as a mother to all mankind," you will no longer see others as strangers; you will recognize and love all children of the world as your own. All forms of human love, in the perfect state, are encased in the love of God.

Judge yourself no more a sinner; cast off your wrong habits and pray, "Mother, I am Thy child. Reveal Thyself!" If you send this appeal to God as the Divine Mother night and morning, unceasingly, She will manifest Herself unto you.

Let us give thanks to God, and pray for His blessing on all mothers, that they be enabled to manifest His qualities.

May all the sons and daughters of the world be filled with that motherly affection which is the reflection of the Divine Mother's unconditional love; and may they give that unconditional motherly love to one another, that we have peace and heaven on earth.

The Art of Developing Memory

*Self-Realization Fellowship international headquarters,
Los Angeles, California, August 28, 1932**

By virtue of the faculty of memory, human beings are unique. The souls of all creatures, through unconscious recollection of their divine origin, tend naturally to seek their Source. This accounts for the upward evolution of everything in the universe. But, in conformance with God's plan for creation, it is only upon attaining a human body, with its superior brain and nervous system, that each soul is at last endowed with the means to remember consciously its original oneness with Spirit.

Memory is that power by which we mentally reproduce our experiences. If it were not for memory we would forget all our perceptions of life; we would have to start afresh, like infants, every day. A person who has "lost" his mind, and hence his memory, behaves like a child.

There is no value in having experiences if we cannot recall and relive them. We learn by introspection and by analyzing our past behavior. In man's memory lies the value of being a human creature. John *remembers* that he is John each morning upon awakening; and it is through memory that he associates his life experiences with his identity as John.

Whenever we wish it or need it, any experience that we have had can be reproduced by the subconscious mental faculty. By remembering what we have done before, we can perform again some skillful action that we have learned, or reason out which actions to repeat or avoid in a particular situation.

* This talk was one of a series of outdoor Summer School classes that Paramahansaji conducted at the headquarters on Mt. Washington. He taught under a large pepper tree that he called "The Temple of Leaves."

The subconscious mind is always active, recording experiences during the daytime and working even in sleep, looking after the bodily house like a night watchman. Upon waking, one always knows whether he has had a good or a bad sleep. That memory power of the subconscious mind is a faculty of the ever-awake, ever-joyous Lord. Implanted in each soul is the memory seed of that consciousness, for the soul knows itself to be ever living in God. Memory is the seed of immortality by whose cultivation we may recall all the events of this life and of our past lives.

Develop Divine Memory

If we can remember all our experiences as mortal beings in this life, why is it that we do not recollect all the divine experiences that have happened in the soul? Memory has two natures: mortal memory reproduces the experiences of this life, and divine memory reproduces the experiences of the soul throughout all its incarnations. Most people are aware only of mortal memory.

Why is our divine memory asleep? Some people are able to recall many experiences, both mortal and divine; others cannot well remember even their recent past. Memory has different grades in different people according to brain capacity. Education, concentration, meditation, and various memorable experiences are required to develop a good memory. Without developing memory one cannot become a well-educated person. If one has an experience and subsequently forgets it, all values of that experience are lost to the conscious mind.

By improving the quality of memory, we can make it powerful enough to remember all things, even our divine origin. By awakening the divine memory, whereby we can recall every experience of all our past lives and ultimately realize our immortal soul nature, salvation is attained.

Effect of Physical Exercise on Memory

*Asanas** and proper physical exercise are useful in developing memory power. Today, when machines have replaced

* Bodily postures of *Hatha Yoga.* (See *Hatha Yoga* in glossary.)

manual activity in so many functions and departments of life, man is becoming physically lazy and is in dire need of regular exercise. He has begun to devise mechanical and other types of indoor equipment to help him exercise his body.

When one performs physical exercises, it is necessary to concentrate the mind on the activity in order to reap the fullest benefit. It is not just the flexing of muscles, but the inner power of concentration to awaken and redirect the life force that gives the body strength.

Foods That Increase Memory Power

There are certain foods that are brain foods; and there are muscle foods, nerve foods, and foods that help to build up and maintain the different body organs. As an aid in developing memory we should eat foods that increase brain power. Proteins are helpful in developing memory. Ground-up pecans and almonds, mixed with a few drops of lime or orange juice and taken before bedtime, will improve one's brain power, yogis say; milk and cheese also are good brain foods.

Yogis suggest that, at times of worry or strain, one should drink the juice of one or two limes in a glass of water, rinse the head with cold water, and apply cold water on the temples, between the eyebrows, and at the nostrils and ears. The nerve processes are calmed immediately, the mind becomes more peaceful, and good memory returns.

Avoid eating too many fatty foods, which tend to cause fatty deposits to build up in the blood vessels on the surface of the brain. The Hindus say that pork and beef are injurious to man's health; these two meats contain much uric acid. The pig and cow have poor memories. By eating their flesh, man may develop their physical and mental traits.

Practice Exercising Memory

Memory can be developed by exercising it. It is incorrect to say that a man who was born a physical weakling can never become strong. There is always the possibility of becoming and accomplishing something greater in all departments of our lives. One has to know how to seek the right ways. Similarly, according to some doctors, a person who has a hereditary mental weakness will retain that mental defect to the end of his days. But it has been proved that many mental deficiencies may be overcome by the practice of concentration exercises. There has been little research in this direction in the West; hence many psychologists are unacquainted with the art of deep concentration, which has been taught for centuries by India's great yogis.

The correct methods for developing concentration are unknown to most people. The mental faculties are there, but they are not developed. Failure to develop one's mental capacities eventually leads to serious trouble. The brain, like the physical body, requires right exercise for health.

To develop a good memory, therefore, one should not only exercise the body and eat health-building food, but should also engage in mental discipline. Make an effort to remember things. Practice the art of visualization: look at a certain object or at scenery and then try to reproduce that picture in your mind. Trying to recall the strains of songs and chants, and singing them mentally, develops memory. Anything that is done with feeling, or that rouses feeling, develops memory. Both poetry and music have emotional values. All of us remember easily the greatest sorrows and the greatest joys of our lives. Why? Because those experiences were felt deeply. Anything that one strongly feels develops one's power of memory. Writing poetry, and adding and subtracting mentally are also good methods for developing memory and concentration.

Meditation Strengthens Memory

To increase one's power of memory, one should do everything with deep attention. Most people carry on their activities absentmindedly; there is a great gulf between their actions and their thoughts. That is why they cannot remember anything very well. What one wants to recall he should perform with great attention. One should not be fussy, but whatever he undertakes should be done with his whole mind. In church one should listen to the sermon with keen attention. Work at tasks in the home with attention and interest. Keeping the conscious mind on the task at hand does not prevent one from reflecting constantly on God in the background of his mind. But when

one meditates, he should think only of God. The power of
memory is strengthened by meditation.

What is meditation? Becoming one with the soul. It means
banishing the consciousness of being related to the body and to
human limitations, and trying to remember that one is a soul.
When man begins by conscious mental effort to relate himself
to the immortal soul, rather than to the body that he inhabits
for one life only, he will recall more of his past-life experiences,
and will eventually remember that he has come down from the
bosom of God. In Him lies the memory of all the experiences of
one's life and of all lives. When man communes with his soul
within, the forgotten times and powers of the deathless Self
will come back into his consciousness. Meditation means to
remember that one is not a mortal body but an immortal soul,
one with God.

During the daytime we tend to think of ourselves as
human beings, but at nighttime in deep dreamless sleep we
forget our mortal attitude. In meditation we can try consciously to forget our mortal identification; we can abandon
the consciousness of the body and remember we are Spirit.
Those who persevere in this practice will become masters.

Remember Good Experiences

Memory was given to man to reproduce good. To abuse the
power of memory is harmful. To think hatefully of another
person because of some remembered injury he inflicted on you
is a misuse of memory. However, to recall unhappy experiences in order to learn the lessons inherent in them is a proper
use of memory, as then one may analyze his past behavior and
avoid repeating in future the wrong acts that brought painful
results. One should not bring back any wrong thought and relive
it; for then it will stay longer in the mind. Memory was given
to us to keep alive only life's good experiences and lessons. Get
rid of wrong past thoughts by avoiding recalling them. If they
come to mind in spite of you, refuse to entertain them.

Let me repeat: to remember bad experiences and dwell
upon them is an abuse of God's gift to us of memory. Rather
one should vow, "I shall use memory only to recall good
thoughts and experiences. From this moment I banish from my

mind all unpleasant memories. They belong to the mortal being. I am a child of the Spirit. I am going to see, hear, taste, touch, feel, and will everything that is good. I shall take only the good from my life's experiences and shall preserve only the good in my memory." Banish forever the abuse of memory.

A person who feels good emotions, and thinks good thoughts, and sees only good in nature and people, will remember only good. Memory was given to you to practice the recollection of good things until you can fully remember the highest Good, God. Beholding goodness in everything, you will certainly find that one day the Invisible Power will shatter all the little windows of thoughts and sensations and feelings through which you have been seeing only glimpses of the divine harmony in creation; you will behold through an infinite opening the omnipresent Goodness, God.

Rouse the eternal flames of divine memory until they burn away your forgetfulness, and you remember that you always have been, and are even now, one with the Lord.

Man's Eternal Quest

First Self-Realization Fellowship Temple at
Encinitas, California, February 16, 1941

The flowers outside* are so beautiful, but behind them is a garden still more lovely. Though it is very subtle and hard to discern in the beginning, if you can penetrate to the inner realm through the door of the spiritual eye† you will discover it. I live in that garden—a region of exquisite qualities, of tender thoughts more sweet and fragrant than any flower. There the bee of my mind is continuously drinking the honey of God's presence.

As we interiorize our concentration and live more and more in that invisible land within us, we find that our soul qualities take special forms; each materialization is a window through which we perceive the Lord's indescribable sweetness. Don't think that the search for God consists only in meditation. Every good quality that you express in thought and action yields the hidden nectar of God's presence, if your inner perception is deep enough.

When we pass through the door of the spiritual eye, we see inside ourselves the factory of intelligent Life Energy that has created the whole universe. Because we don't concentrate within, we are mystified by the imprints of the invisible Spirit in nature. We behold the productions of God; His name is written in the flower and in the sky, in everything—but He is silent. As human beings we are very much privileged, for among all God's creatures man alone has the physical, mental, and spiritual endowment necessary to seek Him, to find Him, to know Him, and to understand His language of silence.

* Colorful gardens surrounded the first Self-Realization Fellowship Golden Lotus Temple in Encinitas.

† Through the "single eye" within the center of the forehead, man can behold the inner astral and causal worlds behind the gross physical cosmos.

What Is a Successful Life?

A child pictures success as having all kinds of playthings, and perhaps a toy car to ride in. A poor child thinks how happy he would be if only he had a lot of toys. A wealthy child, on the other hand, may be bored with his playthings; he has a restlessness in his soul. In time it may become very difficult to please the child of the rich, for he already has so many possessions. When we are older, we laugh at the desires of our childhood; and who knows but that whatever we are wishing for now, thinking it will bring the fulfillment of our life's dream, will one day have little significance for us? I found this to be so. I didn't want to become drunk with emotions, heedlessly bent on the follies I saw others pursuing, and I looked farther on. If we gaze a little ahead we can see for ourselves that most of the things we think we want are not going to make us really happy.

Success is necessary in order to possess the essentials of life: food, clothing, shelter, and health. If you don't have these to at least a certain degree, you are in a wretched position. You should be able to attain the minimum amount of comfort and happiness that you are seeking. Whether one is a spiritual or a material idealist, all persons can agree that there are a few basic physical needs that must be met so that man can preserve his bodily temple. Unless he maintains this temple, he cannot succeed in anything else.

Happiness Is a Creation of Our Own Mind

But what is real success? If you attained everything you wanted in this life, you would eventually become disillusioned anyway. By analyzing I saw for myself that the only pleasure I had in anything was that which my mind gave to it. If I withdrew my attention, enjoyment of any object vanished. Thus I saw that pleasure is internal, a concept of one's own mind. The beauty of your most valued possession, which you may be holding in front of your eyes, disappears when your thoughts are absent from it. Only when you put your mind on it do you perceive its loveliness. Therefore it is reasonable to say that within us, and not outside us, lies most of the happiness we are seeking.

We can magnify our happiness or minimize it. One person has a little home and says, "I enjoy it more than a palace." Someone else has a palace in which he does not take as much pleasure as the other person has in his unpretentious cottage. The secret of success and happiness is inside you. If you have found success and prosperity outside, but not inside, you are not truly successful. A millionaire who is not happy is not successful. I don't mean that if you have a million dollars you cannot be a success. Whether you are rich or poor, if you get happiness out of life you are a real success.

Pleasure that lasts only for a moment and leaves you with regret afterward is not happiness. In true success, even though the first excitement of delight in some accomplishment fades away, the gratifying memory of fulfillment remains. All the good things that you have done in your life stay on in your memory as a joy forever. They are the real success that you have attained.

To Be Happy Under All Circumstances Is Real Success

Success is not a simple matter; it cannot be determined merely by the amount of money and material possessions you have. The meaning of success goes far deeper. It can only be measured by the extent to which your inner peace and mental control enable you to be happy under all circumstances. That is real success. When you can look within and your conscience is clear, your reason unprejudiced, your will firm yet flexible, and your discrimination strong; and when you are able to obtain at will the things you need and the things you consider worthwhile, you are a success.

As a child you could be happy with little things, but now you tend to think you have to own several homes and cars, even though you can see that those who have them are not invariably happy. Plain living and high thinking make for contentment. Keeping your mind on the plane of ideas will give you more happiness than if you dwell on externals. Those who are preoccupied mostly with looking after their home, their possessions, their dress, are not necessarily civilized. You can dress up a dog, but that doesn't make it civilized. The difference between man and the dog is that man can voluntarily change his consciousness and his nature. He can penetrate deep within, into the region of the Spirit, where the dog cannot. Man's love is transcendental. When we die, the dog may grieve for us a little while, in some cases till death, but human friends never forget us (if they don't want to!) throughout incarnations. So mankind has tremendous advantages over other creatures.

Evolutionary Human Progress Lies in the Power of Thought

As a human being, you make your greatest evolutionary progress by the power of thought. Set aside some time each day to improve your mind. It is more commendable to read awhile than to occupy yourself day and night with housework or with noncreative activities. Plan your life so that you do not live in a haphazard way; but if your tendency is to overorganize your time, get away from that extreme also. Balance is necessary in every avenue of life. Instead of using your mind only to plan your everyday work and other passing activities, or with idle mind letting your time slip away, employ it some of the time in constructive reading. Have at hand some worthwhile reading material, and peruse it during free moments. It is more effective to have a variety of literature—a bit of science, a bit of history, philosophy, biography, travel—anything that will expand and inspire your mind.

Books can be dear friends, and if your selections are choice ones you will experience much benefit from them. It may seem very hard at first when you read Emerson or Milton or Plato, or some of the great saints, but after a while you will find yourself thinking about what they have written. You will feel you have gained something, because all those sages received their wisdom from the infinite treasure-house of God—ideas that otherwise might not occur to you in a lifetime.

However, many people read constantly and yet cannot tell you what they have read. The best way to read a book is to introspect about it. See how it applies to your own life. And learn to discriminate. Do not accept blindly everything that you read; it should meet the tests of your mind. To be worthwhile, books should cause you to think. If they do that, you will find that your mind is developing.

Receive Knowledge Directly from Spirit

People who do not read or meditate, who live only externally, do not develop any deep understanding. Meditation keeps you directly in tune with the Power that evokes all thought. To touch that Supreme Power is meditation. As a human being you do injustice to yourself if you don't read; but to meditate is still better. I would like to read, but I can scarcely finish two pages before I am called to attend to something else, so I have given up reading. I find it more profitable to meditate. As I go deep within, radiant lights appear and great joy comes, joy that remains with me all day long. Such is my experience. Such is the experience of all who commune with the ever blissful Lord.

Don't waste your time. God wants you to be a balanced individual. If you allow your life to become unbalanced you will be punished by the cosmic law. Live simply, have daily physical exercise, study rewarding books, and cultivate the habit of daily meditation. If you meditate you will find much more happiness than you have ever known. All knowledge will be given to you from within.

My life has been that way. I have not read twenty books since I came to America twenty years ago. I am not proud of the fact; I would have been wholly ignorant if I hadn't had, through meditation, the consciousness of Spirit. When I look at a book I see that whatever truth it contains has already been given to me from God. All thought and truth come from Spirit; if you commune with Him you receive His wisdom direct. So, read good books rather than waste time on unproductive activities; but better still, meditate and anchor your mind on the ultimate Truth, which is God.

Man's Evolution Ordained by Cosmic Law

In different ages and places, man has developed, by his thought processes, various ideas about life and the soul. For instance, when members of some primitive tribes have headaches, they think their soul is lost, and they appeal to the medicine man for healing. He goes out in the woods looking for the lost soul, which he brings back in a box. Then he "replaces" the "soul" in the patient's head, and the headache is supposed to go away. It is the custom in another culture, when anyone is sick, to put fishhooks into his flesh so that if he happens to sneeze, his soul will not escape but will be caught by the hooks.

As through the process of faulty thought some people have arrived at erroneous conclusions about the soul, so by true reasoning others have come to a more profound understanding. We know that the soul is not a puff of breath, because there are persons who have lived long in the suspended-animation state without breathing at all, showing that the soul cannot be bound by breath.* The soul is something beyond breath or any other physical condition.

Whether or not one believes in himself as a soul, he is bound by the cosmic law to develop, consciously or unconsciously, his deeper nature. Whatever a person's occupation in life, his consciousness is evolving whenever he is planning something or otherwise using his intelligence creatively. Man evolves through every constructive action he performs.

The trouble with most people is that when they are performing an action they are thinking about something else. They don't know how to concentrate on what they are doing when they are doing it. You should learn to think of one thing at a time with all the power of your mind. Your whole attention should be there. Don't drag along. Doing things in a lackadaisical way leads to failure and misery.

Man should not be a psychological automaton, like the animal, which acts only through instinct. To be unthinking is a great sin against Spirit, which abides in you; we are meant to be conscious of what we do. We should reflect before we act. We should learn how to use our minds so that we can evolve and realize our oneness with the Creator. Everything we do should be the result of premeditated thought.

Aim for high goals. It is a waste to use the power of thought to obtain things that are not important. Learn to remove the weeds that have grown in the garden of the mind. Make your mental garden so beautiful that God will come there. If you want to have such a mental garden, blooming in

---

* See feat of Sadhu Haridas, page 214.

the soil of wisdom, you must make your life simple. By doing everything consciously, not absentmindedly, you can analyze your activities; then choose what is important and cut out the nonessentials. As soon as you are through with your duties, withdraw your mind from them and employ it in other creative pursuits.

God Fulfills Man's Eternal Quest

Learn how to cultivate the consciousness of Spirit. That is why you were born a human being. You were created under the evolutionary law that you might exercise your divine powers to find God. The animal can't find Him. Lahiri Mahasaya was working on the science of helping animals to evolve more quickly; but he didn't live to finish this work. I, also, know of some ways to quicken the evolution of the lower forms of life. But what of the millions of human beings who are living like animals? When they leave this world they haven't fulfilled the purpose of their existence. Why not fulfill it now? You can if you concentrate. The only meaning of life is to find the all-loving God, who has kept us apart from Himself by shyly hiding from us. We must find Him. Mankind is engaged in an eternal quest for that "something else" he hopes will bring him happiness, complete and unending. For those individual souls who have sought and found God, the search is over: He is that Something Else.

Nature Veils God's Presence

Why was temptation given to man? That he might look for the One who is more tempting than any worldly temptation. The earthly lures that surround you are not intended to ensnare you, but to cause you to seek beyond them; to make you ask, "Who created all these things? Who made me? Who am I? Where are You, Lord? Why are You hiding? Talk to me!" When you directly approach God with these questions, He answers. Most people don't call deeply enough to Him, and so they never find Him. You must speak clearly to Him in the language of your soul: "Lord, I want no longer to see only the beauty You have created. I want to behold Your Face, which is more beautiful than the flowers, more entrancing than all other faces. I want to see Who is behind all nature." Even if a person covers himself with a veil you can see that someone is there. So is nature like a great veil bulging with God's presence. He is hiding there, but you take just a casual look, not penetrating to see the shy Indweller. As I sit breathless, silent, watchful in meditation, I become aware of a blissful trembling stir within me, and He whispers: "I am here."

The intelligence God has given us is the gateway to Heaven. It is the outer door to His kingdom, but you don't use it. Why not use it now, today? Don't wait, only to leave the earth like a dog, kicked out by death. It is a crime against your soul. Your intelligence was given to you to discover why you were placed here: to find Him.

How to Discover Spirit

There are various techniques for discovering the Spirit. Silence is one of them. Practicing silence means to silence all desires that try to percolate into your consciousness from outside, so you can go deeper within to feel your soul.

Another step or technique is devotion, or speaking to God purely and simply: "You have created me. I didn't want to be created. It is Your responsibility to reveal Yourself to me." Talking to Him a little while and then forgetting will never bring His response. God is "hard to get" because not everyone "means business" with Him. The technique of prayer is usually ineffectual because most prayers are not deep or devotional enough. You have to repeat and repeat until you go really deep, into the superconsciousness. Prayer in which your very soul is burning with desire for God is the only effectual prayer. You have prayed like that at some time, no doubt; perhaps when you wanted something very badly, or urgently needed money—then you burned up the ether with your desire. That is how you must feel for God. Talk to Him day and night; you will see that He will respond.

Yoga Is the Science of Finding God

The Yoga system of contacting God is the best. It consists of various scientifically effective techniques of meditation. The great sages of India reasoned that logically there must be an exact law by which to approach God, just as there are exact

laws by which He operates His universes. Through their experiments, the spiritual laws of yoga were discovered. The science
of yoga will take hold in this country more than any other form
of spiritual seeking. The entire trend will be away from
churches, where people go only to hear a sermon, and into
schools and quiet places where they will go to meditate and
really find God.

Everyone should practice divine communion with God.
This is what Jesus did when he was with his disciples. I am not
here just to tell you about the sugar of God's presence; my
greatest aim is to make sure you taste it. What is the use of my
talking about God unless you know Him and taste His sweetness? You must realize God, as I have realized Him.

It is not out of pride that I speak this way, but because I am
sent here to testify to you about Him. Day and night I think
about my Lord. I am not wasting my time. Everything I do I am
doing only for Him, so engrossed that I don't notice the passage
of time or feel fatigue from my daily activities. I feel His presence when I work. That is also my meditation. I often give this
illustration: Some worldly men remain drunk for years by hiding now and then to take a little drink to sustain the euphoric
feeling; then they go back to their work. So is the divine man;
he hides from people and meditates upon the Lord. Drinking
deep of the intoxicating wine of God's presence, he whispers,
"Lord, You are so wonderful, so marvelous! I love You." Then
he goes back to his duties. Inwardly he talks to God all the
time, no matter what he is doing.

I am never separated from Him for a second. That is the
state I wanted and worked for. I remember that once in a while
I used to feel that He had gone away from me, and at such
times I wanted to die rather than live without Him. I didn't
find happiness in anything. Thus does the lover of God suffer
when separated from Him. But a time comes when the devotee
beholds the Lord dancing everywhere, and feels the immortal
fountain of His spirit and His bliss ever bubbling in his soul.
This is what you will feel if you meditate. Pray with such intensity that He will come to you. In the Gita is a beautiful
promise from the Lord: "Immerse thy mind in Me alone; con-

centrate on Me thy discriminative perception; and beyond doubt thou shalt dwell immortally in Me."*

The yoga techniques are more scientific than prayer; that is why they lead more swiftly to divine communion. In my youth, when I sought Him with prayer alone, it often took a long time to get results. After I had learned *Kriya Yoga* and practiced it, with deep devotion, I achieved results in a few minutes. Krishna taught that yoga meditation is greater than the path of asceticism, the path of devotion or prayer, the path of right action, or the path of discrimination.† It is a faster way. An airplane will take you from Los Angeles to New York in a matter of hours; by bullock cart the journey would last several months. If you practice yoga, you will find it to be the airplane of spiritual progress.

After you have perfected yourself in the Yoga path, which embraces bodily discipline, mental discipline, and spiritual discipline, the obstacles to spiritual success are overcome and you can commune freely with God. That is why it is the highest path. And that is why I am trying to acquaint people with it. Yoga is not a myth, a creation of someone's imagination. It is a true science.

Why shouldn't you take from India the greatest methods for finding God that have ever been given to mankind? I went to the masters in India for training, and they taught me about Christ in a profound and loving way such as never I heard in the West. I saw Christ in their company. They talked with him. Did St. Francis lie to us? He saw Christ every night. Lord Jesus lives! I have seen him. When you are behind a screen you see everyone else outside, but they can't see you. So the saints and the angels can see you, but you can't see them unless you practice yoga.‡

* Bhagavad-Gita XII:8.
† Bhagavad-Gita VI:46.
‡ There have been mystics of various faiths who, through their transcendent powers of devotion to God, have attained to the breathless state of superconscious ecstasy that alone brings true inner vision. The spiritual fervor of such great souls is beyond the emotional scope of the average person. For mankind as a whole, the only hope of divine illumination lies in the yogic approach to God through daily practice of scientific spiritual methods.

Your Prayer Must Be Intense to Reach God

Last summer I stopped at a monastery, where I met one of the priests. He was a wonderful soul. I asked him how long he had been on the spiritual path as a monk.

"About twenty-five years," he replied. Then I asked:

"Do you see Christ?"

"I don't deserve it," he answered. "Maybe after death he will visit me."

"No," I assured him, "you can see him from tonight if you make up your mind." Tears were in his eyes, and he remained silent.

You must pray intensely. If you sit night after night practicing meditation and crying to God, the darkness will be burned up, and you will see the Light behind this physical light, the Life behind all life, the Father behind all fathers, the Mother behind all mothers, the Friend behind all friends, the Element behind all elements, the Power behind all powers. That is where I live, and where I want you to come.

Practice of Yoga Awakens Soul Longing

You have gone away from God like the prodigal son, and it is only by returning to Him, within, that you will make this vale of tears a haven of heaven. There is no other way. If everyone in this world were a millionaire there would still be troubles and sorrows, for you cannot buy unshakable happiness. That comes only by following a technique of yoga, and by devotion, by going within. Practicing yoga is half the battle. Even if you don't feel enthusiastic in the beginning, if you go on practicing you will come to feel that tremendous longing for God which is necessary if you are to find Him.

Why don't you make the effort? Whence do all the beautiful things in creation continually emerge? Whence comes the intelligence of great souls, but from the storehouse of the Infinite Spirit? And if these wonders you see about you are not enough to induce you to seek Him, why should He reveal Himself to you? He has given you the capacity for love that you may yearn for Him above all else. Don't misuse your love and reason. And don't misuse your concentration and intelligence on false goals.

This World Is Only Pictures of Light

Night is the time for meditation; never go to bed until you have communion. I never do. Last night as I sat on my bed His presence engulfed me. The whole room and everything in it was blinding Light. Even when I slept I remained locked in the arms of the Divine. Never have I felt such joy.

This world is all a motion-picture projection of God's mind. There is no death, no disease, no wickedness. Someday, when He will show you His Light transforming itself into this terrible cosmic motion picture of life and death, and then withdraw the picture so that only His Light remains, you can laugh at the unreality of His light-and-shadow creation. You will know then that He has created everything out of His Light; and that only the Light is real. We must fully shake ourselves out of this dream delusion to realize that we are rays of that immortal Light. This realization comes with the practice of the highest yoga technique of meditation. It cannot be conveyed in lectures.

God Is Our Only True Goal

Every now and then I receive a letter from the Self-Realization students in London. During these terrible air raids they have not missed one Self-Realization Fellowship service. That is the real spirit of England and that is the spirit that will save England. Politicians can never save the world; it is only understanding God that will save the world. He is our true goal in this life. Otherwise there would be no incentive for going on.

Those who love God should worship Him in all religions. "In whatever way people are devoted to Me, in that measure (according to their desire, their degree of understanding, and their manner of worship) I manifest Myself to them. All men, regardless of their mode of seeking, pursue a path to Me."* Criticize no one's faith. There should be a genuine feeling of love and respect for all. Wherever you see a temple or church you should inwardly bow down to the Spirit there. It is not for everyone to be a teacher, but you can always draw the attention of others to spiritual things. Don't waste your time, spending hours listening to the radio and reading useless novels. Be

* Bhagavad-Gita IV:11.

entertained by the divine messages coming from your own soul. Just by a gentle attuning touch of my love, I hear His program here in my heart.

No one can bring you salvation unless you earn it—not through belief, not through following dogma, but by your own knowledge and experience. You should ask yourself these questions every day: If there is a God, why don't I see Him? If there are saints, where are they? The answers will be given you; you can commune with God and His saints if you practice the science of *Kriya Yoga*. My sole desire is to give you the Truth, that you may experience what I experience.

The purpose of this life is to find your Self. Know your Self. Feel the throb of the ocean of God's presence in your heart. Suppose you are floating in the ocean, rocked on the bosom of its mighty vastness, and when you swim ashore, you still feel the whole ocean, surging behind you as you walk onto the beach—this is the way I feel God. He never leaves any of His children for a moment. He will reply to all your questions, and then there will be no more fears.

Find that Power, feel the ocean of His love behind your consciousness, and you will achieve the greatest success man can attain.

The Art of Living

1933

Every man builds his aspirations and forms his desires according to prenatal and postnatal influences. Heredity, and national, social, and family characteristics, tastes, and habits mold each human life. But in the beginning of life, children are about the same everywhere. Jesus said: "Suffer little children to come unto me, and forbid them not: for of such is the kingdom of God."* Divinity is the one nationality of all children the world over; but as they grow older, and family and social characteristics begin to exercise their influence, children begin to manifest national and racial traits.

God has expressed His truth in varying combinations within particular civilizations, nationalities, and individual mentalities. Through this diversity He has placed before us a kaleidoscopic image of man's potential. It is man's duty to glean from this variety the qualities that are highest and best; and to foster them within himself, his nation, and the world. Great men and saints do this. They live several hundred years ahead of their time in exemplifying universal principles of truth that are eternal. These principles are the essence of the true art of living, and are applicable and vital to the success and happiness of all men. The differences among peoples of the various nations, races, and creeds should create, not a division, but a basis of comparison for selection of the best qualities and methods with which to develop the ideal man and the ideal world.

Of all the nations at present, India and America represent, respectively, the acme of spiritually and materially efficient civilizations. India and other Oriental nations have produced the highest types of spiritual people, such as Jesus and Gandhi;

* Luke 18:16.

whereas America has produced the greatest types of business-men and practical scientists, such as Henry Ford and Thomas Edison. A combination of spiritually efficient qualities with materially efficient qualities, as represented in the foregoing life-examples of great men, can offer us an art of living that will produce in every nationality all-round men of the highest type—physically, mentally, morally, materially, socially, and spiritually.

It is important to select, not one-sided national charac-teristics, but all-round universal principles of living from all nations and from all great men. Do not take only those princi-ples that develop the physical at the cost of the spiritual phase of man's life, or vice versa; adopt those principles that develop equally and harmoniously the superman of balanced physical, mental, moral, and spiritual qualities.

Practical Methods for Uniform Development

Following are a few practical methods for uniformly de-veloping body, mind, and soul:

• Include in your daily diet milk and other dairy products, and a good percentage of raw food and fresh fruits; drink a large glass of orange juice with finely ground nuts mixed in. Eat less meat; avoid beef and pork entirely. Read and follow a reliable modern book on dietetics.

• Fast one day a week on orange juice and use a suitable natural laxative as prescribed by your physician.

• Every morning and evening, with deep attention, walk briskly, run, or take some other form of exercise—as vigorous as your constitution allows—until you perspire.

• Read and meditate on some inspiring passage from the Bible and from the Bhagavad-Gita.

• Read Shakespeare and other classics, and suitable por-tions from practical books on such subjects as chemistry, physics, physiology, history of Oriental and Western philosophy, comparative religion, ethics, and psychology. Don't waste your time on cheap writings. Read a dependable health periodical and an inspiring spiritual magazine. Include editorials and health articles when reading newspapers, not just the comics and scandals.

• Visit different temples and churches—Protestant, Catholic, Buddhist, Jewish, Hindu, and so on—to develop your appreciation and understanding of all faiths. Look upon each one as The Temple of Our God.

• Honor God not only in man-made temples, but learn to worship and commune with Him in the inner temple of silence. Practice meditation for one hour in the morning and one hour at night, following the scientific methods taught by the great masters of Self-Realization Fellowship. Do not be side-tracked into forests of blind, untested belief and theology; get on the one highway of Self-realization that leads quickly to God.

• Do not be enslaved by the senses. They are not meant to bind you with material desires, but to serve you with perceptions of good, which reflect God.

• See plays or motion pictures only occasionally, choosing those of the highest quality.

• Obey God's divine laws as applied to family, country, and all nations.

• Speak truth with kindness and understanding, and respect truth wherever you perceive it.

• Expand your love for family and country to include love and service to people of all nations. See God in all men of whatever race or religion.

• Spend less, and have more, by doing away with luxurious habits. From your earnings put aside as much as possible, so that you can live partially on the interest from your savings, without having to dip into the capital.

• See life as divided into four periods, during each of which the main focus should be on developing efficiency in the activities appropriate to that part of life.*

* This is a general application of the ancient Vedic ideal of dividing man's life into four stages, known as the four *ashramas*. (1) Physical, mental, moral, and spiritual education of the celibate student (*Brahmacharya*). (2) Fulfillment of householder or worldly responsibilities (*Grihastha*). (3) Retirement from the world to seclusion or an *ashram* to devote more time to spiritual pursuits and thinking of God (*Vanaprastha*). (4) Complete outer as well as inner renunciation of all ties to the world (*Sannyas*). Though complete renunciation was generally the fourth *ashrama*, it was not confined to that stage, but was advocated

(1) From age 5 to 25 years. The child should receive concentrated character training and become instilled with spiritual ideals and habits. As he grows into adulthood, he should get a general education, learn efficiency by study and observation, and seek specialized training in some work to which he feels suited.

(2) From age 25 to 40 years. As an adult, one should fulfill family and other obligations to this world, while striving to keep a spiritual balance.

(3) From age 40 to 50 years. During this period, adults should live more quietly, studying inspirational writings and keeping abreast of progress in the arts and sciences, and spending more time in meditation.

(4) From age 50 on. One should spend the last part of life in meditating deeply most of the time; and, through the wisdom and spirituality thus acquired, in rendering social and spiritual service to others.

Be Calmly Active and Actively Calm

In short, don't think all the time of just making money. Exercise, read, meditate, love God, and act peacefully at all times. Learn to be calmly active and actively calm, carrying into your daily activities the calmness gained in the spiritual activity of meditation. In the Gita, Bhagavan Krishna teaches: "Remaining immersed in yoga, perform all actions, forsaking attachment (to their fruits). Remain indifferent to success and failure (while performing all actions). The mental evenness during all states of activities (resulting in success or failure) is termed yoga."*

Please join me in this prayer for true brotherhood under the Fatherhood of God:

---

earlier in life for those who felt the supreme desire for God alone.

By following the four *ashramas*, man was taught the art of living and right behavior; given an opportunity to fulfill his material ambitions and responsibilities; allowed a time to contemplate his spiritual life and make a greater effort for Self-realization; and then encouraged to give his life, his all, back to God, from whom all gifts of life, and life itself, have come.

* Bhagavad-Gita II:48.

"Heavenly Father, help us to create a 'United States of the World,' with Thy Truth our leader and president, which will guide us to live in loving brotherhood, and urge us to develop our bodies, minds, and souls perfectly, that Thy Kingdom of Heavenly Peace, which is within us, may be manifest in the actions of our daily life.

"Make us healthy, efficient, perfect in every way, so that we may inspire all our earthly brothers to manifest their true nature as Thy noble children.

"Heavenly Father, may Thy love shine forever on the sanctuary of our devotion, and may we be able to awaken Thy love in all hearts."

If you contact and commune with God in the inner temple of silence, you will have mastered the true art of living. Then health, prosperity, wisdom, love, and joy will be added unto you.

Habit—Your Master or Your Slave?

Date and place unknown

The human brain, with its hilly ranges of cerebral convolutions inlaid with arterial streamlets and dark rivers of veins, presents an epitome of a huge estate. Is this exquisite territory devoid of a Divine Resident? Could there be a book without an author, a child without parents, a clock without a maker, a rose without a designer? Nay! Similarly, the cerebral domain of mystic beauty has been shaped by wondrous intelligent agencies.

Who lives in this marvelous hall whose walls of mortared osseous tissues are fitted with ocular, tactual, auditory, olfactory, and gustatory doors? Beneath the dome of the human skull a colony of myriads of cells pulsating with life and intelligence are playing out scenes of intense activity. Tiny brain cells are engaged in diverse pursuits—banqueting, introspecting, and receiving guests of sensations that enter from the outer sensory doors. There is buying and selling going on: processes of absorption and elimination. Like tiny boats, blood corpuscles paddle along arterial streams, laden with various vital commodities.

Guiding and controlling many of these cellular activities is an unseen band of impish pixies and good fairies—habits. Sometimes great mischief is created when foreign and lawless habits are permitted entry into the cranial commonwealth. They set themselves up as lords, dominating the activities of their hosts, the brain cells. When the latter attempt to resist this encroachment on their freedom, these United States of Flesh become a scene of civil war. The whole bodily country is thrown into disorder while the brain cells furiously debate the right of certain habits to act as petty dictators.

How do habits gain power to tyrannize over human conduct? Every human activity, whether it be performed as an outward physical movement or as an inner process of thought, is a vote for a particular habit. Repetition of that action or thought swells the number of votes in favor of electing that habit to a seat in the bodily government. A considerable number of such actions vote that habit into office. At different periods of life a collective vote of all previous human actions determines which habits are going to predominate and rule supreme.

An election by numerical superiority alone, without adherence to a desirable qualitative standard, may bring disaster upon a country. If the majority of voters are morons or criminals, they are bound to blunder and elect the wrong president. Similarly, unless the votes of human actions are cast according to the supreme law of discrimination, the brain cells may thoughtlessly enslave themselves under tyrannical habit-dictators.

Maintenance of a truly enlightened spiritual democracy in the bodily country requires a thorough education of the brain-cell citizenry. The latter should be trained not to permit habit-candidates to be elected merely on the numerical strength of thoughtlessly repeated actions, but should consciously exercise the qualitative power of discriminative attention with the casting of every action-vote. They should be guided by ideal rationalism, and heed its warnings against accepting the bribe of sentimental attachment to environment, which leads to the misuse of voting power. Discriminative reason should be the sole guide in selection of the presidential habit-candidates.

Are Habit Slaves Born or Made?

Habits of drinking, excessive smoking, overindulgence in coffee or tea; and habitual moods of anger, greed, envy, sloth, and despondency are usually elected to office by the cumulative numerical strength of unwise hordes of little actions performed without any thought of the aftereffect of enslavement. Persons addicted to such habits are not born ineluctably to their unfortunate fate; in this or in a past life, knowingly or unknowingly, they have enslaved themselves through constant repetition of certain actions. The first drink never made a drunkard; the first act of sensuality never made a libertine; the first use of narcotics never made a dope addict. It was a series of mechanical or ill-considered repetitions of such misguided actions that elected these gripping habits to power.* Quantitative strength won against the qualitative voice of attentive reason, which had become weakened through failure to exercise its powers, and had thus lost its vote.

Guard yourself, therefore, against the first performance of a wrong act. What you do once you are likely to do again. It is by repetition that a habit grows stronger and bigger, like a rolling snowball. Use your reason in all your actions; otherwise you may thoughtlessly convert yourself into a helpless slave of undesirable habits.

Impeach a Bad Habit-President and Install a Good One

A strong bad habit presiding for a long time over the bodily country brings chaos and misery. Spiritual famine, mental fevers, and a universal poverty of body and mind exist in that misruled land. A strong bad habit should be impeached before a tribunal of daily introspection under the presiding judge of conscience, who should inform the court of reason that the inevitable outcome of persistence in the offending actions will be an impaired nervous system, wasted powers, and vanished happiness. This constantly sounded note of warning may serve gradually to persuade the jury of reason to the decision to put away forever the guilty victimizing habit.

Sometimes it is difficult to convince the court. Many persons who excessively smoke, drink, or indulge in sex experiences do not seek or even wish to be free of these slavish compulsions. They delusively think that there is nothing harmful about what they are doing because they don't immediately suffer disillusioning painful consequences. Childlike, they fail to visualize the ultimate results of their actions. They do not see

* For people who have established in previous lives the pattern of a harmful habit, such as alcoholism, the "first drink" was taken many lives ago; that is why in this life even the first drink can revive that habit with alarming suddenness and often tragic consequences.

that they have set into motion laws that work impartially for good or ill, according to the nature of human actions; that, although the shovels of harmful habits dig slowly, they yet dig surely a yawning, untimely grave, a pit of misery toward which the slave of wrong habits proceeds through scorching flames of suffering. Of such entrapped persons the Gita says: "Harboring bewildering thoughts, caught in the net of delusion, craving only sensual delights, they sink into a foul hell."*

First convince your mind that you are going to overthrow the tyranny of the undesirable ruling habit; then begin the work of constitutional agitation and actual impeachment. A whining or sorrowing attitude, gentle remonstrance, or even violent but spasmodic rebellion is of little avail. It is through continuous repetition of certain actions that you are the maker of your habits; and you must undo hurtful ones by a similarly regular effort, implemented by conscious exercise of will and the discriminative power of reason.

Relate your actions to new and better habits. Keep them continuously busy, interested, and attentive in serving good habits and in fraternizing with other good actions. If your actions begin to revert to their old dangerous habit-influenced associations, don't become discouraged. Persist in right actions, give them sufficient time and attention, and the voting strength of the new good actions will increase and finally become powerful enough to overthrow the worthless habit and to elect in its place a worthy one.

It Takes Time to Establish Habits, Good or Bad

It takes time for even a bad habit to attain supremacy, so why be impatient about the growth of a rival good habit? Do not despair about your undesirable habits; simply stop feeding them and thus making them strong by repetition. The time that elapses in the formation of habits varies with individual nervous systems and brains and is chiefly determined by the quality of one's attention. Through the power of deep, concentration-trained attention, any habit may be installed— that is, new patterns may be made in the brain—almost in-

* Bhagavad-Gita XVI: 16.

stantaneously and at will. The potency of concentration and will to create good and bad fortune is strikingly summed up in the Biblical verse: "For whosoever hath, to him shall be given, and he shall have more abundance; but whosoever hath not, from him shall be taken away even that he hath." * This truth is particularly applicable to habits. A man of good actions strengthens his will to perform further good actions, and thus increases in virtue with little effort. But a slave of bad habits debauches his will and reason, so that eventually he is not only powerless to create new good habits, but also has weakened his hold on whatever good habits he may have had at the start.

Government of one's actions by intuitional, wisdom-guided discrimination, uninfluenced by either good or bad habits, imparts unbounded power of will. "The individual who, disciplining the senses by the mind, unattached, leads his organs of activity to the proper wisdom-directed, *Karma Yoga*-prescribed channel of actions, he, O Arjuna, succeeds."† A man with such power can instantly fix a new habit in his brain, or stop one at will. An ideal democracy presupposes rational, willing obedience to good laws, without any goading by higher authority or other external influences. Similarly a wise man, one who is really free, avoids error and performs good, not from the compulsion of habit but from free and reasoned choice. Such a one does not permit himself to be dominated by even a good habit, lest in so doing he fail to exercise full discriminative choice of action. A good habit may be in force simply because there has never been any temptation of evil to overthrow it. A good habit thus established is not necessarily fixed permanently in the nature, because it has been maintained not from discriminative choice and reason but as a result of favoring circumstance.

All national tastes and human customs are habits, circumstantially acquired as a result of environmental influence. Love of Americanism or of Hinduism is the outcome of habit and familiarity. If I had had the choice, I would have preferred to be a human "chameleon," free to embrace the desirable aspects of all nationalities and all creeds.

* Matthew 13:12.

† Bhagavad-Gita III:7. (See *Karma Yoga* in glossary.)

We can test our power over our habits by commanding the mind to like or dislike a certain food at will. On one occasion I found this particular test useful: Shortly after I had come to America, I attended a dinner at which Roquefort cheese and crackers were served. No sooner had Mr. Roquefort touched the palate, and no sooner had his arrival become known to the cerebral cells, than the habit-lords of taste instituted a rebellion among the honored guests already gathered in my stomach, who became very upset and began to threaten, "If you let Mr. Roquefort in, we will all leave in a body!" I did not enjoy this sudden embarrassment! Noticing that everyone else at the table was greatly relishing the peculiar food, I strongly urged my senses to elect immediately the Roquefort cheese–enjoying habit. Then I liked the taste at once, and have continued to like it from that time on.

Why is it that you sometimes find yourself acting, or reacting, contrary to your real desires? Because over a period of time you have built up habits that are contrary to those desires, and your actions automatically flatter your habits. You must first establish habits that will influence your actions to cater to your true ideals.

Habit is an automatic mechanism for performing actions without expending the mental and physical labor ordinarily involved in performing actions that are new to us. Wrongly used, this mechanism is an archenemy, threatening man's citadel of free choice. Be practical. Try from today to overcome inimical habits hidden within you, garbed as environmental likes and dislikes. Oust them and be free to act from reason alone. Your habits are not you. Shake off that delusion and you will remember your true Self, the perfect image of God within you.

Creating and Destroying
Habits at Will

Self-Realization Fellowship Temple,
San Diego, California, December 12, 1943

Many are the favors that God does for His children. Some-times He grants a wish immediately. When I asked if the rain might be stopped for the services today, the Voice of the Divine Mother said: "There will be a little sunshine." It is because of the kindness of the Holy Spirit that we have sunshine this morning.

The Lord is the Mother of all mothers, the Father of all fathers, the One Friend behind all friends. If you always think of Him as the nearest of the near, you will witness many won-ders in your life. "He walks with me and He talks with me and He tells me I am His own."* And God will talk with you, also, if by meditation you make definite inroads "with unperturbèd pace" into the divine realm.

The poet Francis Thompson spoke of God as the "Hound of Heaven": God is depicted as pursuing man, rather than as being sought by him. Man, hiding in labyrinthine caves of doubts, escapes from God; still the Divine Hound keeps com-ing, and warning: "All things betray thee, who betrayest Me."

If you so live that you drive God away, you drive love itself away from you. In everything we are seeking—money and sense pleasures—we are actually seeking God. We are search-ers for diamonds, who pick up instead little pieces of glass shin-ing with the sunlight. Momentarily blinded by their attractive-ness, we forget to keep on looking for the real diamonds, which are much harder to find.

---

* From the hymn, *In the Garden*, by Carl Goldmark.

Although more difficult to obtain, your good habits are the diamonds that will give you true and lasting pleasure. And bad habits are the pieces of mere glass that seem to satisfy you, because they are more easily come by; but which, being delusory, will in the end bring disappointment. Satiety will overtake you, so that nothing gives you pleasure. I do not have to go through those experiences; I can see the end of human pleasures, and I have found in God the only real and lasting joy.

The true definition of "old age" is that state wherein one has become bored with the world. I tired of the pleasures of life very quickly;* and this world would have been extremely boresome to me had I not sought and found the joy of God. The happiness and abundance I find in Him are measureless. Eternity is not long enough for me to explain the joy of the devotee's heart when God enters. This is not exaggeration, because God's joy *is* eternal—unceasing, ever new, boundless. All of us have glimpses of it now and then—soul recollections of a state of eternal happiness.

In this world everybody wants to use us for his own purpose. Only God—and a real master who knows God—can truly love us. The ordinary human being does not know what love is. When someone's company gives you pleasure, you tend to think you love that person. But in reality it is yourself you love; your ego has been pleased by the other person's attention, that is all. Would you go on "loving" that person if he should cease to please you? What it means to love someone else more than oneself is very difficult to understand, and even more difficult for the average person to practice. To illustrate, I will tell you a true story of real love.

There was in India a devoted husband who loved his wife very deeply. Another man became infatuated with her. She ran away with her lover, who eventually left her without friends or funds. One day her husband came to see her. He spoke gently.

---

* The death of Paramahansaji's mother when he was about eleven was a turning point in his life, strengthening his already ardent spiritual inclinations into an iron resolve to find God. The divine wisdom garnered in previous incarnations manifested early in this one; thus he was able by discrimination to see the inherent disillusionment in the experiences of this world, and to realize that lasting happiness could come only from God. *(Publisher's Note)*

"Are you through with this experience? Come home with me, if you are."

She demurred. "I could not think of disgracing you further."

"What do I care about the opinion of society?" he replied. "I love you. The other man loved only your body. I love the real you—your soul. What has happened doesn't make any difference."

That was real love. The husband wasn't concerned for his honor; he was thinking only of the welfare of his beloved.

One great stumbling-block in the way of giving true love is our habits. In our hearts we all want to be angels, but our habits make us devils. In the morning we make up our minds to adhere to good, but during the day we forget our resolution. "The spirit indeed is willing, but the flesh is weak."* Flesh means habits. Our spirit, our wisdom, is willing; but our good habits are weak. The Gita says, "The eager excitable senses forcibly strive to seize the consciousness of those who seek liberation."†

Many people don't understand the terrible nature of habit. Some persons form habits very quickly. This is all right when establishing good habits; but it is dangerous when performing actions that may create bad habits. If you give such a person one cigarette, he may become a habitual smoker. Or a taste of one drink may make him a lifelong drinker.‡

Since you do not know what type of subconscious mind you have, or what your hidden tendencies may be, it is best to avoid actions that may lead to harmful habits. If the mind is not strong in wisdom and discrimination, it acts like a blotting paper, absorbing bad habits quickly.

So many people need help in this world! And God does help them, through those who are willing instruments of His

---

* Matthew 26:41.
† Bhagavad-Gita II:60.
‡ This is particularly true of persons in whose subconscious minds are latent strong bad habits from previous lives. The first acceptance of the temptation to perform that same wrong action in this life triggers an already long-established habit mechanism from before.

love. The other day a pitiable case came to me. This person, when not drinking, is a good man; but as soon as he starts drinking he becomes a fiend. He would go to extremes to do good when he is sober; but when drunk he beats his wife and causes terror. He has come for healing, and I know that if he tunes in just a little bit he will be helped. But see how terrible evil habits are! When this man is not under the influence of liquor, you wouldn't be able to see a trace of evil in him; and at such times he is so filled with remorse about his evil habit of drinking that he wants to destroy himself. But still he drinks! That is what habit does.

If you make up your mind to do something good you must *do* it. Don't let anything stand in your way. But before you make a resolution, determine that it is a good one. When I make up my mind I absolutely do not listen to any contradictions. I sometimes take a long time to make my decision, but when I do, nothing can stop me. A law of God operates for you when you strongly make up your mind and then adhere firmly to that resolution.

All of us mean well; but habits sometimes make us do things, against our will, that are harmful to others and to ourselves. Therefore, make up your mind not to be imposed upon by bad habits.

Why Let Your Habits Dictate to You?

Your forefathers came here to escape from rules that took away freedom to act according to one's conscience. Freeborn Americans don't like to have anyone dictate to them. Why then should you let yourself be dictated to by your habits? Such as when you don't want to eat, and still you eat; or when you don't want to fight with others, yet you do. What is the matter? You have allowed yourself to become a slave to bad habits.

Just being born in America or in other democratic lands does not guarantee freedom of the mind and heart. To be free is to be able to perform right actions according to the dictates of one's own soul-wisdom, not out of compulsion of habit, or blind obedience, or unreasoning fear. Wisdom confers true freedom, and that is the real spirit of America.

Doing whatever you please is not freedom; it is an abuse of freedom. Suppose you live in a house with twenty other people, each of whom regards freedom as the right to do what he pleases, and each of whom wants to do something that conflicts with the desires of the others? There can be no real freedom under such circumstances. Freedom comes only by following the law of self-government. To do freely *what you ought to do, when you ought to do it*—to be guided by your wisdom—is the only real freedom.

Slavery to habits is slavery in its worst form. Resolve to be free. Awaken the divine memory of your soul's freedom by affirming: "Even though I have had some bad habits since childhood, I can discard them by exercise of my wisdom and will. I am master of my own body-house."

Be Guided by Wisdom, Not Convention

What makes one person act differently from another? Habits of living and doing and thinking; habits of environment and of nationality. In the latter case, habits are imposed upon us. I follow my own ways. When I started for America in 1920, I had a long beard. You would think that men with beards would appear more venerable; and in India beards are admired for this reason. But while still aboard ship, I was persuaded that Americans, on seeing a man with a long beard, would be more inclined to remark, "There goes a wild man from the jungle!"

After I understood that few American men wear a beard, I was willing to abandon mine; but I resolved to keep my hair long, because my guru, Sri Yukteswarji, wore his hair long. So no one was able to influence me to cut my hair short. If I were to cut off my long hair now, the same people who ridiculed its length years ago would laugh at me for having short hair, and would feel that the stature of the inner man also had been shortened.

We don't really know what is right or real, because we are always comparing things on the basis of outer appearances. Therefore we are often incorrect in our judgments. Who is able to say what is right and what is wrong, merely on a basis of appearances?

You should make an effort gradually to free yourself from

slavery to any habit, be it of dress or food or anything else. Many people feel they have to eat meat three times a day. Others are convinced they should eat nothing but lettuce and nuts; that if they vary their diet they will become ill! Such beliefs are a form of slavery. You should not permit yourself to be bound by any habit of living; be able, rather, to change your habits as wisdom dictates. Learn to live rightly, using your power of free choice, guided by wisdom. Be able to sleep comfortably on a soft bed one night and just as comfortably on the floor the next night. That divine nonattachment to habit is the freedom advocated by the masters of India.

True Freedom Versus Whim Freedom

In the West many people believe in freedom of a different kind—I call it *whim* freedom. Because of a mistaken conception of the real nature of freedom, some parents make their children habit-slaves for life by indiscriminately giving in to their desires. The child grows up thinking that so long as his desires are satisfied he will be happy; and that the purpose of life is to satisfy desires. Later he realizes that he has been misled; the world outside is much different from what he has seen at home. To satisfy every whim is not so easy in the world! Others may push him around in order to gain their own ends; and he too becomes callous in order to satisfy his whims and desires. "Believing that fulfillment of bodily desires is man's highest aim, confident that this world is 'all,' such persons are engrossed till the moment of death in earthly cares and concerns."*

Parents should try to equip their children with firm will and discrimination, so that they can make their way in the world and still remain apart from its bad habits. Teach children how to be really free. Don't let them become slaves to the body and to undesirable habits. It is good to train a child in regularity of daily habits, but he should be trained also in evenmindedness: if he gets to sleep on time, all right; if not, all right. If he has his dinner on time, fine; if he cannot eat on time, fine. Children should be taught to respect the rights of others; but to be free of habit slavery to anything or anyone.

* Bhagavad-Gita XVI:11.

Fight Bad Habits with "Won't" Power

When a mule wants to be agreeable, it is quite obedient, but when it makes up its mind to stop cooperating, nobody can move it. You should develop that kind of *won't* power. *Be master of your moods and habits.* Then when you make up your mind not to do something that is wrong, nobody can make you do it against your will. In other situations, however, should you find yourself to be mistaken, be able quickly to change your mind. This flexibility comes when you do not permit yourself to be governed by habit, but act instead by wisdom-guided free will. Be free! Don't be a slave even of good habits; do right for its own sake.

Some people have to be told every day what to do, even though their duties may be substantially the same; but ordinarily people perform routine daily activities as a matter of habit. This is fine if they have cultivated good habits; but it is unfortunate for those who have adopted bad habits. Most people possess a combination of both.

Habits Are Mental Phonograph Records

Repeated performance of an action creates a mental blueprint. Every action is performed mentally as well as physically, and repetition of a particular action and its accompanying thought-pattern causes the formation of subtle electrical pathways in the physiological brain, somewhat like the grooves in a phonograph record. After a time, whenever you put the needle of attention on those "grooves" of electrical pathways, it plays back the "record" of the original mental blueprint. Each time an action is repeated, these grooves of electrical pathways become deeper, until the slightest attention automatically "plays" those same actions over and over again.

Yet by concentration and will power you can erase even deep grooves of long-standing habits. If you are addicted to smoking, for example, say to yourself: "The habit of smoking has long been lodged in my brain. Now I put all my attention and concentration on my brain and I *will* that habit to be dislodged." Command your mind thus, again and again. The best time of the day to do this is in the morning, when the will and attention are fresh. Repeatedly affirm your freedom, using all the strength of your will power. One day you will suddenly feel that you no longer are ensnared by that habit.

I know a man who wanted to get rid of the smoking habit. He was a chain smoker, but he had great faith that he could overcome the habit. I told him: "After I have given you a healing I want you to smoke. It will taste just like a bundle of rags and you will not enjoy smoking anymore." And this was so. When he tried to smoke the next day he became nauseated. He had been receptive to my strong thought, and I had momentarily been able to transmit my consciousness to him. After that he was freed from this bad habit.

Biting the nails is another foolish, useless habit. Why should you do such things against your will when you are the king of the castle of your life?

Maintain Your Freedom as a Child of God

If your mind is strong, and if you surrender yourself to God and forget the body, you will be able to maintain your freedom as a child of God. Make up your mind that no habit has a permanent hold on you. If your wisdom is strong, you can convince yourself in a second what you should do. Awaken that wisdom which revives in you the power of free will, enabling you to rise above the compulsive instinct of ordinary habits. "Even if thou art the chief sinner among all sinners, yet by the (sole) raft of wisdom thou shalt safely cross the sea of sin."*

The best way to get rid of habits is to will them out of your mind at once! Do not linger over them, lest your resolve weaken. Wisdom is your salvation from habits. If one tells a little boy not to eat candies, he will want them more than ever. Suppose that when he grows up he has diabetes, and his doctor tells him he will die if he eats more candy. It is wisdom then that tells him the doctor is right, and that encourages him quickly to give up the candy habit of many years. Through wisdom man learns—sometimes!

I remember in my school in Ranchi, India, a boy who liked to do just the opposite of what he was told to do. Therefore I

* Bhagavad-Gita IV:36.

often told him to do what I *didn't* want him to do, and in that way got him to do what I wanted. In time he "got wise," in a double sense, and changed himself for the better.

This is my message to all who suffer from slavery to habit: turn against those slave-driving habits that have been telling you what to do, and say, "I have a whip with which I will make you get out. You cannot make me do things against my will any longer. I am a freeborn child of God. I am made in His image. I will use my divinely bestowed wisdom and free will to do the right thing that I should do in everything."

Many times I have used the divine power of will to destroy a habit that was seeking to get hold of me. When I have eaten certain foods and found myself becoming bound by a wish for them, I stopped eating those foods until the desire was gone.

When I went to Singapore I found there a certain fruit that is delicious; but I watched myself that I didn't form a craving for it. I knew that if I did not take care I could find myself wanting it morning, noon, and night. That is the way we enslave ourselves. So although I had full enjoyment of the fruit that one day, I didn't regret its absence on the next day. If we are watchful of the things we enjoy, there is no need to fear. We should keep our freedom at all costs.

So many people go on eating foods that they know are not good for them. But if I say I won't eat a food, that is the end of it. Isn't that freedom? to do things, not because your habits compel you, nor because your friends persuade you, but because your own wisdom tells you? With wisdom comes such power of conviction that you don't need habits to lean on to do the right thing you should do. As soon as you are convinced of the wisdom of doing a thing, nothing should be able to turn you away from doing it. But you have to be guided by wisdom. You can install habits at will by the power of wisdom. I can make myself like anything that wisdom demands.

The mental habit-patterns of most people have become set, making it difficult for them to change. Those who keep their minds pliable through discipline and self-control can easily change. The mind should be like putty. Wisdom keeps the mind plastic. That is freedom. I want all mankind to enjoy that freedom from habits. When you have liberated yourself from habit slavery, you will know there is no happiness greater than in acting as a freeborn child of God.

Never let life beat you down. Beat life! If you have a strong will you can overcome all difficulties. Affirm, even in the midst of trials: "Danger and I were born together, and I am more dangerous than danger!" This is a truth you should always remember; apply it and you will see that it works. Don't behave like a cringing mortal being. You are a child of God!

Developing Dynamic Will

Self-Realization Fellowship international headquarters,
Los Angeles, California, January 11, 1949

God sent man on earth empowered with certain physical, mental, and spiritual forces that he can wield, and, by their wise use, produce intended definite results. The force that runs machinery is electricity. And this complex human machine that God has given us, a movable structure of bones covered with tender flesh and consisting of trillions of cells, is run by *prana,* intelligent life force, traveling like electricity through the wires of the nerves.

In childhood the body is more responsive to the mind; it can more easily make the body do its bidding. But later on, as the child develops various habits, the body and mind do not work in the same harmony as before. Although, as I have often pointed out, the material form is only a dream in the consciousness of God, so long as you have to use the physical body, it should be under the control of your mind.

Troubles will always strike at the body, for this is a law of life; in spite of difficulties, you should keep such mental neutrality that the mind is not affected by outer conditions.

St. Francis of Assisi suffered terribly, yet he was mentally unaffected. Shortly before his death he was going blind. The doctor advised a treatment that required cauterization of the saint's face, from the eyebrows back to the ears, with a white-hot iron bar. There were no anesthetics then. The disciples present could not bear the sight, but St. Francis told the physician to proceed with the treatment. He welcomed Brother Fire with sweet words and never showed that he felt even the slightest connection between the mind and the body. The Lord wants you also to understand this truth: that within your perishable body is an inviolable, immortal soul.

It is an error to suppose that masters do not suffer at all. Jesus let his body suffer the pains of crucifixion, even though he was already redeemed, for he thereby willingly worked out on his own body some of the karmic suffering due his disciples and the world. But he knew the relationship between mind and body; he saw them as a delusory creation in the cosmic dream of God. The body is merely a cluster of sensations. It is not easy to cut off sensations, but you can do so by remaining constantly in the consciousness that you are a soul, one with Spirit. When the mind is almost wholly dominated by the body and its demands, as is the case with most persons, it is best to begin gradually, in little things, to dissociate the mind from the body.

One difference between an ordinary man and a superman is that the ordinary man cries and gives in to suffering if he is hurt, but the yogi is established in the consciousness that he is not the body, that he is apart from it. This realization is with me all the time. Sometimes I see myself walking, and I am simultaneously aware that I have no body. In the divine consciousness you realize that you, as soul, have no hands, eyes, ears, or feet, nor any need of these physical adjuncts; yet you can use and move these bodily instruments. It is possible to hear, see, smell, taste, and touch with mind power alone. In clairaudience, for example, one hears through the power within. Many saints hear the voice of God or one of His angels guiding them. They hear not with ears but with mind. Such a state of consciousness is a real experience, not imagination. But it cannot become your experience unless you meditate. If you meditate with the greatest devotion, someday when you least expect it you will have the same experience, and you will understand what I am speaking of.

God is constantly showing me this truth, that the body is unreal. He has also shown me that this body shall suffer. But the physical suffering this body will endure has nothing to do with my consciousness. It comes from taking on the negative *karma* of others, and has no connection with misery-producing desires of self. If this body does some good to the world and to others, fine. A master does not care what happens to his body. He just looks after it that others may be benefited.

The only time the ordinary person is not conscious of the body is during sleep; yet upon waking, he is immediately conscious of how well or poorly he slept. Some materialists think that we are wholly unconscious when we are asleep, but this is not true. How could we know, upon waking, how well or ill we slept, unless we were conscious during sleep? We can safely say that the mind can exist without the body.

Wisdom and Will Govern Body and Mind

What, then, are the principal powers that govern body and mind? Wisdom and will. Wisdom is the soul's intuitive, direct knowledge of truth. During warfare, range finders are used to determine where to fire shells; once the range is found, the guns are effectively fired. Wisdom is your range finder, and your will gives the firing power to accomplish your ends according to the dictates of your wisdom. Your will should always be guided by wisdom. One without the other is dangerous. If you have wisdom but not sufficient will to follow through as wisdom dictates, it is hurtful to your well-being; if you have a strong will but no wisdom, there is every chance of "misfiring" and destroying yourself.

Your intelligence is not guided by true wisdom if it fails to show you the right thing that you should do. And, if it doesn't encourage the strength of will necessary to carry out the behests of your soul, then that power of intelligence is not fulfilling its true purpose. "The senses are said to be superior (to the physical body); the mind is superior to the sense faculties; the intelligence is superior to the mind; and the one that is superior to the intellect is He (the real Self, the soul)."*

Most people are like automatons. They breakfast, go to work, have lunch, go back to work, come home to dinner, watch TV, and go to bed; then the body machine is shut off for the night. Those who live in this way are using only mechanical will, performing most of their actions as a matter of habit, accomplishing their duties always in a certain way. They make little or no effort to exercise their will consciously. True, they are using will power all the time in performing these habitual

* Bhagavad-Gita III:42.

actions, but it is purely mechanical; it is not *dynamic* will.

Physiological Will—First Expression of Will Power

When human beings are born, the initial expression of will power is the baby's first cry, which opens up the lungs and causes breathing to begin. Sages say that the soul doesn't like being caged in the feeble little baby body; its first experience in that form is to cry. The soul realizes that in the human form it will again go through many struggles, and says, "Lord, why did you put me here again?" Many babies' hands are folded at birth. Their soul is worshiping God in this way and praying, "O Spirit, release me in this life."

Will is a tremendous factor in life. It is the power by which you can reach the heights of God-realization, or go down into the deepest strata of ignorance. The cry of a newborn child is an expression of physiological will; the baby wills to remove the discomfort it feels. Most people have not risen above that state of babyhood. They immediately want to be rid of any discomfort, and whenever they see anything that attracts them, they cry for it. They think they have got to have it, that they can't live without it. The will that is thus overpowered by the senses is called physiological will—body-bound will, following the dictates of the senses.

It is terrible to use any kind of drug, for the drug enslaves the will to the body. I once knew a man who used opium. All day long he slept in a stupor. It took him years to overcome his slavery. To use narcotics is one of the greatest sins against Spirit. Drink is the same. Both mean destruction of will power. The great saints have warned against them. Under no circumstance should you let yourself be tempted, for in a short while you can be lost. Drink and drugs are sins against the soul because they paralyze the will, without which soul-realization and salvation are impossible.

Many people are bound by physiological will. The very power that governs *prana* and enables it to efficiently operate the human machine is destroyed when strong habits of sex or drink or hatred take over. And once they are established they are very difficult to conquer. Once you are in the habit of showing temper whenever you are crossed, you follow that habit in spite of your wish to behave otherwise. Habit destroys the supreme gift of heaven—will power—by which you can work out your own salvation.

Without Wisdom, Will Becomes Habit-Bound

If God and heaven were imposed on us, then we would be their slaves. But the Lord has given us free choice by which we can accept good or cast it out, accept evil or cast it out. The powers that God has given you by which you can make this choice are wisdom and will. Find out whether you have control over your will or not. Don't let your will be devitalized by bad habits.

After physiological will comes habit-bound will. Your will automatically enters this second phase unless it is guided by wisdom. Sometimes a good man's child is lacking in truthfulness and good habits. Certainly the child has had every opportunity to learn to be good; yet the moment he becomes old enough to start using his own will, he gets into all kinds of mischief. Why? Usually in such cases the child's nature from past lives is karmically inclined toward wrong thinking and habits. Through his family training in this life he learns to perform good actions; but they are only superimposed on his real nature. Because his will is controlled only by mechanical good habits, rather than by soul wisdom and true understanding, he readily succumbs to temptations when he is free of the good influence of the family.

If you ask thieves and habitual drinkers if they like their way of life, they usually say "No." They thought when they started their wrong actions that they would be happy. They never realized that the effects would be hurtful to them. For this reason I deeply feel for people who have done wrong. I cry for them. "But for the grace of God, there go I." Evil is a sort of opiate. That is why we should have places where people who have gone wrong can learn how to live and how to think. Jail is not a suitable place of reform. Such persons need to mix with superior men who can help them.

All around you are thieves of circumstances, trying to steal your vitality of will; but no one can take away your will but yourself. The child wants his own way. When he grows up, unless his will has been curbed and guided by wisdom, he finds that he is a slave to desires. Are you not doing things today that you know you ought not to do, and which you know will bring you unhappiness later on? Overstimulation of the senses devitalizes the will, so do not create an unnatural craving for anything. Suppose you like a certain food very much. Your will power should be such that you can do without it henceforth.

It is impossible to say what you really like and don't like, because your inclinations are always changing. If you analyze yourself you will see that in the matter of likes and dislikes we are all crazy. We don't know why we like certain things and don't like others. What you like through the influence of your wisdom, and what you like as a result of your physiological habits, are two different things. I can make myself like something, and the next minute I can make myself repelled by it.

To be guided by wisdom is to be king of the world. The wise man tries first to determine if he is right; then he acts. But if he makes a decision and then finds out he was wrong, he immediately acknowledges his mistake. Never use your will power to be stubborn. You can talk with some people for an hour, and they seemingly agree with you, and then they turn around and say just the opposite. They don't want to give up their own way. That is not will power, but slavery to the ego. You can see such slaves all around you. They think they are free, but their will is chained; they perform actions mechanically, guided by good or by evil habits. But when you can say, "I stay away from evil because evil works against my happiness," or "I am good, not because I am forced to be, but because good leads to my own happiness"—that is wisdom. Such was my guru's training. One thing we should always remember: If will is guided by wisdom, it will produce something constructive in our life.

When Jesus said to the Heavenly Father, "Thy will be done,"* it was not because he lacked will power, but because he wanted his will to be guided by God's. When the Divine Will intimated, "Give up the body," Jesus had to use a great deal of will power to conquer the weakness of the flesh. Hu-

---

* Matthew 26:42.

man will has become divine will, completely attuned to Spirit, when even though it is necessary to give up the body, one is able to do so willingly, as Christ did. A body-bound slave would have said, "They are trying to crucify me; I must try to save myself." If Jesus had done that, he would not have been the Christ who lives in our hearts today.

Stages of Will Development

Man progresses from the physiological will of infancy to the unthinking will of childhood. That is when he is used to obeying his mother, doing whatever she tells him to do. After unthinking will comes blind will; he gets away from the mother's will and begins to feel his own will power. This comes in youth. He tests his own will and begins to use it to get what he sets his heart on.

As a child I wanted a bicycle and I got it. Then I wanted a horse, but I didn't get it. A long time after, though, I did receive it. Every desire that I have had has been satisfied by the Lord. Everything I have wished for has come to me. That was His blessing.

I was always careful that my wish was right before I used my will to carry it out. It is good to be stubborn in good things, but never otherwise. When you are wrong, you should correct yourself. If you don't blind yourself to good by using your will for wrong things, then you progress from blind will to thinking will.

After Mother died, when I was only eleven years old, and so grief-stricken! my eldest sister Roma loved to guide me. Others tried to use force, but Roma won me by love. Even when I was obstinately saying to her, "Go away, go away," I found myself obeying her wishes.

The nature of a saint is tender like a flower, but stronger than thunder when he makes up his mind about something good, because his will is guided by wisdom. It was not the easiest thing to convince my guru when I felt I had a better idea, but as soon as he saw that I offered a different angle he would say: "You are right. Let us do it that way." But when I was wrong, he couldn't be moved.

Thinking will is the most marvelous instrument you can imagine. Are you governed by thinking will, or by blind will, or by physiological will? Thinking will is the way toward wisdom. When you get a notion in your mind that you must go to the movies, that is physiological will. And when you decide, "Well, it doesn't matter, I will go some other time," that is thinking will.

Will that is not guided by habit is thinking will. If you don't want to smoke, you should not smoke. If you do not feel hungry, don't eat just because of habit. Whenever I wish to refrain from taking food, no one can tempt me to eat. Another habit amongst those hardest to control is that of harsh speech. Speaking unkindly to others paralyzes your will. Never be cranky. Whenever you get angry you make your face ugly. Be so loving and kind that everyone who meets you says of you, "I would like to see that person again." When you control your own speech you will not be so sensitive to others' remarks about you. I quit anger when I was a little child. But I often discipline with strong words those understanding ones whom God has sent me for training. To those who don't understand, I never say anything.

See how wonderful will power is. After you have developed thinking will, you begin to reason, "I must produce something worthwhile with this power," and you take up one thing at a time and try to accomplish it. You revolve that will around a problem of health or of finances or of controlling a habit, or around the desire to know God. If you will and act until victory, then you have attained dynamic will.

The World Will Try to Trick You

Everything in life tempts you away from God. In the beginning most devotees fall down, because they don't use their divine will; they put off meditation. Day after day, week after week, they put it off. You know you want to love God, you know you ought to get busy making the effort now, and still you procrastinate. I remember a period in my childhood when I lost a great deal of time in this manner. I was already meditating every day, and I had resolved to meditate much longer each day. But I kept putting it off until suddenly I realized a whole year had gone by. Then I remembered the story about the cat and the sparrow.

The cat caught a sparrow, but the sparrow was wise. He reminded the cat that it was proper first to lick clean his face and paws in preparation for the sparrow meal. This made sense to the cat, so he let the sparrow go and took his time washing himself. In the meantime the sparrow flew away to a high branch. The cat finally said, "You can come down now. I am ready for my dinner." But the sparrow chirped, "Too bad; I am now at the top of the tree." So the cat resolved: "Henceforth, I will eat my sparrow first and then wash myself."

First things must come first. When you awaken in the morning, meditate. If you don't, the whole world will crowd in to claim you, and you will forget God. At night, meditate before sleep claims you. I am so strongly established in the habit of meditation that even after I lie down to sleep at night, I find I am meditating. I can't sleep in the ordinary way. The habit of being with God comes first.

In Your Will Power Lies the Image of God

Will power means freedom. Will power means Heaven. If you don't permit your will to be weakened by the attractions of the world, you will reach your divine goal. But most of you have allowed your will to be sapped by bad habits—many of you indulge in them every day—smoking, drinking, angry speech. You think you can't do without these things. But there was a time when you didn't know what smoke was, or what drink was, or what anger was. You have given up your freedom by acquiring these habits. Must you remain a slave to them? How can you find God unless you free your will power, by eliminating these worldly habits and by using that will to meditate instead?

No matter what happens to your body, meditate. Never go to sleep at night until you have communed with God. Your body will remind you that you have worked hard and need rest, but the more you ignore its demands and concentrate on the Lord, the more you will burn with joyous life, like a globe afire. Then you will know that you are not the body. In your will power lies the image of God. That image has been desecrated because you have made a slave of your mind. When I left India to come to America, my guru said: "Forget you were born among Hindus, and don't adopt all the ways of the Americans.... Be your true self, a child of God." By following his wise advice, I have kept my will free. If the whole world stood against me, and I saw that I was right and others were wrong, I would not change my mind.

Nothing Is Impossible When Will Becomes Dynamic

Choose a good, wholesome, constructive goal and then determine that you are going to achieve it. No matter how many times you fail, keep on trying. No matter what happens, if you have unalterably resolved, "The earth may be shattered, but I will keep on doing the best I can," you are using dynamic will, and you will succeed. That dynamic will is what makes one man rich and another man strong and another man a saint.

It is not Jesus and a few others who alone know God. If you make the right kind of effort, *you* will find God. What is the value of using dynamic will today to be a great doctor, or a successful businessman, when tomorrow you may die? This is why Jesus said, "Seek ye first the kingdom of God."* Use your will to know God first; then He will direct your path in life.

You are using dynamic will when day and night you whisper within, "Lord, Lord, Lord," with the deepest desire to find Him. It is better to use your will to seek God than for anything else. I am so happy that He blessed me with the divine will power that my guru, Sri Yukteswarji, awakened in me. Before I met Master I was exercising that will power right and left in useless things. But even then, whenever I started something, I employed dynamic will to complete it.

I remember the first time I used dynamic will to help others. My friend and I were just little boys then. One day I said to him, "We are going to feed five hundred people."

"But we haven't a cent!" he exclaimed. "We are going to do it just the same," I assured him. "And I think the money is going to come through you."

"That is impossible!" he scoffed. An intuitive conviction

---

* Matthew 6:33.

prompted me to say: "Don't offend your mother in any way. Do whatever she asks you to do."

One day later he came running and told me this story. "I was bathing and Mother called me. I was going to say, 'Don't bother me now while I am bathing,' but instead I asked her what she wanted. She told me to go and see my aunt who lived nearby. I said, 'All right.'

"When I went to see my aunt, the first thing she said to me was, 'Who is this crazy boy you are mixing with? Have you lost your mind? What is this I hear about your feeding five hundred people?' I was angry with her. 'I must leave now,' I told her, and started to go. But she stopped me, saying, 'Your friend may be crazy, but his idea is good. Here are twenty rupees.'"

The boy had nearly fainted with surprise. He ran to me at once to tell me the news. When we went to buy the rice and other things, the people in the neighborhood had already heard of our plan, and added more food. In the end we fed two thousand people! The same divinely charged will power also brought about the first library I founded, Saraswat Library in Calcutta.

When you make up your mind to do good things, you will accomplish them if you use dynamic will power to follow through. No matter what the circumstances are, if you go on trying, God will create the means by which your will shall find its proper reward. This is the truth Jesus referred to when he said: "If ye have faith, and doubt not,...if ye shall say unto this mountain, Be thou removed, and be thou cast into the sea, it shall be done."* If you continuously use your will power, no matter what reverses come, it will produce success and health and power to help people, and above all, it will produce communion with God.

This is the kind of will power you must develop—the will power that will run the ocean dry if necessary in order to accomplish what is good. The greatest will should be used to meditate. The Lord wants us to discover our divine will and use it to find Him. Develop this God-seeking dynamic will. It is not profound words that will give you emancipation, but your own efforts through meditation.

* Matthew 21:21.

Seek God Now!

Self-Realization Fellowship international headquarters,
Los Angeles, California, July 15, 1941

God-realization is attained only by great effort on the part of the yogi, and by divine grace. Though God can be approached by law, still, as the Searcher of Hearts, He must be convinced that a devotee really wants Him before He sends His grace. God withholds final illumination from a devotee, however perfected he may be in the science of Yoga, who does not wholeheartedly desire Him.

I recall a time in the *ashram* of my guru, Swami Sri Yukteswar, when month after month, with the greatest devotion, I was seeking God; yet I was experiencing a sort of stagnation. When I questioned Master about my problem, he said, "You think that if you had more mental power or more miracle power you would realize more fully that God is with you. But that is not so. Suppose He responded by giving you control over the whole universe. Possession of such power would leave your heart still unsatisfied. God is the Ever-New Joy you already feel in meditation. When man loves that Joy above everything else in this world, desiring it more than money and fame, more than his indulgences in moods and habits and sensory experiences, God will open the way." Few devotees are prepared to make such "sacrifices."*

It is at once very easy and very hard to please God. He is playing with His devotees even in tests, and He tests them all the time.

How easy it is to pack the day with foolishness, how difficult to fill it with worthwhile activities and thoughts! Yet God is not so much interested in what we are doing as in where the mind is. Everyone has a different difficulty, but God doesn't listen to any excuses. He wants the devotee's mind to

---

* "The harvest truly is plenteous, but the laborers are few" (Matthew 9:37).

be engrossed in Him in spite of any troublesome circumstances. Even as I am engaged in talking to you now, my mind is ever on God. I am with Him inwardly all the time. I live in His joy. Loving and craving naught else but that joy, I find that all obstacles to God-union give way before me. This declaration is not a fairy tale; it is true. But not until God has received all of the devotee's love will He come. It will seem that He has forsaken us sometimes, but such tests are inescapable; if we steadfastly refuse to give up our search, God receives us as His own.

In worldly ambitions there is always an element of uncertainty. Some people spend year after year trying wholeheartedly but unsuccessfully to make money. But in the spiritual path no wholehearted devotee is ever unsuccessful. His labors are never in vain.

Perseverance Is the Whole Magic of Spiritual Success

The greatest enemy of divine realization is the body; it becomes easily tired and wants to give up. A true devotee never relaxes his effort nor admits the supremacy of the body. Continuous vigilance is required. We must believe, against all seeming odds, that He will come. Even an agnostic who thinks that there is little likelihood that God exists, but who perseveres in the search for Him, will ultimately find Him. Even though God may not seem to respond, one should not succumb to doubts but should unremittingly continue in the holy quest. *Perseverance is the whole magic of spiritual success.* If the Lord responded easily and openly to the devotee's prayers for divine illumination, all men would immediately seek Him—not for love of Him, but for the illimitable rewards.

This world is God's playhouse. It is part of His intricate drama here that He has made it very difficult to discover His presence. Because the search is not easy, we tend to forget Him. Even when we see our loved ones pulled away into the mysterious unknown, we do not think seriously about our having to go too, sometime. But one should not wait for the approach of death to realize the importance of seeking God. It is every man's supreme and immediate duty. Each minute of life should be a divine quest. The burning question in our hearts should be: "When shall I find Thee, O Lord?"

No matter what happens, never give up the vital search. Suppose one sits to meditate, and friends arrive. There is nothing to do but to cut the meditation short; yet one may still keep his mind on God. Whatever the activity, the inner attention should be on Him. He is so necessary to us!

Get busy *now;* time is passing, and one day the fearful realization will come that life has gone by as though in a twinkling, and still He has not been found. Let no day pass without your having made an effort to meditate on Him. Soon, surprisingly little effort will be needed. Great happiness comes to the devotee who is steadfast. Without unquenchable enthusiasm nothing can be gained.

The Bhagavad-Gita teaches the importance on the spiritual path of rising above bodily sensations. The contact of the senses with outer environment produces sensations of heat and cold, pleasure and pain, and other oppositional states. The average man is easily affected by these sensations, but the Gita teaches that one should be neutral to them. This is not a recommendation to be rash! If the yogi finds the sensations of heat or cold are extremely difficult to bear, he should seek an outward remedy without becoming inwardly involved. He who can practice mental neutrality is on the way to becoming a saint. He who lives in the bodily temple without being affected by changing sensory perceptions, remaining evenminded during pleasure and pain, cool and heat, and so on, becomes a true king among men. Having attained changelessness, he is one with the changeless Spirit.

All who came to my guru's *ashram* for spiritual training were disciplined in this way. The aspiring yogi of the West as well as of the East must discipline himself similarly. He should refrain from making too much fuss about the body. If he sees he is finding time for everything else but is too busy for God, he should take the whip of discipline to himself. Why be afraid? There is everything to gain. If a man will not himself cry and struggle to attain his own salvation, will anyone else do it for him?

God-realization is the most difficult state to reach. Let no one fool himself, nor think that someone else can "give" it to him. Whenever I fell into a state of mental stagnation, my guru could do nothing for me. But I never gave up trying to keep in tune with him by cheerfully performing whatever he asked me to do. "I have come to him for God-realization," I reasoned, "and I must listen to his advice." At his *ashram* we young disciples seemed to be always cooking, and there were many other excuses not to meditate. Yet even though I worked harder there than in my own home, I found the environment of the *ashram* to be spiritually helpful to me.

Keep a Daily Appointment with God

Let no devotee miss his daily appointment with God. The mind may suggest the movies or some other distraction; but when the time comes for God each day, keep that sacred engagement. Otherwise you will be a long time finding Him.

There is a personal element in the search for God that is more important than mastery over the whole science of Yoga. The Heavenly Father wants to be sure that His children desire only Him, that they will not be satisfied with anything else. When God is made to feel that He is not first in the devotee's heart, He stands aside. But to him who says, "O Lord, it matters not if I lose sleep tonight, so long as I am with Thee," He will come. Positively! From behind the countless screens of this mysterious world the Ruler of creation will come forth to reveal Himself behind each one. He talks to His true devotees, and plays hide-and-seek with them. Sometimes He suddenly unveils a comforting truth when one is worried. In time, and in direct or indirect ways, He grants every wish of His devotee.

Fulfillment of a particular desire seems necessary only if one lacks conviction that he can find perfect fulfillment in God. One who is at peace in God is not tortured by unfulfilled earthly desires. "Taking shelter in Me, all beings can achieve the Supreme Fulfillment...."* No one can hurt me by thwarting me in some outward matter, because to me God is sufficient; His joyous presence is the only conditioning factor in my happiness. Each of you should try resolutely to meditate

* Bhagavad-Gita IX:32.

and to feel His presence, and see how quickly you will become aware of His favor.

The world worships men of power, like Alexander the Great and Napoleon, but think of their mental states! Then think of the peace that Christ had. His peace could not be taken from him. We think we will seek that peace "tomorrow." Anyone who reasons this way will never find it. *Seek it now.* We do not neglect eating and our other duties to the body. They are very important to us. But one who loves God intensely loses all worry about the body. This is what Jesus meant when he said: "Take no thought for your life, what ye shall eat; neither for the body, what ye shall put on." *

Not until you feel in your consciousness the absolute importance of God will you reach Him. Do not permit life to cheat you. Form those good habits that make for true happiness. Follow a simple diet, exercise the body, and meditate daily—no matter what happens, rain or shine. If you are unable to exercise and meditate in the morning, do it at night. Pray to Him every day, "Lord, even if I die, or if the whole world crumbles away, I am going to find time daily to be with Thee."

Who is interested in God alone? Very few. Most people want to talk about spirits and miracles and so on. But he who knows God will be told by Him everything he has ever wanted to know.

Kriya Yoga—Highest Method of God-Contact

Kriya Yoga is the highest method of God-contact. In my own search for God I traveled all over India, and heard wisdom from the lips of a number of her greatest masters. I can therefore vouch for the fact that in Self-Realization teachings are the highest truths and scientific techniques given to mankind by God and the Great Ones.

The aftereffects of *Kriya* bring with them the utmost peace and bliss. The joy that comes with *Kriya* is greater than the joys of all pleasurable physical sensations put together. "Unattracted to the sensory world, the yogi experiences the ever-new joy of Being. His soul engaged in the union with Spir-

* Luke 12:22.

it, he attains indestructible bliss."* From that joy experienced in meditation I receive the rest of a thousand sleeps. Sleep becomes virtually unnecessary to the advanced *Kriya Yogi.*

When by *Kriya Yoga* the devotee enters *samadhi,* wherein his eyes, breath, and heart are quieted, another world comes into view. Breath, sound, and movement of the eyes belong to this world. But the yogi who has control of the breath † may enter the heavenly astral and causal worlds and commune there with God's saints, or enter cosmic consciousness and commune with God. The yogi is not interested in anything else.

Whoever will give less importance to everything else, remembering what I have said, will get to God without fail. Everyone must eventually get there. But what is the use of my telling these truths to you unless you practice them? My loving attention on you is not wanting; but even if I were to remind you each day of these truths, they would not help anyone who does not himself make the effort to practice meditation. No one is greater than God, enthroned in the heart of every man; yet even He does not force us to seek Him. He has given us free will. But he who follows a true guru, and keeps faith with him by adhering to his instructions, will transform his whole life. "Comprehending that (the wisdom from a guru), thou wilt not again fall into delusion."‡

To Find God, Be Loyal to God

It is easy to see in a person's face whether or not he is a lover of God. True devotees may be called fanatical in their devotion to Him. The only right kind of fanaticism is loyalty to God—night and day, night and day, thinking of Him. Without this kind of loyalty it is impossible to find God. Those who never miss *Kriya,* and who sit long in meditation and pray intensely to God, will discover the longed-for Treasure.

This world is but a dream. Just as in the movies there is no essential difference between the ocean and the sky, which are simply two different rates of light-vibration, so it is in this

* Bhagavad-Gita V:21.

† See glossary.

‡ Bhagavad-Gita IV:35.

world. Sorrow and joy, pain and pleasure, cold and heat are but dreams of this world. The Lord is the only Reality. We should always pray that no test or temptation will ever have the power to make us forget Him. When I pray thus I receive more result than at any other time. Then, even if something very serious comes to divert me, I nevertheless see immediately that I am safe in His arms.

It is difficult to know Him. The path to God is like a razor's edge. But discouragement is never justified, because we don't have to acquire or win anything; we have only to realize that God is already within us. That is why negativeness should be completely put out of one's mind. Cooperating with the guru's thoughts makes the path easy. If the disciple says, "I can't do this; it is too hard for me," he is held back. No one has entangled us in moods and habits and desires but ourselves, and no one but ourselves will free us.

Keep a diary of your spiritual life. I used to make a record of how long I had meditated daily and how deep I had gone. Seek solitude as much as possible. Do not spend your leisure in mixing with people for merely social purposes. God's love is hard to find in company. The Lord is discovered in silence, and *Kriya* shows you the way.

To establish God-consciousness in the souls of men is my great interest. I see that everything else is futile. The one purpose of Self-Realization Fellowship is to teach the individual the way to personal contact with God. Those who make the effort cannot miss Him. Make a solemn promise in your heart and pray to the Father that He bless you with the haunting desire to find Him, that you may not waste any more time in the useless diversions of this earth.

Pray to the Father: "As we are bound by Thy laws of creation to work, may we perform our duties only to please Thee. Bless us every moment, that we realize Thou art more important than eating or sleeping or anything else. Bless us that we be able to meet Thy tests and to avoid the terrible temptations of the flesh. May we all, thy princely children, be diademed in Thy bosom."

And my prayer for each of you is that from today you will

make a supreme effort for God, and that you never give up until you are established in Him. If you love Him you will practice *Kriya* with the greatest devotion and faithfulness. Continuously seek Him through prayer and *Kriya Yoga*. Be of good cheer, for as Babaji once said, quoting from the Bhagavad-Gita:[*] "Even a little bit of the practice of this religion will save you from dire fears and colossal sufferings."

[*] Bhagavad-Gita II:40.

Why Waste Time?
God Is the Joy You Seek

An informal talk to resident renunciants and guests
at Self-Realization Fellowship international headquarters,
Los Angeles, California, on Christmas Day, 1939

This Christmas will remain in my memory always, for it is a great joy and privilege to be with devotees of the Lord. Yesterday, when we communed with Christ in our all-day meditation here, we felt that we are all one family in God. In meditation, souls meet on the plane of the heart and rejoice in Spirit.

May all men and all churches be inspired by the humble example of our spiritual celebration of Christmas to devote, as we have, one day entirely to worship of the Christ Consciousness. The eight hours that we meditated yesterday passed like eight minutes! The love of God is greater than all the pleasures of the senses. If once we experience His love in the heart, we become so imbued with it we can never forget it. Last night I had no sleep, but I didn't need sleep. For in the eternal joy that I feel in the Christ Consciousness nothing else matters at all.

Dear ones, my greatest gift to you this Christmas is my love. To love all, to sacrifice for all, and to have boundless pleasure in helping others—this is the grace I have received. We should do for others as if it were for ourselves. If a coat that we need costs fifty dollars, we spend it gladly. When we can do that for another with the same sense of joy, we know the true spirit of giving.

"My Words Shall Not Pass Away"

May the Christmas spirit you feel not end with today; rather may it be with you every night as you meditate. Then in the silence of your own mind, as you drive away all restless

439

thoughts, Christ Consciousness will come. If we all follow the spirit of Jesus we shall surely experience every day his presence within us. For the Christ Consciousness that was manifest in Jesus was not meant to be the light of one century only, but of all centuries for eternity. That is why Jesus said: "Heaven and earth shall pass away, but my words shall not pass away."* The joy that Christ felt, the joy that he told the world to seek, and the spiritual rules of conduct he exhorted us to follow—to love our enemies and to turn the other cheek—are timeless. The commandment to love God with all your heart, mind, and soul was not intended merely for the biblical generations; it is an eternal law.

Life Is a Caravan

Many who were with us last Christmas are not with us now, and who knows who will be here next Christmas? Such is the way of life. And still life goes on. It is a caravan in which we are traveling for a little while. Some of our companions have fallen into ditches of folly and ignorance, but when they are tired of the suffering they experience, they will begin to seek the safe guidance of the Owner of the caravan, who is also the Owner of this earth—none other than the Heavenly Father. Even though we part in this caravan, and the beginning and end of our journey are shrouded in darkness, still, life has a deep meaning: to teach us to seek God earnestly.

This world may also be likened to a play. The actors do not come out of nowhere; there is a backstage. After their part is over, the players do not cease to exist; they only go behind the scenes for a rest. It is the scheme of the Stage Manager that we come here to play for a time on this stage of life; then we depart. We are not dead—only backstage, hidden behind the screen of time, according to the direction of the Stage Manager. And we will be seen on this stage of life again and again, until we become such good actors that we can play our parts perfectly, according to the Divine Will. Then He will say: "You need go no more out. You have done My Will. You have played your part, and acted well. You did not lose courage. Now you

---

* Matthew 24:35.

have come back to Me, to be a pillar of immortality in the temple of My Eternal Existence."*

Good Company Is of Supreme Importance

To play your part well on earth is not easy. It is only by good associations that you can find your way out of the darkness of ignorance. The blind cannot lead the blind. Mixing with those who love only social gatherings will waste your time, but association with those who love God will give you the love of God. The Lord said in the Bhagavad-Gita: "Only one among thousands of men strives for salvation; and, among those exalted seekers, perhaps only one will perceive Me as I am."† Very few people are interested in God. It is said that the child is busy with play, the youth is busy with sex, and the adult is busy with worries. How few think of the eternal bliss of Spirit! But he who seeks God, and who seeks with all the depth and fervor of his soul until he finds Him, is wisest of all men. The Lord knows what you think; and if you love Him He will reveal Himself to you.

Never Forget God

Since last Christmas, no matter what I have gone through, my joy has been like a silent stream continuously flowing beneath the sands of my thoughts. These silent rivers of divine joy cannot be seen with the eyes, but whenever you dig deeply through the outer layers of consciousness you discover them. Let not anyone else know how deeply you feel for the Lord. The Master of the Universe knows of your love; don't display it before others, or you may lose it.

When in the silence of the soul and in every phase of life you turn within and say, "Father, I have not forgotten You"—when that kind of devotion wells up from the depths of your heart—God comes to drink from the fountain of your love. The only purpose of life is to enjoy Him. *It is possible.* I would not speak of it if I didn't know His limitless joy and bliss. You too must find Him. God *is.* The saints have not lied to you. And

---

* "Him that overcometh will I make a pillar in the temple of my God, and he shall go no more out" (Revelation 3:12).

† Bhagavad-Gita VII:3.

I am not lying to you. Then why waste time? Why be forgetful of Him? I know how terrible are the consequences. Forgetfulness of that inner Source of happiness is the cause of all human suffering and misery.

We put forth our hands to receive His gifts of life and sun and food and all the other things He bestows on us; but even as we receive them, we are unmindful of the Giver. If you have lovingly given presents to someone and then find out that he never thinks of you, how hurt you feel! God feels that way, too. Every day we use His gift of sight to see the world; we accept His gifts of thought and reason, but we are oblivious of Him.

If God is ever a beggar, it is to ask your love. He is continuously pursuing you; He coaxes you through the words of the saints. Do not ignore Him!

March on Toward the Lord's Kingdom

The joy that you felt yesterday after eight hours' meditation is continuous with me. Naught else could give me so much happiness. Everything else is a waste of time. Why hang on to worldly delusions? Every minute that I am with you I will try to impress on your consciousness the importance of seeking God. Remember, when you are trying to improve spiritually, you are moving toward His kingdom; and when you are not trying, you are standing still, or slipping backward. March on! Use your nights for meditation. That is the way to discover Him. It seems very hard to find God, yet He is the easiest to please as soon as you convince Him that He means everything to you. That day He will come to you.

Dear friends, I hope this Christmas will not end tonight for you. My Christmas never ends. It is with me day and night. The Lord is with me, and I am with Him. This is His promise in the Bhagavad-Gita: "He who seeth Me everywhere and seeth everything in Me, of him will I never lose hold, and he shall never lose hold of Me."*

Those who are addicted to wine are all the time drunk. Whether they are working or playing, their mind is on liquor. The Divine Nectar is a million times more intoxicating. When I am talking to you I am just as much with Him as when I am

* Bhagavad-Gita VI:30.

meditating. Such love! No tongue can ever describe this happiness. The Bible mentions that on the day of Pentecost the Apostles were enveloped by the Holy Ghost. Doubters said, "These men are full of new wine."* They were drunk, indeed, but with the wine of divine bliss!

The wellspring of undiluted joy of Spirit lies buried within your soul. Dig with the pickax of meditation until you discover it, and bathe in that fountain of eternal bliss.

And so, dear ones, my Christmas will go on forever, in ever increasing joy everlasting. If this joy were limited, as worldly happiness is, a time would come when all would be finished. But no saint will ever be able to exhaust the ever-new bliss of God. Even though the masters know Him fully, His joy is ever new to them throughout eternity. If the delights of Spirit were not endless, even the saints would want to come back to earth now and then for diversion, like ordinary mortals who return again and again. But the saints are eternally happy, as no one else is. This is the wealth they receive when they give up everything else for love of the Lord. Nothing can destroy the joy and peace of their being. That is Christhood.

Please Man by Pleasing God

Therefore seek only to please God. Try to please man, too, but not at the cost of pleasing Him. To attain the recognition of man by your own God-realization is the greatest thing you can do. Time is flying. Why are you waiting? There is no reality to worldly life. Though you have to eat and sleep, one day the switch of your heart will be suddenly pulled, and you will have to leave everything behind. When a visitor said to me, "I am too busy to meditate," I replied: "When you die, all your engagements will be canceled. What then? Where will you be if you haven't found God? Your friends will mourn briefly and

---

* "And when the day of Pentecost was fully come, they were all with one accord in one place....And they were all filled with the Holy Ghost....Others mocking said, These men are full of new wine. But Peter, standing up with the eleven, lifted up his voice, and said unto them...these are not drunken, as ye suppose....But this is that which was spoken by the prophet Joel; and it shall come to pass in the last days, saith God, I will pour out my Spirit upon all flesh" (Acts 2:1-17).

then resume their usual preoccupations. Why neglect your one
Eternal Friend?"

Wisdom becomes dimmed when you use your mind
wrongly, or mix with bad company. To seek God is the highest
way to happiness. Neither human love nor any other mortal
experience comes near His bliss. Anyone who tells you that
something else is more important than seeking the Lord is
wrong. Nothing can be greater than finding Him who created
you. This is why the Hindu scriptures say: "Forsaking all
duties, if it is necessary, pursue Me. For the forsaking of all
duties you will incur sin, but I shall forgive that because no
duties can be performed without receiving power from Me."*
Duty to God nullifies all other duties. When you resolutely
leave everything else to attain Him, then you are on the path to
realization.

To be able to do duty to God and to man is wonderful. To
do duty to God without duty to the world is all right. And to do
duty to the world and not to God is to be like a mule carrying a
bag of gold. The mule knows only the weight of the gold; he
cannot use it. To do duty to God first, and then, with His consciousness to help the world, is divine. And this is what the
Self-Realization Fellowship teachings stand for: to gain fellowship with God through realization of the Self; and, having that
divine fellowship, to help others to attain it.†

Wherever your heart is, there your mind is also. Wherever
those you love may be in the world, your heart is drawn to
them. You must feel that way about God; you must love Him
with all your heart. And love Him also with all your mind; if
your thoughts are roaming as you pray, it is a mockery. Last of
all, love God with all your soul. As you approach God, defeat-
ing all your temptations with the sword of wisdom, closing one
by one the doors of the senses, and one by one saying good-bye
to restless worldly thoughts, then you will love God with all
your heart, all your mind, and all your soul. The moon's reflection in a cup of water that has been stirred appears distorted,

* In part, a free translation from the Gita, XVIII:16 (see p. 310).
† "With sins obliterated, doubts removed, senses subjugated, the *rishis* (know-
ers of God), contributing to the welfare of mankind, attain emancipation in
Spirit" (Bhagavad-Gita V:25).

but the moon's reflection is seen perfectly when the water in the cup becomes quiet. Similarly, the soul image has become distorted by the restlessness of your mind, but when you still the mind, by loving God with all your heart, mind, and soul, you behold, within, the clear reflection of the Divine.

God is twinkling in the Milky Way, and through our intelligence and reason. He is present in every blade of grass; every flower mirrors His smile. In every good thought there is the joy of Spirit. He is everlasting. As you develop spiritually you see that He is your true Self, reflected in you as the soul, just as the moon can be reflected in a vessel of water; you realize that you are the pure image of Divinity. By greater effort you become able to break the vessel of the mortal ego; then the reflected soul image within it becomes one with the moon of Spirit.

Seek the Recognition of God

We don't want the praise of man; the recognition of God is what we are seeking. "For what everyone is in Thy sight, so much is he, and no more," said St. Francis. If before Him we are immaculate, nothing else matters. In doing good we must sometimes suffer. To find the Lord we must be willing to suffer. What is it to endure discomfort of the flesh and discipline of the mind to gain the eternal solace of Spirit? Christ's joy in God was so great he was willing to give up the body for Him. The purpose of life is to attain that tremendous happiness—to find God.

Renunciation is not an end; it is the means to an end. The real renunciant is he who lives for God first, regardless of his outer mode of existence. To love God and conduct your life to please Him—that is what matters. When you will do that, you will know the Lord. Every noble thought in your mind brings you closer to Him. Those thoughts are like a river leading to the ocean of Spirit.

Devotion is the one offering that tempts God. He is not moved by all the rich gifts and promises that are made to Him. But into the garden of a life redolent with sweet devotion God is tempted to come. When the fragrance of your devotion oozes forth unceasingly from the rose of your heart, the mighty Deity must come to you.

No matter how our thoughts run away from the Lord or how forlorn we feel, still the footsteps of our devotion lead us to the haven of Spirit. No matter how far we have strayed away, through devotion we can still reach Him; our lives need not be spent in vain.

Although you have regular duties, they are no excuse for saying you cannot seek God. While others sleep, you concentrate on Him. You will find you are a hundred times more happy and rested. Do this night after night, without thinking of time. When you are meditating, just remind yourself, "I am with Him, and that is all that matters."

When you plant a seed in the ground, you must not take it out every day to see if it is germinating; you will only hamper its growth. So with the seeds of your spiritual efforts. Once they are planted, leave them there, and tend them carefully.

I hope you will make a greater spiritual effort from tonight on. Don't lose sight of Him. The world will go on without you. You are not as important as you think. Countless men have been thrown into the dustbin of the centuries. Do not let your life pass uselessly. If in your heart you love God, you are greater than the most materially accomplished man. When you please God, you come closest to pleasing everybody. So learn to love Him. Don't feel that you have to mix with people all the time. When you do mix, do everything you can to help others; but when you are alone, be alone with God. When you attain Him, all things else will be added unto you.

It is not what you hear that redeems you, but what you do with what you hear. Many hear what they should do, but few act upon it. Don't paralyze your determination. When you know a thing is right, why shouldn't you go after it? Why shouldn't you cry for the Lord until the skies are shaken with your prayers? Surrender to Him completely. And never doubt Him.

Dive deep in the ocean of meditation. If you don't find the pearls of His presence, don't blame the ocean, blame your diving. Dive again and again until you find Him. "Seek, and ye shall find; knock, and it shall be opened unto you."* Re-

* Matthew 7:7.

member, it is the naughty baby who gets the mother's attention. The easily pacified infant is soon satisfied with toys. But
the naughty baby wants the mother only, and goes on crying
until she comes. Cry until the Divine Mother comes!

God is so real to His devotees! Every word they have said
about Him is true, but His play is shrouded in mystery. Your
seeking must be continuous. You cannot summon God by a
little cry; it must be unceasing, and not quelled by toys of
money, fame, and human love. When your desire is only for
Him, He will come. Then your lessons in the world are
finished. You are filled evermore with the joy of the Infinite.
"He who works for Me alone, who makes Me his goal, who
lovingly surrenders himself to Me, who is nonattached (to My
delusive cosmic-dream worlds), who bears ill will toward none
(beholding Me in all)—he enters My being."*

* Bhagavad-Gita XI:55.

God as Light and Joy

Self-Realization Fellowship Hermitage,
Encinitas, California, November 14, 1937

All nature is unreal. The supernatural is the only real Substance. Today I was walking on the Hermitage grounds, beholding the sunshine all around me. As I passed the stairway to the beach, I stopped and turned on the electric stair-lights to see if they were working. But I could not see them; for as I stood there the great light of God suddenly came and made it impossible to distinguish lesser lights. Even the sun I could not see at all. Vividly I understood that neither the sunlight nor the electric light is real. The only true light is the light of God.

> If there should rise
> Suddenly within the skies
> Sunburst of a thousand suns
> Flooding earth with beams undeemed-of,
> Then might be that Holy One's
> Majesty and radiance dreamed of.*

In that great vision He showed me worlds upon worlds— endless manifestations of His light. These things that I beheld are but expressions of His consciousness. And if we are attuned to Him, our perception is limitless, pervading everywhere in the oceanic flow of the Divine Presence.

When the Spirit is known, and when we know ourselves as Spirit, there is no land or sea, no earth or sky—all is He. The melting of everything in Spirit is a state no one can describe. A great bliss is felt—eternal fullness of joy and knowledge and love. I can see it in a devotee's face if inwardly his soul is trembling with that joy, as a leaf trembles in the wind. Such is the yogi. This ecstasy can only be known by balancing the activity of ordinary life with deep, soulful, undiscourageable meditation.

---

* Bhagavad-Gita XI:12, Sir Edwin Arnold's translation.

The Way to True Freedom

Egotism, pride, greed, anger, and other ugly outgrowths of self-centeredness are barriers to spiritual development, preventing man's escape from the misery of soul ignorance. The right course is to follow the teachings of a spiritual master who has wisdom and who loves God above all else, and to tune in with the wishes of such a guru. That way leads to freedom. Your wishes are guided by habits of past lives and by new habits you are constantly creating. These hold the soul prisoner and make it impossible for you to race along the road to everlasting liberty.

On one side of the path of life is the dark valley of ignorance, and on the other side the eternal light of wisdom. When you follow the guidance of a true guru, you will safely tread the road to freedom. Then everything that you wish for will be born of wisdom, and will come to you without the slightest effort. The whole universe has been created by the Divine Will, and when you are attuned to it, whatever you want is accomplished just by mere willing. I dare not even wish anymore, for I know that whatever is in my mind will come to me.

The true devotee says, "Lord, I have no desires. I have found all that I want in You; no other gain could be greater."* Possessing His wisdom, love, and joy, all desires of the heart are satisfied. This is a tremendous state. When you are united with Spirit, you are king—a king of quietude and bliss, fully satisfied and complete within your Self. In your oneness with Him, you see the whole world standing before you, ready to do your bidding. Because God made man in His image, all those who find Him find also that His will in them fulfills their slightest command.

With God-Realization Comes All Power

So long as you have any desire to dominate other people, or to show them how powerful you are spiritually or in any other way, you will not find soul freedom. God-awareness begins in humbleness, love, and meditative bliss; but with the realiza-

---

* "The state that, once found, the yogi considers as the treasure beyond all other treasures—a state in which he is immune to every grief" (Bhagavad-Gita VI:22).

tion of God comes all power. If the little wave knew that behind it is the great ocean, it could say, "I am the ocean." You
should realize that just behind your consciousness is the
Ocean of God.

When Jesus was being crucified he could have reduced his
enemies to ashes with one look; but he didn't do it. Instead, he
forgave them. That is the divine nature: peace, love, humbleness, omnipresence, omniscience. He who becomes one with
God has no need to prove to himself or to others the extent of
the power he possesses. He knows within that he has all power
at his command, and there is nothing to fear. But he uses his
power only when God directs him to do so.

The accomplished yogi is awake in his infinite nature and
asleep in his material nature.* You should attain this self-
mastery. Don't fool yourself, giving all your time to the world.
Outwit the world and its lures: the best way to conserve your
time and use it to greatest benefit is to put your whole mind on
seeking God day and night, no matter what activities you engage in outwardly.

The cow calmly grazing with its calf in the pasture does
not show any sign of worry about the calf, but if you go near it,
the cow comes at you immediately. So is the yogi, outwardly
busy with his work but inwardly keeping his attention always
on the Lord.

Jesus said, "If thy hand offend thee, cut if off."† He didn't
mean that you should maim your body, but rather that you
should cut off enslaving sense attachments, which prevent you
from finding God. Like an insistent child, constantly call to the
Divine Mother until She says: "All right, what is it you want?"
She is so busy with creation, She doesn't reply at once; but to
the naughty child who cries and cries for Her, She will come.

The Divine Mother is most anxious to have you back with
Her, but first you must prove to Her that you want Her alone.
You must cry urgently and unceasingly; then She smiles and is
with you instantly. Divine Spirit has no partiality; the Mother

* "The seeming state of wakefulness of the ordinary man is perceived by a sage
to be, in reality, a state of delusive sleep" (Bhagavad-Gita II:69).

† Matthew 18:8.

loves all. But Her devotees appreciate Her love, respond to Her love. I see the effect on people who have gained a little human love, or a little money—how happy they are! But if they could see what strength, what joy, what love is in the Divine Mother, they would fly away from all else.

God Speaks Only Through His Devotees

To the world God speaks only through His enlightened devotees. Therefore, the wisest of all actions is to tune in with the will of the guru who is sent to you by the Lord as a response to your soul's desire. He is not a guru who is self-proclaimed as such; he is a guru who is asked by God to bring others back to Him. When there is a little spiritual desire, the Lord sends books and teachers to further inspire you; and when your desire is stronger, he sends a real guru. "Understand (this truth): By surrendering thyself (to the guru), by questioning (the guru and thine inner perception), and by service (to the guru), the sages who have attained supreme wisdom will be thy teachers." *

There are teachers who expect their followers to be always at their beck and call, ready to obey instantly; and if they don't, the teacher becomes angry. But a spiritual teacher who knows God and is truly a guru never thinks of himself as a teacher at all. He beholds God's presence in everyone, and feels no resentment if some students disregard his wishes. The Hindu scriptures say that those who tune in with the wisdom of a true guru make it possible for the guru to help them. "Comprehending that (the wisdom from a guru), thou, O Arjuna! wilt not again fall into delusion."†

The friendship that exists between guru and disciple is eternal. There is complete surrender, there is no compulsion, when a disciple accepts the guru's training.

Human friendship is often selfish; when a person ceases to be useful to us, we lose our love for him. This is the defect of human love.

In friendship that is divine, love that is divine—not conditioned by material forms but by spiritual law—there is a

---

* Bhagavad-Gita IV:34.   † Bhagavad-Gita IV:35.

consciousness of mutual responsibility. When you try to understand a person, it is easy to please him. But when you don't try to understand, it is impossible to keep harmony. I can get along with strangers, but I can best help those who tune in with me. I never would want to hurt anyone. I like to please all—not by sanctioning their wrong desires, but by encouraging them in their right aspirations, that they may really live in the consciousness of God.

God Is the Only Guru

One who loves God can never take pleasure in being a teacher. He knows that God is the only Guru. I feel as the dust at your feet. This I say out of the realization of that mighty Spirit I behold in each one of you.

I was to have gone from this earth a long time ago. I would like to melt this body in the Divine Flame and burn the dross, so that the body is no more a part of me that appears separate from the Infinite. One day I shall be gone, but so long as I live on earth, my greatest pleasure is to tell those who tune in with my wishes, and who trust me, that the only thing I want is to interest them in that Light which has given me consolation and freedom and assurance indescribable. "The Light of All Lights, beyond darkness....He is seated in the hearts of all."*

In that Light I see all those who have come and gone. I see all creation, and events that happened many years ago. The history of the world is preserved in the archives of the eternal sphere beyond. It is another dimension. Here in this finite world we behold length, breadth, and thickness, but there is another plane where the three dimensions do not exist; all is transparent. Everything is consciousness. The sense of taste is consciousness. The sense of smell is consciousness. Our feelings, our thoughts, and our body are nothing but consciousness. Just as we can see, hear, smell, taste, and touch in a dream, so in that higher sphere we experience all these sensations through pure consciousness.

This is what I am seeing now even as I speak to you. I am not in this body; I am a part of all that exists. These things I am

* Bhagavad-Gita XIII:18.

beholding are just as real to me as are you who are in this room. You have to awaken in order to perceive that God is everywhere and to realize that you have been dreaming. All of you are sitting here in this dream, and you are part of the dream. Many times I see this room in Eternity, and other times I see Eternity in this room. All things have borrowed life from that Eternal Source.

I Cried and Prayed, Day and Night

Everything is God. This very room and the universe are floating like a motion picture on the screen of my consciousness. When you look back at the booth, you see only the beam of light that is projecting the pictures on the screen. That this creation is naught but a motion picture, created out of God's light, seems incredible; but it is true. I look at this room and I see nothing but pure Spirit, pure Light, pure Joy. "He dwells in the world, enveloping all—everywhere."* The picture of my body and your bodies and all things in this world are only rays of light streaming out of that one sacred Light. As I see that Light I behold nothing anywhere but pure Spirit.†

It seems so simple now; but when as a boy I sat praying night after night, no answer came. On one side I beheld unenlightened humanity and on the other side Eternity, which would not speak to me. It was a very cruel state—forsaken by God, I thought. But I was not forsaken by Him; He was hiding behind my thoughts, behind my feelings all the time. When I began to see the light within, my soul would be mysteriously filled with divine fragrance; I would see revealed all the roots of trees and the sap flowing in them. Then I began to feel the great Spirit near. Again and again I cried and prayed, day and night, and when nothing any longer meant anything to me, when inside I renounced everything—even happiness, lest it be material happiness—then He came to me. Now He is with me evermore. The world may forsake me, but He forsakes me never.

---

* Bhagavad-Gita XIII:14.

† Of such great lovers of God the Gita (VII:19) says: "At the termination of many births, the sage, perceiving that (all creation) is pervaded by God, obtains Me. Such a devotee is hard to find (in this world)." *(Publisher's Note)*

I don't know why I am telling these things to you, but I feel I must do so. I used to talk of them, but in the presence of those who became indifferent I couldn't speak—my mouth wouldn't open. This time He has made me tell, that you may know there is nothing to live for except Him. All else will go. Pray only for That which is abiding.

Pray Only to Know God

Don't yearn for human love; it will vanish. Behind human love is the spiritual love of God. Seek that. Don't pray for home or for money or for love or for friendship. Don't pray for anything of this world. Enjoy only what the Lord gives to you. All else leads to delusion. Man has come on earth solely to learn to know God; he is here for no other reason. This is the true message of the Lord. To all those who seek and love Him, He tells of that great Life where there is no pain, no old age, no war, no death—only eternal assurance. In that Life nothing is destroyed. There is only ineffable happiness that will never grow stale—a happiness always new.

So that is why it is worthwhile to seek God. All those who sincerely seek Him will surely find Him. Those who want to love the Lord and yearn to enter His kingdom, and who sincerely wish in their hearts to know Him, will find Him. You must have an ever-increasing desire for Him, day and night. He will acknowledge your love by fulfilling His promise to you throughout eternity, and you shall know joy and happiness unending. All is light, all is joy, all is peace, all is love. He is all.

Have I Found God?

May 1938 *

This is the message of my heart to you. Mark it well. Read and inwardly digest it, and put into practice the truths that God has expressed through me.

First, ask yourself: "Have I found God?" If your answer doesn't satisfy you, get busy sincerely with meditation, as taught by the Self-realized masters who have found Him.

India's saints experimented through the ages to perfect the universally scientific yoga methods of emancipation, of attaining oneness with God. For your own satisfaction, apply those methods in your spiritual seeking, for you cannot find the Supreme without following the law of concentration and meditation, which alone leads to Him. Material scientists are gathering secrets from nature every day by applying the physical laws that lead to discovery. Without similarly utilizing spiritual laws, dogmatic theology becomes stagnant, powerless to open the doors to God.

Absentminded prayers and affirmations, and untested decrees and beliefs will not give you God. The step-by-step yoga techniques of Self-realization, the help of a guru (one who has traveled beyond the forest of theology and *knows* God), and daily deep effort in yoga meditation will lead you to the Divine Goal. In the Gita we find the testimony of the Lord Himself: "Thou canst not see Me with mortal eyes. Therefore I give thee sight divine. Behold My supreme power of Yoga."†

---

* This selection was written by Paramahansa Yogananda. We have included it in this compilation of talks because it expresses one of the most important aspects of his universal message to mankind: "It is not what you read that can give you liberation, but what you do with what you read. Salvation comes from practice, not theory; realization, not blind belief." *(Publisher's Note)*

† Bhagavad-Gita XI:8.

To reach God you must find some time every day to be alone with Him; you must get away from too many distractions, too many fruitless engagements, too many desires, too much waste of time; and you must follow a spiritually awakened teacher who has found Him. Use your common sense and intuition to recognize the true teachers who know Him. Those alone who have experienced God can lead you to Him.

Use the night hours as much as you can, and the early morning, and all free moments between demanding duties, to pray inwardly to God with all your soul: "Reveal Thyself!" Solitude is the price of God-realization. Wake! Waste no more time in blind believing; follow the tested methods of attaining Self-realization, and know God.

The Purpose of Life Is to Find God

Self-Realization Fellowship Temple,
Hollywood, California, October 8, 1944

I am working for God alone. Earth has no illusions for me; I have seen through them all. You too should realize that you are visiting this earth only temporarily; you are here solely to learn necessary lessons and to help all who cross your path. You do not know why you have been cast in a particular role, so you must learn what God expects of you. Don't harbor personal desires; your only desire should be to follow the Lord's will and to live and work for Him.

We are here today, tomorrow we are gone: mere shadows in a cosmic dream. But behind the unreality of these fleeting pictures is the immortal reality of Spirit. Life here on earth appears futile and chaotic until we are anchored in the Divine.

This is why, as I have often told you, I am here to testify to the supreme importance of Spirit. Do not concentrate upon ephemeral worldly goals and human attachments. Such fanaticism takes your mind away from the Lord and your eternal Self in Him. "He who has overcome attachment both to sense objects and to actions, and who is free from ego-instigated plannings—that man is said to have attained firm union of soul with Spirit." *

You came here through the will of God, but He gave you freedom to live according to your own will. You should learn now to be obedient to the will of the Almighty. This is how I try to be. Every morning I ask Him to tell me what He wants me to do; then I see Him working through my hands and brain, and everything goes as He wishes.

That is the Power you should trust, the Power through which you can find guidance, happiness, strength, and free-

* Bhagavad-Gita VI:4.

dom. That is the Power which will give you emancipation.

No other duty is important if it takes your thought and desire away from your duty to God; all else is illusion. To grasp this truth I had to remove all worldly hallucinations from my brain, through meditation and the company of great masters. I want to instill this understanding in your hearts: until you realize that God is more important than anything else, and until you spend your life in seeking to please Him, you are not spiritually evolved at all.

To Ignore God Is Not Common Sense

Is it not true wisdom to do His will and to be directly helpful in bringing others back to Him? My greatest joy is to remind others of the importance and necessity of remembering God. This earth is a foreign land; we are not in our own Home. In an instant you may be required to leave this world; you will have to cancel all your engagements. Why then give any other activity first importance, with the result that you have no time for God? That is not common sense. It is because of *maya*, the net of cosmic delusion which is thrown over us, that we entangle ourselves in mundane interests and forget the Lord.

Jesus said: "If thy right eye offend thee, pluck it out, and cast it from thee: for it is profitable for thee that one of thy members should perish, and not that thy whole body should be cast into hell."*

He was speaking not literally but metaphorically; it is only if the mind has become enmeshed in wrong desires that any of the senses can offend the divine soul image within man. Christ meant that so long as wrong desires lead the senses astray, we shall remain oblivious of God, in whom our real happiness lies. Therefore it is better, he said, to be maimed of the senses than to misuse them. Christ spoke in a dramatic way to point out that nothing in life, not even the body, is of any value if we remain in ignorance of God. Without knowing Him, life becomes a "hell"—a hornet's nest of troubles. There is no security in this world; one never knows from what quarter disaster may strike.

* Matthew 5:29.

A man with cancer lies in the hospital. "Well," you say, "that is not I; it is somebody else." But I have mentally put myself in such bodies and I know how hopeless those people feel. While you are well and strong, do not spend your time on foolishness. God understands everything; He knows He has sent us to this terrible place. He grieves in His heart at our sufferings. Nothing hurts Him more than to see us grovel in the mud of delusion. He wants us to come back Home. And to those who make the effort to know Him, He responds: "From sheer compassion I, the Divine Indweller, set alight in them the radiant lamp of wisdom that banishes the darkness of ignorance."*

For every man who retraces his steps to God, there is a great celebration among the angels. They actually appear and receive that returning soul in great joy.

There is no way back Home if you weave around you a snare of worldly desires. You came to play your part on the stage of time, to fill the role that you were designed for in the divine drama; but the essential part of your role is to think of Him and to do His will, naught else. Every thought, every act, is deluded that does not place Him first. The Hindu scriptures say: "As soon as you feel the desire for God, immediately change your life and plunge into Him."

Each soul must find its way back alone. No one but you is responsible for your mistakes and habits. Once you have found your Self in your soul, you are free. But so long as you are not free, so long there is danger; you will have to come back to earth and work out all the desires that remain unfinished.† Your body is mortal, but the soul outlasts the body. If you die wanting a Cadillac you will have to come back here for it; you will not be able to get it in heaven, where cars are not used.

Although the force of desires is strong, the potency of Divine Will is stronger. That Will is in you and will work through you, if you permit it, and if you refuse to let worldly motivations weave nets of incarnations around you.

* Bhagavad-Gita X:11.
†Desires may be worked out by material fulfillment or, according to one's spiritual development, by the mental process of discrimination or the spiritual process of deep meditation.

Seek God while you are young and strong, because in old age and disease you may not be able to seek Him. By the time most people begin to understand the true meaning of life, the body is weakening; they have to spend their time looking after the frail physical machine instead of pursuing the search for Reality.

The only purpose of life is to find God. If you are married, you and your loved one should seek the Divine together. But if you are unmarried, obey at once Christ's command: "Seek ye first the kingdom of God." When you know Him, He will tell you what to do. Otherwise, you don't know what fate may await you in marriage. The tragic stories that come to my ears are unimaginable! Terrible tales of human incompatibility. People should be taught in youth how to control their emotions. I don't think anyone should marry without first having learned to control his impulses. Until one is emotionally stable, he is not fit to have a family. The greatest thing is to possess self-control; then, if you want to marry, the right person will be drawn magnetically into your life.

Ignorance is like a great poison in the system. Because of it we don't realize our true nature, made in the image of God. First of all, find out by ceaseless prayer what the Lord wants you to do. There is nothing greater than obeying His will. It is your desires that enslave you and make you think, "I want this" or "I want that." Do not act on what your enemy, the ego, dictates; seek rather to do the will of the Heavenly Father, your sole Friend.

So long as ignorance remains, you cannot tell how many incarnations of suffering may be ahead of you. Eliminate ignorance by meditation. The longer you meditate, the more completely you will "cauterize" the injurious mental bacteria that have been infecting you for ages. For instance, some people are prone to anger; they do not realize that they have been cultivating the habit of wrathfulness for many lives. Others are slaves to the sex instinct as a result of bad habits for incarnations. It is best to struggle to get rid of bad habits now. "Him that overcometh will I make a pillar in the temple of my God, and he shall go no more out (reincarnate no more)."*

* Revelation 3:12.

Daily say with me to the Lord: "I am working for You. Whenever You want to take me, I am ready. I am Your child." He will give you the same freedom I am enjoying. I take on more and more work but I never feel I am overburdened, because I do everything for Him. I love Him. That surrender to God has destroyed in me the *karma* of ignorance. So long as there is a weeping brother by the wayside, I will come again into this world to wipe away his tears. Why should I be content to enjoy the blessings of heaven while others are suffering?

The Romance of Divine Love

Reform your life. Every night commune with Him; talk to Him; pray to Him sincerely. Give up the mockery of half-hearted prayer. Say, "Lord, I know You are here. You must talk to me! Come out of the cave of silence." This prayer is expressed in a song I wrote to the Divine Mother when I visited the desert near Palm Springs.

> Mother, I give You my soul call!
> You can't remain hidden anymore.
> Come out of the silent sky,
> Come out of the mountain glen,
> Come out of my secret soul,
> Come out of my cave of silence.

I had just finished the song when I saw a wondrous form, the Divine Mother! appear from out of the sky. In response to my soul call, I beheld everywhere, in everything, the Cosmic Mother. I prayed and worshiped Her. She blessed me and talked with me.

The greatest romance is with the Infinite. You have no idea how beautiful life can be. "Unattracted to the sensory world, the yogi experiences the ever-new joy of Being. His soul engaged in the union with Spirit, he attains indestructible bliss" (Bhagavad-Gita V:21). When you suddenly find God everywhere, when He comes and talks to you and guides you, the romance of divine love has begun.

GOD! GOD! GOD!

By Paramahansa Yogananda

From the depths of slumber,
As I ascend the spiral stairway of wakefulness,
I whisper:
God! God! God!

Thou art the food, and when I break my fast
Of nightly separation from Thee,
I taste Thee, and mentally say:
God! God! God!

No matter where I go, the spotlight of my mind
Ever keeps turning on Thee;
And in the battle din of activity my silent war-cry is ever:
God! God! God!

When boisterous storms of trials shriek
And worries howl at me,
I drown their noises, loudly chanting:
God! God! God!

When my mind weaves dreams
With threads of memories,
On that magic cloth I do emboss:
God! God! God!

Every night, in time of deepest sleep,
My peace dreams and calls: Joy! Joy! Joy!
And my joy comes singing evermore:
God! God! God!

In waking, eating, working, dreaming, sleeping,
Serving, meditating, chanting, divinely loving,
My soul constantly hums, unheard by any:
God! God! God!

AIMS AND IDEALS
of
Self-Realization Fellowship

As set forth by Paramahansa Yogananda, Founder

Sri Daya Mata, President

To disseminate among the nations a knowledge of definite scientific techniques for attaining direct personal experience of God.

To teach that the purpose of life is the evolution, through self-effort, of man's limited mortal consciousness into God Consciousness; and to this end to establish Self-Realization Fellowship temples for God-communion throughout the world, and to encourage the establishment of individual temples of God in the homes and in the hearts of men.

To reveal the complete harmony and basic oneness of original Christianity as taught by Jesus Christ and original Yoga as taught by Bhagavan Krishna; and to show that these principles of truth are the common scientific foundation of all true religions.

To point out the one divine highway to which all paths of true religious beliefs eventually lead: the highway of daily, scientific, devotional meditation on God.

To liberate man from his threefold suffering: physical disease, mental inharmonies, and spiritual ignorance.

To encourage "plain living and high thinking"; and to spread a spirit of brotherhood among all peoples by teaching the eternal basis of their unity: kinship with God.

To demonstrate the superiority of mind over body, of soul over mind.

To overcome evil by good, sorrow by joy, cruelty by kindness, ignorance by wisdom.

To unite science and religion through realization of the unity of their underlying principles.

To advocate cultural and spiritual understanding between East and West, and the exchange of their finest distinctive features.

To serve mankind as one's larger Self.

GLOSSARY

Arjuna. The exalted disciple to whom Bhagavan Krishna imparted the immortal message of the Bhagavad-Gita (*q.v.*) around 3000 B.C.; one of the five Pandava princes in the great Hindu epic, the *Mahabharata*, in which he was a key figure.

ashram. A spiritual hermitage; often a monastery.

astral body. Man's subtle body of light, *prana* or lifetrons; the second of three sheaths that successively encase the soul: the causal body (*q.v.*), the astral body, and the physical body. The powers of the astral body enliven the physical body, much as electricity illumines a bulb. The astral body has nineteen elements: intelligence, ego, feeling, mind (sense-consciousness); five instruments of knowledge (the sensory powers within the physical organs of sight, hearing, smell, taste, and touch); five instruments of action (the executive powers in the physical instruments of procreation, excretion, speech, locomotion, and the exercise of manual skill); and five instruments of life force that perform the functions of circulation, metabolization, assimilation, crystallization, and elimination.

astral light. The subtle light emanating from lifetrons (see *prana*); the structural essence of the astral world. Through the all-inclusive intuitive perception of the soul, devotees in concentrated states of meditation may perceive the astral light, particularly as the spiritual eye (*q.v.*).

astral world. The subtle sphere of the Lord's creation, a universe of light and color composed of finer-than-atomic forces, i.e., vibrations of life energy or lifetrons (see *prana*). Every being, every object, every vibration on the material plane has an astral counterpart, for in the astral universe is the blueprint of our material universe. At physical death, man goes in his astral body of light to one of the astral planets, according to merit, to continue his spiritual evolution in the greater freedom of that subtle realm. There he remains for a karmically predetermined time until physical rebirth.

Aum (Om). The basis of all sounds; universal symbol-word for God. *Aum* of the Vedas became the sacred word *Hum* of the Tibetans; *Amin* of the Moslems; and *Amen* of the Egyptians, Greeks, Ro-

mans, Jews, and Christians. *Amen* in Hebrew means *sure, faithful.*
Aum is the all-pervading sound emanating from the Holy Ghost
(Invisible Cosmic Vibration; God in His aspect of Creator); the
"Word" of the Bible; the voice of creation, testifying to the Divine
Presence in every atom. *Aum* may be heard through practice of
Self-Realization Fellowship methods of meditation.

"These things saith the Amen, the faithful and true witness, the
beginning of the creation of God" (Revelation 3:14). "In the beginning was the Word, and the Word was with God, and the Word was
God.... All things were made by him [the Word or *Aum*]; and without him was not any thing made that was made" (John 1:1,3). See
also *Sat-Tat-Aum.*

avatar. From the Sanskrit *avatara,* with roots *ava,* "down," and *tri,*
"to pass." Souls who attain union with Spirit and then return to
earth to help mankind are called *avatars,* divine incarnations.

avidya. Literally, "non-knowledge," ignorance; the manifestation in
man of *maya,* the cosmic delusion (*q.v.*). Essentially, *avidya* is
man's ignorance of his divine nature and of the sole reality: Spirit.

Babaji. See *Mahavatar Babaji.*

Bhagavad-Gita. "Song of the Lord." This scripture consists of eighteen chapters from the *Mahabharata* epic. It is chiefly a dialog between the *avatar* Lord Krishna and his disciple Arjuna on the eve of
the historic battle of Kurukshetra, about 3000 B.C. The Gita is al-
legory as well as history, a spiritual treatise on the inner battle between man's good and bad tendencies. Depending on the context,
Krishna symbolizes the guru, the soul, or God: Arjuna represents
the aspiring devotee. Of this holy scripture Mahatma Gandhi wrote:
"Those who will meditate on the Gita will derive fresh joy and new
meanings from it every day. There is not a single spiritual tangle
which the Gita cannot unravel."

The quotations from the Bhagavad-Gita in the text and footnotes
of this book are from the translation by Paramahansa Yogananda.

Bhagavan Krishna. An *avatar* who lived as a king in India three millenniums before the Christian era. One of the meanings given for
the word *Krishna* in the Hindu scriptures is "Omniscient Spirit."
Thus, *Krishna,* like *Christ,* is a spiritual title signifying the divine
magnitude of the *avatar*—his oneness with God. The title *Bha-*
gavan means "Lord." In his early life, Krishna lived as a cowherd
who enchanted his companions with the music of his flute. In this
role Krishna is often considered to represent allegorically the soul
playing the flute of meditation to guide all misled thoughts back to
the fold of omniscience.

Bhakti Yoga. The spiritual approach to God that stresses all-surrendering love as the principal means for communion and union with God. See *Yoga*.

Brahma-Vishnu-Shiva. Three aspects of God's immanence in creation. They represent that triune function of the Christ Intelligence (*Tat*) that guides Cosmic Nature's activities of creation, preservation, and dissolution. See *Trinity*.

Brahman (Brahma). Absolute Spirit.

breath. "The influx of innumerable cosmic currents into man by way of the breath induces restlessness in his mind," Paramahansa Yogananda wrote. "Thus the breath links him with the fleeting phenomenal worlds. To escape from the sorrows of transitoriness and to enter the blissful realm of Reality, the yogi learns to quiet the breath by scientific meditation."

caste. Caste in its original conception was not a hereditary status, but a classification based on man's natural capacities. In his evolution, man passes through four distinct grades, designated by ancient Hindu sages as *Sudra, Vaisya, Kshatriya,* and *Brahmin.* The *Sudra* is interested primarily in satisfying his bodily needs and desires; the work that best suits his state of development is bodily labor. The *Vaisya* is ambitious for worldly gain as well as for satisfaction of the senses; he has more creative ability than the *Sudra* and seeks occupation as a farmer, a businessman, an artist, or wherever his mental energy finds fulfillment. The *Kshatriya,* having through many lives fulfilled the desires of the *Sudra* and *Vaisya* states, begins to seek the meaning of life; he tries to overcome his bad habits, to control his senses, and to do what is right. *Kshatriyas* by occupation are noble rulers, statesmen, warriors. The *Brahmin* has overcome his lower nature, has a natural affinity for spiritual pursuits, and is God-knowing, able therefore to teach and help liberate others.

causal body. Essentially, man as a soul is a causal-bodied being. His causal body is an idea-matrix for the astral and physical bodies. The causal body is composed of 35 idea elements corresponding to the 19 elements of the astral body plus the 16 basic material elements of the physical body.

causal world. Behind the physical world of matter (atoms, protons, electrons), and the subtle astral world of luminous life energy (lifetrons), is the causal, or ideational, world of thought (thoughtrons). After man evolves sufficiently to transcend the physical and astral universes, he resides in the causal universe. In the consciousness of causal beings, the physical and astral universes are resolved to their thought essence. Whatever physical man can do in imagination, causal man can do in actuality—the only limitation being thought itself. Ultimately, man sheds the last soul covering—his causal body—to unite with omnipresent Spirit, beyond all vibratory realms.

chakras. In Yoga, the seven occult centers of life and consciousness in the spine and brain, which enliven the physical and astral bodies of man. These centers are referred to as *chakras* ("wheels") because the concentrated energy in each one is like a hub from which radiate rays of life-giving light and energy. In ascending order, these *chakras* are *muladhara* (the coccygeal, at the base of the spine); *svadhisthana* (the sacral, two inches above *muladhara*); *manipura* (the lumbar, opposite the navel); *anahata* (the dorsal, opposite the heart); *vishuddha* (the cervical, at the base of the neck); *ajna* (traditionally located between the eyebrows; in actuality, directly connected by polarity with the medulla; see also *medulla* and *spiritual eye*); and *sahasrara* (in the uppermost part of the cerebrum).

The seven centers are divinely planned exits or "trap doors" through which the soul has descended into the body and through which it must reascend by a process of meditation. By seven successive steps, the soul escapes into Cosmic Consciousness. In its conscious upward passage through the seven opened or "awakened" cerebrospinal centers, the soul travels the highway to the Infinite, the true path by which the soul must retrace its course to reunite with God.

Yoga treatises generally consider only the six lower centers as *chakras*, with *sahasrara* referred to separately as a seventh center. All seven centers, however, are often referred to as lotuses, whose petals open, or turn upward, in spiritual awakening as the life and consciousness travel up the spine.

chitta. Intuitive feeling. When feeling is unclouded by selfishness, anger, or fear, it is intuitive. The perception is felt in the heart.

Christ center The *Kutastha* or *ajna chakra* at the point between the eyebrows, directly connected by polarity with the medulla (*q.v.*); center of will and concentration, and of Christ Consciousness (*q.v.*); seat of the spiritual eye (*q.v.*).

Christ Consciousness. "Christ" or "Christ Consciousness" is the projected consciousness of God immanent in all creation. In Christian scripture it is called the "only begotten son," the only pure reflection in creation of God the Father; in Hindu scripture it is called *Kutastha Chaitanya* or *Tat*, the cosmic intelligence of Spirit everywhere present in creation. It is the universal consciousness, oneness with God, manifested by Jesus, Krishna, and other *avatars*.

Great saints and yogis know it as the state of *samadhi* meditation wherein their consciousness has become identified with the intelligence in every particle of creation; they feel the entire universe as their own body. See *Trinity*.

Concentration Technique. The Self-Realization Fellowship Technique of Concentration (also *Hong-Sau* Technique) taught in the *Self-Realization Fellowship Lessons*. This technique helps scientifically to withdraw the attention from all objects of distraction and to place it upon one thing at a time. Thus it is invaluable for meditation, concentration on God. The *Hong-Sau* Technique is an integral part of the science of *Kriya Yoga* (*q.v.*).

consciousness, states of. In mortal consciousness man experiences three states: waking consciousness, sleeping consciousness, and dreaming consciousness. But he does not experience his soul, superconsciousness, and he does not experience God. The Christman does. As mortal man is conscious throughout his body, so the Christ-man is conscious throughout the universe, which he feels as his body. Beyond the state of Christ consciousness is cosmic consciousness, the experience of oneness with God in His absolute consciousness beyond vibratory creation as well as with the Lord's omnipresence manifesting in the phenomenal worlds.

Cosmic Consciousness. The Absolute, beyond creation. Also the *samadhi*-meditation state of oneness with God both beyond and within vibratory creation. See *Trinity*.

cosmic delusion. See *maya*.

cosmic energy. See *prana*.

Cosmic Intelligent Vibration. See *Aum*.

Cosmic Sound. See *Aum*.

dharma. Eternal principles of righteousness that uphold all creation; man's inherent duty to live in harmony with these principles. See also *Sanatan Dharma*.

diksha. Spiritual initiation; from the Sanskrit verb-root *diksh*, to dedicate oneself. See also *disciple* and *Kriya Yoga*.

disciple. A spiritual aspirant who comes to a guru seeking introduction to God, and to this end establishes an eternal spiritual relationship with the guru. In Self-Realization Fellowship, the guru-disciple relationship is established by *diksha*, initiation, in *Kriya Yoga*. See also *guru* and *Kriya Yoga*.

Divine Mother. The aspect of God that is active in creation; the *shakti*, or power, of the Transcendent Creator. Other terms for this aspect of Divinity are *Aum*, *Shakti*, Holy Ghost, Cosmic Intelligent

Vibration, Nature or Prakriti (*q.v.*). Also, the personal aspect of God embodying the love and compassionate qualities of a mother.

The Hindu scriptures teach that God is both immanent and transcendent, personal and impersonal. He may be sought as the Absolute; as one of His manifest eternal qualities, such as love, wisdom, bliss, light; in the form of an *ishta* (deity); or as Father, Mother, or Friend.

egoism.   The ego-principle, *ahankara* (lit., "I do"), is the root cause of dualism or the seeming separation between man and his Creator. *Ahankara* brings human beings under the sway of *maya* (*q.v.*), by which the subject (ego) falsely appears as object; the creatures imagine themselves to be creators. By banishing ego-consciousness, man awakens to his divine identity, his oneness with the Sole Life: God.

elements (five).   The Cosmic Vibration, or *Aum*, structures all physical creation, including man's physical body, through the manifestation of five *tattvas* (elements): earth, water, fire, air, and ether (*q.v.*). These are structural forces, intelligent and vibratory in nature. Without the earth element there would be no state of solid matter; without the water element, no liquid state; without the air element, no gaseous state; without the fire element, no heat; without the ether element, no background on which to produce the cosmic motion picture show. In the body, *prana* (cosmic vibratory energy) enters the medulla and is then divided into the five elemental currents by the action of the five lower *chakras* (*q.v.*), or centers: the coccygeal (earth), sacral (water), lumbar (fire), dorsal (air), and cervical (ether). The Sanskrit terminology for these elements is *prithivi, ap, tej, prana,* and *akash.*

Energization Exercises.   Man is surrounded by cosmic energy, much as a fish is surrounded by water. The Energization Exercises, originated by Paramahansa Yogananda and taught in *Self-Realization Fellowship Lessons,* enable man to recharge his body with the energy, or *prana,* that is all around him.

ether.   Sanskrit *akash.* Though not considered a factor in present scientific theory on the nature of the material universe, ether has for millenniums been so referred to by India's sages. Paramahansa Yogananda spoke of ether as the background on which God projects the cosmic motion picture of creation. Space gives dimension to objects; ether separates the images. This "background," a creative force that coordinates all spatial vibrations, is a necessary factor when considering the subtler forces—thought and life energy (*prana*)—and the nature of space and the origin of material forces and matter. See *elements*.

gunas. The three attributes of Nature: *tamas, rajas,* and *sattwa*—obstruction, activity, and expansion; or, mass, energy, and intelligence. In man the three *gunas* express themselves as ignorance or inertia; activity or struggle; and wisdom.

guru. When a devotee is ready to seek God in earnest, the Lord sends him a guru. Through the wisdom, intelligence, Self-realization, and teachings of such a master, God guides the disciple. By following the master's teachings and discipline, the disciple is able to fulfill his soul's desire for the manna of God-perception. Such a guru, ordained by God to help true seekers in response to their deep soul craving, is not an ordinary teacher: he is a human vehicle whose body, speech, mind, and spirituality God uses as a channel to attract and guide lost souls back to their home of immortality. A guru is a living embodiment of scriptural truth. He is an agent of salvation appointed by God in response to a devotee's demand for release from the bondage of matter. See *master*.

Gurudeva. "Divine teacher," a customary Sanskrit term of respect that is used in addressing and referring to one's spiritual preceptor; sometimes rendered in English as "Master."

Gurus of Self-Realization Fellowship. The Gurus of Self-Realization Fellowship (Yogoda Satsanga Society of India) are Jesus Christ, Bhagavan Krishna, and a line of exalted masters of contemporary times: Mahavatar Babaji, Lahiri Mahasaya, Swami Sri Yukteswar, and Paramahansa Yogananda. To show the harmony and essential unity of the teachings of Jesus Christ and the Yoga precepts of Bhagavan Krishna is an integral part of the SRF dispensation. All of these Gurus, by their sublime teachings and divine instrumentality, contribute to the fulfillment of the Self-Realization Fellowship mission of bringing to all mankind a practical spiritual science of God-realization.

Hatha Yoga. A system of techniques and physical postures (*asanas*) that promotes health and mental calm. See *Yoga*.

Holy Ghost. See *Aum* and *Trinity*.

intuition. The all-knowing faculty of the soul, which enables man to experience direct perception of truth without the intermediary of the senses.

Jadava Krishna. *Jadava* refers to the clan of which Bhagavan Krishna was king, and is one of many names by which Krishna is known. See *Bhagavan Krishna*.

ji. A suffix denoting respect, added to names and titles in India; as, Gandhiji, Paramahansaji, Guruji.

Jnana Yoga. The path to union with God through transmutation of the discriminative power of the intellect into the omniscient wisdom of the soul.

karma. Effects of past actions, from this or previous lifetimes; from the Sanskrit *kri*, to do. The equilibrating law of *karma*, as expounded in the Hindu scriptures, is that of action and reaction, cause and effect, sowing and reaping. In the course of natural righteousness, each man by his thoughts and actions becomes the molder of his destiny. Whatever energies he himself, wisely or unwisely, has set in motion must return to him as their starting point, like a circle inexorably completing itself. An understanding of *karma* as the law of justice serves to free the human mind from resentment against God and man. A man's *karma* follows him from incarnation to incarnation until fulfilled or spiritually transcended. See *reincarnation*.

The cumulative actions of human beings within communities, nations, or the world as a whole constitute *mass karma*, which produces local or far-ranging effects according to the degree and preponderance of good or evil. The thoughts and actions of every man, therefore, contribute to the good or ill of this world and all peoples in it.

Karma Yoga. The path to God through nonattached action and service. By selfless service, by giving the fruits of one's actions to God, and by seeing God as the sole Doer, the devotee becomes free of the ego and experiences God. See *Yoga*.

Krishna. See *Bhagavan Krishna*.

Krishna Consciousness. Christ Consciousness; *Kutastha Chaitanya*. See *Christ Consciousness*.

Kriya Yoga. A sacred spiritual science, originating millenniums ago in India. It includes certain techniques of meditation whose devoted practice leads to realization of God. Paramahansa Yogananda has explained that the Sanskrit root of *kriya* is *kri*, to do, to act and react; the same root is found in the word *karma*, the natural principle of cause and effect. *Kriya Yoga* is thus "union (*yoga*) with the Infinite through a certain action or rite (*kriya*)." *Kriya Yoga* is praised by Krishna in the Bhagavad-Gita and by Patanjali in the *Yoga Sutras*. Revived in this age by Mahavatar Babaji (*q.v.*), *Kriya Yoga* is the *diksha* (spiritual initiation) bestowed by the Gurus of Self-Realization Fellowship. Since the *mahasamadhi* (*q.v.*) of Paramahansa Yogananda, *diksha* is conferred through his appointed spiritual representative, the president of Self-Realization Fellowship/ Yogoda Satsanga Society of India (or through one appointed by the president). To qualify for *diksha* Self-Realization members must fulfill certain preliminary spiritual requirements. One who has received this *diksha* is a *Kriya Yogi* or *Kriyaban*. See also *guru* and *disciple*.

Lahiri Mahasaya. *Lahiri* was the family name of Shyama Charan Lahiri (1828–1895). *Mahasaya*, a Sanskrit religious title, means "large-minded." Lahiri Mahasaya was a disciple of Mahavatar Babaji, and the guru of Swami Sri Yukteswar (Paramahansa Yogananda's guru). A Christlike teacher with miraculous powers, he was also a family man with business responsibilities. His mission was to make known a yoga suitable for modern man, in which meditation is balanced by right performance of worldly duties. He has been called a *Yogavatar*, "Incarnation of Yoga." Lahiri Mahasaya was the disciple to whom Babaji revealed the ancient, almost lost science of *Kriya Yoga* (*q.v.*), instructing him in turn to initiate sincere seekers. Lahiri Mahasaya's life is described in *Autobiography of a Yogi*.

Laya Yoga. This yogic system teaches the absorption of mind in the perception of certain astral sounds, leading to union with God as the cosmic sound of *Aum*. See *Aum* and *Yoga*.

Lessons. See *Self-Realization Fellowship Lessons*.

life force. See *prana*.

lifetrons. See *prana*.

mahasamadhi. Sanskrit *maha*, "great," *samadhi*. The last meditation, or conscious communion with God, when a perfected master merges himself in the cosmic *Aum* and casts off the physical body. A master invariably knows beforehand the time God has appointed for him to leave his bodily residence. See *samadhi*.

Mahavatar Babaji. The deathless *mahavatar* ("great *avatar*") who in 1861 gave *Kriya Yoga* (*q.v.*) initiation to Lahiri Mahasaya, and thereby restored to the world the ancient technique of salvation. Perennially youthful, he has lived for centuries in the Himalayas, bestowing a constant blessing on the world. His mission has been to assist prophets in carrying out their special dispensations. Many titles signifying his exalted spiritual stature have been given to him, but the *mahavatar* has generally adopted the simple name of Babaji, from the Sanskrit *baba*, "father," and the suffix *ji*, denoting respect. More information about his life and spiritual mission is given in *Autobiography of a Yogi*. See *avatar*.

Mantra Yoga. Divine communion attained through devotional, concentrated repetition of root-word sounds that have a spiritually beneficial vibratory potency. See *Yoga*.

master. One who has achieved self-mastery. Paramahansa Yogananda has pointed out that "the distinguishing qualifications of a master are not physical but spiritual.... Proof that one is a master is supplied only by the ability to enter at will the breathless state (*sabikalpa samadhi*) and by the attainment of immutable bliss (*nirbikalpa samadhi*)." See *samadhi*.

Paramahansaji further states: "All scriptures proclaim that the Lord created man in His omnipotent image. Control over the universe appears to be supernatural, but in truth such power is inherent and natural in everyone who attains 'right remembrance' of his divine origin. Men of God-realization...are devoid of the ego-principle (*ahankara*) and its uprisings of personal desires; the actions of true masters are in effortless conformity with *rita*, natural righteousness. In Emerson's words, 'all great ones become "not virtuous, but Virtue; then is the end of the creation answered, and God is well pleased."'"

maya. The delusory power inherent in the structure of creation, by which the One appears as many. *Maya* is the principle of relativity, inversion, contrast, duality, oppositional states; the "Satan" (lit., in Hebrew, "the adversary") of the Old Testament prophets; and the "devil" whom Christ described picturesquely as a "murderer" and a "liar," because "there is no truth in him" (John 8:44).

Paramahansa Yogananda wrote:

"The Sanskrit word *maya* means 'the measurer'; it is the magical power in creation by which limitations and divisions are apparently present in the Immeasurable and Inseparable. *Maya* is Nature herself—the phenomenal worlds, ever in transitional flux as antithesis to Divine Immutability.

"In God's plan and play (*lila*), the sole function of Satan or *maya* is to attempt to divert man from Spirit to matter, from Reality to unreality. 'The devil sinneth from the beginning. For this purpose the Son of God was manifested, that he might destroy the works of the devil' (I John 3:8). That is, the manifestation of Christ Consciousness, within man's own being, effortlessly destroys the illusions or 'works of the devil.'

"*Maya* is the veil of transitoriness in Nature, the ceaseless becoming of creation; the veil that each man must lift in order to see behind it the Creator, the changeless Immutable, eternal Reality."

meditation. Generally, interiorized concentration with the objective of perceiving God. True meditation, *dhyana*, is conscious realization of God through intuitive perception. It is achieved only after the devotee has attained that fixed concentration whereby he disconnects his attention from the senses and is completely undisturbed by sensory impressions from the outer world. *Dhyana* is the seventh step of Patanjali's Eightfold Path of Yoga, the eighth step being *samadhi*, communion, oneness with God. See *Patanjali*.

medulla. The principal point of entry of life force (*prana*) into the body; seat of the sixth cerebrospinal center, whose function is to receive and direct the incoming flow of cosmic energy. The life force is stored in the seventh center (*sahasrara*) in the topmost part of the brain. From that reservoir it is distributed throughout the body. The subtle center at the medulla is the main switch that controls the entrance, storage, and distribution of the life force.

Mt. Washington. Site of, and, by extension, a frequently used name for the Mother Center and international headquarters of Self-Realization Fellowship (Yogoda Satsanga Society of India) in Los Angeles. The 12½-acre estate was acquired in 1925 by Paramahansa Yogananda. He made it a training center for the Self-Realization monastic order, and the administrative center for disseminating worldwide the ancient science of *Kriya Yoga*.

paramahansa. A spiritual title signifying a master (*q.v.*). It may be conferred only by a true guru on a qualified disciple. *Paramahansa* literally means "supreme swan." In the Hindu scriptures, the *hansa* or swan symbolizes spiritual discrimination. Swami Sri Yukteswar bestowed the title on his beloved disciple Yogananda in 1935.

paramguru. Literally, "supreme guru" or "great guru"; the guru of one's guru. To Self-Realizationists (disciples of Paramahansa Yogananda), *paramguru* refers to Sri Yukteswar. To Paramahansaji, it meant Lahiri Mahasaya. Mahavatar Babaji is Paramahansaji's *param-paramguru*.

Patanjali. Ancient exponent of Yoga, whose *Yoga Sutras* outline the principles of the yogic path, dividing it into eight steps: (1) moral proscriptions (*yama*), (2) right observances (*niyama*), (3) meditation posture (*asana*), (4) life-force control (*pranayama*), (5) interiorization of the mind (*pratyahara*), (6) concentration (*dharana*), (7) meditation (*dhyana*), (8) union with God (*samadhi*).

prana. Sparks of intelligent finer-than-atomic energy that constitute life, collectively referred to in Hindu scriptural treatises as *prana*, which Paramahansa Yogananda has translated as "lifetrons." In essence, condensed thoughts of God; substance of the astral world (q.v.) and life principle of the physical cosmos. In the physical world, there are two kinds of *prana:* (1) the cosmic vibratory energy that is omnipresent in the universe, structuring and sustaining all things; (2) the specific *prana* or energy that pervades and sustains each human body through five currents or functions. *Pran* current performs the function of crystallization; *Vyan* current, circulation; *Saman* current, assimilation; *Udan* current, metabolism; and *Apan* current, elimination.

pranayama. Conscious control of *prana* (the creative vibration or energy that activates and sustains life in the body). The yoga science of *pranayama* is the direct way to consciously disconnect the mind from the life functions and sensory perceptions that tie man to body-consciousness. *Pranayama* thus frees man's consciousness to commune with God. All scientific techniques that bring about union of soul and Spirit may be classified as yoga, and *pranayama* is the greatest yogic method for attaining this divine union.

pronam. A form of greeting in India. The hands are pressed, palms together, with the base of the hands at the heart and the fingertips touching the forehead. This gesture is actually a modification of the *pronam,* literally "complete salutation," from the Sanskrit root *nam,* "to salute or bow down," and the prefix *pro,* "completely." A *pronam* salutation is the general mode of greeting in India. Before renunciants and other persons held in high spiritual regard, it may be accompanied by the spoken word, *"Pronam."* (Also *pranam.*)

Raja Yoga. The "royal" or highest path to God-union. It teaches scientific meditation (q.v.) as the ultimate means for realizing God, and includes the highest essentials from all other forms of Yoga. The Self-Realization Fellowship *Raja Yoga* teachings outline a way of life leading to perfect unfoldment in body, mind, and soul, based on the foundation of *Kriya Yoga* (q.v.) meditation. See *Yoga.*

Ranchi school. Yogoda Satsanga Vidyalaya, founded by Paramahansa Yogananda in 1918 when the Maharaja of Kasimbazar gave his summer palace and twenty-five acres of land in Ranchi, Bihar, for use as a boys' school. The property was permanently acquired while Paramahansaji was in India in 1935–36. More than two thousand children now attend Yogoda schools at Ranchi, from nursery school through college. See *Yogoda Satsanga Society of India.*

reincarnation. The doctrine, set forth in the Hindu scriptures, that human beings, entangled in a web of unfulfilled material desires, are forced to return again and again to earth until they consciously regain their true status as sons of God: "Him that overcometh will I make a pillar in the temple of my God, and he shall go no more out" (Revelation 3:12).

The early Christian Church accepted the principle of reincarnation, which was expounded by the Gnostics and by numerous Church fathers, including Clement of Alexandria, Origen, and St. Jerome. The doctrine was first declared a heresy in A.D. 553 by the Second Council of Constantinople. Today many Western thinkers are beginning to adopt the concept of the law of *karma* (*q.v.*) and reincarnation, seeing in it a grand and reassuring explanation of life's seeming inequities.

rishis. Seers, exalted beings who manifest divine wisdom; especially, the illumined sages of ancient India to whom the Vedas were intuitively revealed.

sadhana. Path of spiritual discipline. The specific instruction and meditation practices prescribed by the guru for his disciples, who by faithfully following them ultimately realize God.

samadhi. The highest step on the Eightfold Path of Yoga, as outlined by the sage Patanjali (*q.v.*). *Samadhi* is attained when the meditator, the process of meditation (by which the mind is withdrawn from the senses by interiorization), and the object of meditation (God) become One. Paramahansa Yogananda has explained that "in the initial states of God-communion (*sabikalpa samadhi*) the devotee's consciousness merges in the Cosmic Spirit; his life force is withdrawn from the body, which appears 'dead,' or motionless and rigid. The yogi is fully aware of his bodily condition of suspended animation. As he progresses to higher spiritual states (*nirbikalpa samadhi*), however, he communes with God without bodily fixation; and in his ordinary waking consciousness, even in the midst of exacting worldly duties." Both states are characterized by oneness with the ever-new bliss of Spirit, but the *nirbikalpa* state is experienced by only the most highly advanced masters.

Sanatan Dharma. Literally, "eternal religion." The name given to the body of Vedic teachings that came to be called Hinduism after the Greeks designated the people on the banks of the river Indus as *Indoos*, or *Hindus*. See *dharma*.

Satan. Literally, in Hebrew, "the adversary." Satan is the conscious and independent universal force that keeps everything and everybody deluded with the unspiritual consciousness of finiteness and separateness from God. To accomplish this, Satan uses the weapons of *maya* (cosmic delusion) and *avidya* (individual delusion, ignorance). See *maya*.

Sat-Tat-Aum.   *Sat,* Truth, the Absolute, Bliss; *Tat,* universal intelligence or consciousness; *Aum,* cosmic intelligent creative vibration, word-symbol for God. See *Aum* and *Trinity.*

Self.   Capitalized to denote the *atman* or soul, as distinguished from the ordinary self, which is the personality or ego. The Self is individualized Spirit, whose nature is ever-existing, ever-conscious, ever-new joy. Experience of these divine qualities of the soul's nature is achieved through meditation.

Self-realization.   Paramahansa Yogananda has defined Self-realization as "the knowing—in body, mind, and soul—that we are one with the omnipresence of God; that we do not have to pray that it come to us, that we are not merely near it at all times, but that God's omnipresence is our omnipresence; that we are just as much a part of Him now as we ever will be. All we have to do is improve our knowing."

Self-Realization Fellowship.   The society founded by Paramahansa Yogananda in America in 1920 (and as Yogoda Satsanga Society of India in 1917) for disseminating worldwide, for the aid and benefit of humanity, the spiritual principles and meditation techniques of *Kriya Yoga* (*q.v.*). The international headquarters, the Mother Center, is in Los Angeles, California. Paramahansa Yogananda has explained the meaning of the organization's name in this way: "Self-Realization Fellowship signifies fellowship with God through Self-realization, and friendship with all truth-seeking souls." See also "Aims and Ideals of Self-Realization Fellowship," page 465.

Self-Realization Fellowship Lessons.   The teachings of Paramahansa Yogananda, sent to students throughout the world in a series of lessons, available to all earnest truth seekers. These lessons contain the yoga meditation techniques taught by Paramahansa Yogananda, including, for those who qualify, *Kriya Yoga* (*q.v.*).

Self-Realization Magazine.   A quarterly journal published by Self-Realization Fellowship, featuring the talks and writings of Paramahansa Yogananda; and containing other spiritual, practical, and informative articles of current interest and lasting value. *Satsangas* (informal spiritual talks) of Sri Daya Mata, president of Self-Realization Fellowship, are also a regular feature.

Shankara, Swami.   Sometimes referred to as Adi ("the first") Shankaracharya (Shankara + *acharya,* "teacher"); India's most illustrious philosopher. His date is uncertain; many scholars assign him to the ninth century. He expounded God not as a negative abstraction, but as positive, eternal, omnipresent, ever-new Bliss. Shankara reorganized the ancient Swami Order, and founded four great *maths* (monastic centers of spiritual education), whose leaders in apostolic succession bear the title of Jagadguru Sri Shankaracharya. The meaning of *Jagadguru* is "world teacher."

siddha. Literally, "one who is successful." One who has attained Self-realization.

soul. Individualized Spirit. The soul is the true and immortal nature of man, and of all living forms of life; it is cloaked only temporarily in the garments of causal, astral, and physical bodies. The nature of the soul is Spirit: ever-existing, ever-conscious, ever-new Joy.

spiritual eye. The single eye of intuition and omnipresent perception at the Christ (*Kutastha*) center (*ajna chakra*) between the eyebrows. The deeply meditating devotee beholds the spiritual eye as a ring of golden light encircling a sphere of opalescent blue, and at the center, a pentagonal white star. Microcosmically, these forms and colors epitomize, respectively, the vibratory realm of creation (Cosmic Nature, Holy Ghost); the Son or intelligence of God in creation (Christ Consciousness); and the vibrationless Spirit beyond all creation (God the Father).

The spiritual eye is the entryway into the ultimate states of divine consciousness. In deep meditation, as the devotee's consciousness penetrates the spiritual eye, into the three realms epitomized therein, he experiences successively the following states: superconsciousness or the ever-new joy of soul-realization, and oneness with God as *Aum (q.v.)* or Holy Ghost; Christ consciousness, oneness with the universal intelligence of God in all creation; and cosmic consciousness, unity with the omnipresence of God that is beyond as well as within vibratory manifestation. See also *consciousness, states of; superconsciousness; Christ Consciousness.*

Explaining a passage from Ezekiel (43:1–2), Paramahansa Yogananda has written: "Through the divine eye in the forehead, ('the east'), the yogi sails his consciousness into omnipresence, hearing the word or *Aum,* the divine sound of 'many waters': the vibrations of light that constitute the sole reality of creation." In Ezekiel's words: "Afterward he brought me to the gate, even the gate that looketh toward the east; and behold, the glory of the God of Israel came from the way of the east; and his voice was like a noise of many waters; and the earth shined with his glory."

Jesus also spoke of the spiritual eye: "When thine eye is single, thy whole body also is full of light.... Take heed therefore that the light which is in thee be not darkness" (Luke 11:34–35).

Sri. A title of respect. When used before the name of a religious person, it means "holy" or "revered."

Sri Yukteswar. Swami Sri Yukteswar Giri (1855–1936), India's *Jnanavatar*, "Incarnation of Wisdom"; guru of Paramahansa Yogananda, and *paramguru* of Self-Realization Fellowship *Kriyaban* members. Sri Yukteswarji was a disciple of Lahiri Mahasaya. At the behest of Lahiri Mahasaya's guru, Mahavatar Babaji, he wrote *The Holy Science,* a treatise on the underlying unity of Christian and Hindu scriptures, and trained Paramahansa Yogananda for his spiritual world-mission: the dissemination of *Kriya Yoga* (*q.v.*). Paramahansaji has lovingly described Sri Yukteswarji's life in *Autobiography of a Yogi.*

superconscious mind. The all-knowing power of the soul that perceives truth directly; intuition.

superconsciousness. The pure, intuitive, all-seeing, ever-blissful consciousness of the soul. Sometimes used generally to refer to all the various states of *samadhi* (*q.v.*) experienced in meditation, but specifically the first state of *samadhi,* wherein one drops ego-consciousness and realizes his self as soul, made in the image of God. Thence follow the higher states of realization: Christ consciousness and cosmic consciousness (*q.v.*).

swami. A member of India's most ancient monastic order, reorganized in the ninth century by Swami Shankara (*q.v.*). A swami takes formal vows of celibacy and renunciation of worldly ties and ambitions; he devotes himself to meditation and other spiritual practices, and to service to humanity. There are ten classificatory titles of the venerable Swami Order, as *Giri, Puri, Bharati, Tirtha, Saraswati,* and others. Swami Sri Yukteswar (*q.v.*) and Paramahansa Yogananda belonged to the *Giri* ("mountain") branch.

The Sanskrit word *swami* means "he who is one with the Self (*Swa*)."

Trinity. When Spirit manifests creation, It becomes the Trinity: Father, Son, Holy Ghost, or *Sat, Tat, Aum.* The Father (*Sat*) is God as the Creator existing beyond creation. The Son (*Tat*) is God's omnipresent intelligence existing in creation. The Holy Ghost (*Aum*) is the vibratory power of God that objectifies or becomes creation.

Many cycles of cosmic creation and dissolution have come and gone in Eternity (see *yuga*). At the time of cosmic dissolution, the Trinity and all other relativities of creation resolve into the Absolute Spirit.

Vedanta. Literally, "end of the Vedas"; the philosophy stemming from the *Upanishads,* or latter portion of the Vedas. Shankara (ninth century) was the chief exponent of Vedanta, which declares that God is the only reality and that creation is essentially an illusion. As man is the only creature capable of conceiving of God, man himself must be divine, and his duty therefore is to realize his true nature.

Vedas. The four scriptural texts of the Hindus: Rig Veda, Sama Veda, Yajur Veda, and Atharva Veda. They are essentially a literature of chant, ritual, and recitation for vitalizing and spiritualizing all phases of man's life and activity. Among the immense texts of India, the Vedas (Sanskrit root *vid,* "to know") are the only writings to which no author is ascribed. The Rig Veda assigns a celestial origin to the hymns and tells us they have come down from "ancient times," reclothed in new language. Divinely revealed from age to age to the *rishis,* "seers," the four Vedas are said to possess *nityatva,* "timeless finality."

Yoga. From Sanskrit *yuj,* "union." The highest connotation of the word *yoga* in Hindu philosophy is union of the individual soul with Spirit through scientific methods of meditation. Within the larger spectrum of Hindu philosophy, Yoga is one of six orthodox systems: *Vedanta, Mimamsa, Sankhya, Vaisesika, Nyaya,* and *Yoga.* There are also various types of yoga methods: *Hatha Yoga, Mantra Yoga, Laya Yoga, Karma Yoga, Jnana Yoga, Bhakti Yoga,* and *Raja Yoga. Raja Yoga,* the "royal" or complete yoga, is that which is taught by Self-Realization Fellowship, and which Bhagavan Krishna extols to his disciple Arjuna in the Bhagavad-Gita: "The yogi is greater than body-disciplining ascetics, greater even than the followers of the path of wisdom or of the path of action; be thou, O Arjuna, a yogi!" (Bhagavad-Gita VI:46). The sage Patanjali, foremost exponent of Yoga, has outlined eight definite steps by which the *Raja Yogi* attains *samadhi,* or union with God. These are (1) *yama,* moral conduct; (2) *niyama,* religious observances; (3) *asana,* right posture; (4) *pranayama,* control of *prana,* subtle life currents; (5) *pratyahara,* withdrawal of the senses from external objects; (6) *dharana,* concentration; (7) *dhyana,* meditation; and (8) *samadhi,* superconscious experience.

yogi. One who practices Yoga (*q.v.*). Anyone who practices a scientific technique for divine realization is a yogi. He may be either married or unmarried, either a man of worldly responsibilities or one of formal religious ties.

Yogoda Satsanga Society of India. The name by which Self-Realization Fellowship is known in India. The Society was founded in 1917 by Paramahansa Yogananda. Its headquarters, Yogoda Math, is situated on the banks of the Ganges at Dakshineswar, near Calcutta. Yogoda Satsanga Society has a branch math at Ranchi, Bihar, and many branch centers. In addition to Yogoda meditation centers and groups throughout India, there are twenty-two educational institutions, from primary through college standard. The literal meaning of *Yogoda*, a word coined by Paramahansa Yogananda, is "that which yoga imparts," i.e., Self-realization. *Satsanga* means "divine fellowship," or "fellowship with Truth." For the West, Paramahansaji translated the Indian name as "Self-Realization Fellowship" (*q.v.*).

yuga. A cycle or subperiod of creation, outlined in ancient Hindu texts. Sri Yukteswar (*q.v.*) describes in *The Holy Science* a 24,000-year Equinoctial Cycle and mankind's present place in it. This cycle occurs within the much longer universal cycle of the ancient texts, as calculated by the ancient *rishis* and noted in *Autobiography of a Yogi*, chapter 16:

"The universal cycle of the scriptures is 4,300,560,000 years in extent, and measures out a 'Day of Creation.' This vast figure is based on the relationship between the length of the solar year and a multiple of pi (3.1416, the ratio of the circumference to the diameter of a circle).

"The life-span for a whole universe, according to the ancient seers, is 314,159,000,000,000 solar years, or 'One Age of Brahma.'"